STEPPING
ON THE SERPENT
THE JOURNEY OF TRUST WITH MARY

Fr. Thaddaeus Lancton, MIC

D.T. THOMPSON

Available from:
Marian Helpers Center
Stockbridge, MA 01263
1-800-462-7426
marian.org
ShopMercy.org

Library of Congress Catalog Number: 2017907831
ISBN: 978-1-59614-400-2

Imprimi Potest:
Very Rev. Kazimierz Chwalek, MIC, Provincial Superior
The Blessed Virgin Mary, Mother of Mercy Province
Congregation of Marian Fathers of the Immaculate Conception
July 17, 2017

Nihil Obstat:
Dr. Robert A. Stackpole, STD
Censor Deputatus
July 17, 2017

Cover image and inside front cover: Close up of the Immaculate Conception painting by Peter Paul Rubens c. 1628. RestoredTraditions.com. Public Domain.

MARIAN PRESS
STOCKBRIDGE MA 01263

Printed in the United States of America

Acclaim for
Stepping on the Serpent

At the time of the French Revolution, Blessed William Joseph Chaminade encouraged Catholics to stomp out the devilish spirit of the revolutionaries by acting as the "heel of the woman" (Gen 3:15). In *Stepping on the Serpent*, Fr. Lancton echoes this biblical wisdom for the people of our times. He encourages us to overcome the distrustful spirit of our age by being like Mary, acting like Mary, and saying with Mary, "Jesus, I trust in You!" This book is a veritable *summa* on trust and will change your life!

— **Fr. Donald Calloway, MIC**
Author of *Champions of the Rosary: The History and Heroes of a Spiritual Weapon*

When we open our hearts to Scripture and the liturgy — especially the feasts of the Virgin Mary — we learn to trust Jesus. Only she was with Him from the beginning. She was close to Jesus to the last, and she remained with Him in His Church after the Ascension. She teaches us to trust amid the most trying circumstances. Father Thaddaeus demonstrates this in a deeply biblical, authentically Catholic, and truly practical way.

— **Dr. Scott Hahn**
Author of *Rome Sweet Home*

God and His Word are infinite and rich, deep and inexhaustible. The life of the Church and her saints draws us into this ecstasy of joy and fulfillment as we abandon ourselves to God and the spiritual life. Father Thaddaeus takes us by the hand and walks with us into this world of meditation and enrichment. Using Scripture, the life of Mary and the saints, and his own bountiful experience, he continues what the Church has always done — leading us deeper into trust and the love of God to better know and appreciate the mysteries and depths of our Lord and all that He wants us to experience in this life and the next.

— **Steve Ray**
Author of *Crossing the Tiber* and *Upon This Rock*

Acknowledgments

I cannot take credit for the thoughts in this book, since all these thoughts are *borrowed*. They came from the Lord and Our Lady through prayer, through study, or through the innumerable people from whom I have learned about the Lord. Ultimately, however, "every good endowment and every perfect gift is from above, coming down from the Father of lights" (Jas 1:16-17). May God our Father be glorified through this book, and may all thanks be given to Him.

Contents

Introduction

This book is the fruit of many years of personal prayer and my own journey of learning to live the short but important prayer, "Jesus, I trust in You." Together, we will make this journey — to the depths of our souls and through history — a pilgrimage of faith, encountering the Risen Lord by the help of the Holy Spirit. Jesus Himself leads us, His Church, by the Holy Spirit along this path of trust, for He Himself is the Way to the Father (see Jn 14:6). We have not only Jesus and each other on the journey, but also the Immaculate Mother of God, who, as the first disciple of her Son, "advanced in her pilgrimage of faith and loyally persevered in her union with her Son unto the cross,"[1] as St. John Paul II said, describing "this lively sharing in Mary's faith that determines her special place in the Church's pilgrimage as the new People of God."[2] Her special place is that of Mother, accompanying her exiled children as they journey home.

For that reason, her "exceptional pilgrimage of faith represents a constant point of reference for the Church."[3] The Immaculata herself is our sign of hope and solace along our journey, for in Mary, we see the fulfillment of our pilgrimage. We will have reached the goal of our pilgrimage of faith when each member of the Church will be immaculate, without spot or wrinkle (see Eph 5:27).[4] Precisely because Mary has already traversed her path to perfection, she stands before us as a model of holiness and virtue. She is the Star of the Sea who illumines and guides us along the journey of faith and trust, teaching us to walk on water as St. Peter did.[5]

Unfortunately, there is another companion who attempts to journey with us: the serpent, Satan, who injects the venom of distrust, original sin, and concupiscence into us when he strikes at our heel. Our *distrust* in the Father is our Achilles' heel, but Mary will teach us how to trust in the Father as the antidote to the serpent's poison and avoid any further bites. We will learn how to step on the serpent and crush his head ourselves — not just once, but with every step on our journey. We must always be aware that Mary, the Mother of Trust, always desires to accompany us; but so, too, does Satan, the father of distrust, desire to ambush and sting us at times along our journey. To be sons or daughters of the Immaculata, we need to commit to trusting as she did and share

---

[1] *Lumen Gentium: Dogmatic Constitution on the Church*, in *Vatican II Documents* (Vatican City: Libreria Editrice Vaticana, 2011). See also John Paul II, *Redemptoris Mater*, Encyclical Letter (Vatican City: Libreria Editrice Vaticana, 1987), n. 2.

[2] Saint John Paul II, *Redemptoris Mater*, n. 27.

[3] Ibid., n. 6.

[4] *Lumen Gentium*, n. 68.

[5] See Saint John Paul II, *Redemptoris Mater*, n. 6.

in her total surrender. This means we must be at enmity — as she is — with the devil and step firmly upon the serpent who tempts us with distrust.

In the Roman Seminary, there is an image of Our Lady entitled *La Madonna della Fiducia* — "Our Lady of Confidence" or "Our Lady of Trust" — to whom the seminarians recite a short prayer in Latin: "*Mater mea, Fiducia mea!* My Mother, my Confidence, my Trust!" Since we have all been bitten by the serpent at one time or another, I invite you to make this prayer your own. Just as Mary taught her own Son to walk, so will she guide our steps and watch over our spiritual growth. Call upon Mary, the Refuge of Sinners, to wrench you free from the serpent's bite, remove the venom of distrust, and gently bring you back onto the path of trust. I also invite you to share in the mystery of her Immaculate Conception, a mystery that continued throughout her entire life and was manifested in her faith and trust in the Father.[6] By trusting after the example of Mary — confessing both our misery and His Mercy and walking in daily trust that expresses itself in obedience — we participate in the grace of this mystery of Mercy.

To help describe the path of this journey, I have included quotations, definitions, and theology. This book is not meant to be merely informational, however, since knowledge "inflates with pride" if it's not put into practice (see 1 Cor 8:1). This often happens when our knowledge of God simply piles up in our minds and doesn't affect the way we live. When this is the case, the Word of God sown in our souls bears little fruit (see Mt 13:18-23). Pope Benedict XVI emphasized that the Gospel is not only "informative speech, but performative speech — not just the imparting of information, but action, efficacious power that enters into the world to save and transform."[7]

Mary is our model of truly being transformed through the Word of God. She is transformed by the Holy Spirit because she hears, cherishes, and keeps the Word of God (see Lk 1:28, 11:28). Learning to pray "Jesus, I trust in You," with Mary is not only about being *informed*, but rather, about being *transformed*. Part of this *transformation* occurs through suffering, and the serpent striking at the heel is a vivid image of the suffering caused by his presence along the journey. The Father allows the serpent to strike at us so we will not be complacent and will not *think* we trust in Him when in truth we do *not* trust.

All suffering is a fork in the road, where we are forced to make a choice between *trust* and *distrust*. If we want to live the prayer "Jesus, I trust in You," only two paths exist: Either we step on the serpent with Mary, or we fall prey to Satan. The *Didache* (*The Teaching of the Twelve Apostles*), states: "There are two ways: one is the Way of Life, the other is the Way of Death; and there is a mighty difference between these two ways."[8] We are called to walk the Way

---

[6] See Saint John Paul II, *Redemptoris Mater*, n. 6.
[7] Benedict XVI, *Jesus of Nazareth: From the Baptism in the Jordan to the Transfiguration*, trans. Adrian J. Walker (New York: Doubleday, 2007), 47.
[8] Thomas O'Loughlin, *The Didache: A Window on the Earliest Christians* (London and

of Life — Mary's path of trust in Jesus, the Way to the Father. Only by this path are we led to Heaven. We step off this path onto the Way of Death — the serpent's path — when we distrust Jesus. Both paths include suffering, but only one conquers it: Jesus crushes the head of the serpent, and by her trust, Mary shares His victory. By choosing to trust in her Son, we will also share in the victory over Satan, sin, and death.

To traverse the path of trust amid suffering, we must first ask these questions: Do I know how to trust in Jesus, as our Sorrowful Mother did at Calvary? Do I know what I am saying when I pray, "Jesus, I trust in You"? If your trust in Him is weak or you do not fully understand how to trust in Him, do not be discouraged. This entire book arises from my realization of how little I trust in Jesus or even understand what those words mean. We all walk a path of trust to Heaven; let us do so with Mary, learning how to share her faith and trust by living the prayer "Jesus, I trust in You" in all circumstances.

In order to trust like Mary, we need to more fully understand the goodness of our Heavenly Father — goodness that has been manifested throughout salvation history, but is often clouded over by the squalls of our sinfulness and the suffering that sin causes. We will learn how to walk upon the violent waters in every storm with Mary, the Star of the Sea, and with St. Peter. We will learn how to confidently and boldly trust in Jesus, knowing that suffering is never pointless or meaningless. You will see that by praying, "Jesus, I trust in You," we express our certainty that the Father uses our suffering for our true good, for our true happiness, to allow us to share once again in His divine life of self-giving love. By shedding light on the purpose of suffering, we will learn how to trust without reserve in Jesus, for Jesus is worthy of trust, most especially when we suffer.

Hence our journey may seem a bit circuitous and repetitive – because to be able to discuss trust we need to describe all its various forms: listening, obedience, patience, and more. Trust, in and of itself, encapsulates the entirety of the Gospel and all Christian spirituality; trust is the great synthesis of Christ's teachings in the Gospel. If we live the prayer "Jesus, I trust in You" as Mary did, we will be lifted with her to Heaven to be near Jesus.

Saint Faustina wrote: "The soul gives the greatest glory to its Creator when it turns with trust to the Divine Mercy" (*Diary of Saint Maria Faustina Kowalska*, 930). Think about that for a moment: the greatest glory we can give to Jesus is through our complete and unconditional trust in Him! Let us join Mary Immaculate, St. Peter, St. Faustina, St. Thérèse of Lisieux, and the host of other saints who brought the greatest glory to the Creator by their trust in the Divine Mercy in their ordinary daily lives!

Before jumping into the book itself, I want to mention a few details. You might notice that I alternate between trust in the Father and trust in Jesus.

Grand Rapids, Michigan: Society for Promoting Christian Knowledge and Baker Academic, 2010), 161.

Jesus reveals the Mercy of the Father, so whoever sees Jesus sees the Father (see Jn 12:45). Jesus is the Face of Mercy, as Pope Francis titled Him in his bull (*Misericordiae Vultus*) declaring the Jubilee Year of Mercy. The Father invites us to trust in Him by learning to trust in His Son, Jesus Christ, the Word made flesh. The prayer "Jesus, I trust in You" will lead us to say with Jesus: "*Abba,* Father, I trust in You."

Throughout the book, you will notice that certain words — Mercy, Love, Power, Goodness, etc. — are sometimes capitalized. When we entrust ourselves to the Mercy of the Father, we are not entrusting ourselves to a mere attribute, but to a Person. The Holy Spirit is the Person-Love in the Trinity.[9] When He is poured out upon us in our sinfulness, He is the Person-Mercy.[10] Therefore, the prayer "Jesus, I trust in You" also includes the Holy Spirit, who pours forth in the Blood and Water coming from the pierced Sacred Heart. We can also say then, "Holy Spirit, Spirit of Mercy, I trust in You."

I invite you to take your time with this book, reading slowly and pondering as you go, meditating upon what you read, imitating Mary, who held all things in her heart (see Lk 2:19). Learning to pray the prayer "Jesus, I trust in You" with Mary is life-changing because it is challenging.[11] This journey of trust will deepen our knowledge both of ourselves and of God, because self-knowledge and knowledge of God are two pillars of the bridge of trust that connects us in our misery to the Father's Mercy. The goal of this knowledge is to share the faith and trust of Mary, so I propose meditating on the words of the book the Father Himself wrote: Mary Immaculate. As St. Stanislaus Papczynski, the Founder of the Marians, wrote:

> My soul, you've been clinging so far to books containing various kinds of knowledge, but today look into a new book, a fresh book, unknown to you so far — the most Blessed Mother of God; I'll tell you that this book is written, illustrated, and published by God Himself. Could you find elsewhere what you could not get from Mary? Could anyone else give to you what Mary can? This is a book of virtues, of every perfection. It has as many chapters as the number of virtues it discusses. Thus, immerse yourself completely in the reading of this book and gather the flowers necessary for you in your walk of life.[12]

What flowers of virtues shall we gather from the book that is Our Lady herself? Her greatest virtue is her unconditional trust in the Father. As we learn

---

[9]   See Saint John Paul II, *Dominum et Vivificantem,* Encyclical Letter (Vatican City: Libreria Editrice Vaticana, 1986), n. 50.

[10]   Ibid., n. 10.

[11]   Benedict XVI, *Spe Salvi,* Encyclical Letter, (Vatican City: Libreria Editrice Vaticana, 2007), n. 10.

[12]   *Saint Stanislaus Papczynski* (Stockbridge, Massachusetts: Marian Heritage Press, 2016), 116.

to trust as Mary did, we not only direct our steps to the Father along the Way of her Son, but also grow in devotion to Mary, our Mother, in whom we trust.[13] Vatican II teaches that true devotion to Mary proceeds from faith and filial love, and that it consists in imitation of her virtues.[14]

As we prepare to take our first steps along this journey of trust with Mary Immaculate, take a moment to quiet yourself and read these words, hearing them as if the Lord Jesus Himself were speaking directly to you:

This is at the heart of the Christian life: Will you trust Me?
Everything I AM, I have given to you. Will you trust Me?[15]
Through every trial and tribulation, will you trust Me?
Behold, I stand at the door of your heart and knock. Will you trust Me?[16]
This is an open invitation, and if you should accept,
eternal life is opened up to you.
I AM the Way, the Truth, and the Life. Will you trust Me?[17]
Through the way of the Cross, will you trust in Me?
I will lead you to the resurrection as My adopted sons and daughters,
Will you trust Me?[18]
Trust is the greatest virtue, for it is contained within love, queen of all virtues.
Will you trust in Me? Will you love Me?
For I have loved you with an everlasting Love.[19]
I will never stop pursuing you and proving My love to you,
for you are worthy of My love.
I have bought you at a price: My own Precious Blood.[20]
Trust in Me: I will never fail you.[21]

---

[13] Saint John Paul II, *Redemptor Hominis*, Encyclical Letter (Vatican City: Libreria Editrice Vaticana, 1979), n. 22.

[14] *Lumen Gentium*, n. 67.

[15] "God said to Moses, 'I AM WHO I AM.' And he said, 'Say this to the sons of Israel, "I am has sent me to you."'" (Ex 3:14)

[16] "Behold, I stand at the door and knock; if any one hears my voice and opens the door, I will come in to him and eat with him, and he with me" (Rev 3:20).

[17] "Jesus said to him, 'I am the way, and the truth, and the life; no one comes to the Father, but by me'" (Jn 14:6).

[18] "Even as he chose us in him before the foundation of the world, that we should be holy and blameless before him, He destined us in love to be his sons through Jesus Christ, according to the purpose of his will" (Eph 1:4-5).

[19] "I have loved you with an everlasting love; therefore I have continued my faithfulness to you" (Jer 31:3).

[20] "You were bought with a price. So glorify God in your body" (1 Cor 6:20); see also "You know that you were ransomed from the futile ways inherited from your fathers, not with perishable things such as silver or gold, but with the precious blood of Christ, like that of a lamb without blemish or spot" (1 Pet 1:18-19).

[21] "Be strong and of good courage, do not fear or be in dread of them: for it is the Lord your God who goes with you; he will not fail you or forsake you" (Dt 31:6); see also "Love never

Trust in Me: I will always be with you.[22]
Trust in Me: I will lead you home.[23]
I love you, My beloved children, and you are Mine.[24]

---

ends; as for prophecies, they will pass away; as for tongues, they will cease; as for knowledge, it will pass away" (1 Cor 13:8).

[22] "Fear not, for I am with you, be not dismayed, for I am your God; I will strengthen you, I will help you, I will uphold you with my victorious right hand" (Is 41:10); see also "teaching them to observe all that I have commanded you; and behold, I am with you always, to the close of the age" (Mt 28:20).

[23] "At that time I will bring you home, at the time when I gather you together" (Zeph 3:20).

[24] "But now thus says the LORD, he who created you, O Jacob, he who formed you, O Israel: 'Fear not, for I have redeemed you; I have called you by name, you are mine'" (Is 43:1).

CHAPTER 1

Steps of Trust into the Future

"For I know well the plans I have in mind for you — oracle of the Lord — plans for your welfare and not for woe, so as to give you a future of hope" (Jer 29:11).

Idistinctly remember meditating upon these words of the Lord during my ordination retreat in the first days of May 2015. Every seminarian is required to make such a retreat before taking the step of priestly ordination. I was a bit uncertain about taking that step, not because of any doubts about my vocation, but rather because of my fears about the "future of hope" in store for me. Though in my mind I believed these words to be truly inspired by the Holy Spirit, I nevertheless had a very human doubt in my heart: *Just what kind of plans do you have in store for me, Lord?*

My question was influenced by the presence of a large crucifix above the altar in the chapel of the Marian seminary in Lublin, Poland, where I was praying. Plans that would involve suffering certainly did not seem to be plans for my welfare or a future of hope. And if the Father did not even spare His sinless Son such terrible suffering, how could I expect Him to spare me, a sinner?[25] I asked, "Father, if your 'plans for my welfare' include the Cross, what kind of 'future of hope' is this?"

Gazing upon the crucifix, I wondered how I could recite — and mean — the words on the Divine Mercy Image: "Jesus, I trust in You"? As a deacon in perpetual vows, I knew where my steps along the journey of my priesthood would be directed: toward Calvary, to the crucifix. I had been told as I was clothed with my profession cross for perpetual vows, "May you never boast except in the cross of our Lord Jesus Christ."[26] I admit that I was not too enthusiastic about the prospect of such a future. Questions began to flood my head, and I began to doubt the Father's goodness as I worried about His plans for me.

The serpent of distrust was near, ready to strike at my heel. I could see only the crucifix and the sheer pain and agony of such an excruciating experience. I could not understand the deeper meaning of the Cross, because I was crushed by

---

[25] "He who did not spare his own Son but gave him up for us all, will he not also give us all things with him?" (Rom 8:32); see also "For the Lord disciplines him whom he loves, and chastises every son whom he receives" (Heb 12:6-8).

[26] "But far be it from me to glory except in the cross of our Lord Jesus Christ, by which the world has been crucified to me, and I to the world" (Gal 6:14).

the weight of my distrust and doubt about the Father's Goodness and Mercy.[27] Nor did I notice the image directly to the left of the Crucifix: Our Lady, Mother of Mercy, beside Jesus Crucified. I failed to recognize the presence of Mary, who herself had already traversed the path to Calvary. She had persevered in her trust in the Father even while gazing upon her crucified Son. In my doubt and fear, I was unaware that Mary, the Mother of Hope, was now gazing upon me. This journey of trust is indeed lonely without Mary, and I daresay that without her, it simply cannot be made — for without sharing in her deep faith, we, who have already been stung with the venom of distrust, will flee from the Cross.

As a priest, I know that this experience of fear in the face of the future is not unique to me. If we watch 30 minutes of the evening news, we are often overwhelmed by the tsunami of reports of disasters, murders, and corruption from around the world. If there are plans for our welfare and a future of hope, they do not seem to be coming true; instead, it seems that the world is spiraling out of control and evil will have the last word. In addition, you might be undergoing any one of a number of personal problems: the death of a loved one, the loss of a job, a divorce, prolonged sickness. In such moments of trial, the serpent begins to whisper into our ears all sorts of doubts, just as he tempted Adam and Eve to distrust and disobey. We might wonder: What kind of Father allows all this evil? Why does He allow Satan to strike at our heels, causing so much suffering along our journey to Heaven? Is this the same Father who promised a future of hope? How can I trust Him in the face of all this evil?

My own doubts flowed from my gaze upon the crucifix: Can I trust a Father who allows the crucifixion of His Son, who allows me to suffer, and even includes suffering in His plans for me? How does the crucifix lead to happiness or a future of hope? During my prayer, I became aware of how much the serpent's venom of distrust had poisoned my heart. I had thought that the words of Jeremiah were meant to bring emotional peace and encouragement in times of trouble, but in my heart, I had difficulty believing that they were true.

As I continued my search for answers, I remembered that the final word the Father spoke in the earthly life of Christ was not the Cross, but the Resurrection and Ascension.[28] My trust in the Father had begun to fail because I had shifted my gaze from Jesus upon the Cross and Mary beside Him to the pain and the suffering involved in the Cross itself. Thus the end of my journey seemed to be suffering and death. Since I had forgotten the Resurrection — the true fulfillment of Jeremiah's prophecy — I was thinking that the "future of hope" promised by the Lord extended only to blessings in this earthly life.

My doubts and distrust regarding this supposedly "good" Father are strikingly similar to those of many lapsed Catholics and nonbelievers who reject

---

[27] "For the word of the cross is folly to those who are perishing, but to us who are being saved it is the power of God" (1 Cor 18:18).

[28] Tomáš Halík, *Chcę, abyś był*, trans. Andrzej Babuchowski (Kraków: Wydawnictwo Znak, 2014), 27-43.

Him precisely because of the evil in the world. Indeed, if we expect the Father to give us only an obviously bright and beautiful future in this life, then He cannot be trusted. But the Father leads us by the Holy Spirit through the Cross to the Resurrection, through union with the Jesus Crucified continuing into union with the Jesus Resurrected. The Father can be trusted because He sent Jesus to accompany us in this valley of the shadow of death (see Ps 23:4). Even more, Jesus entrusted His Mother to us and to the Church, and she will walk with us unto eternal life. By the grace of the Holy Spirit, we can begin to grasp that the Cross is our greatest blessing because it purifies us of sin and makes us fit to enter Heaven.[29]

The Heavenly Father manifests His goodness not in indulging our self-will with its superficial hopes and dreams, but in fulfilling our deepest desires for eternal life, which begins already upon earth through faith and trust. Jesus leads us always through the Cross to the Resurrection. For this reason, St. Faustina calls suffering the greatest treasure upon earth (*Diary*, 342) and once asked, "Mary, my Mother, do You know how terribly I suffer?" Mary answered her, "*I know how much you suffer, but do not be afraid. I share with you your suffering, and I shall always do so*" (*Diary*, 25). There at the Cross stands Mary, the "Gate of Heaven," who shares in our suffering, too, even if she cannot take it away, just as she stood by the Cross of her Son, helpless to prevent His suffering.

As St. Ignatius of Loyola taught us: "We must always remind ourselves that we are pilgrims until we arrive at our heavenly homeland, and we must not let our affections delay us in the roadside inns and lands through which we pass, otherwise we will forget our destination and lose interest in our final goal."[30]

As stated in the introduction, there are two paths in this life: one of immediate pleasure and eternal pain; the other of immediate suffering and eternal blessing. One is the path of the serpent and distrust; the other is the path of Mary Immaculate and trust. Saint Faustina also describes those paths (see *Diary*, 153).

As we travel along the path of trust, we will fall many times, but the mark of the saints is that they stand up immediately and go on, just as did the Lord along the Way of the Cross. For the Father allows the sufferings of this life to prevent our eternal suffering in hell. This is the dilemma of the Psalmist who sees the lives of the wicked filled with blessings and free from suffering (see Ps 73). He asks why he should continue to suffer by keeping the law of the Lord every day. His temptation is to imitate those who lead a life free of suffering, but he realizes

---

[29] "Thy cross is the fount of all blessings, the source of all graces." Leo the Great, *Sermons*, in *Leo the Great, Gregory the Great*, ed. Philip Schaff and Henry Wace, trans. Charles Lett Feltoe, Vol. 12a, A Select Library of the Nicene and Post-Nicene Fathers of the Christian Church, Second Series (New York: Christian Literature Company, 1895), 173.

[30] Saint Ignatius of Loyola, *Epistolae et instructiones*, Vol. 12 (Madrid: 1903-1911), 6:523. Retrieved from: "Prayerful Thoughts: Passages 51-75," Georgetown University Library, accessed July 11, 2017, http://www.library.georgetown.edu/woodstock/ignatius-letters/passages-51-75.

that there is a great difference in the reward they will receive. They will meet destruction, while he will have an eternal reward: God Himself, the surpassing reward for all our suffering and the fulfillment of all our desires (see Ps 17:15; Rev 22:4). As disciples of Jesus, we realize that our reward is not in this present life; we can be sure that the Father will bless us with crosses and trials in order to help transform us into His own adopted sons and daughters, restoring and perfecting in us the image and likeness of His only begotten Son, Jesus Crucified and Risen (see Mk 10:30).

The Paschal Mystery — Jesus' suffering, death, Resurrection, and Ascension into Heaven — is the mystery of trust par excellence, in which Jesus entrusts Himself into the hands of the Father (see Lk 23:46). In a way unique to her, Mary participated in this Paschal Mystery as well, by entrusting her Son and herself entirely into the Father's hands. She gives us comfort and strength in our own weakness, encouraging us to trust in the Father even when we cry out with Jesus: "My God, my God, why have you abandoned me?" (Mt 27:46). The healing balm for the suffering of this world is Mary's trust and the Mercy of Jesus, as He Himself stated: **"Mankind will not have peace until it turns with trust to My mercy"** (*Diary*, 300).

Jesus also said to St. Faustina: **"I am Love and Mercy itself. When a soul approaches Me with trust, I fill it with such an abundance of graces that it cannot contain them within itself, but radiates them to other souls"** (*Diary*, 1074). This means that when we trust in the Divine Mercy in moments of suffering, the transformative power of the Gospel is released in the world through the Holy Spirit at work in our hearts, radiating from our faces. By trusting, we can most successfully change the world for the better and encourage others to do the same. Trust in the Divine Mercy manifests itself primarily when we deny our own will, take up our cross, and follow Jesus to Calvary with Mary by our side (see Lk 9:23).

SACRAMENTAL INITIATION INTO THE PASCHAL MYSTERY

Every Sunday we come together around the altar and crucifix to celebrate the fidelity of our Father to His promises and to gather strength for the journey toward Heaven (see Dt 7:9). These symbols of the Catholic faith remind us that the Father can indeed be trusted, even to the point of death, for the path to Calvary is the path to eternal life. The Father desires to provide for our welfare and prepare a future of hope for us. His Son's Paschal Mystery proves that nothing — not even the worst possible sufferings of this present life and even death — can separate us from the love of Christ if we persevere in trust after the examples of Jesus and Mary (see Rom 8:37-38).

We celebrate the Paschal Mystery because it is at the darkest moments that the Father reveals Himself most fully as the God of Love and Mercy. As the prayer at the end of the Chaplet of Divine Mercy states: "Eternal God, in whom mercy is endless and the treasury of compassion inexhaustible, look kindly upon us and increase Your mercy in us, that in difficult moments we might not despair nor become despondent, but with great confidence submit ourselves to Your holy will, which is Love and Mercy itself" (*Diary,* 950). If we do not give in to despair, but remain firm in hope, we will see how the Father most fully reveals Himself against the backdrop of the suffering and crosses in our lives.

Is that not why Jesus Himself is the only light in the Divine Mercy Image? The darkness surrounding Jesus serves only to highlight Him, the true Light that shines in the darkness and has overcome it (see Jn 1:5). Through Baptism and faith, we share in that paschal light, and even become light in Christ (see Mt 5:14; Eph 5:8-9; *Catechism of the Catholic Church,* 1216). In the Image, Jesus is wearing a white tunic, reminding us of our own baptismal garment, which we shall wear forever in Heaven (see *CCC,* 1243).

In Baptism, we were washed in the water flowing from the pierced Heart of Jesus and immersed in the Paschal Mystery (see Rom 6:3-5). In Confirmation, we were given courage to bear witness to Christ amid suffering, confident that an eternal weight of glory awaits us for the suffering we endure for Christ and His Kingdom (see *CCC,* 1303). The Eucharist provides strength for our journey. By faith and trust in Jesus, we draw strength from these Sacraments. Unless we trust, the Sacraments cannot fill us with the Holy Spirit. Think how important this prayer "Jesus, I trust in You" is! Without trust, we are unable to receive the graces of the Sacraments or grow in holiness and union with Jesus. The serpent will try to intrude and, if he doesn't succeed, he will attempt to take away our trust so that sacramental grace cannot pour into our hearts. But with Mary as our companion and teacher, we will reach the destination of our journey, which is the Father Himself. Jesus is the Way to the Father — and the Holy Spirit leads us by giving us the hands and loving presence of Mary Immaculate.

PERSONAL WITNESS: MY FIRST STEP

I want to return now to the chapel in Lublin. During the time I spent contemplating my future, I realized that I had often repeated the prayer "Jesus, I trust in You," but without comprehending the full force of what I was saying. Those words acknowledge that only through my trust in Jesus can His plans for my welfare and a future of hope be realized, but I had to ask Him, "Jesus, how do I really trust in You?" I discovered that in praying those words, "Jesus, I trust in You," I give permission to Jesus to lead me — with His Mother — to the Father. The real question is how to live out that prayer when our trust will be proven and tried in tribulation (see *CCC,* 2734), especially when the One we trust leads us to the Cross.

It is no coincidence that most of the apostles fled at the Crucifixion, their distrust turning their steps away from Calvary. Like the disciples walking to Emmaus, they did not imagine that the future of hope they thought would be ushered in by the Messiah included His own crucifixion (see Lk 24:19-21; 25-26). Nor is it a coincidence that today, when darkness and suffering hover on the horizon, we, too, begin to doubt and distrust the Father and walk away from the Cross. In the Gospels and in the *Diary*, however, Jesus challenges us to trust the Father always, most particularly in the moment of darkness and abandonment, and set our faces firmly toward Calvary (see Lk 9:51) and thus toward the Resurrection.

There have been many times throughout the journey of my own life when I made the decision to follow Jesus to Calvary. During my meditation on those words from Jeremiah, I decided to do so once again — with Mary gazing upon me with her tender eyes of mercy. I admit that I have been amply rewarded for my decision. On the day of my ordination (May 30, 2015), I was deeply at peace and filled with spiritual joy. Only at the end of the Mass did my tears of joy begin to flow.

The Marian Fathers have a tradition of placing a rose (or a bouquet of roses) before Our Lady at the end of our ceremonies for perpetual vows and ordinations. I knelt before a statue of Our Lady of Fatima that was similar to the statue before which I had prayed since childhood in my own home. In an instant, my heart was abundantly filled with her maternal love for me, and I began to weep profusely — something I rarely do. During those few minutes, my entire life replayed in my heart, but not simply as I remembered it. Kneeling before Mary, I understood that she had truly adopted me as her son when my own mother died when I was 2 years old. Mary was also there the night when my father died before my eyes, shortly after I had graduated from high school, and she comforted me in my sorrow. I saw how she had walked with me throughout my life, every step of the way, especially in moments of abandonment. Time and again, she defended me and crushed the serpent's head, encouraging me never to give in to discouragement and distrust. I understood that I had made it to the day of my ordination — amid so many trials, sufferings, difficulties, and setbacks — only because *she*, our faithful Mother, had watched over me, held my hand, and taught me to take each step along my path.

I invite you to trust that, if you take the hand of Mary as I was privileged to do, she will be with you through every Cross, so that you may always remember: The one who is crucified upon the Cross with Christ will also be raised to new life with Him as well (see Rom 6:4).

CHAPTER 2

Foreseeing Our Path:
Trusting in Divine Providence

"For your Father knows what you need" (Mt 6:8).

Although one must decide whether to take steps of trust or distrust, the fact that we are on a journey, a pilgrimage to (or a digression away from) the Father, is built into creation itself by the Father. He created the world to be very good; and in resplendent ways, this world reflects His perfection and beauty (see Wis 13), but it has yet to reach its ideal. The world is in a "state of journeying" toward its completion, and the Father's guidance of this journey comes from His Divine Providence. That we are on such a journey is not within our control. The only part of the journey we can control is whether we walk with Mary and step on the serpent to reach our goal of sanctity and Heaven, or whether we fall prey to the serpent along our path and never attain that goal.

Since we are by nature *in status viae* (in the state of journeying), Jesus speaks eloquently about the need for absolute trust in Divine Providence (see Mt 6:24-34). He uses beautiful words and images to describe the Father's provision of our food, clothing, and shelter, and His reassurance that we need not worry about tomorrow is encouraging. But we may have some inner doubts about His unconditional and infinite Goodness and Mercy, and we may believe that, in the end, what we need to do is be practical and provide for ourselves by our efforts alone. Such trust and reliance upon the Father do not preclude, however, our efforts to provide for our basic needs; rather, Jesus simply refocuses us upon the Father, who desires to give us an abundance of what we need if we but ask for it and, with the strength He supplies by the Holy Spirit, work for it in accord with His will.

Nevertheless, Jesus' words describe such an ideal vision that one might ask, "What does this have to do with me and my daily life?" The supposedly indispensable need to be *practical* was the basis for the temptation of Jesus in the desert when Satan enticed Him to provide bread for Himself. The message of the serpent is always clear: Trusting in Divine Providence will get you nowhere, and if you want to have enough to live on, you must fight for it and obtain it with your own two hands.

Today this is seen above all in the political arena. Secular society has removed God from the public sphere because He is seen as irrelevant to solving the real problems of the world. Ironically, when religion attempts to leave the church building in order to assist secular society, it is forbidden to "meddle" with the affairs of this world (e.g., in education, health care, and child care). Hence religion is permitted to enter the public sphere only insofar as it addresses problems according to the logic of this fallen world, and any reference to faith is seen as impractical because it impedes obtaining the goals of the secular world.[31]

The serpent wants us to use our technology and intelligence to pursue our own worldly well-being, not to bring glory to God. The serpent tempted Jesus to use His power for His own welfare, but Jesus refused and chose to trust in the Father rather than abuse His power for His personal gain. One of the primary temptations of Satan is to use one's gifts, not for the glory of God (as He desires), but according to one's own will. There is a great lack of trust reflected in this secular attitude of self-importance and materialistic primacy, and it reveals how often we live, not as Jesus has taught us, but as pagans do.

LIVING AND JOURNEYING "AS IF" WE HAVE A FATHER

In His discourse on Divine Providence during the Sermon on the Mount, Jesus makes it clear that pagans seek clothing, food, etc., because they do not believe they have a Father who watches over and cares for them (see Mt 6:31-32). Christians are to live as sons and daughters precisely because we *do* have a Father, and our Father has *immediate* and *concrete* solicitude about and guidance over every event and detail of our lives (see *CCC*, 303).

Pope Benedict XVI said: "Only when we meet the living God in Christ do we know what life is. We are not some casual and meaningless product of evolution. Each of us is the result of a thought of God. Each of us is willed, each of us is loved, each of us is necessary."[32] That is important for us to understand. We are not accidents. We are not mistakes. We were created out of nothing by our Maker, but we are not "nothing." We came from God, have been given names, and are destined to return to God. Saint John Paul II stated this clearly:

> Faith in divine Providence obviously remains strictly connected with the basic concept of human existence, with the meaning of human life. Man can face up to his own existence in an essentially different way, when he has the certainty that he is not at the mercy of a blind destiny (fate), but depends on someone who is his Creator and Father. "For man would not exist were he not created by God's love and constantly preserved by it; and he cannot live fully according to

---

[31] See Benedict XVI, *Jesus of Nazareth*, chap. 2: "The Temptations of Jesus."

[32] Benedict XVI, "Mass, Imposition of the Pallium and Conferral of the Fisherman's Ring for the Beginning of the Petrine Ministry of the Bishop of Rome. Homily of His Holiness Benedict XVI," April 24, 2005: Mass for the inauguration of the Pontificate, accessed July 11, 2017, https://w2.vatican.va/content/benedict-xvi/en/homilies/2005/documents/hf_ben-xvi_hom_20050424_inizio-pontificato.html.

truth unless he freely acknowledges that love and devotes himself to his Creator."[33]

Trust in the Father means nothing other than trust in Divine Providence. Sometimes people imagine this "providence" as an anonymous force that governs the universe, but Divine Providence is not a force; it is a *Person* — the Father, our Creator — who sustains and guides all of creation. Behind every apparent coincidence of our lives, there is Divine Providence: the Father with His guiding hands, that is, the Son and the Holy Spirit. Nothing escapes His plan, and all things obey His will (see Sir 18:3). As St. Gianna Molla wrote: "God's Providence is in all things, it's always present."[34]

Some may see life as a series of impersonal causes and effects. Impersonal causes and effects certainly do exist, but we are not to live with the presupposition that reality is fundamentally impersonal, or that we are not provided for, that there will not be enough and we must fend for ourselves. The Christian looks beyond that and sees a Person, the Father, who governs all creation through His Word. The Christian lives in trust, as did Mary Immaculate, because we are called not to seek the things of this world, but rather to seek first the Kingdom of God, within ourselves and in the world, and trust that the rest will be given to us in abundance (see Mt 6:33; Mk 10:30).

THE FATHER'S MATERNAL HAND: THE PRESENCE OF MARY

What is Divine Providence? The word "providence" comes from two Latin words: *pro + videre,* meaning "to see ahead" or "to see beforehand." The English version of this word is "foresight." Divine Providence refers to the plan of the Father — the plan He has from all eternity for each one of us, to make us His own beloved, adopted sons and daughters through the Holy Spirit (see Eph 1:9). In the Christian sense, to trust is to live constantly under the gaze of the Father, knowing that even when our faith seems weak and we cannot "see" the Father amid the vicissitudes of our lifelong journey, we nonetheless have confidence that the Father gazes upon us with Love and Mercy.[35] Moreover, we trust in the Father precisely because — unlike us — He can see ahead of us, far into the future. As we walk along this pilgrimage, our task is not so much to peer into the future as it is to take the hand of our Lord Jesus and follow Him wherever He may lead us, for we know that His destination is Heaven.

However, it is not only paternal providence that watches over us. Since Mary is the Queen of Heaven and earth, her Maternal Providence gazes upon us and provides for us. She does not guide creation as the Father does, for she is

---

[33] Saint John Paul II, *Audiences of Pope John Paul II (English)* (Vatican City: Libreria Editrice Vaticana, 2014). Catechesis given on May 7, 1986.

[34] "Reflections of Saint Gianna Beretta Molla," Saint Gianna Beretta Molla: Catholic Pro-Life Saint, accessed July 11, 2017, http://saintgianna.org/reflectionosst.htm.

[35] See Wilfrid Stinissen, *Drogocenna perła: Lectio divina — medytacje biblijne*, trans. Justyna Iwaszkiewicz (Poznan: Flos Carmeli, 2016), 38-42.

not God, but she is closely united to her Son and filled with the Holy Spirit, so we can say that — because of the power of her intercession and mediation on our behalf — there is also Maternal Providence. Thus we can say that Divine Providence has both a fatherly and a motherly face, in Jesus and Mary. In other words, Mary is the Father's maternal hand that gently guides us along our pilgrimage of trust.

The Immaculate Conception of Mary reveals the divine purpose of creation, the divine plan as it was originally: that we would be holy, pure, spotless, and immaculate before our Heavenly Father, able to live with Him and worship Him. In Mary, we see the Providence of our Father revealed and His desire to help us be like her, all-beautiful before Him. In Mary, we also see the sorrows that He allows for the sake of her being the perfect Mother of His Son and the Mother of all, for we see in her journey of trust that the Father guided her through Calvary to Heaven. The Father transformed her many sorrows into the glory she now shares with her Son.

What exactly does Divine Providence mean for us? First, it means that someone else oversees our lives. As much as we moderns, especially Americans, want to strive for independence and control, we need to be careful not to take such independence too far, for sin is nothing other than independence from the Father and from His plan of Providence. Satan declared independence from the Father by halting along his journey and forging a new path to happiness. He attempts to persuade us to do the same and reject the path offered by the Father; but we ought not follow Satan's path, which is one of distrust and destruction.

We are to follow Mary, who, because of her Immaculate Conception, never knew a single moment of "independence" from God or from His plan of salvation. Mary lived in total freedom, not by opposing God's will, but by living in unison and harmony with it. Union with God does not take away our freedom or make us puppets or slaves; rather, it increases our freedom and enables us to live as His sons and daughters. Mary never sought to find a new path; she accepted the one Providence had marked out for her from all eternity.

Because of this singular grace, Mary never participated in the rebellion of Satan, since she always trusted without reserve in the Divine Providence of God our Father — even when His itinerary for her journey included the Cross. By faith, Mary believed that the Father wants to reveal the depths of His Mercy and lead her — and now us — to complete participation in His divine life by His Divine Providence. Therefore, His Providence is expressed resplendently in the mystery of the Immaculate Conception, for in Mary Immaculate, we see manifested the destination of the journey: We see that, like her, we would be perfect and holy. This understanding of Divine Providence is the paradigm that can and should guide our response to His Mercy.

Many of us have difficulty trusting in Divine Providence. The cruelties of fate, as when young children die for seemingly no reason, may cause us to ponder whether these events are indeed caused by a loving Father, or could in some way be man-made, or even a consequence of other people's sins. Our hearts balk at evil, especially when it seems impossible to explain, and we can begin to wonder if the Father is really in control. In describing my own experience of doubt in the first chapter, I pointed out that sometimes we even question His plans and the paths along which He leads us to attain our goal of union with Him.

For this reason, Mary is for us a model of trust, since those paths upon which the Lord leads us are often unknown and unfamiliar, as He tells us: "And I will lead the blind" — that is, those who walk by faith and not by sight — "in a way that they know not, in paths that they have not known, I will guide them" (Is 42:16). With the psalmist, we ought to beg: "Make me to know your ways, O Lord, teach me your paths. Lead me in your truth, and teach me, for you are the God of my salvation; for you I wait all the day long" (Ps 25:4-5).

When we pray these words with Mary, we will learn to trust with her, and the Lord's promise will be fulfilled: "I will turn the darkness before them into light, the rough places into level ground. These are the things I will do, and I will not forsake them" (Is 42:16). Indeed, if we stay on the paths given by the Father, we can be certain He will never forsake us. Even if we cannot seem to find Him or to look upon Him, we can be confident He looks upon us along our journey.

"ALL CREATURES ... ALWAYS FULFILL MY WILL"

The serpent loves to emphasize these apparent contradictions between what we know about God (that He is good and trustworthy) and what we know about life (that it is filled with horrible evils). The serpent overemphasizes evil to increase our distrust in the Father, wanting to convince us that if the world is so filled with evil, then God is not good and should not be trusted. Our failure to trust is part of the serpent's plan, for he has his own false "providence": The devil wants to usurp the power of the Father and guide all of creation to his own goals of destruction and hell. Distrust serves his diabolical plan to guide creation to destruction, but by trusting in the Father, we step on the serpent and thwart his hellish plan.

This means that sometimes we might wonder whether God is truly good. We may lose a job or a loved one; we may suffer illness or injury; or any number of tragic events may happen. It is difficult to believe in Divine Providence in such instances. We need to keep in mind that we humans exiled ourselves from the Kingdom of God through original sin and the fall. We live in the realm where man's fallen will — or worse, Satan's will — is often fulfilled. But the Kingdom of God is where Divine Providence, the Father's will and plan, is always carried out as He desires. Mary always and everywhere chose to fulfill God's will: She trusted in the Father's plan of Providence, even when it took the way of the Cross.

We could say that Divine Providence has two tiers. On one tier, we remain in communion with God and are spared the unnecessary suffering caused by sin. On the other tier, we choose to leave God's particular care and concern and suffer the consequences. Both tiers are incorporated into His single divine plan. We see the difference between these two tiers in the Garden of Eden. His original plan was paradise, even on earth. However, by our sin, we exiled ourselves from that perfect plan, and to restore the full unity between our will and the Father's, we must pass through crucifixion so as to be a new creature in Christ (see 2 Cor 5:17).

The Father's Providence foresees all things that happen. Saint Thomas Aquinas teaches that nothing escapes the will of our Father, that what might seem random to us, because we do not know all the causes, is not random to God — who knows exactly why everything happens.[36] For this reason, Jesus could tell Faustina, **"And know this, too, My daughter: all creatures, whether they know it or not, and whether they want to or not, always fulfill My will"** (*Diary*, 586).

That statement sounds strange in a world where so much sin occurs, but our trust in Divine Providence teaches us that evil does not, and cannot, cancel out or ruin the plan of God. Evil is not stronger than good, and Satan is not more powerful than Jesus. Evils committed by ourselves or others can be used by God, just as easily as He can use good, to accomplish His plan. We know, for example, that manure is excellent fertilizer to yield a rich harvest. Cannot the Father use the "manure" of this world to re-create it and make it more beautiful than before? He can, and this means we must not "get rid" of the manure, but entrust it into His almighty hands!

Saint Augustine wrote, "For almighty God ... , because he is supremely good, would never allow any evil whatsoever to exist in his works if he were not so all-powerful and good as to cause good to emerge from evil itself" (*CCC*, 311). This is most visible in the Cross. The worst event in history — the murder of Jesus — was used by the Father to bring about our salvation (see *CCC*, 312).

Only in light of this trust in Divine Providence can we understand the rest of Jesus' teaching in the Sermon on the Mount. Only if we have a good, merciful Father should we turn the other cheek or go the extra mile (see Mt 5:38-42). Only if we have such a Father who can bring good out of evil can we be perfect, and so repay evil with good, bless those who curse us, and love our enemies (see Mt 5:43-48). This is the center of Jesus' teaching: We fight the serpent by countering evil, not with evil, but with the "weapon" of trust with which we crush his proud head (see *Diary*, 1685).

---

[36] Saint Thomas Aquinas, *Summa Theologica*, trans. Fathers of the English Dominican Province (New York: Benziger Bros., 1947-1948), I, q. 19, a. 22.

"All Manner [of] Things Shall Be Well"

Does the Father have to use evil to accomplish His plan? No. He never intended to in the first place. But can God use even our human free will, with its sin, to accomplish His will? Yes. That is the mystery: that, try as we may, try as others may, our human freedom is limited and cannot frustrate or destroy the plan of our Heavenly Father. In other words, our finite sin is always bounded by His infinite Mercy.

In his *Conformity to the Will of God*, St. Alphonsus Liguori points out that we have nothing to fear, for even the sins of others are part of God's plan to bring us to holiness and help us become more united to Him. But how often we are scandalized by what befalls us, and how often we rebel against what the Father permits! Saint Catherine of Siena said, "Everything comes from love, all is ordained for the salvation of man, God does nothing without this goal in mind."[37] Julian of Norwich wrote, "Here I was taught by the grace of God that I should steadfastly keep me in the faith ... and that at the same time I should take my stand on and earnestly believe in what our Lord shewed in this time — that 'all manner [of] things shall be well.'"[38] Indeed, as Jesus Himself said, we would reach the heights of sanctity if we would accept the will of God in all situations: "**Entrust yourself completely to My will saying, 'Not as I want, but according to Your will, O God, let it be done unto me.' These words, spoken from the depths of one's heart, can raise a soul to the summit of sanctity in a short time**" (*Diary*, 1487).

If we had this attitude, we would retain peace — deeper than emotions — amid the disturbing events and fluctuating reactions of our journey through life. For in the end, nothing that befalls us can deprive us of what sustains us and gives us life: Jesus (see Rom 8:31-39). We do not see the entire plan that the Father sees, however; we see only a part, and Satan often uses what little we do see to convince us not to trust in the Father. He attempts to convince us — as he attempted to convince me in the chapel in Lublin — that our lives end at the Crucifixion without the Resurrection. But at the Last Judgment, we will see how the Father used everything for the great symphony called history, and how even those notes that seemed to be wrong at the time were, in fact, included in His plan (see *CCC*, 314).

What are we to do in the face of these evils that we encounter every day? Jesus tells us that all our activity — every step of our journey — must be based upon trust in Divine Providence. He reminds us that rooting our relationship with God in trust is most important, and that from the relationship of trust, everything else will flow. This is the meaning behind "seek first the Kingdom" (Mt 6:33). Jesus is not saying, "Forget about yourself; you are not important — focus on Me and the Kingdom." No. He is saying, "If you really believe in what

---

[37] Saint Catherine of Siena, *Dialogue on Providence*, ch. IV, 138. Quoted in *CCC*, 313.
[38] Julian of Norwich, *The Revelations of Divine Love*, trans. James Walshe, SJ (London: Paulist Press, 1961), ch. 32, 99–100. Quoted in *CCC*, 313.

I am saying — that God is Father — then trust will enable you to have all you need to live in peace and joy."

Everything flows from our relationship with God, and the Immaculate Conception teaches us how to live and thrive on trust in Him in every moment. Absolute trust is to be the "trademark" of a Christian, who, like Jesus, is privileged to be a child of Mary. By her Immaculate Conception, everything Mary has, she has received from the Father. That makes her entirely poor; there is nothing in her that has come from herself. The only thing that truly belongs to us is our sin — and Mary has no sin! The only thing Mary "possesses" is Divine Providence.

To trust in the Father means not to have inordinate attachments to creatures; such attachments are manifested through worry or anxiety. To trust like Mary is to be always under the gaze of Providence, accepting and living as radically poor creatures: Everything we have, we received from Him — and we are to offer everything to Him in return, even our sin: **"Give Me your misery, because it is your exclusive property"** (*Diary,* 1318). Having done that, we will be immaculate, like her.

THE GREATEST OBSTACLE TO HOLINESS: EXAGGERATED ANXIETY

While we are still along our journey, however, we will be able to make only steps toward imitating Mary. We, her beloved children, often fall into a particular sin, and it emerges from what is perhaps the most difficult aspect of trusting in Divine Providence. This sin is worrying, or being anxious. The word "worry" comes from the Old English *wyrgan,* which is akin to the Old High German *wurgen,* meaning "to strangle," and Lithuanian *veržti,* "to constrict."[39] How true to life! When we worry, our concerns for various matters strangle us and constrict our hearts, closing them off from the grace of God and preventing us from serving Him. For this reason, Jesus taught St. Faustina: **"My child, know that the greatest obstacles to holiness are discouragement and an exaggerated anxiety. These will deprive you of the ability to practice virtue"** (*Diary,* 1488).

"Worry denotes excessive concern and anxiety that monopolizes the heart's attention."[40] This definition highlights the choice of serving either God or material wealth and security. If we worry excessively, we show that our hearts are not fully at peace with the Father's will. This is exactly what the serpent wants: He is the one who injects the venom of worry into our hearts, so that we will distrust the Father and, thinking that we can do a better job of "running the show," we will no longer allow Him to guide our lives.

---

[39] Merriam-Webster, Inc., Merriam-Webster's Collegiate Dictionary (Springfield, Massachusetts: Merriam-Webster, 2003).
[40] Curtis Mitch and Edward Sri, *The Gospel of Matthew*, Catholic Commentary on Sacred Scripture (Grand Rapids, Michigan: Baker Academic, 2010), 110.

We may wonder, "At what point is worry sinful?" If we think we cannot be truly happy without a particular blessing as an end in itself (without reference to God), then that is a sin — because we would be basing our deepest happiness, not on God, but on a creature. An indication of sinful worry is when we cannot let go of a particular matter during prayer. We can always bring our worries and anxieties to prayer and entrust them to the Father, for such is the will of God, and Scripture says that we are to place all our hope in Him (see Ps 130:7; 1 Pet 1:13). When we do this, we will be able to live as Jesus taught St. Faustina: **"Do not value any external thing too highly, even if it were to seem very precious to you. Let go of yourself, and abide with Me continually. Entrust everything to Me and do nothing on your own, and you will always have great freedom of spirit. No circumstances or events will ever be able to upset you"** (*Diary*, 1685).

When we cannot let some care or concern go, even after pouring our hearts out to God, then we have a problem that comes from our attachment to the material world. This attachment stems from our lack of trust that God really will provide what we need, and it prevents us from being free. We have a problem when we are so concerned with material things that we can no longer worship God.

Saint Faustina, for instance, resolved not to give in to sorrow even in the midst of terrible torment: "Satan always takes advantage of such moments; thoughts of discouragement began to rise to the surface — for your faithfulness and sincerity — this is your reward. How can one be sincere when one is so misunderstood? Jesus, Jesus, I cannot go on any longer. Again I fell to the ground under this weight, and I broke out in a sweat, and fear began to overcome me. I had no one to lean on interiorly. Suddenly I heard a voice within my soul, **Do not fear; I am with you.** And an unusual light illumined my mind, and I understood that I should not give in to such sorrows. I was filled with a certain strength and left my cell with new courage to suffer" (*Diary*, 129).

This does not mean that we may not still feel some anxiety or sorrow over a loved one in sickness or some other difficulty — even after we have entrusted the matter to the Father; rather, it means that we allow the peace that surpasses all understanding to come into the midst of the anxiety and sorrow (see Phil 4:7), knowing that everything takes place under the watchful care of a loving, tender Father.

Jesus does not actually command us to stop worrying by an act of will, since we would then paradoxically worry about trying not to worry. Rather, He encourages us to introduce trust in the Father into the midst of our worry, so that worry will not overwhelm us. We make our problems even worse by not entrusting them into His hands. When we try to deal with problems beyond our strength without the omnipotent Father, we are in an even worse situation, for only He can guide such problems to a good conclusion!

Even during sickness, St. Faustina experienced the peace that comes from submission to His will. "On the eve of the retreat, I started to pray that the Lord Jesus might give me just a little health so that I could take part in the retreat, because I was feeling so ill that I thought perhaps it might be my last. However, as soon as I had started praying I felt a strange dissatisfaction. I interrupted the prayer of supplication and began to thank the Lord for everything He sends me, submitting myself completely to His holy will. Then I felt profound peace of soul" (*Diary*, 724).

When we constantly try to solve our problems on our own with no reference to trusting in God, we are simply trying to find ways to obtain our own desired result. It is ironic, then, that if we worry, our hearts are no longer open to receive what the Father wants to give us when He does provide it! Such worry is a matter of sin, not just in the sense that we are morally culpable or guilty by giving in to it, but because it means that we are living outside the Love of the Father, who wants to fill us with joy and peace.

Sin is living in darkness when we could dwell in light. Sin is choosing sadness when we could be overflowing with joy. Our Lord's teaching in Matthew 6 is not so much a condemnation of material wealth as an invitation to true wealth: faith and trust in the Providence of our Father, who gazes upon us with Love. Trust is the door that opens our hearts to the reality of the happiness, joy, and love of the Kingdom even while we are still making steps along the paths of this life toward the Father. Trust allows us access to the eternal exchange of love, which we call the Trinity. As St. Gianna Molla wrote: "The secret of happiness is to live moment by moment and to thank God for all that He, in His goodness, sends to us day after day."[41] Trust will give us the strength needed to run along these paths with Mary and not grow weary, as the Lord promises through Isaiah: "Even youths shall faint and be weary, and young men shall fall exhausted; but they who wait for the Lord shall renew their strength, they shall mount up with wings like eagles, they shall run and not be weary, they shall walk and not faint" (Is 40:30-31).

"You Have Accomplished All We Have Done!"

Does Jesus' teaching about not worrying mean that we ought not to work, or that we ought to be lazy, thinking that everything is simply in the Father's hands anyway? In other texts of the Gospel, Jesus tells us that we ought to increase our talents (see Mt 25:14-30), to work in the vineyard (see Mt 20:1-16), to care for those in need (Mt 25:35), and even to make careful plans lest we find we don't have enough material to finish a project (see Lk 14:28).

Jesus encourages us, therefore, to be engaged with our whole heart in our work, since at creation, the Father gave us a world that still needs our work to be perfected (see Gen 1:28). Those who are of a phlegmatic temperament might

---

[41] "Reflections of Saint Gianna Beretta Molla."

justify their inactivity by focusing more upon Jesus' encouragement to trust, while those who work too much might justify their lack of trust by focusing more upon Jesus' teaching to work with prudence and commitment.

What does Jesus want, then? He desires that we work, even work more, spending less time on the passing things of this world. However, He wants us to work in a new manner: without excessive worry, without haste, without anxiety, without fear or panic. Jesus wants us to remember that we are always cocreators, coworkers: He stands by our side, working with us, transforming everything to good. Hence, amid our hard work, there ought to be a river of peace, flowing from our trust that God Himself is with us and works and fights on our behalf. Indeed, we ought to work with all our being for the glory of God, but never without Him by our side (see Col 3:17, 23-24). Saint Faustina made this resolution: "I will not allow myself to be so absorbed in the whirlwind of work as to forget about God" (*Diary*, 82).

Jesus does not ask us to be merely active or passive. We are to be receptive, for we have received everything from Him already: Even our ability to work is a gift we have received. We are to use what He has given us with peace, joy, and the other fruits of the Holy Spirit; and once we have done our human best with His grace, we are to entrust everything back into His hands, saying with Isaiah: "Lord, you will decree peace for us, for you have accomplished all we have done" (Is 26:12, NAB-RE).

If we cannot honestly repeat this line from Isaiah, we may be falling into pride, thinking that we have accomplished something without God or without His help. Trying to work — or trying to advance along our pilgrimage of trust — without His help is the primary source of our worry or anxiety, because we are working without our foundation, without the One who sustains us.

A good way to examine our work in light of the Gospel is to remember a basic principle: work is created for man, not man for work.[42] This means that work is to help man grow in holiness and virtue. Very often, though, in a consumerist society that values production over the one who produces, the question of personal growth in work can be left on the sidelines. If we trust, we will grow in holiness through our work, following the example of St. Joseph the Worker, remembering that Jesus spent most of His life performing such humble work in Nazareth. We must remember that the two "bookends" of Jesus' life were these: "Behold, I come to do your will" (Heb 10:9) through active work, modeling for us trust in His grace to aid us; and "Into your hands I commend my spirit" (Lk 23:46), demonstrating passive trust, trusting not in our work, but in the Father. We ought to follow His lead!

What I have written about work can be said also about this journey of trust. We are called to be engaged with all our hearts in striving to progress along this journey, but we are always to entrust everything into the Father's hands through

---

[42] Saint John Paul II, *Laborem Exercens*, Encyclical Letter (Vatican City: Libreria Editrice Vaticana, 1981), n. 9.

Jesus. The path of trust is not one of passivity: Rather, trust engages our entire being and leaves everything in the hands of the Father.[43]

Saint Thérèse of Lisieux describes this paradox of trust and effort in a beautiful image:

> You make me think of a little child that is learning to stand but does not yet know how to walk. In his desire to reach the top of the stairs, to find his mother, he lifts his little foot to climb the first step. It is all in vain, and at each renewed effort he falls. Well, be like that little child. Always keep lifting your foot to climb the ladder of holiness and do not imagine that you can mount even the first step. All God asks of you is good will. From the top of the ladder, He looks lovingly upon you and soon touched by your fruitless efforts He will Himself come down and taking you in His arms will carry you to His kingdom never again to leave Him.[44]

In the end, the child cannot climb up the stairs on its own; the good God Himself must come down to the level of the child — as happened in the Incarnation. What is our part to play? As St. Thérèse wrote, simply goodwill and confidence. Even when we have worked much, we must remember to remain poor and little! The attitude of trust moves around two poles: the conviction of our nothingness and weakness and, at the same time, wholehearted effort. Saint Thérèse told a novice about this paradox: "One must do all in one's power. Give without counting, constantly renounce oneself, in a word, prove one's love by all the works in one's power. But in truth, since that is very little, it is urgent to put one's confidence in Him who alone sanctifies the work and to confess oneself to be a useless servant."[45]

As we progress along this journey with Mary, let us keep these words of St. Thérèse in mind: we must do all that is within our power as we learn to take steps of trust, while placing all our confidence, not in our own efforts, but in our good Father who alone sanctifies our efforts and makes them fruitful. Let us trust in Mary, our Mother, who is by our side and helps us to take each step of trust.

---

[43] Stinissen, *Drogocenna perła: Lectio divina — medytacje biblijne*, 47-51.

[44] Marie-Eugène de l'Enfant-Jésus, *I Am a Daughter of the Church: A Practical Synthesis of Carmelite Spirituality*, Vol. 2, trans. Henri Grialou and M. Verda Clare (Notre Dame, Indiana: Christian Classics, 2010), 406.

[45] Ibid., 409.

CHAPTER 3

What Is Trust? Taking the First Step

*"Trust in the Lord with all your heart,
on your own intelligence do not rely"* (Prov 3:5).

As we take our first steps along the journey of trust together with Mary Immaculate, I want to ask the most basic question: *What is trust?* Even though definitions and etymologies of words can be dry, please indulge me in a brief digression. I was taught to study the roots of words by my father, who would purposely use "educated" words at dinner. When I didn't understand him (as when he told me I looked like a *troglodyte* because I hadn't shaved), he would tell me to look the word up. So, I follow his example, and introduce you to the old-fashioned use of dictionaries and etymology.

Why start here? The word *trust* alone appears 198 times in the *Diary* of St. Faustina; *distrust* appears 24 times. Clearly, trust is important in the *Diary*! If we do not understand the precise meaning of the word, we cannot take the first step of this journey or crush the serpent who lies in wait to bite us with the venom of distrust. As Jesus' disciples, we need to fully understand the word *trust* to live the prayer "Jesus, I trust in You," and it is important to examine how lived trust manifests itself in our Christian life: through the theological virtues of faith, hope, and charity, and the cardinal virtues of prudence, justice, fortitude, and temperance.

One definition of trust is "an assured reliance on the character, ability, strength, or truth of someone or something." Another is "a dependence on something future or contingent: hope."[46] The verb *to trust* means "to place confidence in, believe, or rely on someone or something." As a noun, *trust* stems from the word *true*, from the Old English *triewe,* meaning "faithful, trustworthy, honest." *Triewe* in turn comes from the Old English *treo, treow,* "tree" — related to the Sanskrit *dru* ("tree"), since wood and trees were understood to be "firm, solid, steadfast."[47]

Hence, we trust the one who is firm, hard, and solid like a tree (particularly amid wind or storms). This link between trust and something hard and solid is found in the Old Testament, where the Hebrew word 'ā·măn is used to describe trust. 'A·măn is related to *amen,* and signifies something that has "stability, is

---

[46] Merriam-Webster's Collegiate Dictionary.
[47] "*deru-,*" Online Etymology Dictionary, accessed July 11, 2017, http://www.etymonline.com/index.php?term=%2Aderu-&allowed_in_frame=0.

reliable, solid, and can provide support."[48] The Hebrew word for truth, 'ĕmet, is also related to 'ā·măn, and signifies the "condition of being secure, stable, or dependable." Thus we see that trust "communicates a basic sense of duration, permanence, certainty, and dependability."[49] Our response "Amen" to the Word of God or prayer expresses certainty, and when we reply "Amen" in receiving the Eucharist, we acknowledge that despite all appearances, we can stand on the truth that the consecrated Host is the Body of Christ.

We trust in someone or something that provides security for us. We depend on another to provide help in time of need. Those who trust in the Lord cannot be shaken, for He provides solidity, security, and protection: "Those who trust in the Lord are like Mount Zion, which cannot be moved, but abides forever" (Ps 125:1). Indeed, as Blessed Michael Sopocko wrote: "Trust in God should be strong and enduring, without doubts or hesitations. ... Trust, then, may be compared with a chain hanging from Heaven, and to which we attach our souls. God's hand draws the chain upward; as it ascends, it carries with it all who hang on tightly. If we clutch it firmly, we shall get to Heaven, but those of weak will, those who, instead of hanging on manfully, grasp it feebly — or do not grasp it at all — will fall ignominiously, unresistingly, into the abyss."[50] When we say "Amen," we grasp the chain and allow the Father to lift us up to Him!

In other words, trust "may be defined as a quiet, steady, unwavering trust in the goodness, wisdom, and faithfulness of God. No matter what trials or seeming disaster may be encountered, the person who has cultivated this form of fruit remains calm and restful amid them all. He has an unshakable confidence that God is still in complete control of every situation and that, in and through all circumstances, God is working out His own purpose for blessing each one of His children."[51]

Pistis, a Greek word often used in the New Testament to mean "faith," also indicates trust. The Jerusalem Bible, for instance, translates *pistis* as "trust-fulness." Notice that faith refers to a set of beliefs about someone or something, and trust describes the dynamism of faith, whereby we entrust ourselves entirely to another. By looking closely at these words, we see that faith and trust are so closely related that "Christian faith is, essentially, trust in the person and character of God."[52]

---

[48] William Lee Holladay and Ludwig Köhler, *A Concise Hebrew and Aramaic Lexicon of the Old Testament* (Leiden: Brill, 2000), 20.

[49] Aaron C. Fenlason, "Belief," *Lexham Theological Wordbook*, ed. Douglas Mangum et al., Lexham Bible Reference Series (Bellingham, Washington: Lexham Press, 2014).

[50] Blessed Michael Sopocko, *The Mercy of God in His Works*, Vol. 3, trans. R. Batchelor. (Hereford: Marian Apostolate, 1972), 179-180.

[51] Derek Prince, *Faith to Live By* (New Kensington, Pennsylvania: Whitaker House, 1997), 48-49.

[52] Martin H. Manser, *Dictionary of Bible Themes: The Accessible and Comprehensive Tool for Topical Studies* (London: Martin Manser, 2009).

NECESSITY OF TRUST

Why is faith necessary? There are two ways of coming to know something.[53] We can choose to see or experience it for ourselves, or we can trust what another says. In other words, we can rely on verifiable facts or on verifiable people. In our scientific age, we often place our hope and trust on empirical facts that science can verify by experimentation. But even then, one scientist must trust the findings of another and consider them to be trustworthy; otherwise, every scientist would have to start from square one, unable to use the findings of others.

Faith is the kind of knowledge that comes from trusting and knowing the truth about a person. Faith in Jesus means that I believe what Jesus says, not because I can verify it, but because I know what kind of person Jesus is. We trust people because we know their character; we know who they are by their words and actions. The dogmas and doctrine that we, as Christians, believe are simply literary formulations describing the Persons whom we trust: the Father, the Son, and the Holy Spirit (see *CCC*, 177). The Gospels prove the character of Jesus by His words and actions, so that we might trust and have faith in Him (see Jn 20:31).

Saint John Paul II, explaining the phrase "I believe," wrote: "'I believe you' means that I trust you, and I am convinced that you are telling the truth. 'I believe in what you are saying' means that I am convinced that the content of your words corresponds to objective reality. In this common use of the word 'believe,' some essential elements are given prominence. 'To believe' means to accept and to acknowledge as true and corresponding to reality the content of what is said, that is, the content of the words of another person (or even of more persons) because of his (or their) credibility. This credibility determines in each case the authority of the person — the authority of truth. By saying 'I believe,' we express at the same time a double reference — to the person and to the truth; to the truth in consideration of the person who enjoys special claims to credibility."[54] Simply put, to say "I believe" means to "abandon oneself to the truth of the word of the living God."[55]

When *pistis* is used in an objective way to denote confidence and trust, it refers to the trustworthiness of those in whom we trust: in our case, God our Father. Reading the Bible through the lens of trust, we know that the only Person who is the ultimate source of such character and strength, and of every other good attribute, is the Father. He is infinitely good, merciful, and wise, and therefore infinitely worthy of our trust: "God's Mercy is the basis of our trust."[56]

---

[53] See Josef Pieper, *Faith, Hope, Love*, trans. Sr. Mary Frances McCarthy, SND (San Francisco: Ignatius Press, 1997). www.ignatius.com. Used with permission.

[54] Saint John Paul II, *Audiences of Pope John Paul II (English)*. Catechesis given on March 13, 1985.

[55] Saint John Paul II, *Redemptoris Mater*, n. 14.

[56] Blessed Michael Sopocko, *The Mercy of God in His Works*, Vol. 3, 169.

The Father is trustworthy because His ways are perfect and He keeps His promises and covenant forever (see Dt 7:9; Ps 18:30). The Word the Father speaks — Jesus — is trustworthy because He never passes away, even when everything else passes away (see Mt 24:35). He is Truth itself (see Jn 17:17). As stated above, *trust* and *truth* are intrinsically related in many languages. Truth is what gives solidity and firmness to reality; truth is the rock on which we can stand without wavering. Think of Jesus' example of building a home on the bedrock of His Word: Only the house built upon the foundation of His Word will endure the storm (see Mt 7:24-25). Since Jesus is Truth itself, He is worthy of our trust precisely because there is no greater foundation upon which we can find support and security (see *CCC*, 215).

Moreover, Jesus is worthy of our trust because He is our faithful and merciful High Priest and knows how to lead us through the trials of this life to the bliss of Heaven (see Heb 2:17-19). The Holy Spirit is trustworthy because He is the Spirit of Truth who leads us into the fullness of the Truth — Jesus Christ (see Jn 14:16-17). And the work proper to the Holy Spirit is to reveal to us the Face of the Father — Jesus — so that we can cry out, "*Abba*, Father!" and trust the Father as Jesus did (see Rom 8:15). Mary, our Mother, is herself the *Mother of Trust*, for she dependably leads us to her Son to be washed in the Blood and Water that flowed from His side (see Jn 19:25). She also is herself a woman of trust and is "blessed" because she believed and trusted in the Word of the Lord, and teaches us to do the same (see Lk 1:45).

The subjective basis of *pistis* is personal and refers to "me." Do I choose to trust? In whom or in what do I place my trust? Do I choose to trust in the Lord Jesus, the "Amen," who is called Faithful and True (see Rev 3:14, 19:11)? Trust means that I recognize the trustworthiness of the One I trust, and trust Him with my very self and all that pertains to me. Such recognition means that I believe what He says is true and want to obey Him, that I believe He will help me, and that I believe He can be depended on to fulfill His promises, particularly in times of need and danger: "Trust is the expectation of someone's help."[57]

REQUIREMENTS FOR TRUST

To trust in Jesus, we must be docile, like children, and allow ourselves to be led by Him to the Kingdom of God; we must trust Him completely and be entirely dependent upon Him (see Mt 18:3). Looking at our own strength, we see that we are feeble and weak, especially in moments of suffering. But just as children seek refuge and help from their parents when facing a difficulty, we are privileged to turn to God our Father amid any danger or trial (see Is 45:22). For this reason, trust requires that we admit two things: first, that we have limitations and needs; and second, that there is someone to help us. These two go together. If either one is lacking, trust breaks down.

---

[57] Blessed Michael Sopocko, *The Mercy of God in His Works*, Vol. 3, 169.

Trust is the most basic human act; it is the glue that binds us to one another and is necessary for life in this world. Trust is an essential mark of being a limited creature — we can trust only when we admit our inability to attain something. We are not omniscient, so we must ask others to teach us and alleviate our ignorance; therefore we have teachers and schools. Nor are we omnipotent, so if we want to do something beyond our own ability, we must trust another to help us. We go to doctors when we are sick and trust them to help because they have the knowledge and skill to heal us. Remember that trust also refers to the character or reliability of the person in whom we place our confidence — thus the doctor often puts his diploma from medical school in a visible place. If we were not convinced he had sufficient knowledge and training to help us, we would not go to him.

Because of our limitations, we must depend on others in order to live peacefully in this world and achieve our goals in life. God the Father told St. Catherine of Siena: "And so I have given many gifts and graces, both spiritual and temporal, with such diversity that I have not given everything to one single person, so that you may be constrained to practice charity towards one another. … I have willed that one should need another and that all should be my ministers in distributing the graces and gifts they have received from me" (CCC, 1937; see 340). When we cooperate in trust with others, we can attain what we could not on our own. We cooperate with the Father by admitting our limitations, sinfulness, and need for His Mercy, knowing that He works in all things for our salvation (see Rom 8:28). Indeed, by trusting in Jesus, we can do things beyond our human strength and power.

So, trust is necessary for us to accomplish human tasks beyond our ability, and it is even more necessary for our spiritual life. We need to trust our Creator precisely because we are limited creatures and rely on His help. Trust is a journey from our own weakness to the strength of another who can help us, ultimately leading us out of our own misery into the infinite Mercy of our Father. The result of such trust is joy in the Father's care for us. Mary herself sings of this magnificent interplay between weakness and strength, between our lowliness and God's greatness: "My soul magnifies the Lord, and my spirit rejoices in God my Savior, for he has regarded the low estate of his handmaiden. For behold, henceforth all generations will call me blessed; for he who is mighty has done great things for me, and holy is his name" (Lk 1:46-49).

As can be seen from Mary's exuberant joy in the Magnificat, trust is not simply an abstract idea or a philosophical notion. Trust is a lived reality that enables a living relationship between oneself, God, and others. Saint Francis de Sales wrote: "Trust is the life of the soul: take away trust from the soul, and you cause it to die."[58] We trust, then, in Jesus, who is the Truth, the solid foundation of reality upon which we can stand. The foundation of all reality is the eternal

---

[58] Jan Malicki, *Zawierzyć Bożemu miłosierdziu: świadectwo św. Teresy od Dzieciątka Jezus i św. Faustyny Kowalskiej* (Kraków: Wydawnictwo Karmelitów Bosych, 2010), 23.

dialogue of love between the Father and the Son in the Holy Spirit. As creatures, we depend upon the Father Himself for our support, for He Himself, because of His Goodness and Mercy, sustains us in existence at every moment. If He did not sustain us at each moment, we would cease to exist (see *CCC*, 301).

Trust is therefore our *response* to the trustworthiness of the other, gained by the goodness of another toward us in our neediness and limitations. It comes not so much by our own initiative as by an instinctual reflex in which we trust someone who is trustworthy. Think of certain flowers: They open in the morning in response to sunlight and close in the evening when the sun sets. The same is true of our hearts. We open our hearts in trust to the Father when we bask in the light of the truth that Mercy is the Father's Love seeking to help us in our misery.

As Jesus told St. Faustina: "**I am Love and Mercy Itself. There is no misery that could be a match for My mercy, neither will misery exhaust it, because as it is being granted — it increases. The soul that trusts in My mercy is most fortunate, because I Myself take care of it**" (*Diary,* 1273). In these words, Jesus tells us the secret to happiness or "good fortune." We will not be blessed by ridding ourselves of our poverty and misery on our own; rather, we will be fortunate only by trusting Him to fill our misery with His Mercy. We must therefore beware of the serpent. He teaches us to hate and abhor our limitations as creatures precisely because in desiring to be like God, he rejected his own limitations. Such abhorrence of our limitations is pride; hence, humility is required for trust. The only true misery we should hate and abhor is sin and distrust, but even then, we ought to rejoice that our sinfulness is permitted to keep us humble and aware of our misery and need of His Mercy.

Mary teaches us to step on the serpent by accepting and even rejoicing in our poverty and limitations, for these are the "entry points" for the Father's Mercy — His way into our hearts. As St. Faustina wrote near the end of her life: "One day during Holy Mass, the Lord gave me a deeper knowledge of His holiness and His majesty, and at the same time I saw my own misery. This knowledge made me happy, and my soul drowned itself completely in His mercy. I felt enormously happy" (*Diary,* 1801). The key to happiness is an awareness of both our misery and His Mercy — secured through the bridge of trust. "Nothing disturbs the depths of my peace. With one eye, I gaze on the abyss of my misery and with the other, on the abyss of Your mercy" (*Diary,* 1345; see also 55).

CHAPTER 4

Trust Is a Journey:
Agreeing on the Destination

*"'Inquire of God, we beg you, that we may know whether the
journey on which we are setting out will succeed.'
And the priest said to them, 'Go in peace.
The journey on which you go is under the eye of the Lord'"*
(Judges 18:5-6).

By Divine Providence, we are all on a pilgrimage in this life, and to choose the appropriate path on this journey, we must first agree on our destination. If the goal is to be a saint in Heaven, then we must take the path of trust, which Mary will tread with us if we invite her. If our goal is not Heaven, we will miss the mark and lose the one thing for which we were created. As the French author Léon Bloy once stated, "There is only one tragedy in the end, not to have been a saint."[59]

In this life, to reach our destination requires simply fulfilling the will of the Father, for Heaven, with its happiness, consists primarily in this: that His will is fulfilled and accomplished always, everywhere, and in everything. Hence, St. Faustina could write: "My goal is God ... and my happiness is in accomplishing His will, and nothing in the world can disturb this happiness for me: no power, no force of any kind" (*Diary*, 775). When God is our destination and goal, no one can take our happiness from us!

We are not yet in Heaven, however. We are still on the journey, so I want to delve more deeply into this idea of life as a pilgrimage. The fact that we have the desire to achieve goals reveals that we are not yet complete, not yet fully happy. Our desires reveal that we seek something "more" to satisfy our hearts. As St. Augustine said, "We all want to live happily; in the whole human race there is no one who does not assent to this proposition, even before it is fully articulated."[60] Since we were made by God and are destined to live with God for all eternity, the "more" that satisfies our hearts is God Himself. He created us to share in His divine life, here on earth and forever in Heaven (see *CCC*, 1).

---

[59] Quoted in Peter Kreeft, *Catholic Christianity: a Complete Catechism of Catholic Beliefs Based on the Catechism of the Catholic Church* (San Francisco: Ignatius Press, 2014). www.ignatius.com. Used with permission.

[60] Saint Augustine, *De Moribus Ecclesiae*, 1, 3, 4: PL 32, 1312. Quoted in *CCC*, 1718.

In theological terms, sharing in the blessed life of the Trinity is called the *beatific vision* — the vision of the Triune God that makes us truly blessed and happy for all eternity (see *CCC*, 1024). Since the Trinity is our happiness, by seeking the beatific vision, we seek our true happiness. Saint Augustine asks, "How is it, then, that I seek you, Lord? Since in seeking you, my God, I seek a happy life, let me seek you so that my soul may live, for my body draws life from my soul and my soul draws life from you."[61]

But if we seek only temporal happiness, we will not trust Jesus — for He never promises His disciples such earthly happiness. Rather, He promises eternal life — a share in the life of the Trinity. Temporal happiness and eternal happiness need not be mutually exclusive; however, the serpent offers us apparent temporal happiness all too quickly while hiding the destination to which he's leading us — eternal loss. Jesus, on the other hand, openly declares the need for sacrifice if we are to persevere in journeying toward His destination — eternal life, whose happiness is indescribable (see *Diary*, 777).

In this life, true happiness is not simply the sum of everything going "right" or "my way." As Mary told St. Bernadette at Lourdes, "I do not promise to make you happy in this life, but in the next." Mary is not saying that St. Bernadette or we will never be happy in this life; rather, we ought not to fool ourselves into thinking that we can find in this life the complete, satisfying happiness that is possible only in Heaven. For true happiness is sharing in the life of the Triune God in a dialogue and communion of Love, and we taste this happiness in the vestiges or echoes of the Trinity in all of creation, particularly in family life and in all relationships that are built upon this Love.

The Triune God is the source of the happiness we should desire and seek above all, rather than merely pursuing the superficial happiness that this world can offer apart from God. Mary's own life was not one of temporal, superficial, merely earthly happiness, although she did experience many true joys through her relationship with the Father, Jesus, and Joseph (which we meditate upon in the Joyful Mysteries of the Rosary). But she is called Our Lady of Sorrows because she also endured many crosses (as in the Sorrowful Mysteries). By her trust, she crushed the head of the serpent and transformed her suffering into eternal happiness (the Glorious Mysteries).

When we sin, we sacrifice the true happiness of being the Father's beloved children for the passing happiness of getting "what we want" — "as we want it" — in this world. In other words, when we venially sin, we take a detour, whether long or short, away from our destination, Heaven. When we mortally sin, we totally redirect ourselves and no longer aim at our true destination, Heaven, or at our goal of becoming a saint.

Sin and trust create a dramatic issue seen time and again in the pages of Sacred Scripture: Do we trust the Father's Word (Jesus) and His promises

---

[61] Saint Augustine, *Confessions*, 10, 20: PL 32, 791. Quoted in *CCC*, 1718.

enough to avoid the false promises of happiness that the world offers and to seek the true happiness the Father offers us, both in this life and in the next?

By obeying the Father's will through a virtuous life of trust, we will find true happiness even on earth, but this happiness does not exclude suffering. Rather, the happiness promised by Jesus is present even amid it. Hence Our Lady taught St. Faustina never to take her eyes off the Cross, even when joyful, because the Cross always remains the source of true happiness (see *Diary*, 561). Even amid the greatest joys of this life, we ought never to lose sight of the Cross. So often the serpent tricks us into distrust because we immerse ourselves in the joys of this life — even the good joys given by God Himself — but forget about the Cross. Then, when the Cross comes, we become upset, discouraged, or distrusting, and we can come to see Jesus as the enemy of our joy and well-being. We may even (like the Gadarenes who lost some of their livelihood because of Jesus when He allowed the demons to enter the herd of swine) ask Him to leave, because His presence means the Cross is never lacking as He attempts to cast out evil (see Mt 8:28-34). If you want to maintain the status quo, Jesus will surely leave you disappointed or, worse, upset.

My emphasis on the Cross throughout this book is not intended to negate joy; rather, it is meant to indicate the source from which true joy flows: the pierced Heart gushing forth the Blood and Water. As St. Faustina wrote, "For Jesus is our Hope: Through His merciful Heart, as through an open gate, we pass through to heaven" (*Diary*, 1570).

"THE MORE A SOUL TRUSTS, THE MORE IT WILL RECEIVE"

This desire for the true happiness of Heaven, and our reliance upon God to help us attain it, is what we call the theological virtue of *hope* (see *CCC*, 1817). Attaining the true happiness of Heaven on our own is not possible, because there is an infinite abyss between creature and Creator; we are not strong enough or holy enough to cross the abyss unaided. In fact, Jesus clearly states that we cannot do anything for our eternal salvation without Him (see Jn 15:5).

But Jesus bridges that gap by His Love, as St. Faustina wrote: "Jesus, my Love, today gave me to understand how much He loves me, although there is such an enormous gap between us, the Creator and the creature; and yet, in a way, there is something like equality: love fills up the gap. He Himself descends to me and makes me capable of communing with Him. I immerse myself in Him, losing myself as it were; and yet, under His loving gaze, my soul gains strength and power and an awareness that it loves and is especially loved. It knows that the Mighty One protects it" (*Diary*, 815).

Trust enables us to open our hearts to that Love, which "fills the gap"; trust places us beneath the Blood and Water, receiving His Love and Mercy. If we want to receive that Love, we must trust: "The decisive factor in obtaining

God's Mercy is trust."[62] Charity (divine love) is the greatest of all the virtues, for it gives us a share in the Triune God who is Love, enabling us to love as God loves by the power of the Holy Spirit. That Love — the Holy Spirit — is the one who makes us saints, who guides us along our journey of trust to Heaven. Only by trust can we become saints, for only trust allows His Mercy to make us "capable of communing with Him." For this reason, Jesus Himself taught St. Faustina: **"The graces of My mercy are drawn by means of one vessel only, and that is — trust"** (*Diary*, 1578). The only means to sanctity, to communion with Jesus, is trust, and the more we trust, the more we are filled with His Mercy.

Such trust is important because it integrates all the other virtues: "[Trust] does not constitute a separate virtue [on its own], but is an essential condition of the virtue of hope, and an integral part of the virtues of fortitude and generosity. Because trust springs from faith, it strengthens hope and love, and is, moreover, linked up, in one way or another, with the moral virtues. It may, therefore, be called the basis on which the theological virtues unite with the moral. The moral virtues, originally natural, become supernatural if we practice them with trust in God's help."[63]

Hence, by hope we trust in the help of another, and by faith we trust in the Father — because we believe that His Word is Truth itself (see *CCC*, 1814). Faith implies trusting God always (see *CCC*, 227) and is manifested through charity — loving the Father above all things, and our neighbors as He has loved us (*CCC*, 1822). Charity is exemplified by Christ's gift of Himself on the Cross: the complete and total gift of self to God and neighbor. As a total gift of self, the Cross is also the visible manifestation of complete and total trust, of the abandonment of oneself into the hands of the Father.

This entrustment of oneself in charity is called the obedience of faith, which is the proper response to the Father's revelation of Himself in His Word, Jesus Christ. By this obedience of faith, we entrust our entire self freely to God. This means we accept that the Word the Father has given us is true and we submit our will to Him in obedience to that Word. Such complete trust is not possible without the grace of the Holy Spirit, who moves our hearts and turns them to the Father, as revealed in Jesus Christ.

Trust in the Mercy of God is therefore a *synthesis* of the three theological virtues of faith, hope, and charity, by which we participate in the life of the Trinity here on earth (see *CCC*, 1812). Trust integrates the moral virtues of prudence, justice, fortitude, and temperance with the theological virtues, enabling us to order our lives to God to share in His supernatural life.

If we trust, we already share, within our hearts, in the life of the saints in Heaven. When we trust, we believe in who the Father is and in what the Father reveals in Jesus (faith); we count and depend on the Father to fulfill the Word of promise He has spoken (hope); and we entrust not only our possessions,

---

[62] Blessed Michael Sopocko, *The Mercy of God in His Works*, Vol. 3, 169.
[63] Ibid.

but our very selves, with Jesus, to the Father, by the power of the Holy Spirit (charity). To trust means to make these three theological virtues the foundation of our spiritual lives.

Jesus wanted St. Faustina to spend her time on earth and in Heaven exhorting souls to trust in His mercy: "**Fight bravely, because My arm is supporting you; fight for the salvation of souls, exhorting them to trust in My mercy, as that is your task in this life and in the life to come**" (*Diary,* 1452). Saint Faustina wrote: "All for You, Jesus. I desire to adore Your mercy with every beat of my heart and, to the extent that I am able, to encourage souls to trust in that mercy, as You Yourself have commanded me, O Lord" (*Diary,* 1234).

TRUST AS THE KEY TO THE DIVINE MERCY DEVOTION

We could ask: "Why does God so strongly urge us to trust?" The answer is because trust is homage to the Divine Mercy. Anyone who expects God to help him is thereby acknowledging that God is almighty and good, that He can help us, and wants to do so, and that He is, above all else, merciful."[64]

The message and devotion of the Divine Mercy are first and foremost about trust in Jesus Christ and believing the truth about who He is. Without trust, the devotion and message lacks all meaning. Without trust, we cannot expect the Lord to fulfill any of His promises, because all that the Lord revealed to St. Faustina depends directly upon our trust in His Goodness and Mercy.

Emphasis is often placed on those elements of the Divine Mercy message that we can "do" — the Chaplet, the Feast, etc. However, He first wants us to learn to receive more, because Heaven is not something we "reach" or "attain"; rather we receive it with an open heart. For this reason, Jesus wants us to learn to receive, so that we may do more with Him (as discussed in the previous chapter about work and cooperation).

Through trust, we receive the truth about God and ourselves, and only after accepting the truth do we begin to act. Many of our difficulties in the modern world and in our personal lives spring from not receiving or accepting reality as it is and instead imposing our own designs, plans, and manipulations. Living in a technological age when we have tools to manipulate things according to our desires, we find it easy to give free rein to our selfishness and to our fallen human nature.

The receptive aspect is essential when it comes to our trust in the Father. If we do not accept the truth of our own limitations and those of others, we cannot trust; if we do not accept ourselves and others as we and they really, truly are right now (physical appearance, wounds, sinfulness, and all), we cannot trust; if we do not accept the truth of the Father's Mercy and His desire to help make us saints in Heaven, we cannot trust.

---

[64] Ibid., 170.

When we receive the truth as a *gift*, our gratitude provides a firm foundation for trust, and we thank God for His Providence and wisdom in all that He allows and wills. We can then begin to obey, which is nothing other than to act in accord with the truth, for the fruit of trust is obedience to the Father's will. Taking this to heart can free us from the heavy burden of putting much effort into things that cause much frustration and bear little fruit, for what pleases God is not the amount of effort alone, but trust that manifests itself in obedience: **"No action undertaken on your own, even though you put much effort into it, pleases Me"** (*Diary,* 659).

If the Divine Mercy is part of a worldview in which "I" am in the center and am simply "doing" the devotion, then I am sadly fooling myself and need to discover the essence of the message: patient, persevering, humble trust in the Word of the Lord gained through prayer (see *CCC,* 2728). As I will explore later, this is exactly why the Lord allows suffering — to teach us that the Father is not another "thing" that fits into our lives. Rather, the Father is to be "all in all" — the source of all our happiness (see 1 Cor 15:28).

To place the Father at the center of one's life, so that He alone might be our "all in all," we always need to keep in mind the Commandment Jesus said is the most important — "Hear, O Israel: The Lord our God, the Lord is one; and you shall love the Lord your God with all your heart, and with all your soul, and with all your mind, and with all your strength" (Mk 12:29-30).

In the context of this journey of trust, I might suggest replacing the word *love* with the word *trust,* since, as we have seen, entrusting oneself to another is the height of love. Thus the First Commandment would sound like this: "You shall trust the Lord your God with all your heart, and with all your soul, and with all your mind, and with all your strength." Do we fulfill this commandment to that degree? Or do we trust the Father only in part, or only to a certain degree? The destination of our journey is just this: to love and trust in the Father with all our heart, soul, mind, and strength. That is what it means to be a saint.

As a faithful daughter of Israel, Mary would have prayed the First and greatest Commandment — the *Shema* — daily. By her life, she proved her trust in the Lord. If you feel that your trust in the Father is weak or if you cannot confidently say that you fulfill this Commandment, then ask Mary for her help, for her presence, for her guidance — beg her to share her trust with you.

The goal of this book is to teach you to fulfill that First and most important Commandment: to trust in the Lord your God with all your heart, soul, mind, and strength — after the example of Mary. Will you take the first step with Mary along this journey that remains always "under the eye of the Lord"?

PERSONAL WITNESS:
"FULFILL YOUR PROMISE ..."

During my sixth grade and seventh grade years, I moved an hour out of my hometown, Houston, Texas, and was homeschooled. By the summer between those two grades, all my siblings had left for college and I was alone with my father, who was recovering from heart attacks, strokes, and triple-bypass heart surgery. We lived in a small town called Simonton, which had only a post office and a few stores. The community was composed largely of retirement-age couples (which is why our house had originally belonged to my grandparents, who were deceased).

At an age when children are often seeking to make contacts with new friends and to form their identity, I spent most of my time isolated in the house with my father. Because of his sickness, I could not get out very often; my only contact with my peers was during CCD once a week on Wednesday nights. I was rather miserable and sad, but I began to read the lives of the saints and pray more often. I picked up *The Story of a Soul*, since St. Thérèse of Lisieux was the patron of my family. Inspired by her desire to become a saint for Jesus, I once promised my father — amid many tears one day during seventh grade — that I would become a saint. My logic was simple: Nothing else was working in my life, so I had just one thing left at which I could succeed, becoming a saint — something that no one could take from me.

I persevered in my resolution for some time, but as I started high school, I began to waver because I wanted to be more popular and well-liked. Later, I fortunately found some friends who were practicing their faith with joy, and I began to do so as well. By that time, I had forgotten about my resolution — until May 21, 2005. That was the day of the baccalaureate Mass for my high school graduation at Strake Jesuit.

On May 20, 2005, my dad sat me down at the dinner table with my brother Jonathan and shared with me news he had just received: He had stage IV lung cancer (probably from his habit of smoking, which he had stopped too late). Tumors riddled his entire body, and he told me that he was given a prognosis of only six to 12 months.

The evening of May 21, we pulled into the carport at the house in Simonton. About to get out of the car, my father began to speak to me in his usual deep, serious voice: "Thaddaeus, I want you to fulfill your promise to me." I had forgotten the promise he was referring to. He continued: "Your promise to become a saint." That was my father's last, dying wish. He died — unexpectedly before my eyes — only two weeks later, on June 7. In this, his "last will and testament," I see the request not only of an earthly father but of the Heavenly Father, whose one desire for me — and for each of us — is to become a "saint."

What has become clear to me since then is that the only way to fulfill my promise is through unconditional, total, complete, unreserved trust. I needed a lot of time to understand this because at age 18, I felt I could do anything I set my mind to: I was physically very strong as a result of being a competitive swimmer, highly intelligent and so did well in academics, and competent at almost anything I wanted to do. I had one major flaw, however: I relied almost entirely on myself and my own talents and gifts. During my novitiate in the Marians from 2007 to 2008, my novice master repeated to me often the words of Jesus: "Apart from me you can do nothing" (Jn 15:5). I had the correct destination, but I realized that my own "fuel" was not sufficient for the journey; I needed, not the "gasoline" of human effort and zeal, but the rocket fuel of an open heart filled with trust in His Mercy. Only trust in Him would allow me to reach my heavenly destination and fulfill my promise to my earthly father and Heavenly Father.

That transition — from effort, works, and zeal to complete and total trust — took place through Mary Immaculate, who guided me during my formation as a Marian, helping me understand that true strength comes from accepting our weaknesses and allowing the Father to fill us with the Holy Spirit. Mary teaches me that holiness is not the fruit of my efforts, but rather the effect of allowing the Father to love me as I am, and so transform me into His son in the Son by the Holy Spirit. All that is required for that to happen is trust — trusting as Mary trusts.

CHAPTER 5

Trust Is the Key to Heaven

"Let us make human beings in our image,
after our likeness" (Gen 1:26).

In the preceding chapter, I drew a broad outline of trust and explained that it is essential because we are limited creatures who need others to help us attain what we want. Trust in our Heavenly Father is necessary if we are to reach our destination — Heaven. We must rely on Jesus, His Son, to help us get there by becoming saints already along the journey through faith, hope, and charity. The Holy Spirit — particularly through Mary's maternal presence — gives us the inner strength to take each step along the journey and crush the serpent's head. Now I want to delve deeper into what Heaven is and why trust is the key that unlocks the gates of Heaven.

TRUST: THE NATURAL RESPONSE TO GOODNESS

How does the Father awaken our trust? Trust is our natural response to His goodness. Just as a child opens his heart to his mother because of the mother's tenderness and love, so our hearts open to God our Father only in the context of His Mercy and Love. Trust is not something we command ourselves to possess, but something evoked as we grow in our awareness of the Father's love and mercy toward us. Creation is the very first act of God's Mercy — God's merciful love pouring itself out upon nothingness to bring creatures into existence. We cannot bring ourselves into existence; that is something only God can do! Saint Faustina reflected upon the Mercy of the Father shown through His creating us (see *Diary*, 1743).

The Father reveals His trustworthiness not only by creating us but also by creating an ordered world governed by natural laws that foster life on this planet. By the very existence of the created world that surrounded them, Adam and Eve were invited to trust in this good Father who had made the entire universe and provided them with all they needed for food and shelter (see Rom 1:20; Wis 13:1-5). By trusting in the Father, they entered into loving communion with Him. Their minds were filled with the Truth, and the Love of God was poured into their hearts by the Holy Spirit (see Rom 5:5). They were, by that same Holy Spirit, to make all of creation a reflection of the Trinity by immersing it in the Trinitarian life, shaping it to be a cosmos of dialogue and communion.

In the beginning, the Father manifested His goodness by giving Adam and Eve dominion over all of creation (see Gen 1:28). He also desired to give them His most precious gift — the ability to share in His divine life. In His abundant goodness and generosity, God desired to give Himself to Adam and Eve. How would He do that? We see in Genesis that the Father created Adam and Eve in His own image and likeness (see Gen 1:27).

When we were without sin at the time of creation, we were capable of knowing the truth with our intellect and choosing to do only what is good with our will. Our emotions would have confirmed that choice with joy, a feeling that is the result of possessing something good.

Before sin, man lived in paradise in a state of holiness and *original justice*, undergirded by a relationship of trust with God. Original justice subjected the flesh to the spirit. After the truth was discerned by the intellect, the will, informed by the truth, would choose what was truly (and not just apparently) good. Then, the emotions would conform to the truth and to goodness. Thus all three — the intellect, the will, and the emotions — would be whole and in harmony, in one accord.

Original justice consisted primarily in sharing in the divine life through the theological virtues of faith, hope, and charity; this original justice manifested itself in harmony between God and man, between man's soul and his body, between man and the rest of creation, and among all men. This meant that man would not have to suffer or die, and that there was an inner harmony within him that prevented the soul's separation from the body (see *CCC*, 376). Moreover, mankind was given mastery over himself by the Father, such that man was free from the disordered desires that impel him to misuse God's creation (see *CCC*, 377).

Mary Immaculate is an example of this original plan of the Father. Her mastery of self was perfected, so she could always trust in the Father. Because she was without sin, her flesh was always subjected to her spirit, her emotions to her will, and her will to her intellect. She enjoyed harmony between her soul and body, and between herself and other creatures, although this friendship with God meant also enmity with sin and with those who live in sin — the serpent and his fallen angels. She assented to and lived according to the Truth of His Word. She submitted her will to His.

Even amid her sorrows, she never ceased abandoning herself without reserve to God, whose ways are inscrutable and beyond our understanding (see Rom 11:33). Even when she did not understand His will, she always submitted her intellect and will to the Father through faith and trust. In this way, she accepted everything that was decreed in the Father's plan — even the crucifixion of her Son. This was Mary's greatness: she never ceased to trust in the Father, since she always knew the Truth and chose the good.[65]

---

[65] Saint John Paul II, *Redemptoris Mater*, n. 14.

Mary is a sign of hope for us. She is proof that the grace we once lost can be regained through the Blood and Water from the pierced Heart of Jesus. If we ask her, she will share this grace with us, so that with her we might once again fulfill the original plan of the Father. Mary teaches us how to trust the Father with our whole being — our intellect, will, and emotions — and so fulfill the *Shema,* the First Commandment: to love and trust the Lord, our God, with all our heart, soul, mind, and strength.

TRUST AND THE TRINITY

God possesses both intellect and will. When I write "God" here, I am referring to the Trinity: a communion of three Persons who know and love each other. To be created in the image and likeness of God means that we are also called to be in communion with other persons — the Divine Persons of the Trinity, angels, and other human beings.

Let us delve more deeply into trust in relation to the Trinity. The Father begets or "speaks forth" the Word (*Logos* in Greek) in eternity, and this Word is His Son. Beholding the Son, the Father loves the Son; seeing the Father, the Son loves the Father. This interchange of love is called spiration ("breathing"). The Father and the Son spirate (breathe) forth the Holy Spirit through their mutual love.

Within the Trinity, there is a dialogue between the Father and the Son. The Father speaks forth the Word (*Logos*) and the Word responds to the Father in *dialogos* (*dia,* "across"; *logos,* "word"), their eternal dialogue of love. The Holy Spirit, because He is the bond of Love, is the "place" where this dialogue between the Father and Son occurs. The Triune God is therefore a dialogue and communion of love. If we are made in His image and likeness, then we are called to a dialogue and communion of love with each other and with God. Living in this dialogue and communion is what is meant by sharing in the life of the Trinity. This is revealed significantly in marriage: the communion of love between a man and a woman whose mutual love brings forth children.

The foundation for this dialogue and communion includes two basic realities: truth and love. In the Hebrew of the Old Testament, the words ʾĕmet ("truth") and ḥĕsĕḏ ("steadfast love") are used to describe God, who is truth (fidelity) and love. For example, the Lord tells His name to Moses in this manner: "The Lord, a God merciful and gracious, slow to anger, and abounding in mercy and faithfulness" (see Ps 86:15; Jn 1:18). This Truth is what the Father speaks forth in the Word, and Love is the Holy Spirit who is breathed forth by the Father and the Son. Note that, in the Hebrew mind, truth is not an abstraction. Truth can be translated as fidelity, because fidelity denotes steadfastness and unwavering commitment, just as truth is what is firm and solid, and does not pass away. Furthermore, this Truth is so far from being abstract that the Word took on flesh and dwelled among us in human form (see Jn 1:14).

Extending our analogy from our earthly experience to the life of the Trinity, we realize that a certain element of trust is needed for the dialogue and communion to take place. Remember the connection between *trust* and *truth:* to trust others means to believe that what they say is true. For a dialogue to take place, there first must be trust. If we do not believe what another says is true, there is no possibility for a dialogue with that person. In fact, there is likely to be an argument, because agreement is always based on the truth. If there is no dialogue, there is no communion of love, either. Such a situation describes hell: the place where there is no dialogue and no communion of love — only isolation and mutual hatred (see *CCC*, 1033-1035).

Trusting God means we believe that what the Father speaks, the Word, is true. For instance, Mary simply believed the Word of the angel, without requiring proof, as Zechariah demanded. Through such trust, we on earth already enter the dialogue of love within the Holy Trinity itself. Such participation in the dialogue and communion of the Trinity is what we mean by the word *Heaven*, and the fulfillment of our being made in the image and likeness of the Triune God.

The implications of being made in the image and likeness of God are profound and far-reaching, for if the Triune God is an eternal dialogue and communion of Persons, and we are made in His image and likeness, then we are human persons who are called to participate in that same dialogue and communion. Faith is the door through which we can enter the reality of the Trinitarian life on earth and fully in Heaven (see Acts 14:27). It is by the key of trust that we open this door!

In Heaven, we find our fulfillment and completion by adoring the Father, believing the Word, and receiving the Holy Spirit. But we do not have to wait until death to begin experiencing such happiness and bliss. Because Mary always trusted, she never interrupted this dialogue of love; she participated in the life of the Trinity from the moment of her conception, and her participation continues now in Heaven. For Christians, Heaven begins here on earth in our hearts through Baptism, faith, and prayer. Prayer is emptying ourselves so that the Father can speak His Word into our hearts and fill us with the Holy Spirit.

This life of the Trinity dwells within us through faith and Baptism: "By the grace of Baptism 'in the name of the Father and of the Son and of the Holy Spirit,' we are called to share in the life of the Blessed Trinity: here on earth in the obscurity of faith, and after death in eternal light" (*CCC*, 265). Saint Thomas Aquinas states that one effect of faith "is that eternal life is already begun in us; for eternal life is nothing else than knowing God."[66] Through faith, we believe the Word of the Father and live in obedience to that Word by the power of the Holy Spirit. If we live the grace of Baptism well, such faith and obedience will blossom into eternal life in Heaven.

---

[66] Saint Thomas Aquinas, "Expositio in Symbolum Apostolorum: Commentary on the Apostles' Creed," accessed July 11, 2017, http://dhspriory.org/thomas/Creed.htm.

Who would not want to partake of this harmonious life of God, this dialogue and communion of love? This life of the Trinity is the Kingdom that Jesus proclaimed in His public ministry. If we only understood how beautiful that Kingdom — the inner life of God — is, we would never want to leave the dialogue and communion. We would be willing to give up or endure anything — even suffering and death — to enter this Kingdom and remain in His divine life! Just as Jesus Himself said in the Gospels: "The kingdom of heaven is like treasure hidden in a field, which a man found and covered up; then in his joy he goes and sells all that he has and buys that field. Again, the kingdom of heaven is like a merchant in search of fine pearls, who, on finding one pearl of great value, went and sold all that he had and bought it" (Mt 13:44-46).

The early Christians referred to themselves as *hoi zoontes:* "the living ones."[67] They believed, as we do today, that Christ came to bring us true life — to make us truly alive, not only in body but especially in our souls. "I came that they may have life, and have it abundantly" (Jn 10:10). The life we now live, marked by sin and suffering, is merely *bios*, the Greek word for "life," referring to the life of the body.[68] Eternal life — the life that Jesus Christ brings — is *zoe*, from which comes *zoontes*, "living ones."

The early Christians understood that, even while yet living *bios*, they began to share in *zoe* through trust manifesting itself in faith, hope, and charity.[69] Both *bios* and *zoe* were given to Adam and Eve at creation, and they partook of the intimate life of God. They walked in trust before God and could be naked without shame (see Gen 2:25). Sin and distrust, however, separated *bios* from *zoe,* and now we are born merely with *bios*. In Baptism, Christ returns *zoe* to us — the life of the Trinity, the life of joy, peace, and eternal happiness. Rupert of Deutz (1075/1080-1129 A.D.), a Benedictine theologian, went so far as to say, "Now we live only inasmuch as we know the blessed Trinity."[70] I would slightly rephrase this, "Now we live only inasmuch as we trust, for when we trust we come to participate in the life of the Trinity."

By walking in trust, we live and foster *zoe* in our lives, as Habakkuk states: "the righteous shall live by his faith [*emunah*]" (Hab 2:4). Without trust, we live mere *bios*, which leads to death. From the moment of her conception, Mary Immaculate always possessed *bios* as well as *zoe*, and she teaches us how never to separate the two through sin and distrust. She teaches us how to truly live.

---

[67] Joseph Ratzinger, *Jesus of Nazareth*, Part 2, *Holy Week: From the Entrance into Jerusalem to the Resurrection* (San Francisco: Ignatius Press, 2011), 82. www.ignatius.com. Used with permission.

[68] "Life," *Lexham Theological Wordbook*.

[69] Ibid.

[70] Rupert of Deutz, *De Trinitate*, 42, 24. Quoted in Gisbert Greshake, *Trójjedyny Bóg*, trans. Jan Tyrawa (Wrocław: Wydawnictwo TUM, 2009), 194.

CHAPTER 6

Stepping on the Serpent of Acedia

"Duc in altum! Set out into the deep!" (Lk 5:4).

I want you to reflect now on this question: Are you truly interested in sharing the life of the Trinity, *zoe*? At the beginning of the *Spiritual Exercises,* St. Ignatius of Loyola wrote that our goal is to serve, praise, and worship God our Lord. Seen from this perspective, everything else is secondary (which means not that it is unimportant, but rather that everything else is to serve the primary purpose).[71]

In the world today, there is unfortunately a fair amount of *acedia,* or "spiritual sloth," carelessness regarding our spiritual lives. Acedia is the vice that leads us to ignore our dignified vocation of sharing in the divine image and life. The paradox of acedia is that because it is often translated as "sloth," those who work hard for a living often assume they do not suffer from it. However, acedia refers not to a lack of diligence in our work, but rather to a lack of diligence regarding our vocation before God.

Unfortunately, all too often acedia is marked by workaholism; people work only for this world and forget about the next. Acedia is manifested by a lack of joy in response to the offer of divine grace and sharing in the Trinitarian life. To understand the danger of acedia, imagine what your reaction would be if I told you that you were to receive $50,000 later today. What emotions do you feel? Now compare that reaction with the emotions you feel when you receive Holy Communion.

Even though $50,000 might be incredibly helpful, Holy Communion ought to evoke a stronger emotion, for there is nothing greater than Jesus Himself. A practical way to gauge how much we desire God Himself is to ask ourselves how much we desire to receive Holy Communion. Saint Faustina wrote: "The most solemn moment of my life is the moment when I receive Holy Communion. I long for each Holy Communion, and for every Holy Communion I give thanks to the Most Holy Trinity" (*Diary,* 1804). Indeed, as Blessed Michael Sopocko wrote, "Our trust ought to engender within us a great longing to be with the Lord."[72]

Acedia manifests itself in two primary ways. First, we feel sadness about or indifference to our vocation and dignity as Christians. Second, we lack the

---

[71] Saint Ignatius of Loyola, *The Spiritual Exercises of St. Ignatius of Loyola,* trans. Elder Mullan (New York: P. J. Kenedy and Sons, 1914), 19.
[72] Blessed Sopocko, *The Mercy of God in His Works,* Vol. 3, 175-76.

motivation or the willingness to take up the necessary means to live out that vocation and guard our dignity.[73] In the second manifestation of acedia, we are willing to endure hardship to obtain money, but are we willing to endure such hardship to enter Heaven, to suffer with and for Christ and the Church? Acedia flows from lack of interest and lack of love: only if we truly love someone or something will we feel a desire for this love and take the necessary steps — even difficult and painful ones — to obtain it. The cause of indifference and lack of motivation is our lack of love for God and neighbor, as well as our sinful tendency to focus on this world. Just like Adam and Eve, we choose *bios* over *zoe*, fooling ourselves by supposing that we are content and happy in this earthly paradise while forgetting the true paradise that awaits us.

Why do we do this? Our hearts are naturally filled with many desires, but ultimately we desire the Infinite (God). When we think that attaining the Infinite is impossible, however, we turn to a myriad of finite things. The very word "desire" comes from the Latin words *de* + *sidera*, meaning "down, away from the stars."[74] Our human hearts cannot withstand a vacuum, so when we lack the spiritual joy of participation in the inner life of the Trinity, we turn to temporal joys as a substitute. Sin is the substitution of what is only apparently good for what is truly good — exchanging spiritual joys for temporal joys, eternal gratification for immediate satisfaction.

We can get so bogged down in the practical difficulties and problems of our everyday life, however, that participation in the Trinitarian life may seem too high a calling, unimportant, or even completely impractical. A parent might ask, "I have to feed my children and pay off college debt, so why is this important?" If we get swamped with practical matters, we allow the seed of the Word to be choked by daily worries and anxieties (see Mt 13:22) and miss the most important fact of our lives: We are created by Love for Love. Saint John Paul II wrote, "Man cannot live without love. He remains a being that is incomprehensible for himself, his life is senseless, if love is not revealed to him, if he does not encounter love, if he does not experience it and make it his own, if he does not participate intimately in it."[75] The same can be said of the Trinity: replace the word *love* with *Trinity*!

Sharing in the divine life is important precisely because our life is not simply about the practical aspects. Life is much more than what we do; it is about who we are and with whom we are in a relationship. When we mistakenly think that if something is not practical, not good, or not worthwhile from a materialistic way of thinking, then it's not any use at all, our vocation to participate in the inner life of the Trinity will seem the most useless thing of all. Paradoxically, that is

---

[73] See Jean-Charles Nault, *Noonday Devil: Acedia, the Unnamed Evil of Our Times*, trans. Michael J. Miller (San Francisco: Ignatius, 2015), 61-78.

[74] See Livio Melina, *The Epiphany of Love: Toward a Theological Understanding of Christian Action* (Grand Rapids, Michigan: William B. Eerdmans, 2010).

[75] Saint John Paul II, *Redemptor Hominis*. n. 10.

true! God is not "useful." We do not "use" God, because God is the end. He is the goal. Ultimately, everything else is useful only as a means of participating in His life and thereby entering Heaven. The paradox is that we are most useful to the Church and the world through holiness, as St. Faustina wrote: "I am striving for sanctity, because in this way I shall be useful to the Church" (*Diary*, 1505).

Do you desire to participate in the divine life, *zoe*? Or are you more interested in this earthly life, *bios*, and in what this world offers? It is true that sometimes *zoe* can seem boring and earthly life more exciting than the divine life, but we must remember that God is spirit, and participating in His divine life is incomparably greater than superficial earthly pleasures, such as a suspenseful movie or a vacation in Cancun. Rather, sharing in God's divine life is the fulfillment of our deepest desires — to love and be loved, to be in a dialogue of love with another. Heaven is echoed in a husband and wife spending a meal together, being able to talk with each other from the heart, and in the marital embrace. That sharing of love is a foretaste of Heaven.

Because the divine life of mutual, self-sacrificing love may not seem exciting to us sinners, we can easily be distracted by this world, which promises us that if we purchase this or do that, we will be happy. But to the saints, the divine life in Heaven is never boring, as St. Faustina wrote: "Incomprehensible is the happiness in which the soul will be immersed. O my God, oh, that I could describe this, even in some little degree. Souls are penetrated by His divinity and pass from brightness to brightness, an unchanging light, but never monotonous, always new though never changing. O Holy Trinity, make yourself known to souls!" (*Diary*, 592).

In a similar vein, St. Augustine wrote: "There is no more perfect joy possible for us than this: to delight in the Triune God, in whose image we have been created."[76] Trust is the road toward happiness because it leads us out of the limitations of this world into the divine life of God, happiness itself. We cannot be happy on our own and are happy only when we trust in the goodness of a God who wants to share His eternal happiness with us, beginning here on earth in Baptism.

DESIRE TO BE WITH GOD

When we judge everything in terms of productivity and utility, we unwittingly judge from our limited point of view and act as though we were the center of the universe. But we exist not just to *do*, not simply for productivity and utility, but to *be*. We exist to be with the Trinity in a dialogue of trust and a union of love that results from loving adoration, united to the Father through the Son in the power of the Holy Spirit. We are called to gaze upon the Father for all eternity with our brothers and sisters.

Now, we cannot desire what we do not know through our senses, and that is true also of our desire for God. If we do not spend time with God in prayer, do

---

[76] Saint Augustine, *De Trinitate*, I, 8, 18. Quoted in Greshake, *Trójjedyny Bóg*, 388.

not see and hear Him in the Liturgy and the Word of God, how can we desire Him? The key to desiring union with God more and more is to be able to taste the *sweetness of the Lord* (see Ps 34:9). If we do so, we will desire Him so much that we will take steps to obtain what we desire, including maintaining a regular prayer life and making an effort to live virtuously. The final step in desiring God is not something we do, but something we endure: suffering. As Jesus said to St. Faustina, **"But there is no way to heaven except the way of the cross. I followed it first. You must learn that it is the shortest and surest way"** (*Diary*, 1487). All of this — a regular prayer life, a virtuous life, and an acceptance of suffering — requires trust.

It is important to remember that everything God has done throughout salvation history is directed toward our entrance into the Trinitarian life (see *CCC*, 260). If we do not pursue this vocation, we show our ingratitude and nullify all of God's attempts to offer salvation. If we do not pursue a life of *zoe*, we negate all that Christ did on our behalf — even His death upon the Cross. If we allow ourselves to be bogged down in everyday life and fail to maintain faith in this ultimate call, then we will miss the meaning of life.

Mary teaches us how to participate in the life of the Trinity. Saint Faustina often asked her for help to grow in the spiritual life, writing: "Mary is my Instructress, who is ever teaching me how to live for God. My spirit brightens up in Your gentleness and Your humility, O Mary" (*Diary*, 620).

So, let me ask you these questions now: Are you fulfilled? Or do you find your life to be boringly repetitive? Do you want something more, without being able to put a finger on what that "more" is? The "more" that we desire is precisely this participation in the inner life of the Trinity: receiving and giving in return the Father's infinite Love — the Holy Spirit. This sense of wanting *more* will never go away until we learn to trust and so allow the Father to fill our hearts with His grace, with His infinite Love, with the Holy Spirit.

The boredom or tedium of life flows from this lack of depth. We tend to focus merely on the horizontal, the immediate reality of life, without ever hearing or obeying the words of our Lord: "*Duc in altum!* Set out into the deep!" (Lk 5:4). This is the way to crush the serpent of acedia: by setting out into the deeps of the spiritual life to encounter the infinite depth of the Father's Mercy.

By repeating "Jesus, I trust in You," we can set out into the deep of the infinite ocean of God's Mercy — and I assure you, you will never be bored! For this reason, St. John Paul II could say: "Discovering Christ, always again and always more fully, is the most wonderful adventure of our life!"[77] Indeed, trusting in Christ is a wonderful adventure! Mary, the Star of the Sea, will guide us as we set out on our journey of trust into the infinite ocean of the Father's Mercy.

---

[77] Saint John Paul II, IV World Youth Day, 1989, November 27, 1988, accessed July 11, 2017, http://w2.vatican.va/content/john-paul-ii/en/messages/youth/documents/hf_jp-ii_mes_27111988_iv-world-youth-day.html.

CHAPTER 7

Stung by the Serpent of Distrust

"Have you eaten of the tree of which I commanded you not to eat?"
(Gen 3:11).

If the Father only wants what is good for us — giving us both *bios* and *zoe*, both now and forever in Heaven — why do we not trust Him? If you struggle to answer this question, do not be discouraged. You are not alone! This is our unfortunate condition after the fall of Adam and Eve.

TRUST PUT TO THE TEST

As described in the previous chapter, the Father created man and woman to be in a relationship of trust with Him. It was His intention and desire to have a free dialogue with Adam and Eve in the Garden. They lived in trust and were naked, meaning that they were completely vulnerable before the Lord and each other. The Father's plan is for humanity to be in a relationship of loving trust with Him, both on earth and forever in Heaven. What happened to ruin this plan?

Adam and Eve shattered the dialogue and communion they had with God by their sin of distrust: "Man, tempted by the devil, let his trust in his Creator die in his heart and, abusing his freedom, disobeyed God's command. This is what man's first sin consisted of. All subsequent sin would be disobedience toward God and lack of trust in his goodness" (*CCC*, 397). Sin is not just a moral problem in the sense of breaking a commandment. What Adam and Eve did was much more than simply "breaking" the commandment not to eat of the forbidden fruit. All sin is at its root a form of distrust, and distrust eats away at the very essence of what it means to be a human person created in the image of the Triune God. Distrust ruptures the communion for which we are destined through dialogue.

The choice Adam and Eve faced — whether to trust in God, others, or themselves — is a choice that confronts each one of us every day of our lives. The story of the fall is not just about something that occurred long, long ago. Rather, the fall is an everyday reality. In fact, the choice made at the fall to distrust the Father and His will for our lives is the foundation of all sin. Remember, the Father's will is to lead us by all means necessary to eternal salvation; but through our distrust, we prevent Him from fulfilling His intention. For that reason, it is important for us to meditate upon the fall, because we often lose sight of the fact that distrust is the root of all other sins.

Distrust wounds Him most, as He told St. Faustina: **"Write this: Everything that exists is enclosed in the bowels of My mercy, more deeply than an infant in its mother's womb. How painfully distrust of My goodness wounds Me! Sins of distrust wound Me most painfully"** (*Diary*, 1076). Indeed, all our sins wound the Lord, but distrust wounds His very Heart: **"My child, all your sins have not wounded My Heart as painfully as your present lack of trust does — that after so many efforts of My love and mercy, you should still doubt My goodness"** (*Diary*, 1486).

Adam and Eve chose to verify the consequences of breaking the law of God for themselves by experience. This is a tragic choice. We are not enduring or permanent by nature. We are here one day and the next day we pass: "As for man, his days are like grass; he flourishes like a flower of the field; for the wind passes over it, and it is gone, and its place knows it no more. But the mercy of the Lord is from everlasting to everlasting upon those who fear him" (Ps 103:15-17).

Adam and Eve did much more than simply eat a piece of fruit. They withdrew from their dialogue with the Father and, by their actions, stated that His Word cannot be trusted. Putting trust in ourselves or others instead of God is always a bad choice, because we have only a limited view of reality and know only a tiny portion of the truth. Indeed, we are rather weak and feeble creatures.

THE CONSEQUENCES OF KNOWLEDGE

Describing the forbidden fruit in Genesis, the author stated that Eve perceived it was "good for food and pleasing to the eyes, and the tree was desirable for gaining wisdom" (Gen 3:6). Adam and Eve and all their descendants (including us) believe that in order to be like God, we must *taste* good and evil so we know the difference for ourselves. Evil enslaves and blinds us; having tasted it, we begin to mistake evil for good and good for evil (see Is 5:20).

After eating the forbidden fruit, instead of going out to meet God in the cool of the day to converse with Him, Adam and Eve hid themselves (see Gen 3:8). Instead of staying in their original intimate communion of love, they were now separated from God. Their actions show that they had come to believe a lie, one that we may also be tempted to believe after we have sinned: that we are "doomed." When we hide in fear, our actions reveal distrust in the Father and a warped perception of Him, as ready to punish instead of forgive.

When we sin, Satan condemns us, saying that God is holy and just, but not merciful. If we give in to his condemnation, we may begin to distrust God. Jesus longs for souls not only to say they trust in Him, but to believe in His Goodness and the justice of God: He tells St. Faustina, **"Oh, how much I am hurt by a soul's distrust! Such a soul professes that I am Holy and Just, but does not believe that I am Mercy and does not trust in My Goodness. Even the devils glorify My Justice but do not believe in My Goodness. My Heart rejoices in this title of Mercy"** (*Diary*, 300).

We flee from this imagined image of a Father who is ready to punish and condemn us, when, ironically, the one who accuses and condemns is the evil spirit, Satan (see Rev 12:10). Satan is true to his name, which in Hebrew means "the accuser."[78] But we must keep in mind always: There is no condemnation for those who are in Christ Jesus (see Rom 8:1).

SATAN: THE SERPENT OF DISTRUST

The evil spirit, Satan, is the father of lies (see Jn 8:44), and demons influence us by lying or deviously changing the Word of God just enough so that we begin to trust them, at least enough to converse with them. That is the mistake Eve made in the temptation in the Garden, when she began to engage with the force of evil. Notice how that interaction began not as an outright invitation to sin, but as a conversation about something good: the command of the Father to eat of all the fruit of the Garden of Eden, except from that one tree. Satan and his fallen angels are very cunning: Beginning with something good, they slowly lead us down a path toward evil (see Gen 3:1).

That is precisely how demons attack us — through temptations that twist the truth in our minds. Demons may be fallen angels, but they still retain their intellect, and that intellect is vastly more powerful than our own. In a battle of wits against angelic intelligence, we will lose. Jesus taught St. Faustina never to converse with demons during temptations: **"Satan gained nothing by tempting you, because you did not enter into conversation with him"** (*Diary*, 1499). In that way, we will gain the victory. Our only defense against such superhuman enemies is to trust in the Word of God.

By basing their choice on what was pleasing to their senses and so trusting in themselves, Adam and Eve fell to the enemy, Satan, and began to efface the likeness of the Triune God in which they had been made. Recall that decision making, rather than following the example of Adam and Eve's choice, should follow this order: Our intellect grasps the truth and guides our will to choose what is truly good. Our emotions then confirm our good choice with joy. If we make a bad choice, we suffer sorrow.

Adam and Eve trusted more in what they saw with their eyes and felt with their emotions than in what they could discern with their intellect, that is, the truth of God's Word. The proper order was reversed, which means that since the fall, our emotions do not always confirm good choices with immediate joy, since sometimes we may feel sorrow when doing a good deed because it goes against what we, in our sinful desires, may want. Or we may feel joy at doing evil, though ultimately we will suffer eternal sorrow if we persist in such evil.

This reversal of this proper ordering within creation is the effect of sin.[79] Our rightly formed conscience doesn't judge something to be good or evil on

---

[78] Holladay and Köhler, *A Concise Hebrew and Aramaic Lexicon of the Old Testament*, 350.

[79] See Augustine, *On Free Choice of the Will*, trans. Anna S. Benjamin (New York: Macmillan, 1989).

the basis of how we feel, but rather on the basis of the truth we know about right and wrong. When we rely on our emotions and our senses — which perceive only a small portion of reality — we cannot discern what is truly good. Satan wants to portray the Father as someone who keeps good things from us because He does not truly love us. Satan feeds us false words that make evil look very good, so we distrust the Father and think He is keeping us from being happy.

INNER UNITY AND DISUNITY

Through original sin, we have lost the harmony of original justice and now bear the burden of interior disunity between our intellect, will, and emotions. This means that the will, instead of always choosing what the intellect knows to be *truly* good, is often influenced more by emotions than by reality. Since emotions are blind to what is truly good and simply respond to stimuli presented to our senses, our desires can be "all over the place," regardless of whether something is good for us or not. That is why we lose control in front of delicious food and overeat, or give in to sexual temptation. We want some good to merely satisfy our desires, not because having it in this way in this amount at this time is objectively good. Our intellect alone can determine that.

To explain this a bit further: Everything that God created is good. We were in fact created to share in God's own divine goodness. It is impossible for us to choose something that is *entirely* evil, so we choose something because we see some amount of good in it. Only our intellect can tell us what is *good for us right here and right now.* The flesh does not always follow the intellect. Saint Paul expressed this conflict well between what is truly good and what we desire when he explained that we often choose to do what we do not truly want, and do not do what we do want. Only Jesus has the power to save us from this division between the flesh and the spirit — the power to heal us and make us holy (see Rom 7:15-25).

DISCORD AND PEACE

We live in discord and forfeit peace until we surrender ourselves to the Father through Jesus Christ. That is why there is so little peace in the world. The world is like a magnified version of the interior of human hearts, and where there is no holiness, there is no peace — because we are in conflict within ourselves.

By God's design, we fundamentally desire what is truly good, what is truly fulfilling. Yet instead of seeking the truly good, we substitute false or apparent goods that cannot satisfy us, and then we wonder why we lack peace. Peace is the result of having our deepest needs and desires satisfied, and when those needs and desires are not satisfied, we may resort to dishonest means to satisfy our untamed flesh. When we do not have peace in our hearts, we feel constantly in need of more and more, to the point of *greed*. This hunger of the soul is the source of evil (see 1 Tim 6:10). When the hungry soul is unable to satisfy itself with God, there will be destruction, because it is searching for infinite Goodness among finite goods.

If you want peace of soul, if you want what truly satisfies, if you want true joy that never leaves you, then you desire holiness (see Mt 5:6). Do not quench the Holy Spirit, for these desires are the fruit of the Holy Spirit within your heart (see 1 Thess 5:19). What you truly desire is the wholeness that comes from interior harmony and peace. To attain what you want — union with the Triune God — you need to persevere in unconditional trust. That is possible only if our intellect, will, and emotions are united rather than divided among themselves, with our mind thinking one thing, our will desiring another, and our emotions pushing us in yet another direction.[80] No person divided against himself can stand or withstand the trials of this life and live so as to enter the Kingdom of Heaven (see Mk 3:24-25; Acts 14:22).

WISDOM AND TRUTH

Adam and Eve desired to obtain *knowledge* or wisdom by eating the forbidden fruit (see Gen 3:6). Tragically, this was displeasing to the Father. The prophet Jeremiah (Jer 17:5-10) describes the vast difference between trusting in creatures and trusting in the Lord.

Adam and Eve thought that what they could independently experience was better than what was promised by God. That misconception is at the root of original sin. That sin has been passed on to our generation and is in full force today. In fact, the major battle of our times is the battle for truth: how to recognize the one who speaks the truth (see Jn 18:38). This is a central problem for humanity, because we cannot love or trust without truth (see 1 Pet 1:22). It is essential for us to be able to identify the people who speak the truth, because those are the people we should trust.

As Christians, we know that Jesus Christ is the Truth. But as sinful creatures, we tend to trust in ourselves and our own understanding. Look around the world and see what this trust in ourselves has led to. Look at the news; look at the failure of all the best-laid political plans; look at how even the greatest technological progress fails to bring us peace and happiness.

Without God, we are nothing and return to nothing — a man's plans go with him to the grave (see Ps 146:3-4). We cannot redeem ourselves. We put ourselves into sin, but cannot get ourselves out of it. We are saved therefore not by our efforts, but by the Father's Mercy: "For by grace you have been saved through faith; and this is not your own doing, it is the gift of God — not because of works, lest any man should boast" (Eph 2:8-9). Of course, it is necessary to

---

[80] Saint Catherine of Siena, *The Dialogue of the Seraphic Virgin Catherine of Siena*, trans. Algar Thorold (London: Kegan Paul, Trench, Trübner and Co., 1896), 116: "I have explained to thee the figure of the three steps, in general, as the three powers of the soul, and no one who wishes to pass by the Bridge and doctrine of My Truth can mount one without the other, and the soul cannot persevere except by the union of her three powers."

cooperate with the Holy Spirit, because without His grace, no amount of effort can save us (see *CCC*, 2008).

Mary of Nazareth

Mary, in her Immaculate Conception, exemplifies the beauty of trust, of living in obedience to the Father. By a singular grace merited by her Son, Mary was preserved from the stain of original sin. In her, we see how salvation is a free gift: The Holy Spirit filled her from the first moment of her existence before she could even begin to contemplate trying to merit salvation or attempting to please God. Turn to her when you are assailed by the remaining effects of original sin, called concupiscence, from the Latin *cum + cupere,* meaning "to desire ardently" — the root of our English word *Cupid*.[81] She will take your hand and teach you to step on the serpent of distrust; she will teach you to trust God, but distrust the serpent.

In Mary, we see the beauty of the grace we were given in Baptism. We were not conceived without original sin, but that sin was washed away in our Baptism. By entrusting ourselves to her, we renew our desire to imitate her and live free of sin — to share in the grace of her Immaculate Conception, the grace of complete and total trust in the Father. I invite you to renew your baptismal vows through Mary as the next step along the journey of trust.

---

[81] Merriam-Webster's Collegiate Dictionary.

CHAPTER 8

Vengeful or Good Father?

"The Lord, the Lord, a God merciful and gracious, slow to anger, and abounding in mercy and faithfulness" (Ex 34:6).

The image we have of the Father plays a key role in establishing trust. Satan's trick is to tempt us to distrust, not once but many times. He disfigures our image of God, presenting Him as angry, vindictive, and condemning, and tempts us to distrust by disobedience. After we fall, he tries to persuade us never to get back up — to convince us that the journey is already ruined, and that there is no hope of reaching the goal of sanctity.

SINNERS AND SAINTS

The difference between saints and sinners is not whether they sinned or not, but rather that the saints arose from their fall while the sinners — still discouraged — never stood up again: "For a righteous man falls seven times, and rises again; but the wicked are overthrown by calamity" (Prov 24:6). All of the serpent's temptations are directed toward the "unforgivable" sin: blasphemy against the Holy Spirit (see Mt 12:31-32). This sin itself, of distrust and disbelief in the Father's Mercy, can be forgiven if we give it up, turn to God with trust, and repent; but the devil's trick is to cause so much fear of God that we don't attempt to arise from the fall and we fail to approach Him for forgiveness.

Why would anyone fall into such a sin? The serpent's greatest trick is not in the original temptation, but in distorting the image of God so much that we have become afraid of Him. In reality, Satan is merely attributing to the Father his own sinfulness: anger, condemnation, hatred, etc. The Lord revealed Himself to Moses thus: "The Lord, the Lord, a God merciful and gracious, slow to anger, and abounding in mercy and faithfulness, keeping merciful love for thousands, forgiving iniquity and transgression and sin, but who will by no means clear the guilty" (Ex 34:6-7).

When the Father says He will not clear the guilty, it does not mean He is vindictive. Rather, like a doctor, the Father will not let His children who are afflicted with the cancer of sin continue to suffer this life-threatening sickness without proper treatment. Hence, He chastises us and disciplines us, not because He hates us, but precisely because He loves us and desires for us, His beloved sons and daughters (see Heb 12:6; Rev 3:19; Prov 3:12), to become saints. We must trust Him, just as we trust a doctor who gives us painful (though necessary) treatment.

As a priest, I often recommend that people come to Confession at least once a month. Continuing this analogy of sin as a cancer of the soul, we know that those with bodily cancer need some intensive form of treatment to be cured. They often visit the hospital regularly, at least once a month, for treatment. If they don't avail themselves of the medicine provided, they can be certain the cancer will spread and they will die. Yet many of us forget this when it comes to spiritual cancer. We go weeks, months, or even years without treatment, and are often surprised that our lives aren't going well or that we're falling into serious sin. For that reason, I recommend confession monthly *at a minimum*, if not more often.

Confession is important not only as a means to visit the doctor of our souls and receive the spiritual medicine of Divine Mercy that flows from the Sacrament. How often we frequent the Sacrament also reveals our perception of the Father. If we truly believe that the Father is forgiving and merciful, then why would we hesitate to approach His Son hidden in the priest in the confessional? Despite our belief in His Mercy, however, we still live distrustfully by avoiding Confession and hiding from the Father, as did Adam and Eve after they had sinned (Gen 3:8). When we must come before Him, like Adam and Eve we often make every excuse for our sins or blame others (see Gen 3:8-13) instead of confessing our sins and trusting in His Mercy!

OUR CONCEPT OF GOD

If we recognize the Father for who He is — the loving, merciful Father who called us into existence to share His own divine life — then we will trust. Why do so many people in our world today not trust or not believe in God? Because they do not know the Father — they know only some distorted image of Him, and we cannot trust what we do not love, and cannot love what we do not know. Some people even say that they hate God. Saint Thomas Aquinas tells us that it is impossible to hate sheer goodness; thus they don't hate God, but rather carry hatred in their heart for what He permits that causes them or others suffering. [82]

That kind of hatred and bitterness can be extinguished only by trust in the Mercy of the Father, trust that redeems even suffering and uses it for our good. To encourage souls to trust again in the Father, St. Faustina desired to tear aside the veil of Heaven to prove that God is good and merciful: "O doubting souls, I will draw aside for you the veils of heaven to convince you of God's goodness, so that you will no longer continue to wound with your distrust the sweetest Heart of Jesus. God is Love and Mercy" (*Diary*, 281). That is precisely what needs to be done for souls to be able to trust in the Father again.

The original temptation by Satan was designed to persuade us to fall so as to disfigure us as images of the Triune God, and to deform the concept of God that we hold in our hearts and minds. In asking Adam and Eve whether the

---

[82] Saint Thomas Aquinas, *Summa Theologica*, II-II, q. 34, a. 1.

Father had forbidden them to eat the fruit of any of the trees, Satan made Him look like a severe, strict God who was jealous of His prerogatives (see *CCC,* 399). No one would want to trust a God who is concerned only about Himself and His prerogatives, but that is not the God who created us!

Our God is the Trinity, who wishes to pour His divine life freely out upon us in order to allow us to share in His eternal happiness and love. The Father has no ulterior motive in creating us. He gains nothing at all from our creation or even from our praise. As we pray in the Mass in one of the prefaces: "For, although you have no need of our praise, yet our thanksgiving is itself your gift, since our praises add nothing to your greatness but profit us for salvation, through Christ our Lord."[83] The Father's love is purely selfless, with no self-interest, since He has no need of anything from us, but only desires to give: **"I am the Lord in My essence and am immune to orders or needs. If I call creatures into being — that is the abyss of My mercy"** (*Diary,* 85).

One of the greatest works of the Holy Spirit is to renew our image of the Father so that we can cry out with confidence again, "*Abba,* Father!" (see Rom 8:15).[84] As Mother, Mary plays a large role in this renewal. In the Syriac tradition, the Holy Spirit is feminine. The Hebrew word *ruah,* meaning "breath" or "wind," is grammatically feminine and, in some instances, is used to mean "Mother."[85] It is not surprising that Mary is given to us to serve as an icon of this motherly aspect of the Holy Spirit, who fills us with Love and unveils the Face of the Father in Jesus Christ.

Saint Maximilian Kolbe uses the analogy of the human family: The mother is the one who teaches the child to say "Dad" and introduces the child to the father.[86] In the same way, Mary Immaculate opens our hearts to the truth about the tender Mercy and Compassion of the Father — the Holy Spirit. By looking upon the feminine face of Mary, we can contemplate the tender Mercy of the Father, and our hearts become more receptive to receiving that mercy through the vessel of trust (see *CCC,* 370).

The Hebrew word for "tender mercy," *rahamim,* comes from *rehem,* Hebrew for "womb." What the mother feels in her womb for her unborn child is the same as what God, personified in the Holy Spirit and revealed in the face of Mary, feels for us in our sinfulness and weakness (see Is 49:15). By revealing the tender Mercy of the Father as a "face" of the Holy Spirit, and pointing to the faithful Love of the Father in Jesus, her Son, Mary crushes the head of the serpent in our lives. She does so by teaching us to trust once again and

---

[83] The Roman Missal, Third Typical Edition (Washington, D.C.: United States Conference of Catholic Bishops, 2011), 616.

[84] Raniero Cantalamessa, *The Gaze of Mercy: A Commentary on Divine and Human Mercy,* trans. Marsha Daigle-Williamson (Frederick, Maryland: Word Among Us Press, 2015), 169.

[85] Eugene F. Rogers, *The Holy Spirit: Classic and Contemporary Readings* (Malden, Massachusetts: Wiley-Blackwell, 2009), 114-27.

[86] H. M. Manteau-Bonamy, *Immaculate Conception and the Holy Spirit: Marian Teachings of St. Maximilian Kolbe* (Libertyville, Illinois: Marytown Press, 2001), 19-23.

encouraging us take a step with her toward the Father, along the Way that is Jesus, her Son.

In Hebrew, *hesed* describes the Father's fidelity to His Word and the profound covenantal love He has for His People, a love so great that it impels Him to send His Spirit to enable us to be faithful in return for His Word and covenant. It is our Father's desire that we enjoy a reciprocal relationship with Him, based on love, mercy, kindness, loyalty, and trust.

HUMILITY AND OBEDIENCE VERSUS PRIDE AND REBELLION

Mary Immaculate teaches us obedience, leading us to do whatever He commands, as she did the servants at Cana (see Jn 2:5). In this way, we fully become sons and daughters of the Father, for St. Paul said that those who are led and are obedient to the Spirit are the children of God (see Rom 8:14). To fully live as God's children, created in His image and participating in His life, we must learn to trust in His Word and not in ourselves.

Trusting in ourselves leads not to dialogue, but to monologue; not to communion, but disunion. Disunion is born of disobedience, and if we do not trust in the Father, if we do not accept what He says as true, then we will not obey. The very word *obey* shows the relationship between trust and obedience, between listening and doing, between word and action. In Hebrew, the verb *shema* means both "to listen" and "to obey." Humility leads us to listen to the Word of God and accept the will of the Father in obedience. If we do not truly listen and accept what another says as true, we will not be able to obey. In turn, if we do not obey, we each live in our own world, according to our own "truth" — what we desire at any given moment.

Pride is born out of distrust and disobedience, out of not accepting objective reality, and out of refusing to listen to the truth as revealed by God but rather relying on experience. Pride is the attempt to create one's own world according to one's own desires instead of entrusting oneself to Divine Providence.

Pride wants to take matters into one's own hands, as if to say, "I know better than God" — He made the world this way, but I am going to change things to be the way that I want them. Pride is essentially attempting to be God and recreating the world according to our own desires. We know we are proud if we get upset when events do not go as we had intended or people do not act according to our plans. This happens in marriages when spouses are unwilling to compromise out of love. It happens when people redefine what is right and wrong so that the world will fit their idea of how it should be, instead of humbly accepting the way that the Father has created the world.

In these and other ways, we try to re-create the world. We do so because we are more interested in this world, and in getting the most out of it, than in patiently awaiting Heaven, where all our desires will be completely fulfilled. That does not mean we should not try to improve the world. It does mean that we should not try to *redefine* the world so as to make it our own paradise.

A personal paradise under our control can never exist upon earth, because pride seeks to create its own little world, separate from everyone else's little world. Such division is the fruit of distrust. Once trust is broken, wars begin to brew. This is the condition of the world in which we live. This is the reason that we have armies, and weapons such as nuclear bombs.

Pride and distrust are also the reason that we have gated communities, which separate people of wealth from those who have less or who might be considered dangerous. According to this attitude of distrust, *we must defend our own little worlds.* But true security, especially political security, is found not in weapons, but in trust in the Lord (see Is 26:1-4). Indeed, security is not found in amassing riches or having all that this world can offer; true security is found in trusting in the Father's Providence (see Mt 6:24-34).

CONSEQUENCES OF DISTRUST AND DISOBEDIENCE

The Garden of Eden was a paradise before the fall because the Father's will was fulfilled there without hindrance. Wherever there is obedience to the Father's will, there is Heaven — even on earth. For this reason, Mary is called *hortus conclusus,* the "enclosed garden," where the Father's will is fulfilled. There, in her Immaculate Heart, paradise still exists: There is only goodness and no presence of evil, for the serpent was never able to enter this enclosed garden.

Where the Father's will is not fulfilled, where there is pride and its daughters, *distrust* and *disobedience,* there is simply "earth" — the earth as we know it, riddled by sin.[87] The more we trust and obey, the more we are able to reenter the Garden, to taste Heaven already on earth. The more we distrust and disobey, the more we taste the torments of hell already on earth. The Father taught St. Catherine of Siena, in fact, that Heaven is tasted by those who are "deprived of the hell of their own will, which gives to man the earnest-money of damnation, if he yield to it."[88] Hell indeed is tasted and experienced on earth when we give in to our own sinful will.

The Father wants to save us from hell, from the place of total distrust and total disobedience, of monologue and disunion. Hell is therefore not simply a place we go to after death — it is a state of being orphaned and separated from the Father. Heaven and hell begin already on earth, and it all depends on whether we enter this relationship of trust with the Father or whether we continue to follow Adam and Eve's example and live outside that relationship. For this reason, the greatest gift of redemption is the Holy Spirit — the Spirit of adoption Jesus promised to send us so that we would no longer be orphans, separated from the Father (see Jn 14:18).

---

[87] Joseph Ratzinger, *Gospel, Catechesis, Catechism: Sidelights on the Catechism of the Catholic Church,* trans. Adrian Walker (San Francisco: Ignatius Press, 1997), 52. www.ignatius.com. Used with permission.

[88] Saint Catherine of Siena, *The Dialogue,* 176.

Adam and Eve chose distrust over trust — trusting in themselves over God. As Jesus pointed out to St. Faustina, this is a problem not just for them. The source of our own daily falls is that we trust too much in ourselves (see *Diary,* 1488).

Time and again, we want to get rid of a certain fault or moral failure, but we cannot. Why does the Lord Jesus allow this? We often see our obvious sins, without recognizing their root — distrust —which is what truly offends and hurts our Lord. If this distrust remains, the sin too will remain, until we are humbled enough to recognize our distrust. Only when we turn away from trust in ourselves can we begin to truly trust in the Lord and walk according to His Commandments (see Ps 119:32).

Trust is at the very core of who we are as human beings. It only makes sense, then, that Jesus would place the prayer "Jesus, I trust in You" at the bottom of the Divine Mercy Image. Jesus wants us to restore our relationship with the Father by repeating that prayer and shake off the dust of original sin and its effects. Jesus Christ is the Image of *hesed*, the Father's faithful Mercy (see Col 1:15), just as Mary, the Mother of Mercy, reveals *rahamim*, the Holy Spirit, the Father's tender and compassionate Mercy.

Moreover, Jesus is the Perfecter of Trust who goes before us, showing how to trust in God as Father, even to the point of being obedient unto death (see Heb 12:2; Phil 2:8). Mary is the Mother of Trust who reveals the tenderness of the Father — the Holy Spirit — by her maternal love and presence. She encourages us to take the step to trust God and crush the lies of the serpent who distorts our image of the Father.

By repeating the prayer "Jesus, I trust in You," we express our desire to restore that broken dialogue and communion with God, and reenter the intimacy with the Father that was lost in Eden. By turning to the Immaculate Heart of Mary, we can already enter that paradise of communion and intimacy with the Holy Trinity now. She will accompany us each step of the way, teaching us how to step on Satan, the serpent of distrust, as we progress along our path of trust. She will be with us, just as she accompanied her Son throughout His life, until one day we share divine communion and intimacy with all the saints in Heaven.

Moreover, as a good Mother, she will pick us up when we fall, showing us the merciful face of the Holy Spirit, who desires to heal us and forgive us our sins. The polar opposite of blasphemy against the Holy Spirit is the eternal Immaculate Conception, which is nothing other than the Spirit of Mercy, who not only forgives sin but prevents it. To avoid the sin of disbelieving the Father's Mercy, grasp Mary's hand and allow her to teach you to discover the true Face of the Father: Jesus Christ, her Son.

CHAPTER 9

Misery and Mercy

"For God has consigned all men to disobedience,
that he may have mercy upon all" (Rom 11:32).

As sinful creatures, we stand in constant need of the Father's Mercy, which sustains us in existence at each moment. In our pride, we can often forget a fundamental truth (one that existed even before sin), that the Father often allows us to sin for this reason: to rediscover, time and again, how frail we are as creatures and how much we need Him. In other words, the Father allows us to fail so as to humble us, so that we learn to trust in ourselves less and in Him more.

MISERY

In the preceding chapters, the word "misery" has appeared multiple times. Before continuing, I want to take a moment to define the term. The English word "misery" comes from the Latin *miser,* meaning "wretched, unfortunate, miserable, pitiable, lamentable."[89] Saint Faustina uses the word "misery" 112 times throughout the *Diary.* Does this mean that she was wretched on a daily basis?

According to Dr. Robert Stackpole, the author of several books on Divine Mercy, we need to understand St. Faustina's misery, not in terms of feeling miserable, but rather as a recognition of *who she is* on her own apart from God: "'Misery' is what she calls the state of her soul — or of any soul — if God is excluded. In other words, take away God's power and grace, and what are we? Nothing but misery. Without God's sustaining, creative power, we are nothing at all: We don't even exist!"[90] As St. Faustina wrote: "During this hour of adoration, I saw the abyss of my misery; whatever there is of good in me is Yours, O Lord. But because I am so small and wretched, I have a right to count on Your boundless mercy" (*Diary,* 237). Later on, she wrote: "Without You, I am weakness itself. What am I without Your grace if not an abyss of my own misery? Misery is my possession" (*Diary,* 1630).

Misery includes sin but is broader than sin, so we can say that Mary Immaculate experienced misery through suffering and her recognition that, apart from

---

[89] Charlton T. Lewis and Charles Short, *Harper's Latin Dictionary* (New York and Oxford: Harper and Brothers, and Clarendon Press, 1891), 1150.

[90] Robert Stackpole. "Was St. Faustina 'Miserable' Most of the Time?" Divine Mercy Library. June 30, 2010. Accessed July 11, 2017. http://www.thedivinemercy.org/library/article.php?NID=3296.

the Immaculate Conception, she is nothing at all. For us who do fall into sin, our misery includes sin because it is a choice to live without God — a choice to turn our backs on Him.

The secret to happiness, according to St. Faustina's experiences recorded in her *Diary*, is to be always aware of one's own misery so as to immerse oneself in the ocean of the Father's Mercy: "From the beginning I have been aware of my weakness. I know very well what I am of myself, because for this purpose Jesus opened the eyes of my soul: I am an abyss of misery, and hence I understand that whatever good there is in my soul consists solely of His holy grace. The knowledge of my own misery allows me, at the same time, to know the immensity of Your mercy. In my own interior life, I am looking with one eye at the abyss of my misery and baseness, and with the other, at the abyss of Your mercy, O God" (*Diary*, 56).

MISERY, MERCY, AND MAGNIFICAT

In a remarkably similar manner, Blessed Pope Paul VI said that his entire spiritual life could be summed up by three words: *miseria, misericordia,* and *Magnificat,* writing:

> The secret of my spirituality is to be found in St. Augustine. In St. Augustine, as there is in each of us, there is a struggle going on inside; I call it a tension of love, between the weaknesses that are within us, the *miseria*, on one hand, and on the other hand, the love of God that seeks us out, to cover over the *miseria* that each one of us is. And this encounter between the love of God and the *miseria* of mankind coming together forms the word *misericordia* — mercy. So on the one hand, every one of us carries baggage, we all have *miseria* within us, we all are broken, but God sent his Son to cover over the brokenness, to redeem it and draw us back into the Father ... Remember, mercy would never have been, were there no sin to be redeemed ... and when *miseria* and *misericordia* encounter each other, *misericordia* becomes prominent in our lives, we become conscious of God's goodness to us.[91]

Our misery and God's mercy always go together, and when they meet, we begin to sing the Magnificat, as Blessed Paul VI told his secretary: "You have the secret of my spirituality ... I am always conscious of my *miseria*, my weakness; I am always conscious of God's great love for me [*misericordia*], and when I allow the two to encounter, I sing my *Magnificat*."[92] Trust, expressing itself in praise,

---

[91] Bishop John Magee, *Untold Stories of Three Popes* (Lighthouse Catholic Media, 2013, CD) Quoted by Lori Pieper, OSF, "The Real Paul VI (Part II) His Spirituality," August 24, 2014, accessed July 11, 2017, http://subcreators.com/blog/2014/08/24/the-real-paul-/ vi-part-ii/.

[92] Ibid.

is the bridge that connects our own misery and the Father's Mercy, and as the Father told St. Catherine of Siena, we ought never to think of our sins without also thinking of the Precious Blood, lest we run into an opportunity to distrust and despair:

> Now I do not want her [the soul] to think about her sins individually, lest her mind be contaminated by the memory of specific ugly sins. I mean that I do not want her to, nor should she, think about her sins either in general or specifically without calling to mind the blood and the greatness of my mercy. Otherwise she will only be confounded. For if self-knowledge and the thought of sin are not seasoned with remembrance of the blood and hope for mercy, the result is bound to be confusion.[93]

Divine Mercy is the Father's Love — the Holy Spirit — poured out in the Blood and Water of Jesus upon us to heal our sins and weaknesses. Father George Kosicki, an author, speaker, and preacher who enjoyed a passion for the Divine Mercy, describes mercy in this way:

> Mercy, then, is God's love poured out upon us; it is when God, who is love itself, loves us. This flowing quality of mercy is most dramatically represented by Christ on the cross as, through the Blood and Water gushing forth from His pierced Heart, He pours His very life out as a fountain of mercy for us . ... And we also find it in the great chant of the Church, the Kyrie Eleison ("Lord, have mercy"), which for centuries has resounded throughout the world at every celebration of the Eucharist and the Liturgy of Hours. The word *eleison*, which in Greek means "have mercy," has the root meaning of "oil being poured out," so whenever we say, "Lord, have mercy," we are really saying, "Lord, pour Your love out upon us, pour Yourself out upon us."[94]

Satan wants to exaggerate our faults so we begin to distrust the Lord. He wants to take away our peace and prevent us from immersing ourselves in God's Mercy — even in the Sacrament of Confession! The *Diary* of St. Faustina reveals how the serpent attempts to cause confusion (see *Diary*, 1801).

Saint Faustina also writes about how deeper understanding of her misery leads to greater trust in God's Mercy (see *Diary*, 832).

Our journey of trust began with the Father's Mercy creating us and will end with His Mercy lifting us to Heaven. Our misery impels us to beg for mercy — and impels the Father to be merciful! Saint Francis de Sales wrote: "If God

---

[93] Saint Catherine of Siena, *The Dialogue*, 124.

[94] George W. Kosicki, *Now Is the Time for Mercy* (Stockbridge, Massachusetts: Marian Press, 2010), 28.

had not created man He would still indeed have been perfect in goodness, but He would not have been actually merciful, since mercy can only be exercised towards the miserable … I ever say that the throne of God's mercy is our misery, therefore the greater our misery, the greater should be our confidence."[95]

It is important to keep in mind that the greater our misery, the greater should be our trust in the Mercy of the Father, for as Jesus told St. Faustina: **"The greater the sinner, the greater the right he has to My mercy"** (*Diary*, 723). Indeed, as Blessed Francis Xavier Seelos wrote, "None of the damned was ever lost because his sin was too great, but because his trust was too small!"[96] In the face of the ocean of her own misery, St. Faustina trusted even more in the Divine Mercy (see *Diary*, 1298).

Expressing similar thoughts in a homily while still a bishop in Kraków, St. John Paul II explained Psalm 42:7 ("deep calls to deep"), saying that the deep or abyss of our misery calls out to the deep of the Father's Mercy.[97] Our misery is limited, however, while the Mercy of God is infinite — and even *increases* when it is given: **"I am love and Mercy Itself. There is no misery that could be a match for My mercy, neither will misery exhaust it, because as it is being granted — it increases. The soul that trusts in My mercy is most fortunate, because I Myself take care of it"** (*Diary*, 1273).

By accepting our misery, we participate more fully in His divine life. As Jesus promised, only those who are poor in spirit — who are aware of their misery, poverty, and nothingness — possess the Kingdom of Heaven (see Mt 5:3). Having received His infinite mercy, we sing with Mary a canticle of praise to our Father for His goodness and mercy (see Lk 1:46-55).

Precisely because Mary was aware of her littleness before the Father, she could rejoice even more in His Mercy. As St. Elizabeth of the Trinity wrote, "The abyss of God's immensity encounters the abyss of the creature's nothingness and God embraces this nothingness" and we read in *Lumen Gentium*: "She stands out among the poor and humble of the Lord, who confidently hope for and receive salvation from Him."[98] She received the fullness of the Kingdom in her Immaculate Conception. In the Incarnation, the King Himself took flesh in her womb. Paradoxically, she did not know the misery of sin, but she knew her misery in full clarity — that she is nothing at all without the infinite Mercy of the Father.

---

[95] Saint Francis de Sales, *The Spiritual Conferences*, trans. Abbot Gasquet and Canon Mackey, Library of Francis de Sales (London; New York, Cincinnati, and Chicago: Burns and Oates, and Benziger Brothers, 1909), 19.

[96] Blessed Francis Xavier Seelos, CSsR, "Wise Words of Francis Xavier Seelos," accessed July 11, 2017, http://www.seelos.org/lifeWritings.html.

[97] Saint Karol Wojtyła, *Odnowa Kościoła i świata: refleksje soborowe*, ed. Andrzej Dobrzynski (Rome: Fundacja Jana Pawła II. Ośrodek Dokumentacji i Studium Pontyfikatu, 2014).

[98] Saint Elizabeth of the Trinity, *Elizabeth of the Trinity: Always Believe in Love*, ed. Marian Teresa Murphy (Hyde Park, New York: New City Press, 2009); *Lumen Gentium*, n. 55.

PRIDE AND HUMILITY

Pride, on the other hand, involves rejoicing in ourselves — in our talents, in our gifts, in who we are — without reference to the Father. Through pride, we attempt to hide our poverty and misery, believing instead that we can solve our problems by our own efforts (or that we don't experience problems, poverty, or misery at all!) and therefore do not need mercy. In the Gospels, such was the attitude of the Pharisees, who believed that by their effort to keep the Law, they could justify themselves. No amount of merely human effort, however, can free us from our sins; only the Holy Spirit, poured forth in Jesus' Blood and Water, can do so. One of St. Faustina's fellow sisters used the image of mountains to describe pride (see *Diary*, 55).

Just as water flows down away from the peaks of mountains to gather in the valleys, so too does the Father's grace — the living water of the Holy Spirit — flow away from our mountains of pride. Only the humble, those in the valleys, can collect and gather the graces of His Mercy. For this reason, the Father humbles our pride so as to prepare us to be united to Himself: "I shall totally shatter you because of your vain affections and your vicious pride; and after that I shall gather you together and make you humble and gentle, pure and holy, by one-ing you to myself."[99]

Humility, then, is rejoicing in the Father. Often the Father allows us to experience our poverty and misery so we can recognize them; but humility recognizes them and even rejoices. As St. Thérèse of Lisieux wrote to her sister Marie: "What pleases God is to see me love my littleness and poverty ... I am not disturbed at seeing myself *weakness* itself. On the contrary, it is in my weakness that I glory, and I expect each day to discover new imperfections in myself."[100]

Humility keeps us in touch with our limitations, so that we will not rejoice too much in the talents and gifts given us by the Father, but rejoice in the eternal joy of God Himself. Indeed, in the worst suffering, this is the only joy that remains — the eternal happiness of the Trinity, who through the Blood and Water pours His Mercy out upon us in our misery.

This joy of the Trinity is unending and inexhaustible! This is the Mercy of our Father: that He incessantly bursts forth with Love, to share the fullness of His own life with us in our misery and pain. "O Holy Trinity, in whom is contained the inner life of God, the Father, the Son, and the Holy Spirit, eternal joy, inconceivable depth of love, poured out upon all creatures and constituting their happiness, honor and glory be to Your holy name forever and ever. Amen" (*Diary*, 525).

Saint Faustina was humbled repeatedly throughout her life, so that she might know her poverty and rejoice in the Mercy of the Father. She wrote that

---

[99] Julian of Norwich, *Revelations of Divine Love*, trans. John-Julian (Brewster, Massachusetts: Paraclete Press, 2016), 66.

[100] Saint Thérèse of Lisieux, *Story of A Soul: The Autobiography of St. Thérèse of Lisieux*, trans. John Clarke (Washington, D.C.: ICS Publications, 1996), 224.

there are unfortunately few souls who understand the infinite Mercy of God, for few accept their nothingness and misery (see *Diary*, 361). For this reason, St. Faustina wrote that there is nothing better for us than humiliations, for through them, we learn humility. She even adds — note well — that only humble souls can be truly happy upon this earth (see *Diary*, 593).

HIDING OUR MISERY

Let us look at the woman caught in adultery and notice how gentle the Lord is — even with someone who is guilty. When they present the misery and sin of the woman to Jesus, the Pharisees, who personify the serpent, wait for Him to condemn her, but that is not what He does. In the face of the woman's misery, He is Mercy itself. Indeed, when Jesus (Mercy Incarnate) encounters the woman caught in adultery (misery personified), He does not condemn her. He justifies her, as He does with all sinners who take refuge in His Mercy (see *Diary*, 1146).

Satan does the same thing as the Pharisees. He wants to convince us that Jesus would condemn us if He saw our misery — our guilt. Commenting on this passage, St. Augustine wrote that at the end of this scene, there remain only misery and mercy: the woman and Jesus. This woman is every one of us, for in the Old Testament, adultery symbolizes the infidelity of the Israelite people espoused by covenant to one God. Through Baptism, we, too, entered a covenant with God. We were even given a wedding garment — our white baptismal gown. We often are not faithful to the covenant, however, and like the woman, commit "adultery" by our infidelity to the one God.

What does this have to do with trust? The woman caught in adultery is an example of someone who trusts. She is almost forced to trust because her misery is already displayed before Jesus and everyone else there. Jesus came precisely to call sinners and to heal their sins (see Lk 5:32), and He does not condemn her. Instead, He condemns the Pharisees. The Pharisees' sin is their attempt to cover their nakedness and shame — their misery — by their pious practices rather than acknowledging their misery and trusting in the Father's Mercy. Such is their hypocrisy: They presume to be good by their own goodness, instead of acknowledging their sin and proclaiming the Father's goodness.

This is the serpent's sin as well, the sin for which he will remain in hell for all eternity. The Father is not sparing in His Mercy, and were Satan capable of repenting and admitting his need for mercy, the Father would forgive Him, but Satan in his pride refuses to admit his need for mercy. He would rather suffer in hell and cover over his misery, pretending it does not exist, than simply admit it and ask for mercy. We step on the serpent when we openly admit our sinfulness, as in Confession, and confess that God's Mercy is greater than our sin. Further, we crush the serpent's head when, like Mary, we not only confess Divine Mercy but proclaim it to others, encouraging them to trust, too, as Jesus told

St. Faustina: **"And even if the sins of souls were as dark as night, when the sinner turns to My mercy, he gives Me the greatest praise and is the glory of My Passion. When a soul extols My goodness, Satan trembles before it and flees to the very bottom of hell"** (*Diary*, 378).

Unfortunately, we often act like the Pharisees. Instead of coming to Jesus as we are and trusting in His Mercy, we trust in ourselves, thinking that we can make ourselves better or more presentable, more pleasing to the Father, by merely multiplying our devotions without trusting in His Mercy. This is not the teaching found in the Gospel, however. No amount of devotions, prayers, or fasting makes us pleasing to the Father by our own efforts. Rather, it is our acknowledgment of our need for His grace and His Mercy that makes us pleasing to Him. Covering up our misery is the worst thing we can do, for it prevents us from receiving His Mercy. It deceives only us, for when Jesus sees just how miserable we are, He wants to pour out His Mercy upon us.

Mary had no doubt that she was nothingness itself before the Father. She knew that she was pleasing to God not because of anything she had done on her own, but only because of what the Father had done in her, in her Immaculate Conception and her lifelong cooperation with His grace. Likewise, we are pleasing to the Father because of what He has done for us — in Jesus Christ, His Son. We are to trust, not in our works, but in the work He has done for us: the Paschal Mystery.

No amount of works of our own, not even a lifetime of good works, will merit Heaven. As Thérèse of Lisieux exclaimed: "After earth's exile, I hope to go and enjoy you in the fatherland, but I do not want to lay up merits for heaven. I want to work for your *love alone*. ... In the evening of this life, I shall appear before you with empty hands, for I do not ask you, Lord, to count my works. All our justice is blemished in your eyes. I wish, then, to be clothed in your own *justice* and to receive from your *love* the eternal possession of *yourself*."[101]

We are to trust only in the Father's Mercy, revealed above all in the Paschal Mystery. Blessed Marie Eugene of the Child Jesus, in fact, states that being a saint consists precisely in *trusting* amid our poverty, misery, and even sinfulness: "To become a saint, one must arrive at such an extreme, to such a great annihilation [of oneself], that only one thing remains: to place one's hope in God. When one is completely impoverished, only an act of trust amidst such complete poverty can save one — an act of hope arising from a complete emptying of oneself. The state of the highest sanctity almost merges with the state of being a sinner, who no longer has anything and whose only treasure is hope placed in the Divine Mercy. The purifications of the soul and the sufferings into which the divine light immerses the soul, have as their only goal the realization of one's own complete poverty and the elicitation of a [single] act of hope."[102]

---

[101] Saint Thérèse of Lisieux, *Story of a Soul*, 277. Quoted in *CCC*, 2011.
[102] Quoted in André Daigneault, *Droga niedoskonałości: Świętość ubogich*, trans. Agnieszka Kuryś (Kraków: Wydawnictwo Karmelitów Bosych, 2010), 5.

In this quotation, we see more fully what it means to be a saint: recognizing one's own poverty and placing one's trust and hope exclusively in the Father. In fact, Mary is holy, not because she had any holiness of her own (Phil 3:9), but because she knew she had nothing except trust in the infinite Mercy of the Father. Mary knew that apart from her own Son's death, she could not be immaculate and would not have attained the holiness necessary to enter Heaven (see Heb 12:14). Mary herself needed a Savior! (see Lk 1:47). Mary's holiness is her act of trust that allows her poverty to continually be filled by the Holy Spirit! Indeed, as St. Thérèse of Lisieux wrote: "Holiness does not consist in this or that practice: it consists in a disposition of the heart, which makes us always humble and little in the arms of God, well aware of our feebleness, but boldly confident in the Father's goodness."[103]

As discussed previously, the unforgivable sin that Jesus speaks of in the Gospel (see Mt 12:23-32) is lack of trust in the Mercy of God and consists in hiding one's misery (presumption or hypocrisy). If one pretends not to need God's Mercy, one will have too much pride to ask for His Mercy at the time of our judgment. Unforgivable also would be plunging so deep into one's misery that one does not reach out to Christ for forgiveness, believing that such forgiveness does not exist or is not possible — despair.

Ironically, the lack of trust in those who despair is more painful to Jesus than all the sins they have committed up to that moment: **"My child, all your sins have not wounded My Heart as painfully as your present lack of trust does — that after so many efforts of My love and mercy, you should still doubt My goodness"** (*Diary*, 1486). For that reason, Jesus tells St. Faustina that despairing souls ought not to drown too much in their own misery, but rather look into His Merciful Heart (see *Diary*, 1486).

Trust precludes presumption: only focusing on the Father's Mercy while not recognizing one's own sin; believing one does not need mercy. Trust also precludes despair: recognizing only one's own sin but not the Father's mercy; believing there is no mercy for oneself. Even if Satan rightly accuses us of our sins because we are guilty, we have an advocate before the Father: Jesus (see 1 Jn 2:1). Trust in Jesus Christ is the bridge that allows our misery to encounter the Father's Mercy, for in Him our miserable human nature is united forever to the divine nature, which is Love and Mercy itself (see *Diary*, 180).

REACTION TO OUR MISERY

Previously, we discussed the need to desire sanctity, as well as the primary vices that impede this: pride and acedia. The Holy Spirit's goal is to *convict* the world of its sin, and Jesus Himself identifies this sin, the root of all particular and actual sins, as disbelief and distrust (see Jn 16:8-9). To sanctify us and remove sin, the Holy Spirit reveals our poverty to us. He helps us accept our misery and, in doing so, He fills us with Himself, who is Mercy itself.

---

[103] Marie-Eugène de l'Enfant-Jesus, *I Am a Daughter of the Church*, 400.

If we wish to know whether we understand anything about trust, then we must examine our reaction when we discover our wretchedness.[104] Sadness and discouragement in the face of our own misery are the result of our own pride, of thinking that we are much better than, as sinners, we truly are. As Jesus taught St. Faustina: "**Sensitiveness and discouragement are the fruits of self-love. You should not become discouraged, but strive to make My love reign in place of your self-love**" (*Diary*, 1488).

On the other hand, humility and trust rejoice in poverty because that is the emptiness into which the Father pours His Holy Spirit. The sign that our trust in the Lord is complete is our recognition that we are blessed when we are poor, for only in poverty can we truly trust in the Lord. Perfect trust is not disturbed even by our sins, for they are seen to be simply occasions to glorify His Mercy by asking for forgiveness (see *Diary*, 1488). In fact, our imperfections can even become occasions for receiving *more* grace (see *Diary*, 1293).

In Mary, we see the victory of Mercy over misery because as a creature, she stands in need of Mercy from the first moment of her existence. What is unique is that, due to her Immaculate Conception, she never denied the need for Mercy; she never fell into pride or distrust; she never became discouraged by her own nothingness. Rather, she rejoices in the Father's Mercy, for she knows that, far from being less indebted to her Son, she is more indebted to Him than all sinners combined. Christ died above all to make her immaculate, and since she experienced more Mercy than anyone else, she is also more indebted to her Son than anyone else!

With Mary, we will recognize ever more, at every step of our journey, how our need for Mercy is not less than we might expect — rather, it is more than we could ever imagine! But the joy of this journey is that we have a Father who rejoices to fill us with Mercy as often as we ask, for Jesus promised that the Father does not ration His portion of the Spirit of Mercy (see Jn 3:34).

---

[104] Wilfrid Stinissen, *The Holy Spirit, Fire of Divine Love*, trans. Sr. Clare Marie, OCD (San Francisco: Ignatius Press, 2017), 49. www.ignatius.com. Used with permission.

CHAPTER 10

Mary, Our Model of Trust

"'Because no word shall be impossible with God.'
And Mary said: 'Behold the handmaid of the Lord: be it done
to me according to thy word'" (Lk 1:37-38, Douay-Reims).

Before the fall, there was unity between God and His adopted children, who obeyed the will of their kind and good Father. As soon as the fall happened, the Father needed to provide a means for the salvation of His fallen children. This first required restoring the image man had of the merciful Father, whose plan it was to share His divine life with His children. This He accomplished through the renewal of man's trust in Him (see *CCC*, 410). In this way, the image of God within man was also restored by allowing man once again to reflect and mirror the dialogue and communion of the Trinity.

We see this plan of the Father in Genesis 3:15, which the Church calls the *protoevangelium* or "First Gospel." Here, the Father promises to crush the head of the serpent under the heel of a woman by her seed. The woman is the Blessed Virgin Mary, and her Son Jesus is her seed. Jesus is the Word become man to uproot the weeds of distrust sown by Satan. The sin of distrust is a rejection of the Word, and also a rejection of the One who sent the Word (see Lk 10:16; 1 Jn 2:23). As God and man, Jesus is the bridge between misery and Mercy, since He is Mercy Incarnate. Through the Incarnation of the Son of God, man will again share in the inner life of the Trinity, the communion for which he was created (see *CCC*, 460). Jesus is the true Image of God the Father, the Face of Mercy (see Heb 1:3; Col 1:15), who emptied Himself in love for His creatures, becoming poor for our sake so that we might become rich in Him (see Phil 2:6-7; 2 Cor 8:9).

Before there was Jesus, however, there was the Virgin Mary, who gave birth to God and is the Mother of all. I want us to look closely at this woman who is our model of trust. The secret of her life and holiness was not that she accomplished great moral feats or had a stronger will than the rest of us (though both of those things are true). Her secret was that she always trusted in the Father. Her trust in His Word was so radical and complete that this same Word became flesh.

Such absolute trust was no easy accomplishment, especially if we keep in mind all that she suffered in her life: the difficulties brought by her pregnancy, her flight into Egypt, her poverty in Nazareth, the Crucifixion of her Son, and the persecution of her spiritual children by Roman and Jewish leaders, to name but a few of her sufferings. Mary always trusted in the Word of the Lord, no matter how difficult her fidelity and trust proved to be, for she believed the words of the angel: "No word shall be impossible for God" (Lk 1:37). Indeed, we honor and venerate Mary so much in the Church precisely because of her faith and trust.

Mary and Eve — Differences in Wisdom and Trust

How did Mary trust? And how did she trust to the very end? To answer these questions, I will use Mary as a foil for Eve, as did the Fathers of the Church. Both were virgins and became mothers, although only Mary remained ever-virgin. Unlike Eve, who listened to the fallen angel (Satan) and ignored the Word of God through distrust, Mary listened to the archangel (Gabriel) and conceived the Word of God through her faith and trust. Whereas Eve, intimidated by the serpent, fell through fear into slavery, Mary, confident in the merciful Father, crushed the serpent's head and set us free from slavery to sin by her *fiat*.

The Vatican II document on the Church (*Lumen Gentium*) states this about Mary: "Hence not a few of the early Fathers gladly assert in their preaching, 'The knot of Eve's disobedience was untied by Mary's obedience; what the virgin Eve bound through her unbelief, the Virgin Mary loosened by her faith.' Comparing Mary with Eve, they call her 'the Mother of the living,' and still more often they say: 'death through Eve, life through Mary.'"[105]

Remember that we trust someone of character and strength who can help us in our weakness, and to trust the right person, we need to pray and discern whether that person is worthy of trust. Notice that the Bible does not mention that Eve stopped to pray before making her decision to eat the fruit, so she did not seek God's counsel. The problem of original sin is not simply that we do not trust at all, but that we begin to trust the wrong person — with terrible consequences. When we trust, we have only three options: trust in God, trust in ourselves or another fallen human being, or trust in the devil. Eve chose to trust in the temptation of the devil.

Look now at Mary. Even when visited by an archangel, she wondered in her spirit what sort of greeting the archangel gave her (see Lk 1:29). To trust appropriately, we must pray with the Word of God and discern whether our own ideas or what others tell us are in accord with that Word. My professor in seminary described Dominican spirituality as simply basking our minds and hearts in the light of the truth and allowing the truth to penetrate further and further. This truth, though, is not just any abstract truth: This is the Truth that is Jesus Christ, the Word made flesh, who is the Light of the Father that shines in our darkness (see Jn 1:9, 12:46).

---

[105] *Lumen Gentium*, n. 56.

This belief is not exclusive to the Dominicans. It is the goal of Christian spirituality — allowing the Word to *penetrate our minds and hearts so that the Word takes on flesh again in us*. In a prayer by St. Elizabeth of the Trinity, she describes the same reality: "O Consuming Fire, Spirit of Love, overshadow me so that the Word may be, as it were incarnate again in my soul. May I be for him a new humanity in which he can renew all his mystery." Upon awaking, St. Faustina would give thanks that each day the mystery of the Incarnation would be repeated in her (see *Diary,* 486). Through our own prayer and meditation upon the Word of God, this repetition of the Incarnation can happen within us.

Our faith is focused upon trust in the Word of God and oriented toward this: that we, like Mary, would conceive the Word of God in our hearts by the same Holy Spirit and allow that Word to become flesh and dwell within and among us. "Mary believed, and in her what was believed came to pass. Let's also believe so that what came to pass in her can also happen to us."[106] By our response of faith to the Word of God, this Word becomes flesh. It is thus at every Eucharist: When we respond in faith to the Word of God, that very Word descends to the altar. By receiving both the Word and the Eucharist, we become the Body of Christ, and the Word becomes flesh in the Church. The Church, after the model of Mary, gives birth to the Body of Christ through hearing and trusting the Word of God and through the Sacraments. "Like the Mother of the Lord, our holy Mother Church conceives them without stain, she gives birth to them painlessly, and leads them with joy to the heavenly realities."[107]

Mary gave us a perfect example by receiving the Word of God with trust — and that Word became flesh. "Answer quickly, O Virgin. Reply in haste to the angel, or rather through the angel to the Lord. Answer with a word, receive the Word of God. Speak your own word, conceive the divine Word. Breathe a passing word, embrace the eternal Word." As the antiphon for Morning Prayer for the Annunciation reads: "Trusting in the Lord's promise, the Virgin Mary conceived a child."[108] Her trust enabled the Holy Spirit to bring about the Incarnation of Jesus; what will our trust enable the Holy Spirit to do in our own lives?

---

[106] Raniero Cantalamessa, "Mary, Mother and Model of the Priest," Father Cantalamessa's Third Advent Sermon, December 19, 2009, accessed July 11, 2017, https://zenit.org/articles/father-cantalamessa-s-3rd-advent-sermon-2/.

[107] Corrado Maggioni, "Mary, an Icon of the Church That Baptizes in Jesus Christ," Vatican website, accessed July 11, 2017, http://www.vatican.va/jubilee_2000/magazine/documents/ju_mag_01091997_p-60_en.html.

[108] International Commission on English in the Liturgy (ICEL), *The Liturgy of the Hours: According to the Roman Rite* (New York, NY: Catholic Book Publ., 2009), Vol.2, 1748.

WISDOM AND DISCERNMENT

Why is this important? If our mind is not bathed in the light of truth, the Word of God, we cannot trust — just like the flower that cannot open except in the sunlight (see *CCC*, 1216). If our mind is not acquainted with the truth and we remain in darkness, we can easily be deceived by falsehood and trust the wrong person, as did Adam and Eve (see Jn 12:46).

The last line of the prayer "Come, Holy Spirit" asks the Father that we may be *truly wise* (emphasis added):

> Come, Holy Spirit, fill the hearts of Thy faithful and enkindle in them the fire of Thy love.
>
> V. Send forth Thy Spirit and they shall be created.
> R. And Thou shalt renew the face of the earth.
>
> Let us pray. O God, Who didst instruct the hearts of the faithful by the light of the Holy Spirit, grant us in the same Spirit to be *truly wise*, and ever to rejoice in His consolation. Through Christ our Lord. Amen.

I suggest saying this prayer every day as an important way to avoid being deceived. The Latin word for wisdom is *sapientia*, which comes from the word for tasting or perceiving.[109] Hence another translation of the prayer reads, "Grant us to *relish* what is right." By praying with the Word of God and asking for the wisdom of the Holy Spirit, we develop a taste for the truth. Being wise is about having a taste for the Word, which is truth. Once we have that taste, that wisdom, the Holy Spirit can lead us into all truth (see Jn 16:13) and Satan will be unable to lead us astray because in our hearts we will be able to *taste* the difference between truth and falsehood. By *relishing* the truth through daily reading of Scripture and invocation of the Holy Spirit, we learn to step on the serpent with Mary.

Notice the difference between the two kinds of wisdom: Mary's wisdom of trusting the Word of God and Eve's wisdom of experiencing and tasting good and evil for herself (see Jas 3:17). In virtue of her trust, Mary received the true Wisdom that Eve attempted to gain by eating the apple. Such wisdom is a gift from on high to the humble and simple of heart, and to receive it, we have only to ask for it (see Jas 1:5).

Mary not only possessed true wisdom; she became the Seat of Wisdom, for she gave birth to Wisdom Incarnate. She tasted the Word of God in prayer and conceived that Word, as St. Augustine said: The Virgin "conceived in her heart

---

[109] "*săpĭentĭa*. good taste, i.e. good sense, discernment, discretion, prudence, intelligence; from *săpĭo*, to taste, savor; to taste, smack, or savor of; to have a taste or flavor of a thing." Lewis and Short, *Harper's Latin Dictionary*, 1629.

before her womb."[110] Mary possessed true wisdom as a gift of the Holy Spirit; by meditating on the Word of God, she could discern the difference between truth and falsehood and be confident about whom to trust and believe in the moment of decision.

Notice also that while Mary received the greeting of the archangel, she accepted his words only with prudence and discernment (see Lk 1:29). Trust does not mean being gullible and just accepting everything at face value. Trust requires the virtue of prudence, the ability to discern. By being familiar with the Word of God, Mary knew whom she should trust. Eve did not weigh the words of the serpent against the Word of God given to her and Adam. She simply gave in to temptation.

Mary also understood that the archangel came from the merciful Father, and so her response was one of unlimited trust. Her response showed her complete surrender to the Holy Spirit, the fruit of her trust in the Lord. The Holy Spirit is Love in person, "the personified capability for surrender and the actual loving surrender/devotion to the Godhead."[111] Because of her Immaculate Conception by the power of that same Holy Spirit, Mary had an open heart and trust in the Father; she was able and willing to trust, surrender, and act with obedience. With her open heart, she received the Holy Spirit that overshadowed her and conceived the Word made flesh (see Lk 1:34).

When we follow the example of Mary, trust means an unconditional surrender to the work and activity of the Holy Spirit upon us, which sanctifies us and makes us children of our Father (see Rom 8:15-16; 1 Jn 3:2). The Holy Spirit makes us sons and daughters in the Son by allowing the Word to take on flesh in our own lives.

Do you ever wish an angel would appear to you and tell you what the Father wants? It seems like an easy alternative to discernment — if only the Father would simply write out His will for us in neon lights. Maybe He does, and we are not open to noticing it! Are we open to the Lord of history entering our own history? The Father who entered Mary's life through the Word is the same Father who wants to enter our lives and invites us to fulfill the good works He has prepared for us from all eternity (see Eph 2:10). If we remain in dialogue with the Father and, like Mary, trust in His Word, we will be addressed by God in prayer and find our own personal mission: His will for our lives. The problem is not that the Father is silent; it is that we do not know how to listen to the Father who speaks the Word in silence. His voice booms with silent power, but we are not attentive to His voice! (see Ps 29:4; Heb 3:15).

---

[110] Saint Augustine, *Discourses*, 215, 4 (PL 38, 1074). Quoted in Pope Francis, *Angelus*, December 8, 2014 — Solemnity of the Immaculate Conception of the Blessed Virgin Mary, accessed July 11, 2017, https://w2.vatican.va/content/francesco/en/angelus/2014/documents/papa-francesco_angelus_20141208.html.

[111] M. Mueller, OFM, *Gotteskinder vor dem Vater: Ihr Werden, Sein, und Leben*.(Freiburg im Breisgau: Herder, 1938), 78.

MEDITATION ON THE WORD OF GOD

Because Mary's intellect was bathed in the light of Truth, the Word of God, she had an appropriate image of the Father. Remember that the strategy of the devil was not to triumph over Eve with an abstract idea of who the Father is, but rather to implant in her heart an image of a God who is "jealous of His prerogatives." Mary was a woman of the Word who meditated on Scripture and had in her heart a correct image of the Father as merciful and faithful.

When she was asked by the Father to trust, she knew that He was worthy of trust precisely because for more than 2,000 years He had revealed Himself to her ancestors as faithful and merciful. Indeed, in Exodus, God named Himself to Moses in these words: "The Lord, the Lord, a God merciful and gracious, slow to anger, and abounding in mercy and faithfulness, keeping merciful love for thousands, forgiving iniquity and transgression and sin" (Ex 34:6-7).

Without meditation on the Word of God, it would be difficult to trust the Father, and without the Sacred Scriptures, we would not know God as merciful, faithful, and worthy of our trust. Philosophically, we know that God is *one, simple, wise, true, just*; but it is only from the Bible that we come to learn that God is *merciful, faithful,* and open to dialogue with man through the covenant. We may use such adjectives to describe God — we may even know many facts about God — but as His beloved children, we need to *know* our Father intimately.

Otherwise, we begin to construct our own version of what the Father is like, and our version reflects what we know from experience (our own sinful selves) rather than the truth about the Father. We even begin to project onto God our own understanding of what the statement that He is merciful and faithful means, instead of acquiring an accurate perception from the Bible.

Such a self-constructed image of the Father may help us until a crisis comes along, but then our own idea of God cannot sustain us through the reality of suffering. Only the God of the Bible measures up to reality and to our suffering, because it is precisely the God of the Bible who created this world, who acted and continues to act in our history.

Such intimate knowledge of the Father flows from meditation on the Word, and that requires silence and contemplation, since silence is God's language: "Silence is so powerful a language that it reaches the throne of the living God. Silence is His language, though secret, yet living and powerful" (*Diary*, 888). Mary speaks only a few times in the Gospels. If we remain in silence with her, she will teach us to listen to and trust the Father's Word, relishing Wisdom by the Holy Spirit. "Only in silence can the word of God find a home in us, as it did in Mary, woman of the word and, inseparably, woman of silence."[112]

Indeed, only in silence can we hear, receive, and learn to trust in that Word.

---

[112] See Benedict XVI, *Verbum Domini*, Apostolic Exhoratation (Vatican City: Libreria Editrice Vaticana, 2010), n. 66.

GOD IS TRUSTWORTHY

Sacred Scripture teaches us that the Father is infinitely trustworthy. Further, in Jesus Christ, this trustworthy God has given His unequivocal "yes" to us: "For all the promises of God find their Yes in him. That is why we utter the Amen through him, to the glory of God" (2 Cor 1:20). The entire story of the Bible tells us that the Father alone is worthy of trust, because human heroes are men and women who fall quite often. The characters of the Old and New Testament are sinful and weak. Even the best are deceptive and cruel at times — think of David and his affair with Bathsheba in 2 Samuel 11, or Jacob and his trickery in Genesis 27. A read through 1 and 2 Kings or 1 and 2 Chronicles reveals that, overall, Israel kept turning away from God.

Biblical history, as well as world history, reveals that in the face of man's sinfulness, the Father is always faithful and merciful. Scripture shows us that the greatest misery man suffers is sin, and that the mercy of the Father conquers sin. The biblical narrative is primarily about the Father and His fidelity to His covenants with humanity, which reaches its apex in the Incarnation and Paschal Mystery.

That is the very meaning of the word *hesed* ("merciful love" or "fidelity"): God maintains His side of the covenant even when we fail to keep ours. When we keep our part of the covenant, we become *hasidim,* faithful and merciful believers who trust in the Father entirely, expecting help from Him to conquer every trial and difficulty and fulfill His will (see Ps 16:10, 18:36, 43:1). Moreover, we become part of the *anawim,* the poor ones, who have only the Father as our support and help.

By meditating on the history of the Chosen People in the Old Testament, Mary became one of these *hasidim* and *anawim* who relied totally upon the Father. She could trust in the Lord, who entered physically into her personal history. The Annunciation was not a random event to which Mary happened to respond well. By remaining in prayer, in dialogue with the Word in her daily life, Mary was already accustomed to waiting in silence to hear the voice of the Father in His Word (see 1 Sam 3:10). As St. John of the Cross wrote: "The Father spoke one Word, which was his Son, and this Word he speaks always in eternal silence, and in silence must it be heard by the soul."[113]

When the moment came that the Father spoke His Word directly to her, she responded with trust and answered with her *fiat:* "Let it be done to me according to your Word." Saint John Paul II states that Mary's faith is in fact the beginning of the new covenant, that her "Amen" allowed the Word to become flesh. Faith in the Word of God allows salvation to enter our lives in Jesus Christ! "It is precisely Mary's faith which marks the beginning of the new and eternal Covenant of God with man in Jesus Christ; this heroic faith of hers precedes the

---

[113] "Sayings of Light and Love," Sayings of St. John of the Cross, accessed July 11, 2017, http://essene.com/B%27nai-Amen/j-saying.htm.

apostolic witness of the Church, and ever remains in the Church's heart hidden like a special heritage of God's revelation. All those who from generation to generation accept the apostolic witness of the Church share in that mysterious inheritance, and in a sense share in Mary's faith."[114]

This is an amazing insight: all of us, through every generation, further salvation history when we are faithful to this new covenant, when we share in Mary's faith and trust in the Word of God. Elsewhere, St. John Paul II wrote: "We can say that the mystery of the Redemption took shape beneath the heart of the Virgin of Nazareth when she pronounced her 'fiat.'"[115] Salvation takes place for us, too, by our learning to utter, "Let it be done unto me according to your Word," as Mary did in her *fiat* — so that this mystery of redemption, continuing today, might reach its conclusion at the Second Coming.

Raniero Cantalamessa, preacher to the papal household for St. John Paul II and Francis, makes an interesting observation regarding the event of the Annunciation: Mary, like most Jews of her time, probably spoke Aramaic and Hebrew. Certain Psalms end with "Amen, amen!" which is translated in Greek as *genoito, genoito,* and in Latin as *fiat, fiat* (see Ps 41:13, 72:19, 89:2). Hence, she most likely did not respond in Greek (*genoito*) or Latin (*fiat*), but rather with the word "Amen." Remember that amen signifies solidity and certainty. In the Jewish liturgy, amen is the answer of trust and faith to the Word of God, stating that the Word is the solid and certain foundation of our lives — the truth we can trust. Mary responded "Amen" to the Archangel Gabriel's message, and the Word entered her womb, just as we respond "Amen" to the priest, and the Word enters our lips and hearts.[116]

Let us respond — as Mary did — "Amen" to the Father's will, whatever it might be in our lives, and so live in trust. Each "amen" steps upon the serpent's head as we walk with Mary along the path to trust. By repeating "Amen" throughout our days, we assent to the Father's will, living in Mary's attitude of humility, obedience, and trust. How often, however, we gladly believe in faith that Jesus is present under the appearances of bread and wine, yet fail to recognize Him hidden under other appearances throughout our daily lives. How often do we fail to say "amen" at those moments! But true faith and a living trust recognize Jesus everywhere, saying "amen" to Him and to His will.

This path of simple trust is the shortest route to sanctity, as Jesus Himself instructs St. Faustina (see *Diary,* 1487). We have only to say "amen" to the Father's will from the depths of our souls!

By saying "Amen," Mary was also saying "no" to the serpent, "no" to distrust, "no" to sin, "no" to everything that is not in line with the Father's will. Her *fiat* meant a firm "no" to vanity, to egocentrism, to self-defense, to preferential treatment. Notice that she did not demand anything in return for

---

[114] Saint John Paul II, *Redemptoris Mater*, n. 27.
[115] Ibid., n. 22.
[116] See Raniero Cantalamessa, *Mary: Mirror of the Church* (Collegeville, Minnesota: Liturgical Press, 1992).

her self-sacrifice. She called herself merely the "handmaid of the Lord." She did not boast of her role but kept silent. She did not rebel or complain about the sufferings that ensued upon her "Amen." She said "no" to selfishness by giving her Son — her greatest treasure — to the shepherds, to the Magi, to her fellow Jews, and to all sinners upon Calvary.

MARY'S OBEDIENCE

Mary's "amen" — her response of faith — was immediately put into action, revealing an additional aspect of trust. The Archangel Gabriel announced the pregnancy of Elizabeth as a sign to confirm his message. After the angel departed, Mary, trusting in the words of Gabriel, left Nazareth to visit and assist Elizabeth, her elderly cousin, who was now also with child (see Lk 1:36, 39). This was no small journey — especially for a newly pregnant young woman in the Judaean hill country — but rather a lengthy one, made on foot over unpaved roads. Nevertheless, Mary believed the words of the angel to be true and acted in obedience.

In Mary, we see how trust leads to obedience, to acting in accord with the truth, with the Word of the Lord, even when we cannot yet verify what has been told to us. Notice that she does not need more proof. She simply accepts and believes because she knows that the Word given to her is from the Father. That is the key: Once we know that it is the Lord who is speaking, then we know we can trust any word that comes from Him, for "no word shall be impossible with God" (Lk 1:37, DR).

We might be used to the other translation of this biblical verse: "nothing is impossible with God." The word in Greek is *rhema* — "word, matter." The point of the Archangel is this: "No word (*rhema*) from God will be void of power," or, differently, "Every word (*rhema*) from God contains the power for its own fulfillment."[117] The idea is this: Every word from God has the power within itself to bring about what it promises; hence, each word or *rhema* from God deserves our trust. Trust gives us confidence in every *rhema* of the Father; we know that each of them contains the power of the Holy Spirit to bring each promise to fulfillment.

We remember that Zechariah was punished because he did not trust as Mary did. He required a further sign because of his doubt that the Father could work the impossible: "How shall I know this? For I am an old man, and my wife is advanced in years" (Lk 1:18). Ironically, being rendered mute was precisely the sign given to him to confirm that the angel had appeared to him! Mary discerned but did not require proof; Zechariah doubted and needed proof beyond the words spoken to him. For Mary, the Word of the Lord was enough in itself — the very Word that has the power to create and redeem the world! (see Jn 1:3; Col 1:20).

---

[117] Prince, *Faith to Live By*, 103.

Mary's trust was the door that allowed the Word to enter and transform her life in a unique way. Just as the angel had given her a name — *Kecharitomene* ("the One Fully Transformed by Grace"; see Lk 1:28) — so too does Elizabeth also give to Mary a new name: *he Pisteusasa* ("the One Who Has Trusted"). Saint John Paul II wrote that this expression is a "key" that unlocks the "innermost reality of Mary," so to understand Mary, we must look at her as *he Pisteusasa*, the One Who Has Trusted.[118] The fact that Mary is full of grace leads her to be full of trust as well, because the two are intimately connected.

In admiring Mary's faith, Elizabeth gives us another beatitude to keep in mind in addition to the Beatitudes from the Sermon on the Mount: "Blessed is she who believed that there would be a fulfilment of what was spoken to her from the Lord" (Lk 1:45). We will also be blessed and happy if we participate in Mary's faith and have unwavering belief in the Lord's Word and promises. "Blessed rather are those who hear the word of God and keep it" (Lk 11:28). Are not Mary's faith and her trust in the Word the reason she is called "blessed" by her Son (and not simply that she nursed Him at her breasts)?

Our path to happiness is the path of Mary's trust. This is not a new path. It is the path of faith, hope, and charity, integrated and reaching their summit in trust and entrustment of oneself to another. Mary walks with us on our pilgrimage of faith, teaching us to entrust ourselves completely to the Father, while cooperating with the Holy Spirit to fulfill the Father's will as adopted sons or daughters in the Son. Consecrating and entrusting ourselves to Mary means consciously participating in the faith of Mary, seeking to live in the Spirit of Mary — the Holy Spirit.

---

[118] Saint John Paul II, *Redemptoris Mater*, n. 19.

CHAPTER 11

The Challenges of Trusting like Mary

"They did not understand the saying which he spoke to them"
(Lk 2:50).

Let us now consider the difficulties Mary faced because she accepted the Word of God into her life. We have an immense advantage because we already know the end of the story, but when meditating on Mary, we must remember that she did not yet know the ending. Nor did she always understand the Father's will or plan (see Lk 2:50). She could only hold all these words and events in her heart, trusting the Word of God even when things were not clear or understandable (see Lk 2:19).

Mary's Daily Faith

Trusting in the Lord in everyday life can be far from easy. Saint Faustina experienced the challenge of trying not to be dragged back down to earth: "I fervently beg the Lord to strengthen my faith, so that in my drab, everyday life I will not be guided by human dispositions, but by those of the spirit. Oh, how everything drags man towards the earth! But lively faith maintains the soul in the higher regions and assigns self-love its proper place; that is to say, the lowest one" (*Diary*, 210).

Mary, too, experienced multiple challenges along her path of trust. She was probably misunderstood by others around her, possibly even by St. Joseph — imagine being a young fiancée and pregnant! Her life was filled with suffering because of her trust in the Word. Mary had to persevere in this trust despite the tedium and monotony of her daily life. She had to live by faith, for only by faith could she see who her Son was, since He looked the same as anyone else. Faith alone allows us, and Mary, to have contact with the living God. Faith is the veil between the natural and the supernatural, between what is visible and what is invisible. Even in her daily life in Nazareth with Jesus and St. Joseph, Mary continued to take steps of trust along her pilgrimage of faith. "[Mary], his Mother, is in contact with the truth about her Son only in faith and through faith! She is therefore blessed, because 'she has believed,' and continues to believe day after day amidst all the trials and the adversities of Jesus' infancy and then during the years of the hidden life at Nazareth, where he 'was obedient to them' (Lk 2:51)."[119]

---

[119] Saint John Paul II, *Redemptoris Mater*, n. 17.

Saint Joseph also had to live by faith and trust in the Word of God. His trust in the message that Gabriel gave him in a dream altered the rest of his life — choosing to marry a woman pregnant with a child conceived by the Holy Spirit is no small decision! But Joseph believed the Word of God despite the difficulties he would probably have faced in terms of his reputation, desires, and plans for having children of his own. However, precisely because of their trust in the Word of God, both Mary and Joseph could participate in the Father's plan of salvation, and their trust helped Christ to bring us salvation!

We have the same potential to serve the plan of salvation. How many souls depend upon our trust in and obedience to the Word of God — especially when trust and obedience demand sacrifice of us? As St. Faustina wrote: "We do not know the number of souls that is ours to save through our prayers and sacrifices; therefore, let us always pray for sinners" (*Diary*, 1783). It can be easy to claim that others are the "big players" in the Father's plan of salvation, not us, and seek to excuse ourselves from such a responsibility. We must remember that just as chess is played with different pieces, so does the Father's plan include different persons. No Christians can consider themselves unnecessary, for all belong to the one Body of Christ (see 1 Cor 12). No chess game is won without the pawns; often the "weaker" players are the ones God chooses to use to bring about His victory.

VALUE OF WEAKNESS

The story of Mary and Joseph in the Gospels teaches us that God often chooses the weak and the despised of the world to reveal His wisdom and power (see 1 Cor 1:27-29). He allows His treasure to be held in clay vessels so that the vessels' surpassing power to work His will might come from Him (see 2 Cor 4:7). By recognizing that we are weak and incapable of anything good on our own, we become fit instruments for the Father's Mercy, the Holy Spirit, to be at work and do great things in our lives!

This is precisely what causes Mary to sing her Magnificat (see Lk 1:46-55). By being poor and lowly, one of the *anawim*, Mary allowed the Mighty One to do great things in her and for her. By trusting the words of the Archangel Gabriel, she experienced the blessings, the great things, of the Father. By entrusting our own poverty and lowliness to the Lord, we will experience His Mercy — Mercy that endures to all generations for those who fear Him. This fear of the Lord is not servile. It is a gift of the Holy Spirit and enables us in our misery to stand in awe at the mystery of the Father's Mercy.

Saint John Paul II wrote that in the Magnificat, Adam and Eve's sin of distrust and "little faith" is uprooted. The suspicion the serpent had injected into their hearts is cast out, and Mary steps on the serpent, her song proclaiming the "undimmed truth" about God: that He can be trusted to do great things.[120]

---

[120] Ibid., n. 35.

A sign of the strength of our trust is our ability to *sing*. When we are confident in the Father's Mercy and have strong faith, we sing with Mary. Do we not sing while we are on journeys? We listen to the radio while we drive and sometimes sing with others while we walk. As we walk along the path of trust with Mary, let us sing with her. In this way, we boldly step upon the serpent of distrust, for such confident praise and song are our defense, our shield, and our weapon. In fact, when the Israelites went to battle, those who sang praise of God's Mercy were at the front (2 Ch 20:20-23).

We will crush our true enemy — the serpent of old, Satan — if we sing each step of our way along our journey of trust with Mary. In moments of fear, of doubt, of ambush by the enemy, remember to take up your weapon: *singing praise* of the Lord's mercy. Notice that their song is not praise of just anything: it is praise of His Mercy! We, too, will make all of hell shudder by our praise of His Mercy (see *Diary*, 378). An excellent way to sing of the Lord's mercy is singing the Divine Mercy Chaplet, for, as St. Augustine says, "He who sings prays twice."[121]

WORTHINESS

Aware of our misery, we can easily look at ourselves and say, "Who, me? God would not choose me to become a saint, I am just Joe (or Jane) Regular!" This attitude is called *pusillanimity,* meaning "smallness of spirit." We have probably heard of its opposite: *magnanimity,* or "greatness of spirit." According to St. Thomas Aquinas, pusillanimity is worse than presumption because it causes us to withdraw from the good things we are capable of accomplishing, whereas presumption causes us to suppose we are able to do things we are not capable of.

Pusillanimity is the attitude of the fainthearted who feel unworthy.[122] It is the attitude, very common among Christians, that we are just ordinary and should not set our eyes on the goal of becoming heroic saints. Pusillanimity should be confessed, because it is a sin to waste the great gifts of the Father and not develop and share those gifts with others (see Lk 19:20-23). We must always be careful to avoid confusing being *little* with being pusillanimous. Being a *little soul* means being a magnanimous soul, for a *little soul* never relies on itself apart from the Father, but rather trusts in the Holy Spirit, who enables us to use all our skills and talents for His glory. A pusillanimous soul is little in a different sense, relying neither on itself nor on the Father — remaining paralyzed in fear. The Little Way of St. Thérèse of Lisieux is not the pusillanimous way, but rather Mary's way: a path of unlimited trust.

Pusillanimity is often present with acedia — sadness in the face of the Father's goodness — a condition we have discussed earlier. It is manifested as a lack of conviction that we are worthy of our vocation as children of the Father — either because of our sins or because of weakness of character. It can also be a

---

[121] Saint Augustine, *En. in Ps.* 72, 1: PL 36, 914; quoted in *CCC*, 1156.
[122] See Saint Thomas Aquinas, *Summa Theologica*, II-II, q. 133.

certain cowardice in the face of the obstacles we must face to achieve our goal. For this reason, St. Thomas Aquinas discusses magnanimity and its opposite, pusillanimity, in the section on the cardinal virtue of *fortitude* — the virtue of courage that enables us to face difficulties. To be generous in our trust and in our response to the Father's vocation for us — as Mary and Joseph were — we must be courageous and firm in the face of obstacles that would prevent us from trusting.

Consider the fact that we are called to be filled with the Love of the Father, the Holy Spirit. If our hearts are small because we are pusillanimous, how can they contain the infinite Love and Mercy of the Father? They can't! We need to expand our hearts, just as Jesus opened wide His Sacred Heart to us on the Cross. We are constrained, however, because our sinful hearts are too small; they are not open wide enough to receive and contain all the Love the Father wants to give us (see 2 Cor 6:11-13). Pusillanimous souls are those who ask for little — those who do not widen their hearts to receive more, but instead cling to present blessings and close their hearts to future blessings. For this reason, Jesus is bereaved when we ask for only a little, for it is easier for Him to give much to us than to give us little. Saint Faustina once told the Lord, "Jesus, You know that for You it is easier to grant much rather than a little." Jesus responded to her:

> **That is so, it is less difficult for Me to grant a soul much rather than a little. ... Souls that trust boundlessly are a great comfort to Me, because I pour all the treasures of My graces into them. I rejoice that they ask for much, because it is My desire to give much, very much. On the other hand, I am sad when souls ask for little, when they narrow their hearts** (*Diary*, 961, 1578).

The trials and difficulties that we undergo on the path of trust are used by the Father to stretch us and expand our hearts to trust in Him without measure, so as to receive without measure, for more trust allows us to receive more grace — the more we trust, the more we can receive. Through trust, we comprehend and receive the fullness of the Father's Love poured out in the Blood and Water! One of my favorite prayers from St. Paul is his prayer that the Ephesians would be able to fathom the abyss of the Father's Love: "For this reason I bow my knees before the Father ... you, being rooted and grounded in love, may have power to comprehend with all the saints what is the breadth and length and height and depth, and to know the love of Christ which surpasses knowledge, that you may be filled with all the fullness of God" (Eph 3:14-19).

Suffering empties our hearts of our disordered attachments to creatures, so that our hearts can be filled with the love of our Creator. Saint Bernard of Clairvaux wrote: "The soul must grow and expand, so as to be capable of God. And its largeness is its love, as the Apostle says, 'Widen yourselves in love' (2 Cor 6:13). It grows and extends spiritually, not in substance, but in virtue. The greatness of each soul is judged by the measure of love that it has: he who has great love is great, he who has little love is little, while he who has no love at all is nothing."[123] Saint Augustine illustrates this point when he says that the Father delays in answering our prayers precisely to expand our hearts to allow us to receive all that He desires to give us — namely, Himself, the infinite, Triune God in Heaven.[124]

VALUE OF EMPTINESS AND MISERY

Let us meditate again on Mary: a young woman from the small village of Nazareth, who did not appear to have any extraordinary qualities. Nor did St. Faustina. Nor did many of the saints. What was extraordinary about Mary and these saints was their interior trust in the Lord. Their seeming lack of talent and skill, their emptiness, is what allowed the Lord to fill them with His graces because of their trust. By trust they opened the emptiness of their misery to the fullness of His Mercy and so became truly rich. They not only became saints, but they shared the wealth of the Father's Mercy — the Holy Spirit — with many other souls to make them into saints as well.

When we turn with trust to the Father, asking Him to fill our emptiness and pusillanimity with His Mercy, we delight His Heart: "For you, I am mercy itself; therefore I ask you to offer Me your misery and this very helplessness of yours and, in this way, you will delight My Heart" (*Diary*, 1775). Misery is, in fact, our own property, something we can give Him: He fills us with graces, not only for ourselves but for others, too. We will overflow with graces, so that our neighbors might be filled with His Mercy as well. As Jesus told St. Faustina: **"The graces I grant you are not for you alone, but for a great number of other souls as well"** (*Diary*, 723).

We need to *aim higher*, as St. Maximilian Kolbe exhorts us to do.[125] We need to aim for Heaven, for greatness. Not because we are great, but because our Father is great and wants to do great things in our lives, just as He did in Mary's life. The Holy Spirit — the Spirit of Mercy — is given to us for this reason alone: to change us from miserable sinners into saints. The greater our misery, the greater our need and our right to the Mercy of the Father which pours forth in the Blood and Water from the Heart of Jesus: the Holy Spirit (see *Diary*, 723).

Trust does not excuse us from our responsibility in the awesome plan that the Father has for each one of us: sharing His divine life with us and making us saints. Trust does not limit what the Father can do with us, or deny or exaggerate our poverty. It sets its gaze upon the omnipotent Mercy of our Father. Jesus told

---

[123] Bernard Walsh and Kilian Walsh, *Bernard Of Clairvaux: Sermons on the Song of Songs*, Vol. I (Kalamazoo, — Cistercian Publications, 1971).

[124] Saint Augustine, *Letter to Proba*, quoted in ICEL, *The Liturgy of the Hours*, vol. 4, 408.

[125] Saint Maximilian Kolbe, *Aim Higher! Spiritual and Marian Reflections of St. Maximilian Kolbe*, comp. Dominic Wisz (Libertyville, Illinois: Marytown Press, 2007).

St. Faustina that our misery does not prevent His Mercy, but attracts it: "**Write, My daughter, that I am mercy itself for the contrite soul. A soul's greatest wretchedness does not enkindle Me with wrath; but rather, My Heart is moved towards it with great mercy**" (*Diary*, 1739).

It is only our voluntary sin — especially the sin of distrust — that prevents His Mercy from being given to us. Such distrust usually manifests itself through pusillanimity and pride, by not allowing the Spirit of Mercy to overflow onto our misery and make saints out of us sinners. "**Your misery does not hinder My mercy. … My bride, you always please Me by your humility. The greatest misery does not stop Me from uniting Myself to a soul, but where there is pride, I am not there**" (*Diary*, 1182, 1563).

Mary is always our model. She did not shy away from becoming the Mother of God. She did not say, "No, I am just a girl from Nazareth; there is no way I could ever become the Mother of God." She did not look to herself or trust in herself. She did not wallow in her misery or claim that her littleness meant she could not be the Mother of God. For that reason, she could accept an amazing vocation. She knew that she was too weak, too poor, and too miserable to be able to fulfill such a mission on her own. She accepted that mission because she trusted in the infinite Mercy of God — the Holy Spirit. "Mary … by yielding in obedience, became the cause of salvation, both to herself and the whole human race."[126] In union with Mary and her Son Jesus, we can become sources of salvation for others by our obedience, fulfilling our vocations each day.

WILLING SACRIFICE

Let us return for a moment now to the Garden of Eden. The words of the serpent seemed to threaten and intimidate Adam and Eve, making them forget their dignity as children of the Father and, through fear, give in to pusillanimity. The serpent's words implied that if they remained faithful to the Word of God, they would pay — even by giving their lives.[127] Adam and Eve were not willing to trust the Father with their lives. In trying to save their lives by declaring them their own, Adam and Eve lost their lives (see Mt 10:39). Mary and Joseph were willing to surrender their lives rather than their trust in the Word of God. We honor them as saints because of this trust in the Word.

This is one of the corollaries of the Immaculate Conception: Mary always chose to trust and surrender everything, even her life — even her own Son — to the Father, rather than attempting to hold on to her life and Son through distrust. She preferred to trust and suffer rather than distrust and sin. In this way,

---

[126] Irenaeus of Lyons, "Irenæus Against Heresies," in *The Apostolic Fathers with Justin Martyr and Irenaeus*, ed. Alexander Roberts, James Donaldson, and A. Cleveland Coxe, Vol. 1, *The Ante-Nicene Fathers* (Buffalo, New York: Christian Literature Company, 1885), 455.
[127] St. Paul Center for Biblical Theology, "Lesson Two: Creation, Fall and Promise," Genesis to Jesus, accessed July 11, 2017, https://stpaulcenter.com/studies/lesson/lesson-two-creation-fall-and-promise.

she crushed the head of the serpent. The serpent's strike at our heel is nothing other than his attempt to make us suffer. Satan uses suffering to intimidate us and make us cower before him, forcing us to give in to fear and obey him instead of the Father.

Mary crushed the serpent's head because she was not intimidated by the temptation to despair in the midst of suffering, a poison injected by the serpent's fangs. Saint Faustina shared in this grace of the Immaculate Conception through her repugnance for sin and her willingness to suffer anything to avoid it. On Good Friday, March 15, 1937, she wrote in her *Diary* (1016) that, meditating upon the Passion, she would prefer to suffer a "thousand hells than commit even the smallest venial sin" because she saw its effects on Jesus.

Saint Gianna Molla shared this grace of repugnance for sin: "If one were to consider how much Jesus has suffered, one would not commit the smallest sin."[128] Mary desires to share with us the graces flowing from her Immaculate Conception, but this requires a deep conversion on our part spurred by frequent meditation on the Passion. Are we ready to suffer out of fidelity to the Word of God? In a world of sin, we will inevitably suffer if we remain faithful to the Father: Jesus Himself was obedient even unto death on the Cross (see Phil 2:8). Will we resist sin? Will we trust in the Lord to the point of shedding our blood as Jesus shed His? (see Heb 12:4) We may not suffer red (physical) martyrdom, but we are all called to lay down our lives in white martyrdom — daily self-denial in order to fulfill the will of our Heavenly Father. This daily self-denial is the greatest proof of our love, for it involves laying down our lives continuously for our Friend: Jesus Christ (see Jn 15:13).

Be not afraid. Mary walks with us all the way to Calvary, for that is where her "Amen" led her, and don't forget that Calvary is the doorway to Heaven. Although the Annunciation was the "culminating moment of Mary's faith in her awaiting of Christ," it is also the point of departure "from which her whole 'journey towards God' begins, her whole pilgrimage of faith."[129] Indeed, from the moment of the Annunciation, her obedience of faith grew, ever leading her to the Cross, where she shared in her Son's obedience unto death, so that the Father's plan of salvation might be fulfilled. As we continue along this journey, let us praise the Father, singing along with Mary while we journey together — just as we will sing with her and the angels and saints forever in Heaven: "I will sing of your mercies, O Lord, for ever; with my mouth I will proclaim your faithfulness to all generations" (Ps 89:1).

---

[128] "Reflections of Saint Gianna Beretta Molla."
[129] Saint John Paul II, *Redemptoris Mater,* n. 14,

CHAPTER 12

The Infant Jesus: Healing Our Distrust

"And the Word became flesh and dwelt among us, full of grace and truth; we have beheld his glory, glory as of the only-begotten Son from the Father" (Jn 1:14, 18).

Now let us turn to the mystery of our Lord's Nativity. By choosing to come into the world as a child, weak, helpless, and vulnerable, Jesus redeems our weaknesses and our helplessness, and enables us to be vulnerable with Him, because He experienced all these conditions Himself.

RESTORING OUR TRUST

The Father in Heaven restores our trust in Him by sending His Son to take on human flesh and thereby share our weakness in all things but sin (see Heb 4:15). We may wonder how, but just consider: Who can resist a baby? The Father knows our soft spot — that even with our hearts weighed down by sin, we cannot resist holding and kissing an infant. We cannot help drawing near to the Word become flesh as an infant. Our hearts are filled with love at the sight! Knowing that we are too afraid to approach the Triune God in His majesty and splendor, the Second Person of the Trinity humbles Himself, becoming an infant so we might not be afraid to approach Him, for sinful, stained man cannot see the living God as He is and remain alive (see Ex 33:17-33). It was for this very reason that Adam and Eve fled the presence of God, and the Israelites begged Moses to converse with God on their behalf while they stayed at a distance (see Gen 3:8-10; Ex 20:18-20).

The Nativity is one of the many instances where the Father's wisdom is greater than our foolishness (see 1 Cor 1:25). Our hearts melt before this Infant, and our love for the Father is restored, because we see in the flesh of His Son, that He is tender, gentle, and warm. Gazing upon the Infant Jesus, we see that our Father is not angry, severe, or vengeful. In Jesus, His Son, the Father wants to be near to us. He wants to press us to His Merciful Heart (see *Diary*, 1588).

In the mystery of the Nativity, Jesus also wants us to hold Him close to our hearts to teach us to trust Him, for the most distinctive quality of a child is his or her trustfulness (see *Diary*, 1481).[130] By pressing Jesus to our wounded, broken

---

[130] Prince, *Faith to Live By*, 48.

hearts, we allow Him to heal our sinfulness and fill us with His Holy Spirit of mercy and love. We allow Him to save us.

How does that work? We allow Him to fill the God-shaped hole in our hearts, to heal us of evil and bring us to supernatural goodness, to sanctity. Evil is a privation, a lack of something that should be present. Blindness is evil because it is a lack of what is proper to the eyes — sight. Sin is the greatest of evils because it causes a lack of what is proper to human beings — the Love of the Father, the Holy Spirit that created each human being and sustains each in existence.

Remember that at the moment of creating Adam, the Father breathed into his nostrils the breath of life (see Gen 2:7). In Hebrew, this breath is called *ruah,* which we often translate as Spirit. To sin is to give up that Holy Spirit, to exhale it, not physically, but through our sin. At its root, sin is a lack of trust, which closes the heart off from the Love of the Father that is the Holy Spirit. Sin is therefore an emptiness within the soul that needs to be filled anew with the breath of divine Love.

To begin to heal sin, we need not do or give more; rather, we need to *receive* more, especially through the Sacraments. Doing more does not fill the vacuum of sin in our souls. Rather, that emptiness is filled only if we open ourselves in trust to the Love of the Father once again. Salvation means being healed from sin, and healing from sin consists of being filled anew with the Holy Spirit (see Rom 5:5). A newborn has a unique power of attraction to open our hardened, closed hearts so they can once again be filled with such Love! Only when we learn to receive can we also give: As the adage goes, *Nemo dat quod non habet —* "You cannot give what you do not have." Or, as St. Paul states: "What have you that you did not receive?" (1 Cor 4:7).

Jesus is the *Messiah* (מָשִׁיחַ), the *Christ* (Χριστός), in Hebrew and Greek respectively. Both words mean "anointed." Jesus is the one *anointed* with the Holy Spirit. To press Him near to our hearts means that we allow the same Spirit that anoints Him to "rub off" on us and anoint us, too. Think for a moment about oil: if you shake someone's oily hand, your hand will become oily as well. This is the point of the Nativity: The Father sends us His beloved Son, covered with "oil" — the anointing of the Holy Spirit — knowing that we will gladly take Him into our arms, be covered with that same Spirit of Love, and thus healed.

Is this not the Father's plan? Notice what happens immediately after the birth of Jesus. Most would expect a time of quiet and silence for the new mother and foster father to be with their Child, but the Father has other plans. A host of heavenly angels notify the shepherds of the birth of Jesus, and when they arrive, Mary, covered with the anointing of the Holy Spirit because of her Son, whom she cradles in her arms, shares her Son with others, so that they, too, might be covered with that same anointing.

This is a theme that will keep reappearing in Mary's personal pilgrimage of faith: Whenever, through trust, she receives the Word of God, she reflexively shares that same Word with others. After the Annunciation, as a living tabernacle, she went to Elizabeth and shared the presence of Jesus. After the Nativity, she shares that same Word with the shepherds. She shares Jesus with the Jews when she allows Him to leave Nazareth and begin His public ministry. She shares Jesus with us sinners by consenting to His death on Calvary. She shares Jesus with all mankind, when, after His Resurrection, she watches Him ascend into Heaven.

RESTING IN LOVE

The Incarnation is a lesson in humility. It reminds us that our most basic need is to be loved, whether we are children or adults. Resting in the arms of the Blessed Virgin, Jesus reminds us that the first way to heal sin is not by doing something. Rather, we are healed when we rest and receive the Love given to us in the Holy Spirit through prayer and the Sacraments of the Church. Redemption and salvation are therefore about resting and being filled with the love that we need but have not previously received (see Is 30:15). Only then — having been filled with His Mercy — are we equipped to cooperate with that same Holy Spirit so as to help others receive salvation, too.

When we do not rest and receive this Love, in our emptiness we begin to affirm ourselves instead of receiving that affirmation from another. But self-affirmation is at the root of pride, and none of us can genuinely affirm ourselves. When others do not validate us, we think we must hide our weaknesses, because we are afraid that no one could love us with all our sins and faults.[131]

Seen in this light, Confession is the Sacrament through which we admit who we are in reality, confident that the Father still loves us, even though we are sinners. For that reason, Confession can be healing, even on a psychological level. We often walk around with our defenses up because we unconsciously believe others would never love us if they saw us as we truly are, with all our wounds and sins. In Confession, we rediscover, time and again, the inexhaustible Love of the Father, poured out in the Blood and Water. No sin, no misery, ever stops that fount of His Mercy for us.

Confession is the best way to heal our pride, because pride is not simply thinking that we are better than others. Pride is above all the emptiness of our hearts — the vacuum that should be filled with His Love. When we believe the lie that we are unlovable, the vacuum remains. We need to remember that when we go to Confession, by confessing our sins, we are, as it were, stripping ourselves naked and immersing ourselves in the Mercy of the Father to be cleansed under the streams of Blood and Water from the side of Christ. If Confession is simply a perfunctory Sacrament in which we state our sins but don't fully open our hearts, we can forget to allow the Holy Spirit to fill those areas of our hearts that were empty. True penance is designed to remove the obstacles that prevent us from trusting the Father, allowing the Holy Spirit to enter us and fill our hearts with Love and Mercy.

---

[131] Conrad W. Baars, *Feeling and Healing Your Emotions* (Alachua, Florida: Bridge-Logos, 2009).

When we acknowledge our misery and our need for love, the Father can fill us in the greatest measure: **"Because you are such great misery, I have revealed to you the whole ocean of My mercy"** (*Diary*, 718; see Jn 3:34). The more we recognize our misery, the greater our trust in the Father's Mercy will grow: "However, this great misery of mine does not deprive me of trust. On the contrary, the better I have come to know my own misery, the stronger has become my trust in God's mercy" (*Diary*, 1406). Our misery will never stop the Father from loving us — and the more misery we have, the more Mercy we can receive. Also, the more miserable we are, the more the Father can reveal the ocean of His Mercy to us, as Jesus instructs St. Faustina regarding Confession (see *Diary*, 1602).

Jesus makes a very important point: On account of our sins, we all suffer from spiritual poverty, from pride and distrust, in various ways throughout our lives. Do we open that misery to His Mercy or, convinced that we are unlovable or not miserable, do we remain always in poverty and misery? When we remain in our misery, we begin to feel a certain tiredness and tedium in our lives. I am referring not to physical tiredness but to spiritual tiredness, a constant search for satisfaction without finding it. If you have that insatiable hunger of soul or are spiritually tired from looking for happiness and joy, then press the Infant Jesus to your heart! He will heal the misery that tires you and fill you with His Mercy. He alone satisfies our hearts.[132]

The Word became flesh — Love Incarnate — so that happiness might be within our grasp. He came near enough that we could press Him to our hearts and receive Him in the Eucharist. In doing so, He shows us how He holds us close to His Sacred Heart, where we find our true rest (see Mt 11:28-29). Heaven is described as a place of rest for this very reason (see Rev 14:13). In Heaven, our search for satisfying Love is over; our desires are finally fulfilled and we can rest in the Holy Spirit, the Love of the Father (see Heb 4:1, 3).

RECEIVING THE LOVE OF JESUS

In the abstract, we know that our sins are painful to our Lord Jesus. Have you ever wondered why this is so? Remember that the Trinity is a communion of Love. This exchange of Love between the Father and the Son is so abundant and life-giving that this Love overflows upon us in the Holy Spirit, the Lord and Giver of Life. Our sin involves refusal to draw near to the Infant who desires to pour this Love upon us.

At its root, sin is a lack of belief in Love, a lack of trust, a failure to open one's heart and one's arms to embrace Mercy Incarnate. When our sin prevents the overflow of Merciful Love from the Heart of God into our hearts and we

---

[132] Saint John Paul II. World Youth Day: Vigil (Tor Vergata, August 19, 2000), accessed July 11, 2017, http://w2.vatican.va/content/john-paul-ii/en/speeches/2000/jul-sep/documents/hf_jp-ii_spe_20000819_gmg-veglia.html.

do not receive the abundance of the Holy Spirit poured forth in the Blood and Water from Christ's side, sorrow builds up in the Sacred Heart. The flames of the Spirit of Mercy then burn Him; He desires to pour out His Mercy, but there are few who will receive that Mercy: **"The flames of mercy are burning Me — clamoring to be spent; I want to pour them out upon these souls"** (*Diary*, 50).

Let us therefore relieve the Lord of His pain and console Him by receiving His Mercy. Often we tire of receiving His love before He tires of giving it to us (see *Diary*, 294). Jesus asks us to draw near to Him, the Anointed One (the Christ), so as to receive all the blessings of His Mercy. Once we Christians are anointed like Jesus, we are to draw near to others and get them "oily" by encouraging them to trust in His Mercy and sharing with them the blessings of His Mercy.

What does such trust look like in light of the Nativity? This mystery reminds us that we are the Father's beloved children who are called to trust in Him by resting on His heart, as the Son has done from all eternity (see Jn 1:18). Our sin is in wandering away from that embrace and thinking we can survive on our own without the Father. Indeed, the first "war of independence" was waged by Satan, who refused to accept God as his Father by the grace of adoption and showed this by his disobedience.

Jesus, however, the Only Begotten Son of the Father, admits clearly His dependence upon the Father in all things: "the Son can do nothing of his own accord, but only what he sees the Father doing; for whatever he does, that the Son does likewise. ... I can do nothing on my own authority" (Jn 5:19, 30). Even though Jesus is God, equal to the Father, He nonetheless never wanders from the embrace of the Father. He never attempts to survive apart from the Father, but lives His earthly life always in union with Him, as manifested by His many nights of prayer.

When we recognize our miserable state, when we recognize that we have become orphaned children through sin, we can turn to the Mercy of God, the Holy Spirit. "All my nothingness is drowned in the sea of Your mercy. With the confidence of a child, I throw myself into Your arms, O Father of Mercy, to make up for the unbelief of so many souls who are afraid to trust in You. Oh, how very few souls really know You!" (*Diary*, 505). We ought to turn to the Father's Mercy not only for ourselves, but on behalf of so many who are afraid to trust in Him because they do not know Him as He truly is: a loving, tender Father.

When we come to Jesus as a little child would, asking for His Love and Mercy, He wants to give us all we ask for "and a thousand times more" (see *Diary*, 229). Let us approach Him with our misery, confident of receiving a "thousand times more" than we expect! Let us reflect on our Father as Mary did in her Magnificat with the words: "[T]he almighty has done great things for me, and holy is His name."

CHAPTER 13

Trusting like a Child:
Embraced by the Father

"No one has ever seen God; the only-begotten Son, who is in the bosom of the Father, he has made him known" (Jn 1:18).

When they are learning to walk, children constantly stumble and fall. The same is true for us as we traverse the path of trust. Jesus Himself had to grow in age and wisdom, so we cannot expect that we will become perfect in a day. Trust must grow and mature like fruit on a tree. Part of the Father's will is that — like children — we will grow, little by little, each day. Like children, when we fall, we ought to cry out to our Heavenly Father and ask for His help — ask for Jesus to be our Savior and for the Holy Spirit to fill us anew with His Mercy.

IMMERSING OURSELVES IN MERCY

Immersing ourselves in Divine Mercy is what we need to do when we realize that we have sinned. If we use the Greek word for Baptism, *baptizein*, meaning "to plunge or immerse," we can think in terms of "baptizing ourselves in that Mercy" (see *CCC*, 1214). Baptism is an immersion in the Holy Spirit, the Mercy of our Father, and we need to immerse ourselves in that Mercy, especially when we have sinned. Confession is a renewal of that immersion, wherein we immerse ourselves in that same water — the water that flowed from the pierced Heart of Christ for the forgiveness of our sins. In a way, every time we ask for forgiveness after we have fallen, we renew the grace of Baptism that has made us sons and daughters of the Father. Indeed, we are freed from our sins by recognizing once again our status as His beloved children.

As discussed earlier, our first reaction when we realize we have done something wrong is to try to *fix* the situation. The problem is that when we try to fix things on our own, they do not necessarily get better. Instead, we are called to run to the Father in our misery and beg for His Mercy, relying on the truth that we are still His beloved children. This truth reopens the door of our hearts, building the bridge of trust between our misery and His Mercy. Since we were afraid to open our hearts to a distant Father — imagined more as an omniscient and omnipotent Judge, who knows all our sins and can punish us for each of them, than as a God rich in mercy — His Son, Jesus Christ, became man to show us that He directs His infinite power toward redeeming and healing us.

As we read in the Liturgy, "O God, who manifest your almighty power above all by pardoning and showing mercy … ."[133]

When we sin, we need to simply return to the embrace of the Father's Love and appear as we are, wounds and all. Resting in the arms of Mary, Jesus is an image in time of what the Son has been doing for all eternity: resting on God the Father's bosom, near the heart of our Heavenly Father (see Jn 1:18). Resting like Jesus is salvific because salvation is the restoration of our status as adopted children of our Father, who rejoices in offering us His Love and Mercy. This transforms us from slaves to sin into adopted sons and daughters — a transformation that is the culmination of our salvation.

We also find rest in the Eucharist — that is, upon the Sacred Heart of Jesus, as did the Beloved Disciple at the Last Supper (see Jn 12:23). John Paul II wrote: "Here we are touching on the culminating point of the mystery of our Christian life. In fact, the name 'Christian' indicates a new way of being, *to be in the likeness of the Son of God*. As sons in the Son, we share in salvation, which is not only deliverance from evil, but is first of all the fullness of good: the supreme good of the sonship of God."[134]

Jesus taught St. Faustina how to reach the heights of sanctity as an adopted daughter. After she firmly resolved to become a saint, the Lord told her not to lose her peace when she fell. Rather, she was told to entrust herself completely to His Mercy, in the knowledge that by humility one can gain more than one has lost by sin (see *Diary,* 1361).

The secret of the saints is that we are not to let our sins turn us away from the Father, as Adam and Eve turned away in the Garden. Once they had sinned, they hid themselves from the Father (see Gen 3:8). They hid their misery and their nakedness. Instead of being confident in the Father's Mercy and confessing their sins, they just passed on the blame. Adam blamed Eve, and Eve blamed the serpent. They hid and blamed others, missing their opportunity to receive the Mercy of God. Jesus speaks explicitly of what we should do once we recognize our nakedness and sinfulness: Throw ourselves into the arms of His Mercy (see *Diary,* 1541).

We are to run with great confidence to the Father to be embraced and loved by Him: "Steadfast love surrounds him who trusts in the Lord" (Ps 32:10). As St. Thérèse wrote to Maurice: "[A child who has sinned] throws himself into his father's arms, telling him that he is sorry to have hurt him, that he loves him, and that he will prove it by being good from now on. … Then, if that child asks his father to punish him with a kiss, I don't think the happy father could harden his heart against his child's filial trust, knowing his sincerity and love."[135]

---

[133] Collect for the 26th Sunday in Ordinary Time. Roman Missal, 486.

[134] Saint John Paul II, *Homilies of Pope John Paul II (English)* (Vatican City: Libreria Editrice Vaticana, 2014). Homily from January 1, 1997.

[135] Patrick V. Ahern, *Maurice and Thérèse: The Story of a Love* (New York: Image Books/ Doubleday, 2001).

The serpent injects his own pride into our hearts, attempting to make us ashamed of our misery and make us try to hide it. The serpent teaches us to cover our misery up with a show instead of admitting it. The Lord harshly critiqued the Pharisees for hypocrisy: They attempted to cover their sinfulness by external acts of piety, presuming that if they seemed good enough, they would be worthy of the Father's Love. But the Father's Love is not given in response to our worthiness. The Father's Love precedes us.

This is the truth of the Immaculate Conception: Our entire existence is brought into being by His Love, just as our conception is preceded by the love of two parents. To walk in this grace given first to Mary, we always need to remember that the Father's Love and Mercy precede our response; we have only to surrender to the reality of His Love, as Mary did by her trust in the Word of God at each moment of her life. On this point, Jesus even tells St. Faustina: **"Without special help from Me, you are not even capable of accepting My graces. You know who you are"** (*Diary*, 739).

Since the Triune God is immutable, our sins cannot change the love He has for each one of us. This is cause for great rejoicing! We did not cause the Father to love us in the first place, and we cannot ever cause the Father to stop loving us. Nor can we cause Him to love us more by growing in holiness, for holiness is simply participation in the Love of the Father through opening our hearts to cooperate with Him as He pours the Blood and Water of His Mercy into us to wash us clean. Cleansed, we can rejoice anew in His forgiveness, for in the Gospels, every time the Father forgives a sinner, there is rejoicing and celebration.[136]

Knowing that we will be redeemed when we approach Jesus with our misery, the serpent will attempt to discourage us and prevent us from seeking the Father's Mercy — just as his venom of distrust caused Adam and Eve to flee from the Father after they had sinned. We must take the words of Jesus to heart on this matter: **"Have confidence, My child. Do not lose heart in coming for pardon, for I am always ready to forgive you. As often as you beg for it, you glorify My mercy"** (*Diary*, 1488). When we ask Jesus for pardon after our sin, we glorify His Mercy. We ought never to be ashamed and run from the Lord when we sin. Our worship includes our request for forgiveness, and every Mass begins with *Kyrie eleison* — the petition "Lord, have mercy!"

Adam and Eve destroyed the bridge of trust that connected them with the Father's Mercy — not simply by their sin, but above all by their fear and by hiding after their sin. The Father has sent forth His Word to seek us out in our own hiding places and restore that bridge of trust. In Jesus Christ, the misery of our human nature has been inseparably united to the Incarnate Mercy of God. In the Latin Vulgate Bible, Jesus is called the great *Pontifex,* the "bridge builder," translated into English as "high priest," because He Himself is the

---

[136] Pope Francis, *Matteo: il Vangelo del compimento: lettura spirituale e pastorale*, comp. Gianfranco Venturi (Vatican City: Libreria Editrice Vaticana, 2016), 195.

bridge between our misery and the Father's Mercy (see Heb 5:1). The Nativity teaches us to approach the Father as His tattered children, orphaned by sin. By this humble approach, we can be assured that we will be embraced with His eternal Love and Mercy, the only remedy for our sins (see Lk 15:20).

The Incarnation is a great blessing, but ironically, we are so wounded that we are not used to letting anyone come so close to us. We have been burned too many times by people who draw near and then hurt us. This is true even in our relationship with Jesus. He wants to be very close to us — closer than we can imagine — so close that it might be discomforting when we are trained to have our defenses up at all times! He wants to be held in our hands and to dwell in our hearts; but for Him to be that close, we must be vulnerable and naked, as Adam and Eve were before sin. As we will see at Calvary, such vulnerability is often very painful in a sinful world: our nakedness will allow us to love and be loved, but it will also allow us to be wounded and hurt.

For many of us, that divine closeness is *too* close. We want a more distant God, one who does not want to be such a big part of our daily lives and routines. As Fr. Ronchi said to Pope Francis and the Curia in his 2016 Lenten retreat:

> Saint Teresa of Avila … writes a letter to her nuns, in which we find these words: "Know, sisters, that God is moving about in the kitchen, among the pots and pans." But how is it that the Lord of the universe can be in the kitchen, moving about among the jugs, crockery, dishes, pots and pans … God is in the kitchen means bringing God into a place of proximity … If you don't feel him at home, that is, in the simplest things, you haven't yet found the God of life. You still remain at the level of the rational representation of the God of religion.[137]

This "God of pots and pans" is the God who dwelled in the home of Mary and St. Joseph in Nazareth!

Being that close is precisely how Jesus can heal our wounds after someone has broken our trust. We can allow Him to heal those wounds by letting Him pour the Spirit of Mercy upon them in the midst of our everyday lives. Jesus made Himself vulnerable so that we would not have to be alone in our vulnerability before the Father. When we appear before the Father — in our nakedness and weakness — as Jesus did in the Incarnation, the Father pours forth the healing balm of the Holy Spirit to raise us to new life.

If you are afraid to approach Jesus Himself — since He is both Savior and Judge — then approach His Mother, who reveals the tenderness and compassion of the Father. She will teach you to rest upon her Immaculate Heart and will share with you that same Holy Spirit who burns as a fire within her. Her Spirit will free you from your sins. In this simple way we participate in the grace of

---

[137] Fr. Ermes Ronchi and Diana Montagna, "'God Is in the Kitchen.' On Retreat with Pope Francis," Aleteia.org, March 11, 2016, accessed July 11, 2017, https://aleteia. org/2016/03/11/god-is-in-the-kitchen-on-retreat-with-pope-francis/.

her Immaculate Conception. By drawing near to Mary and entrusting ourselves entirely to her, just as we are, we experience the power of the Father's Love that embraces us in our sinfulness and releases us from it — and makes us sons and daughters, not only of God, but also of Mary Immaculate.

CHILDLIKE ABANDONMENT AND SURRENDER

This step of assuming childlike trust, humility, and simplicity is essential before we continue on the journey of trust toward the Cross. Without this, we will not be able to be naked with Jesus upon the Cross. Jesus did not allow St. Faustina to proceed to Calvary without first mastering the two primary virtues of spiritual childhood: simplicity and humility (see *Diary*, 184).

At another point, Jesus appeared to St. Faustina as a young boy and taught her, **"True greatness is in loving God and in humility"** (*Diary*, 424; see also *Diary*, 1711). This teaching of the Lord and Our Lady is echoed in the teaching of Diadochus of Photice, who wrote that the measure of our love for God is not how much we love Him, but rather, how much we are aware of His love for us. Saint John of the Cross provides a corollary to this: "To be taken with love for a soul, God does not look on its greatness, but on the greatness of its humility."[138] Indeed, true greatness is not in great deeds, nor in great acts of holiness, but in childlike trust that comes from the humility of living as a son or daughter of the Father. The Father delights not in our greatness, but rather in our littleness, because that humility allows Him to fill us with His Love.

Jesus later told St. Faustina that without such simplicity, we cannot commune with Him (see *Diary*, 332). The key to this step of spiritual childhood is adopting childlike abandon and surrender. In the face of suffering and trials, in the face of the various difficulties of everyday life, we are called to respond with childlike surrender, trusting in His fatherly Providence that arranges all things for our eternal salvation (see Rom 8:28). Such surrender means acceptance of all that happens as the outcome of the Father's Providence. When we let go, particularly of those things beyond our control, and entrust ourselves to the Father, we can rest with peace of heart during even the most difficult of trials, knowing that what is beyond our control is always within His plan.

This surrender to another with abandon — not worrying about oneself at all, but simply handing oneself over — is essential to trust, and flows from our belief in the Word of God. "To believe means 'to abandon oneself' to the truth of the word of the living God, knowing and humbly recognizing 'how unsearchable are his judgments and how inscrutable his ways' (Rom 11:33)."[139] The verb abandon itself means "to give up, surrender (oneself or something), give over utterly; to yield (oneself) utterly." It comes from the French and implies that something or someone is at the "will, discretion or power of another."[140] To

---

[138] "Sayings of Light and Love," Sayings of St. John of the Cross.

[139] Saint John Paul II, *Redemptoris Mater*, n. 14.

[140] "It comes from Old French *abandoner* (12 c.), from adverbial phrase à bandon 'at will,

abandon ourselves to the Father and to Mary means that we submit ourselves to their will or discretion.

We see perfect abandonment manifested in the image of Jesus in the arms of His Mother. As an infant, He was totally at the discretion of Mary and had no defense at all — only her love. For her part, Mary is totally at the discretion of the Father, to whom she has given her unconditional "Amen." When we place ourselves at the discretion of the Father — abandoning ourselves to Him — we receive the greatest gift of all: Jesus Himself, who takes away our sins (see Mt 1:21; Jn 1:29).

On our journey of trust, it is important to be surrounded by Mary's maternal love and care, because there will be many moments when we need to place ourselves in her arms. There, we will be convinced beyond doubt of the Father's unfathomable Mercy and Love, because just as Mary holds us, she is held by our loving Father. There, we will learn to totally surrender ourselves and let go. If we do not have an underlying attitude of simplicity and surrender, it will be much harder to trust when more difficult moments of suffering come. If we do not have a firm attachment to Mary and our Father in moments of consolation and peace, we will not develop the trust necessary to believe that those same arms embrace us in our moments of abandonment when we feel forsaken by the Father, as Jesus did.

In those moments, we must remember being held in Mary's arms, then embraced in turn by the Father and filled with His love, just as Jesus remembered during His Passion. We often do not remember that when Jesus cried, "My God, my God, why have you forsaken me?" upon the Cross (see Mt 27:46), He intended to pray all of Psalm 22, which includes these beautiful verses: "Yet you are he who took me from the womb; you kept me safe upon my mother's breasts. Upon you was I cast from my birth, and since my mother bore me, you have been my God. Be not far from me, for trouble is near and there is none to help" (Ps 22:9-11).

In the movie *The Passion of the Christ*, both Mary and Jesus have flashbacks of the times when they were together; those memories give them the confidence and courage they need to face the Cross. So too will the memory of Mary's embrace give us a firm foundation of trust in moments of trial. Childlike simplicity and humility guard and preserve our trust, most especially in the darkest moments of our lives. Notice that Jesus ended His life on the Cross by recalling the words of Psalm 22 and the memory of being upon His Mother's breast. He could entrust Himself to the Father knowing that He would likewise return to the Father's heart (see Lk 23:46).

All of this helps more fully reveal to us the great responsibility of being a mother or father in a human family: The loving bonds we form with our children

---

at discretion,' from à 'at, to' + *bandon* 'power, jurisdiction,' from Latin *bannum*, 'proclamation.' See "Abandon," Online Etymology Dictionary, accessed July 11, 2017, http://www.etymonline.com/index.php?term=abandon.

have a direct impact upon their relationship with God the Father. When we react with impatience, anger, or harshness to children's weakness, limitations, or even sinfulness, we teach them to fear approaching the Father instead of drawing near to Him to be loved and healed. Children need to feel that they are loved — even in their misery and sin. This is how human families serve as icons of the Trinitarian life: the father has the opportunity as a parent to reflect the face of the eternal Father; and the mother, to reflect the face of Mary, the visible face of the Holy Spirit.

As Christians, we are to proclaim that God's Justice is His Mercy, poured out to redeem, save, and console us in our sins. How Jesus would be hurt by the distrust of innocent children who run from Him because they have not seen His merciful face reflected in their father or mother (see *Diary*, 300)!

THE VALUE OF POVERTY

The Nativity in Bethlehem reveals the important connection between poverty and our trust in the Father. Imagine the trust in Divine Providence that Joseph had as he searched for a place for his pregnant wife! Imagine their flight into Egypt to escape Herod's slaughter of the innocents. There was no room for Jesus in the inn: The world shut its door to Him and, filled with its own concerns and matters, had no room for the King of Kings to be born. Maintaining their trust must have been a challenge for Joseph and Mary. The Word of God was born in poverty — and not by accident.

It may seem like a beautiful ideal to aspire to, but trust can be quite difficult in our daily lives. If the Word of God is to become flesh in our lives, however, trust is necessary, and it is essential if we are to participate in the Father's plan of salvation. Distracted by this world and its passing riches, we ourselves often offer no place for the Lord in our busy lives, but we are called to provide a place for Him in our weak and broken hearts.

Our own poverty is the place where Jesus is born, the place where the Word is made flesh in our own lives, and we must simply empty ourselves of this world so the Lord can enter our poverty and make us rich (see 2 Cor 8:9). At every Mass, the priest exhorts the faithful: "*Sursum corda* — Lift up your hearts." We are to lift our hearts from the matters of this world, which close us to the Word being sown and born in our hearts (see Mk 4:19).

In preparing to receive the Lord in Holy Communion, it is necessary to be emptied, just as Jesus emptied Himself in becoming man, coming as the Infant Jesus. It is necessary to be aware of our poverty and misery and provide a place for the Lord to come and rest (see Phil 2:7). The manger we provide for the Lord in Holy Communion is our own misery, our own poverty. We know we are truly poor in spirit when our joy comes not from this passing world, but from Jesus alone: "Today, before Jesus, the most sublime Wisdom, present in the most Blessed Sacrament, feel yourself to be so weak, that He would feel the need — even the necessity — of descending to you. For it is more beneficial to you to reveal [to Him] your own helplessness than to give [Him] the impression that you are strong: for that — you are not!"[141]

The more aware we are of our misery, the more we will want to draw near to this fount of Mercy in Holy Communion. True devotion to the Eucharist is therefore built upon humility and repentance. If we know our misery well, like St. Faustina, we will have a devotion to the Blessed Sacrament. Her devotion was so great that she chose as her name in the convent "Faustina of the Blessed Sacrament." We can share her glory in Heaven if we share her humility and misery on earth and receive Holy Communion often, as she tells us in her *Diary*: "But I want to tell you that eternal life must begin already here on earth through Holy Communion. Each Holy Communion makes you more capable of communing with God throughout eternity" (*Diary*, 1811).

Saint Faustina prepared for Holy Communion by anticipating the exchange of her misery for the Mercy of God when she received Jesus (see *Diary*, 1817). Her misery did not discourage her or make her falter. Instead, her experience and knowledge of her own misery led her to greater trust in the infinite Mercy of the Father.

When we approach Holy Communion, let us say, "Amen" to Mercy Incarnate coming to fill our poverty, for we press the Infant to our hearts primarily through receiving Jesus in Holy Communion. Let us say, "Amen," as Mary did at the Annunciation, allowing the Word of God to become flesh in our hearts and in our lives. Let us say, "Amen," as Joseph did, and trust in the Word of God, even when it costs us our dreams and our lives. Let us say, "Amen," and provide a throne for Jesus in the manger of our misery, that He might be, in our hearts, the King of Mercy. With childlike surrender and simplicity, let us learn to entrust ourselves with abandon to Jesus in Holy Communion, just as He entrusted Himself to us as a defenseless child, and continues to do so every time He places Himself in our hands and on our tongues. Ask Mary and Joseph to come with you to Holy Communion: Let them teach you how to hold Jesus, caress Him, and pour out your love upon Him. Ask them how to let Jesus love you in return.

Remember that just as we are miserable and poor, so are others — and just as Jesus loves us and makes his home in our misery and poverty, He also loves others in their misery and poverty. This is the challenge for us: we are willing to accept Jesus in His weakness and fragility as an infant, and we beg Jesus to accept our own fragility and weakness, yet we often recoil before that same weakness and fragility in a brother or sister. Do we revere the broken Body of Christ, the Church, with the reverence we give to the Body of Christ in the Eucharist? We cannot separate the two: If we desire the Lord to draw near to us in our poverty, we ought to be willing to draw near to others in their poverty, as well. Do others find a home for themselves in our hearts? Are we willing to draw near to

---

[141] Saint Stanislaus Papczynski, *Pisma Zebrane (Warsaw: PROMIC, 2016)*.

them as willingly as we do to Jesus and say, "Amen — Amen, I believe Jesus is present in this person, amid poverty, misery, and sin"? For hidden beneath their poverty and misery is Jesus "in the distressing disguise of the poorest of the poor," as Mother Teresa said.

God is present everywhere by essence, presence, and power — even in the worst of sinners. But sinners do not possess the Presence of God by sanctifying grace, and our task is to open their hearts to this Presence, that they might share in the life of God Himself. We want to invite others to believe and trust in Jesus just as He invited sinners in the Gospel, with tender mercy and compassion.

Remember that one of the primary characteristics of Mary's faith is that she always shared the Mercy she received. She shared her Son with everyone, without exception. As we progress on this journey, we must not be focused only on ourselves and our own spiritual lives. In order to arrive in Heaven with Mary, we need to invite her other children to walk this journey of trust, too. This task can be daunting and difficult, as it was for Mary. But with each Holy Communion, we exchange our misery for His strength (see *Diary,* 1803).

His Mercy will sustain us at each step of our path. In all the difficult moments of her life, I imagine Mary pressing Jesus to her heart or calling such memories to mind (see Lk 2:19). Let us do the same in difficult moments: let us press Divine Mercy Incarnate, the Infant Jesus, to our hearts in Holy Communion with Mary. If we cannot walk beside Mary, let us ask her to take us into her arms and hold us, together with Jesus, as we walk along this journey of trust. And when we encounter others who have difficulty, let us be the arms and hands of Mary to lead them to trust in Jesus as she trusted.

CHAPTER 14

Trust Amid Poverty

"But those who seek the Lord lack no good thing"
(Ps 34:10).

Before continuing with Jesus' life, I want to return once again to the Nativity, contemplating it anew in light of Mary's trust in the Father. The story of Jesus' birth may unsettle us, as it should. The Father indeed provides, but look at how He provided for His own beloved Son, who was born in a manger. As we recall this familiar story, we might be inclined to worry about the Holy Family because we can imagine the distress of St. Joseph, who would want, just like any good father, an appropriate place for Mary and Jesus. He can find no such place, however, only a cave for animals, and Jesus is placed in the humble feeding trough, making it the cradle of a king. Yet this is how Jesus, Mary, and Joseph lived. This is the path of the Holy Family, who lived in complete trust in Divine Providence. Without that trust, theirs would not be a holy family and we would not honor them.

Our honor is hollow, however, if we do not follow them in their way of life. I cannot help thinking that what Jesus preached in the Gospel emerged from His own family life with Mary and Joseph, who, in their poverty, had to trust in the Father. We recall that Scripture indicates how poor they must have been to offer two turtledoves for Jesus at the Presentation because they could not afford the normal offering (Lk 2:24; see Lev 12:8). In a poor country, they were even poorer than most. In the Magnificat, Mary described herself as the handmaid of the Lord and proclaimed that the Father looked upon her lowliness with favor. Mary clearly saw herself as completely dependent upon God — part of the *anawim*. Mary's life was nondescript (from an earthly perspective) and filled with suffering, but she lived always in union with God.

If we trust as Mary did, we are daily called to entrust everything to the Father — and receive everything back again as a gift (see Mk 10:28). Walking with Mary along this journey of trust requires our willingness to accept poverty, because the serpent will propose the opposite: riches. In his meditation "Two Standards," St. Ignatius of Loyola writes about this strategy of Satan: "[H]ow he tells them to cast out nets and chains; that they have first to tempt with a longing for riches — as he is accustomed to do in most cases — that men may more easily come to vain honor of the world, and then to vast pride. So that the first step shall be that of riches; the second, that of honor; the third, that of pride; and from these three steps he draws on to all the other vices."[142] The door through which the serpent enters our lives is the desire for riches, which then leads to vanity and ultimately to pride. Ironically, it is poverty that protects our trust in the Father, because poverty leads to humility.

Our trust in the Father cannot be by chance or by habit. Each day we must deliberately place ourselves under our Father's heavenly care, for each day the serpent will attempt to bite us and place obstacles along our path. In the Immaculate Conception, the grace of trust was given to Mary as a free gift, but she had to take steps each day to walk in that grace. Baptized and given grace freely and without merit, we are called to walk along the path of trust just as she did. We ourselves are a gift of the Love of the Father. If we truly live our conception in that same Love, we will not hold onto possessions as our security, but will allow the Father to hold on to us instead. We will see that His Love — the Holy Spirit — never fails to watch over and care for us through the maternal hand of Our Lady.

POVERTY AND MERCY

Radical trust requires that we do as Jesus said: Seek first the Kingdom of God. Without that priority, we are no longer disciples of Jesus Christ and simply live as pagans do, even if we have been baptized. John the Baptist warned that it is not enough to say, "I am baptized," just as he warned the Jews that it was not enough for them to say, "I am a son of Abraham" (see Mt 3:9). It is not enough to say, "I have a devotion to the Divine Mercy, I have the Image, or I pray the Chaplet." As Jesus told St. Faustina, our trust is to manifest itself through works of mercy (see *Diary*, 1267). We receive mercy through the vessel of trust, so we are to share that mercy with others through actions and words that inspire others to trust in the Father and glorify Him (see Mt 5:16).

Love never feels that it loves enough or gives enough. This means not that we give more and more to God, but that complacency must be rooted out. It means that we never say, "I did enough." No. We always aim higher, and trust ever more in the Mercy of our Father, encouraging others to do the same. We may ask why God does not fix the problem of material poverty. The answer is that He intends to. And for this reason, He has created you and me. We are the solution to the problem, but only if we choose to trust, be compassionate, and have mercy on those in need.

What are you called to do? Be generous, as God has been generous to you. If you see your life in light of the Immaculate Conception — if you see that, as He endowed the Blessed Virgin Mary, the Father has endowed you with all sorts of good gifts — then be moved by His generosity to be generous to others. We know that Mary must have had this attitude, for how else could she have returned everything to God? She gave up to the Father all that was dear to her, including her own beloved Son.

---

[142] Saint Ignatius of Loyola, *The Spiritual Exercises of St. Ignatius of Loyola*, 74-75.

This is the mystery of the Eucharist — in union with Jesus, we gather together to offer the Father everything we have, and the Father gives us everything in return: He gives us His own beloved Son. The Father has nothing more to give, nothing left. He has given us everything in the Word made flesh. Will we give Him everything, too? Will we follow Mary's example and let go of everything, trusting that everything will be given back to us in due time? In the celebration of the Mass, the Eucharist commits us to the poor. When we receive the Body and Blood of Christ, we must recognize Christ in the poorest, and through the Eucharist, we are privileged to be one with them.

The Church Fathers remind us that giving to the poor is not always a matter of mercy; rather, it is sometimes a matter of justice, of returning what belongs to them as human beings. Richer nations must return to poorer countries what they have obtained by unjust terms of trade, and have a moral obligation to cut down on their expenditures and give to the poor (see *CCC*, 2439). The Gospel is not good news for consumerism, because if we are certain of the Father's goodness and mercy, we will not need to buy the latest gadget or whatever. Consumerism thrives on people's desire for earthly things, *not* on living as Jesus taught.

As Christians, we need to set the standard for the world through our actions as well as our doctrines. We need to buy less and give more to the poor, to those who are in need. Saint John Chrysostom vigorously reminds us, "Not to enable the poor to share in our goods is to steal from them and deprive them of life. The goods we possess are not ours, but theirs." "The demands of justice must be satisfied first of all; that which is already due in justice is not to be offered as a gift of charity" (*CCC*, 2446). Saint Gregory the Great also states: "When we attend to the needs of those in want, we give them what is theirs, not ours. More than performing works of mercy, we are paying a debt of justice" (*CCC*, 2446).

Those of us who have at least moderate wealth might pat ourselves on the back for helping the poor, but Jesus tells us not to let our left hand know what our right hand is doing. In reality, the poor are the ones helping the rich (see Mt 6:3). The poor open the hearts of their wealthier brethren and give an example of how to trust in the Father, for the poor are often more filled with genuine joy than are the rich, for all their security and possessions. By giving the poor what belongs to them, wealthier hearts are opened to the love of God. In fact, at death, we will all owe much to the poor, for they will be the ones who will judge us and invite us into our heavenly home (see Mt 25:31-46; 1 Cor 6:2).

Even if we are not among those who are wealthy, we are all obligated to share our spiritual wealth of faith in Jesus Christ; the poor in particular can give witness to this faith through their trust in the Father's Providence. Indeed, if we have no means for giving materially to others, spiritual works of mercy are even more meritorious (see *Diary*, 317). During the Jubilee of Mercy, Pope Francis strongly emphasized the corporal and spiritual works of mercy. Before Vatican II, these were called "alms deeds." Though I prefer the new name, it can be misleading. Saint Thomas Aquinas places alms deeds, not under the virtue of mercy, but under the virtue of justice; as above, when we give to the poor what is their due, we are simply paying a debt of justice. When we tend to the sick, we are doing what is just: They deserve such care and respect.

In writing on the seven cardinal virtues, Professor Eleonore Stump makes an interesting point: Works of mercy sound "optional"; that is, we can easily believe that if we get to them, they're great, but if we don't have the opportunity to perform them, they're not essential.[143] However, that is not true: we are called and are obligated to seek justice (see Is 1:17; Mic 6:8) and to be merciful. Indeed, as Jesus Himself stated: **"If a soul does not exercise mercy somehow or other, it will not obtain My mercy on the day of judgment"** (*Diary*, 1317). The "works of mercy" are not secondary to our salvation or to trusting in the Father; rather, they are the very fruit of that trust, evidence that indeed, trust is alive in our hearts. If we trust in the Father, we can let go of our time and our possessions, and entrust these to Him through the poor, for Christ assures us that whatever is given to the least of the brethren is given to Him (see Mt 25).

Our goal is not earthly; our goal is Heaven. Rather than seek our treasure in Heaven, however, quite often we turn to what is unstable and perishable — subject to destruction by moth, decay, and theft — instead of what is imperishable: the Word of God. Jesus shows us how foolish it is to place our trust in perishable things that will not support us in our day of trouble. He also reminds us that where our treasure is, so also are our hearts. Often we are not free to serve God, because our hearts are weighed down by the desires and concerns of this world, so that our anxiety suffocates the seed of the Word of God and makes us incapable of trusting in Jesus. *Mammon*, an Aramaic word that means "what one believes in or places one's trust in," is personified as a *master*.

We cannot serve two masters, because neither will receive our full commitment and service. When we seek security in our possessions for their own sake, we serve them instead of the living God. We must be detached from wealth and possessions (see Mt 5:3) — which means recognizing them as gifts of our Creator that prompt us to focus on Him and to trust in His Providence. But we cannot place our trust both in our Father and in mammon (see Mt 6:24). There is a very important connection that I want to highlight now: Trust also leads to service and worship. The English word *worship* comes from the Old English *weorthscipe*, meaning "worthiness," "respect," which we demonstrate by how we dedicate time and attention to whatever we consider worthy of our respect or trust.[144]

Whatever we trust to provide the security we desire, that is what we begin to worship and orient our lives toward. Trust in the Father does not exclude

---

[143] Eleonore Stump, "The Seven Cardinal Virtues and the Indwelling Holy Spirit," Sound-Cloud, February 2017, accessed July 11, 2017, https://soundcloud.com/thomisticinstitute/prof-stump-the-seven-cardinal-virtues-and-the-indwelling-holy-spiritfeb-2017-bloomfield-ct.
[144] *Merriam-Webster's Collegiate Dictionary.*

trusting in others or relying to a certain degree upon material possessions; rather, trust in God properly orders our trust in others, so that our entire lives are ordered to the worship of Him alone. Unfortunately, a lack of worship and of proper ordering is evident in the world today. In the western, secularized countries, we have constructed a world where money and economic success are the measure of security; and a great many serve these idols today — to their own ruin.

Mother Teresa could bring about many conversions precisely because she was poor and trusted in the Father without reserve. Her love and charity were manifested in her ability to bring hope to the poor and dying. She was the face of Divine Providence and enabled those who had lost hope to hope once again, for they could see in her face the Love of the Father and His Divine Providence that weeps over our misery and lifts us from the dust. Do we weep over the misery of others? Do we desire to become the face of the Father's Providence and Mercy, just as Jesus was for us? Or are we content to merely receive and not give? John the Apostle warns us not to be deceived: The love of God cannot exist in a man who has enough of this world's goods and closes his heart to his neighbor (see 1 Jn 3:7). James the Apostle also warns us that faith without works is dead (see Jas 2:14-26). Jesus Himself says that the Divine Mercy Image **"is to be a reminder of the demands of My mercy, because even the strongest faith is of no avail without works"** *(Diary, 742).*

Being a Christian is not about getting or gaining more in earthly terms. Following the example of Jesus, who emptied Himself for our salvation, being Christian entails *kenosis,* the emptying of our self-will that will allow us to open to the will of God, who wants to fill us with the abundance of His Love and Mercy. We are called and enabled by the grace of God to trust completely as Jesus trusted, to empty ourselves utterly and entirely. To trust we must become poor, as Jesus was poor. To be saved we must be empty, so we can receive all the graces the Father has destined for us. If we are already filled with the riches of this world, we will not be able to be filled with the riches of the world to come. Likewise, we cannot be filled with the consolations of the Holy Spirit if we abuse the consolations of this world and so lose our hunger and thirst for the righteousness of God (see Mt 5:6).

The modern ethic is: If you want something, work hard for it, try harder, do it yourself, achieve! But this singular focus on the importance of our own efforts goes against the Gospel. Jesus does not tell us that we should not work hard or should not achieve, but He does tell us that career, money, etc., should not be our ultimate goals. He tells us that we should undertake our work with a spirit of childlike simplicity, trusting that our Father in Heaven supports us, guides us, and helps us. We must seek to be the empty jars of Cana, so we can be filled with the wine of salvation.

TRUSTING EACH OTHER

In our personal relationships, trust is where Divine Providence touches us most intimately — in the fundamental decisions we are required to make regarding exactly to whom we will entrust ourselves. Trust requires not only poverty and obedience, as discussed previously, but also chastity. Even though the vows of *poverty, chastity,* and *obedience* belong properly to religious life in the Church, all Christians are called to live the spirit of the evangelical counsels.

Single people, religious, and priests are to entrust themselves in chastity to the Father without reserve through service to the Body of Christ. In marriage, spouses entrust themselves to the Father through bodily entrustment to the spouse given to them by the Father, so as to bring forth new members to the Body of Christ. In the marital act, which is the visible, physical expression of God's love, everything is to be given and received in reciprocity. This is why the Church forbids contraception: because not everything is given; only part is given, and so we corrupt the love of God in our hearts, for we hold back when God asks us to give all. Just as Christ gave everything for us upon the Cross, so we are called to give everything to Him. Contraception, and all other sexual aberrations, vitiate this pure love, a pure love that is nothing other than the complete entrustment of oneself to the Father through the spouse. Such practices are sinful because they don't involve the total self-gift that the marital act naturally entails, and so they mar the image of God, for He never gives in pieces, in parts, or halfway. God is Love, and He holds nothing back.

PROVIDING A MOTHER

The Father cannot help but take care of us in our need. He is such a loving Father that He cannot forget about us (see Is 49:15). His tender concern is displayed, above all, through Mary. Just as a mother cannot forget her child, so the Father cannot forget us, and He proves this by giving us a perfect Mother. The Immaculate Conception is not simply a theological idea. The "fullness of grace" is a Person — Jesus Christ, the One anointed with the fullness of the Holy Spirit — and Our Lady was filled with that same Holy Spirit from conception to prepare her to conceive Jesus. Mary was disposed from the first moment of her existence to receive this "fullness of grace," and we are destined to receive it at each Holy Communion. Giving oneself specifically to Mary is a particular way of trusting in Divine Providence, and various saints throughout the ages have written on the value of making such a consecration. We are called to imitate the Father, and the Father entrusted *everything* to Mary: His beloved Son. We are to follow this example and give ourselves fully to Mary.

What does giving ourselves to Our Lady mean? It means going to Jesus and accepting the gift He has bestowed on us: the gift of His Mother. It means taking her into all our affairs, concerns, worries, and tasks — letting go of ourselves and being formed anew as children, by Mary. We can learn to think and live as she, the Immaculata, does. We can be in Mary's "school" through the daily recitation of the Rosary.[145] We can talk to her confidently as her children in prayer, entrusting to her our concerns; we can meditate on the Word of God with her, asking her to teach us how to trust and live her *fiat* at each moment. We can learn about her virtues, so as to live as she did.

If we are called to a life of trust, from whom shall we learn but from Mary, for how did Jesus learn to trust in *Abba* in his humanity, if not from her? It means that we follow Mary's path to Nazareth, to the hidden life of the Holy Family, and there learn how to live in deep faith and trust in the everyday circumstances of life. It means not only allowing ourselves to be taught, but giving ourselves entirely to Mary out of love, allowing her to do with us as she wills. Trust was Mary's way of life. Jesus learned from her, and we can learn also. This requires taking steps with her each and every day — steps that not only tread upon the serpent, but move us first toward the Cross and through the Cross to the Resurrection and eternal life.

---

[145] Saint John Paul II, *Rosarium Virginis Mariae: On the Most Holy Rosary*, Apostolic Letter (October 16, 2002), accessed July 11, 2017, https://w2.vatican.va/content/john -paul-ii/en/apost_letters/2002/documents/hf_jp-ii_apl_20021016_rosarium-virginis- mariae.html, n. 1.

CHAPTER 15

Trust as the Door of Faith

"[God] had opened a door of faith" (Acts 14:27).

According to the Evangelist John, the Gospels were written so we might have faith, or trust, in the name of Jesus (see Jn 20:31). How do the Gospels inspire us to have faith? They portray Jesus as One who can be trusted, as He gradually reveals His power over every misery and evil. He has power over sickness by healing, over sin by forgiving sinners, over demons by casting them out, over storms as He calms their wrath, and over death itself in the raising of Lazarus. Ultimately, He conquers sin, death, and Satan altogether by His Resurrection. Plainly, Jesus has power over all the areas of our lives where we are weak and poor.

In our powerlessness, we have a choice. Either we can recognize our poverty and weakness and trust in the Lord, who has power over all that causes us difficulty and pain, or we can trust in ourselves (or other creatures), hoping that we can become perfect again through our own efforts. This was the mistake of the Pharisees (whose descendants in the Church are the Pelagians, those who believe that our effort has priority over the Mercy of God). The Pharisees' intention to strictly keep the Law, thus pleasing God and hastening the coming of the Messiah, was good. But the sin for which Jesus rebuked them was their failure to recognize their poverty and need for mercy. Their self-centered trust led to pride. On the other hand, tax collectors and sinners first accepted Jesus' call to conversion, because they were aware of their need for mercy (see Mt 21:31).

Do we trust in Jesus, who has power over all those things that we are powerless against: sin, death, and suffering? Or do we ignore or even kill Him? By trusting in Jesus, we humbly admit our own weakness and trust in His strength. In his letters, St. Paul is adamant that faith is what justifies and saves us (see Rom 3:28; Gal 2:16). In Scripture, we read that we ought not even trust in our own good works, for they are like filthy rags (see Is 64:6). As mentioned earlier, St. Thérèse declared that she would appear before Jesus in Heaven with empty hands. Her emptiness is what allowed her to receive the fullness of His Mercy.

Christianity is not about "getting it right" or having enough willpower to do the right things to enter Heaven. Rather, the Gospel is about the Father's Mercy toward sinners and the trust they are called to have in the face of such abundant Mercy: "The Gospel is the revelation in Jesus Christ of God's mercy to sinners" (*CCC*, 1846). Far from trusting in what we can do to save ourselves, we ought to trust in what the Father has done, is doing, and will do to save us in His Son and the Holy Spirit.

The Example of Abraham

Trust in the Father does not excuse us from striving to live a moral life. In fact, such trust obliges us to obey the Lord. When discussing faith and salvation, St. Paul utilizes the example of Abraham, whose righteousness and holiness stemmed from his belief in the Word of God (see Gen 15:6; Rom 4:3). Abraham did not have the Law. He heard the Word of the Lord and obeyed it. In other words, he had faith. He trusted. Imagine how difficult that must have been for him! He left his home, his extended family, and all that he knew to obey the Word of God: "Go from your country and your kindred and your father's house to the land that I will show you" (Gen 12:1).

Abraham's trust required him to believe in the promise of God and leave his former way of life behind, and this trust is what filled him with the Father's blessings and let him become a mediator of those blessings to the entire world (see Gen 22:18). Trust empties us of our dreams, desires, pride, and plans, so we can be filled with the Spirit of Mercy instead. Trust in oneself (or in other creatures) and trust in the Father are inversely proportional: the more I trust in myself (or in other creatures), the less I trust in the Father; the less I trust in myself, the more I trust in the Father.

The Father knows we are weak and cannot trust and obey Him without His help, so when we are obedient, He gives us His omnipotence to fulfill His will: **"Yes, when you are obedient I take away your weakness and replace it with My strength. I am very surprised that souls do not want to make that exchange with Me"** (*Diary*, 381). Indeed, through our trust, we are capable of the impossible; when we trust, we rely not on our own resources, but on God Himself. As Blessed Michael Sopocko wrote, "Nothing gives such glory to Divine omnipotence as the fact that God makes those who trust Him omnipotent also … . Trust is, above all, homage to God's Mercy, which, in exchange, bestows on those who trust the strength and courage they need to overcome even the most formidable difficulties."[146] Nevertheless, because we are often so prone to the pride that glories in strength, even when the Father supplies us with His strength, we will likely still feel weak. "Many go around with the illusion that if they give their weakness to God, he will transform it into strength. But God knows man well enough to see that he cannot bear such strength immediately. He would only become more puffed up."[147]

One could say that Abraham obeyed the Word of the Lord because he was given such great promises. Who would not want to be made a father of many

---

[146] Blessed Sopocko, *The Mercy of God in His Works,* Vol. 3, 173, 177.
[147] Stinissen, *The Holy Spirit, Fire of Divine Love*, 48.

nations (see Gen 12:2)? Who would not want to be given the Promised Land for free (see Gen 13:14-15)? Yet we see more than Abraham's easy and obvious blessings; he was also put to the test to determine whether he truly trusted the Lord. When Abraham went to the Promised Land, there was famine (see Gen 12:10); the promised child's birth was long delayed; and after the birth of his offspring, Abraham was asked to give his only son back to the Father to show that he valued God above all His promises and blessings (see Gen 12:10).

Abraham's willingness to sacrifice Isaac showed his complete and total trust in the Father (see Gen 22:12). Abraham could give what was most precious to him to the Father, knowing that he would receive back all that he offered to Him. For us, this is a lesson in trust, a lesson that prompts simple but important questions: What is most precious to us? Are we, like Abraham, able to entrust what we value most into the Father's hands (see *CCC*, 146)? Can we take steps of trust each day, walking in hope that the Father will provide all that we need?

Saint Stanislaus Papczynski identifies Isaac as a type of our free will: The Father asks us each to offer our free will as a holocaust in His sight. "You ought to also consecrate, give and present in offering, to the One, All Good and All Powerful God ... your only son Isaac, that is your one and only will. In all your undertakings or endeavors, always say: *Thy will be done on earth, as it is in heaven.* As to myself, may Your will, Lord, be done at every moment, hour, day, and in eternity."[148]

THE EXAMPLE OF NOAH

Noah is also an example of faith and trust in the Word of God. Imagine for a moment that you are Noah, living amid a corrupt and depraved generation, and the Lord asks you to build an ark because there is going to be a flood (see Gen 5:6, 13-14). We know the end of the story, so we might think, "Well, of course I would build the ark. I would not want to drown!" But at the time that Noah received the Word of the Lord, it is likely that there was no earthly sign of the coming flood. In fact, life continued as normal; people were even celebrating marriages up until the beginning of the Flood (see Mt 24:38-39). Noah believed the Word of God, even when his senses could not yet confirm it. Instead of being caught up in normal life as usual, he prepared the ark and was saved because of his trust and obedience.

We can learn from Noah. Are we prepared for times of desolation when we are living in times of consolation, and do we look forward to times of consolation when we are desolate? Or do we assume that life will always be *this* way, as it is now? Instead of believing the Word of God, are we deceived by our senses and the world into supposing that life is always good or always bad? Like those

---

[148] Saint Stanislaus Papczynski, *Inspectio Cordis,* quoted in *And That Your Fruit Would Remain,* ed. Fr. Andrzej Pakuła, MIC, and Fr. Joseph Roesch, MIC (Przasnysz: J.J. Maciejewscy Publishing House, 2007), 34.

who lived in the time of Noah, we may be tempted to think that no disaster could ruin life as we know it, or that we'll never see relief from the disaster that life is right now. This temptation is particularly acute in relation to the Second Coming: Many live as if Jesus is not coming, as if the world will continue forever just as it is today (see 2 Pet 3:3-4). We do not know the day or the hour of His coming, but we do know that He *is* coming. The hope of His coming will provide stability for those who are already desolate even now, as Isaiah encourages those of a fearful heart: "Be strong, fear not! Behold, your God will come … with the recompense of God. He will come and save you" (Is 35:4).

Noah's salvation came precisely because of his faith and trust in the Word of God. So too does our salvation depend on trust. To be saved, we must trust the Lord and obey His word. This is the foolproof path to salvation, for the devil can fake humility and other virtues, but he cannot fake the obedience that brings salvation: "Satan can even clothe himself in a cloak of humility, but he does not know how to wear the cloak of obedience and thus his evil designs will be disclosed" (*Diary*, 939). The *Diary* is filled with our Lord's repeated pleas to turn to Him with trust, to prepare for tribulation, and ultimately to be ready for the Second Coming. If we are growing in trust in His Divine Mercy, then we are using this time well.

His delay in coming is intended to provide us with an opportunity to repent (see 2 Pet 3:9). We are not to take His patience for granted, however; we are to be vigilant and attentive to the signs of our times (see Mt 16:2-3). Through St. Faustina, Jesus has warned us that this time of mercy is given in preparation for the day of His justice: **"It is a sign for the end times; after it will come the day of justice. While there is still time, let them have recourse to the fount of My mercy; let them profit from the Blood and Water which gushed forth for them"** (*Diary*, 848).

Now is the time to receive His Mercy — the Blood and Water pouring forth from His side — to prepare for the day of justice, for those rays are our only defense on that day: **"These rays shield souls from the wrath of My Father. Happy is the one who will dwell in their shelter, for the just hand of God shall not lay hold of him"** (*Diary*, 299). Even the Father cannot spare us on that day if we do not trust; this not for a lack of divine love, but that God respects free will: **"Before I come as a just Judge, I first open wide the door of My mercy. He who refuses to pass through the door of My mercy must pass through the door of My justice"** (*Diary*, 1146).

Saint Ignatius of Loyola teaches us that times of consolation are given so that we might prepare for desolation by humbling ourselves: "Tenth Rule: Let him who is in consolation think how he will be in the desolation which will come after, taking new strength for then. Eleventh Rule; Let him who is consoled see to humbling himself and lowering himself as much as he can, thinking how little he is … [capable of] in the time of desolation without such grace or consolation."[149] Thus we ought to live in the present with an eye toward the future, receiving all of His Mercy by humbling ourselves and remembering that we are but dust and misery without His grace.

THE EXAMPLE OF MARY AT CANA

Like Abraham and Noah, Mary was called to believe in the Word addressed to her. Even before our Lord's request to the apostles that they leave everything and follow Him (see Mk 10:28), Mary left "everything" precisely because of her trust in the Word.[150] Her *fiat* was uttered in faith, whereby she "entrusted herself to God without reserve and 'devoted herself totally as the handmaid of the Lord to the person and work of her Son.' ... From the moment of the Annunciation and conception, from his birth in the stable at Bethlehem, Mary followed Jesus step by step in her maternal pilgrimage of faith. She followed him during the years of his hidden life at Nazareth; she followed him also during the time after he left home, when he began 'to do and to teach' (see Acts 1:1) in the midst of Israel. Above all she followed him in the tragic experience of Golgotha."[151]

Before she saw any of her Son's miracles, Mary was called to step out in trust at the Annunciation. It was her trust in Jesus that prompted Him to work His first public miracle at Cana. At Pentecost, while Mary was with the apostles in the Upper Room in Jerusalem at the nativity of the Church, her faith, born from the words of the Annunciation, found confirmation after 33 years of taking steps of trust.[152] Her faith kindled the faith of the other disciples, and inspires our own.[153]

Let us take a moment at Cana with Mary now, before going further along this path of trust — the path that requires us to entrust ourselves and everything we have into the Father's hands. It is not by accident that our Lord's first miracle was at a wedding. Jesus is not only our Savior and Lord: He is the Bridegroom, who desires to lavish His love upon His Bride, the Church. The wedding at Cana is a foreshadowing of both Calvary, where the true wine of His Blood poured forth from His side, and Heaven, where, Isaiah promises, the Father will fill us with the choicest of wines — the Holy Spirit (see Is 25:6; Acts 2:13-15).

Remember my personal dilemma in the first chapter, when I wondered with concern what kind of future awaited me and exactly what the Father had in store for me. So often we focus on Christ's suffering and Cross, forgetting what flows forth from the Cross: plenteous redemption in the Blood and Water coming from Christ's side. The plan of the Father is the marriage of the Bride (the Church) and the Bridegroom (Jesus). This marriage is foretold in the

---

149 Saint Ignatius of Loyola, *The Spiritual Exercises of St. Ignatius of Loyola*, 173.
150 See Saint John Paul II, *Redemptoris Mater*, n. 20.
151 Ibid., n. 13.
152 Ibid., n. 13, 26.
153 Ibid., n. 21.

last chapters of the Bible when the Bride, the New Jerusalem, will be spotless, washed in that very Blood of the Lamb, ready for the eternal wedding banquet of Heaven (see Rev 21-22).

A future of joy and bliss awaits us, even though now we "have no wine." In the biblical understanding, wine is not merely a good drink, but rather a sign of abundance, life, and joy (see Ps 104:15; Eccl 10:19). Bread and water are the absolute minimum necessary for life; wine is gratuitous, indicating that life is about more than mere survival. Mary's pronouncement that they "have no wine" is not merely an expression of her concern that the couple not be publicly shamed for running out of wine during a seven-day wedding feast. In the context of salvation history, Mary is pointing out that without God, and especially without the Eucharist, we lack wine — that is, the abundant life and joy that flow from being united to the Lord, the Bridegroom. In other words, we lack the abundance of His love that gives *joie de vivre,* and so she brings us to the Eucharist, to wine transformed into the Blood of Christ, the source of true life and joy.

In Heaven, Mary speaks to her Son on our behalf, not only constantly pointing out our essential needs, but also beseeching Him to fill us to overflowing with His blessings, so that we might be thoroughly convinced of His love. The empty jars are our misery, waiting to be filled to the very brim with His Mercy. Mary asks Jesus to grant us temporal blessings, so we might not give up along the path of trust, and to fill us with His Mercy. The interplay between our weakness and poverty and the infinite power and Mercy of God is displayed at Cana and manifested in various ways throughout the Bible: for example, in the story of the widow of Zarephath, whose oil and flour never ran out, and the multiplication of the loaves and fishes (see 1 Kings 17:7-16; Mt 14:13-21).

At Cana, Mary not only points out the lack of wine but also points to her Son, who can remedy the situation. Notice how discreet she is when she reveals the couple's need to Jesus. She does not expose them to shame or make public their lack of wine. In our case, even though the lack of wine is often caused by our own sinfulness, when Mary brings our need for mercy to Jesus, it is also without fanfare or public display. The serpent does just the opposite: He desires to expose many hidden things to cause us embarrassment, shame, and confusion. When he points out our misery, he does so not to bring us to Jesus, but to cause despair. He would point to the lack of wine — or any misery or sin of ours — and say, "Nothing can be done. Give up. It's impossible to fix this." On the other hand, Mary echoes the words of the angel — that nothing is impossible for God, words repeated by Jesus, her Son: "All things are possible to him who believes" (Mk 9:23).

Mary is a woman of hope. She teaches us never to hesitate to step on the serpent of despair, trusting that Jesus can do all things if we approach Him as she does. As Pope Benedict XVI wrote: "Redemption is offered to us in the sense that we have been given hope, trustworthy hope, by virtue of which we can face our present: the present, even if it is arduous, can be lived and accepted if it leads towards a goal, if we can be sure of this goal, and if this goal is great enough to justify the effort of the journey."[154] We trust that our journey is like this.

When Mary approaches Jesus to ask for His Mercy for our misery, she does not constrain Him or tell Him what He must do. Rather, she simply brings our poverty before Him, knowing that our very poverty moves His Sacred Heart to have mercy on us (see Mt 9:36). The Father desires to shower His Goodness upon us simply because He is Goodness itself. Hence St. Faustina wrote: "Although I understand that, being God, He is happy in Himself and has absolutely no need of any creature, still, His goodness compels Him to give Himself to the creature, and with a generosity which is beyond understanding" (*Diary*, 244).

Jesus desires to fill our emptiness with His divine wine, the Holy Spirit, but our trust and obedience are necessary for this to happen. The Father desires to provide abundantly for us, His children, but He can do so only when He receives our free response of trust. His plan of salvation includes our free will as well as our response of trust. If we want the Father to provide for our every misery and need on our pilgrimage, we must take steps of trust, including doing things that do not seem likely to resolve our misery or solve our problems.

We often attempt to deal with our problems as we think best, by coming up with practical solutions. We forget that the best way to resolve our misery is through patient trust and the willingness to do whatever He tells us. This kind of trust in the face of our daily problems is manifested and made possible through prayer. It may seem that prayer will not solve practical problems and that it is wasting the precious time needed to solve them. But time and again we see in the Bible and in real life that the best way to resolve situations is to imitate Mary by bringing the situation to the Lord with trust, and following His commands in obedience.

At Cana, the means Jesus used to supply the needed wine were, practically speaking, quite odd. Filling the jars used for the ritual washing of hands with water is not the typical way to provide wine. However, Our Lady teaches us that we ought to do whatever He tells us (see Jn 2:5). This command is "an exhortation to trust without hesitation, especially when one does not understand the meaning or benefit of what Christ asks."[155] I know that if I had been one of the servants at Cana, I would probably have complained and asked, "Why do I need to put water in these jars? What good does this do?" But when we make our small efforts in obedience to the Father's will — whether it be filling jars, bringing our small amount of flour and oil, or gathering loaves and fishes — the Father always provides out of His abundant mercy. If we trust as Mary trusted, not waiting for a visible sign, but already believing that the Father will provide, then we will see miracles in our lives every day. Just as Mary's trust unleashed

---

[154] Benedict XVI, *Spe Salvi*, n. 1.
[155] Saint John Paul II, *Audiences of Pope John Paul II*. Catechesis given on February 26, 1997.

Jesus' miraculous power at Cana, so our trust, after the example of Mary, unleashes His miraculous power in the midst of our daily needs and difficulties.

Indeed, our trust "forces" Jesus to bestow His grace upon us when we recognize and admit to Him our misery (see *Diary*, 718). While we are pondering Jesus and Mary at the Wedding Feast at Cana, I want to address married couples in particular for a moment, although what follows can be applied to human relationships in general. The "wine" of joy in marriage can often run dry, due to the many inevitable stresses, crosses, and trials of daily life. We may demand that our spouse fill the empty jars, expecting him or her to take care of things or help us, as Martha complained to Jesus: "Do you not care that I have to serve and suffer so much? Why aren't you helping me?" (see Lk 10:40). How different this is from the way Mary presents the need for wine to Jesus: She brings the need to His attention and awaits His help. In marriage, and in life in general, when we need others to take care of certain matters, we often not only ask them for help but also tell them how it ought to be done. Here, however, Mary waits with trust.

When there is insufficient time for prayer, spouses can begin to demand from each other things that only God can truly provide. Instead of arguing or finding fault, I would suggest a different way to renew the joy of marriage: Go to Mary and ask her to teach you how to approach Jesus with your empty jars — your hearts that bear wounds, pain, and sin. Ask her to accompany you, and go to Jesus together to entrust your difficulties, problems, and trials to Him. Allow her to strengthen your trust in His Word, so that you might be obedient and see the miracles of the Lord in your marriage. Without Jesus, the wine and joy of marriage run dry. Without Jesus, mutual trust runs dry also, for only He can teach us how to forgive "seventy-seven" times (see Mt 18:22). Only through mutual trust and forgiveness will the wine — the Holy Spirit, the source of joy — in marriage be multiplied.

Once our trust in the Lord is restored, we will be able to trust in others as well, and others will begin to trust in us. "We may trust people inasmuch as they are God's instruments — parents, for instance, superiors, and so on."[156] For trust in the Lord does not by its nature exclude others; rather, trusting in the Lord Jesus means being open to Him at work in His Body, the Church, in our brothers and sisters in Christ. Precisely by trusting in the Lord, we will be able to open up to others and share ourselves with them, even if they should cause pain or difficulty, as often happens in marriage on account of sin. Without trust in the Lord, we will become empty and unable to trust in others, because we will become defensive instead of being open to give what we have received from the Lord and receive what He desires to give us through others.

Notice how much the wine was multiplied at Cana: the total amount of wine that Jesus made came to between 120 and 180 gallons (see Jn 2:6).

---

[156] Blessed Sopocko, *The Mercy of God in His Works*, Vol. 3, 174.

Consider also the 12 baskets that remained after the multiplication of loaves and fishes (see Mt 14:20). Jesus not only wants to provide; He wants to provide in great abundance: "I desire to grant unimaginable graces to those souls who trust in My mercy" (*Diary*, 687). Even though Cana is not His hour — for *that* hour is the hour of the Cross, when He will provide the wine of eternal life — the hour of Cana reminds us that along our path to Calvary and Heaven, He will provide in abundance for our needs. Moreover, He will provide us with joy and happiness even amid suffering and trials.

Too often, Christians become gloomy, thinking that they need to just buckle up and get ready for suffering, mistaking Christian suffering for sheer stoic endurance. Jesus never provides us with suffering without also offering us the wine of true joy and love to sustain us during all such trials. Like St. Faustina, we must turn to the source of all true wine, the wounds of Jesus: "In difficult moments, I must take refuge in the wounds of Jesus; I must seek consolation, comfort, light and affirmation in the wounds of Jesus" (*Diary*, 226). There, the wine of His Love never runs dry, and it sustains us in every trial, providing even the temporal blessings we need while seeking His will (see Mt 6:33), just as He provided for St. Faustina's temporal needs (see *Diary*, 548).

I encourage you to take Jesus at His Word. The serpent will attempt to discourage you and tell you not to bring your needs to Jesus. Step on the serpent's head and approach Jesus with Mary, who will teach you to trust in Him without limit, so that you may receive without limit. Having seen the glory of Christ revealed in Cana, the apostles came to believe in Him (see Jn 2:11). But always remember that the miracle that caused the apostles' faith was made possible through Mary's trust, which preceded their faith and enkindled it. The Lord's glory is manifested in His abundant providence for our every need.

For this reason, the Lord can demand of us a superabundance of holiness in the Sermon on the Mount (see Mt 5:20).[157] Indeed, without having first received the abundance of His Mercy, we would never be able to live by Christ's teachings. However, having received freely and without measure the Spirit of Mercy, we are to give freely and without measure — even to our enemies (see Jn 3:34; Mt 10:8).

Leaving All and Giving Thanks

Let us turn now to the Lord's request that we leave everything to follow Him. How could our Lord make such a radical request? Because He asks us to give up temporal goods in order to receive the one and only thing we truly need: God Himself. Jesus promised that if we seek *first* the Kingdom, we will receive every other blessing necessary for our lives here on earth (see Mt 6:33). Moreover, He promised that we will receive a hundred times more on earth than we have

---

[157] Joseph Ratzinger, *What It Means to Be a Christian*, trans. Henry Taylor (San Francisco: Ignatius Press, 2006), 78. www.ignatius.com. Used with permission.

left behind for His sake. "Jesus said, 'Truly, I say to you, there is no one who has left house or brothers or sisters or mother or father or children or lands, for my sake and for the gospel, who will not receive a hundredfold now in this time, houses and brothers and sisters and mothers and children and lands, with persecutions, and in the age to come eternal life'" (Mk 10:29-30). As at Cana, the Lord provides a hundredfold now, in this life of temporal blessings, but the key to receiving all these blessings is detachment.

Are we attached to the blessings of God or to the God who gives such blessings? We ought to seek not the consolations of God, but the God of all consolation (see 2 Cor 1:3).[158] We can see how attached we are to His blessings by examining how often we give thanks to the Father for them, for Jesus instructs us: **"Be grateful for the smallest of My graces, because your gratitude compels Me to grant you new graces"** (*Diary*, 1701). Trust — the vessel for receiving the Father's Mercy — is built of gratitude: When we are grateful, we remember how good the Father is for bestowing His blessings upon us. Tasting how good He is, our hearts open wider in trust, ready to receive even more blessings.

We need not fear enjoying the Father's blessings, but simply ought to enjoy His Mercy more than we enjoy any of His individual blessings. In this way, gratitude is the best means to break the acedia we discussed previously, for instead of being more interested in His blessings, we are more interested in Him alone. With gratitude, we turn our attention to the Father, the Giver, and we trust in Him, rather than focusing on the blessing (for example, money) and beginning to trust in it.

Do we trust in our possessions or do we trust in the Father? Are we willing to leave behind everything to be disciples of Jesus, as described in Scripture: "So therefore, whoever of you does not renounce all that he has cannot be my disciple" (Lk 14:33)? Note that Jesus directs this statement to everyone, not just the apostles. At death, we must leave behind everything. If we are not detached, we will be filled with fear because we are not able to entrust our loved ones and all we have to God. If we are detached, we will have a blessed and peaceful death, because we await with hope what has been promised, knowing that Heaven far surpasses any joy we have experienced in this life: "From of old no one has heard or perceived by the ear, no eye has seen a God besides you, who works for those who wait for him" (Is 64:4; see 2 Cor 2:9).

Mary invites us to allow the emptiness of our spiritual jars — our hearts — to be filled ever more with the Holy Spirit. Hence, if we let go of a creature, it is only so as to be capable of receiving the wine of salvation, the Precious Blood of Jesus filled with the Holy Spirit. He asks us to deny ourselves and give up our own will, hopes, and dreams, so we might allow the Father to fulfill His mighty plan of salvation. Self-denial, a requirement for being Christ's disciple, is built upon trust (see Lk 9:23). If we trust the Lord's promises, we will have little

---

[158] Joseph Glynn, *The Eternal Mystic: St. Teresa of Avila, the First Woman Doctor of the Church* (Durham, North Carolina: Darlington Carmel, 1987).

problem denying ourselves temporal pleasures. In fact, trust is so fundamental that, if we persevere in growing in trust, the Lord Himself will uproot all the weeds of our disordered desires that are at variance with His will until we attain perfect union with Him even in this life. In fact, trust — as a fruit of faith, hope, and charity — is the only adequate means for attaining this union.

The saints could perform penances and suffer so much because they trusted that the Lord would fulfill His promise that they would be repaid a hundredfold. We can be like them if we trust the Lord, who prepares eternal glory for those who remain, even in suffering, faithful to the end: "Do not fear what you are about to suffer. ... Be faithful unto death, and I will give you the crown of life" (Rev 2:10).

When we are ungrateful for the gifts of the Father, our trust begins to flag and the jars, instead of being filled, remain empty. The story of the Israelites in the desert reminds us of the danger of ingratitude and attachment to blessings. Having seen the suffering of the Israelites, the Father was moved to set them free from their slavery so that they need not serve Pharaoh, but could serve Him alone (see Ex 3). When Moses makes his first requests to Pharaoh, the Israelites are forced to work even harder, and so they grumble against Moses and even against God (see Ex 5).

To gain the trust of the people and prove His might to Pharaoh, the Father worked 10 plagues through Moses, and ultimately led the Israelites through the Red Sea. But what happened afterward? Upon enjoying their freedom, they began to use this blessing without reference to the One who had freed them. While Moses was on the mount receiving the covenant that God made with this people, they began worshipping a golden calf. While traversing the desert toward the Promised Land, they began to complain of their lack of food, water, and other blessings that they had possessed in Egypt. Apparently, they had already forgotten all that the Lord had done in Egypt to set them free. They had forgotten because they were ungrateful for the blessings, for gratitude and trust relate to *memory.*

By definition, really, being a Christian means being a person of memory: Our identity is based upon events from the past, particularly the life, death, and resurrection of Jesus Christ. The Eucharist itself is a *memorial,* in which we hear repeated the words of Jesus: "Do this in memory of me." The word "memory" comes from the Greek word *mermēra,* which means "care."[159] The idea is this: Do we *remember* the great deeds of the Lord throughout the ages? Do we remember His blessings during our lives, or even those from yesterday? If we do not remember how the Lord has provided for us in the past, it will be hard to trust in the present. But if we see how He miraculously provides for His People, we can be confident and trust that today, too, He will provide for us.

Without memory, we lose our identity; without memory, we lose hope; without memory, we become ungrateful, because we forget all the Lord's

---

[159] *Merriam-Webster's Collegiate Dictionary.*

blessings. But the point is not to cling to the blessings, but to remember above all the One who gave those blessings, so that our memory points us toward the future, toward the greatest blessing of all: God Himself.

The Israelites were so ungrateful that even while they were receiving the Lord's blessings in their newfound freedom, they attempted to return to Egypt (see Ps 78). They were attached to the gifts instead of to the Giver. In describing the path to holiness, St. John of the Cross says that if we hold on to past graces, we hold on to creatures instead of clinging to the Creator who gave them. This is a major obstacle to spiritual marriage. If we cling to graces instead of to God, we will be like the Israelites who complained that past blessings had been removed and were ungrateful for current blessings. But we look to Mary, who at Calvary entrusted her greatest blessing, her Son, to the Father, and received even greater blessings: Jesus, risen from the dead, and the salvation of all mankind. By her trust at that critical moment of His Crucifixion, she crushed the head of the serpent through her union with her Son.

How was Mary capable of continually walking forward in her own journey of trust? She is a woman of memory: She constantly holds God's saving deeds, told throughout the history of her people, in her mind and heart (see Lk 2:19). She is a woman of gratitude and thanksgiving: She sings the praises of God for all He does in her life (see Lk 1:46-55). She is a woman of trust: remembering His mighty deeds in her past and present as she continues toward the future, confident that this same Father will continue to bless her. At every Mass, we have the opportunity to remember, honor, and imitate Mary. The readings are a memorial of God's saving deeds, and in the Eucharist we remember the saving Passion, Death, and Resurrection of Jesus. We are a people of *memory:* If we forget, we are unable to trust as Mary did. We are a people of *gratitude*: we are formed by the Eucharist, the Sacrament of thanksgiving. We are a people of *trust*: We follow Jesus into the future with Mary by our side, teaching us how to take each step, so that together we may crush the head of the serpent.

One tactic of the serpent is to make us forget the Lord's blessings so that we distrust Him. Satan will gladly point out apparent contradictions between God's promises and the manifestations of His power and will. For example, the Lord promised the Israelites freedom and blessings, but they suffered as they wandered in a wasteland of desert — and therefore, the devil suggests, God should not be trusted. The serpent bit the Israelites with the venom of distrust and rebellion, prompting them time and again to distrust the Lord's promise to provide for them in abundance. Instead of coming to Moses and the Lord with a sincere petition for help, the Israelites complained and murmured, doubting the Father's goodness and intentions in leading them out of Egypt — even going so far as to say that the Lord had freed them only so that they would die in the desert (see Ex 14:11, 16:2-3; Num 14:2).

We cannot expect to receive anything from Him if we ask with a doubting heart: "But let him ask in faith, with no doubting, for he who doubts is like a wave of the sea that is driven and tossed by the wind. For that person must not suppose that a double-minded man, unstable in all his ways, will receive anything from the Lord" (Jas 1:6-8).

The English word "doubt" comes from the Latin *dubius,* meaning "causing uncertainty" and implying a choice between two different options. The ultimate root of "doubt" is the Latin *duo,* meaning "two." Thus a person who doubts is presented with two options and is unable to decide between them. The doubter is "of two minds." When asking something of the Lord, we need to be not "of two minds" but "of one mind" — a mind of confidence and trust in His Mercy. This confidence in the Lord is manifested by Mary at Cana when she approaches Jesus with childlike trust — *parresia* — speaking plainly and boldly about our needs, certain that He will supply what is needed in His way, even in a miraculous way. Mary's faith saved herself and us. She opened the door for the Mercy of God to enter this world and heal our misery and our sin. Jesus could truly say to Mary, His Mother, "Your faith has saved you." Mary shares her faith with us, so that we also might receive salvation from Jesus.

CHAPTER 16

Trust and Salvation

"Your trust has saved you"
(see Lk 7:50, 18:42).

Several times in the Gospels when someone reaches out to Jesus for healing, He responds, "Your faith has saved you." Or, to translate it a little differently, "Your trust has saved you." In an even greater way, the faith and trust of Mary have saved us by giving birth to Jesus.

How is it that trust saves? Trust is essential for salvation: It is the very door to salvation. The Father will do everything possible, but if we do not trust Him, even He cannot save us — just as Jesus could not work miracles when confronted with people's lack of faith (see Mk 6:5-6). In fact, by sending His Son, the Father has already given us what is most precious to Him, and so we can be confident that He will give us *everything else* that proves necessary for our salvation (see Rom 8:32).

Even the act of trusting in Him is not left up to us. Without Him, we cannot trust at all, for trust is a gift of the Holy Spirit, poured into our aching hearts as a healing balm: "O Divine Spirit, Spirit of love and of mercy, You pour the balm of trust into my heart" (*Diary*, 1411). We have only to surrender to that Gift of trust, who is the Holy Spirit Himself, the personified capacity for trust. In doing so, we surrender to the whole Trinity. Trust is a gift of the Lord, to which we must respond with all our hearts. As creatures, we have just one real contribution to this relationship, to either surrender or not: "[S]urrender to God is the only power the creature possesses."[160] When we use that power well, through trust, we receive salvation.

SAVED FROM WHAT?

But what is salvation? What does it mean when we ask the Father to save us? The Greek word for "save" is *sōzō*, meaning both "to heal" and "to save."[161]

---

[160] Gertrud Le Fort, *The Eternal Woman: The Timeless Meaning of the Feminine*, trans. Marie Cecilia Buehrle (San Francisco: Ignatius Press, 2010), 18. www.ignatius.com. Used with permission.

[161] "σῴζω (*sōzō*): 1. rescue from danger (Mt 14:30). 2. save, deliver into divine salvation (1 Cor 1:21, 9:22; Mt 18:11; Mk 16:16; Lk 9:56; Acts 8:37) 3. heal, to make healthy from an illness (Mk 6:56)." James Swanson, *Dictionary of Biblical Languages with Semantic Domains: Greek (New Testament)* (Oak Harbor, Washington: Logos Research Systems, 1997).

Similarly, the Latin word for "salvation" is *salus*, which also means "health."[162] Jesus' very name means "salvation" in Hebrew.[163] Jesus indeed came to bring us salvation, in the healing of our bodies and the saving of our souls. There are several instances in the New Testament where Jesus says, "Your faith has saved you," including His healing of the Syrophoenician woman's daughter, the woman with the hemorrhage, and the two blind men (see Mt 15:28; Mk 5:34; Mt 9:29).

We are often amazed at the miracles Jesus performed and continues to perform even today. However, have you ever wondered what amazes Jesus? There are in fact only *two* times recounted in the Gospels when Jesus is amazed. The first is when there is a lack of faith and trust in Him in Nazareth (see Mk 6:5-6) and the other is when He finds faith in the Roman centurion — the likes of which He hadn't seen in all of Israel (see Lk 7:6-10). The greatest "miracle" in the eyes of Jesus is, in fact, faith and trust in the hearts of men and women — a "miracle" that amazed Jesus!

We need to ask ourselves now: What exactly do we want to be healed of or saved from? What miracle do we ask Him to perform? Many times, for example, we ask the Lord for healing from illness or for help with a financial crisis. Is that what we truly need to be saved from? No. Most of all, we need to be saved from our sin — from our *doubt* and our resulting lack of trust. If you want a miracle, remember that because of the lack of faith, no miracle could be performed in Nazareth. If you want to amaze Jesus, ask Him, as the apostles did: "Increase our faith!" (Lk 17:5).

Trust in the Father and obedience to His will are what will save us. The faith that comes from trust and obedience ultimately brings us to the full and final salvation of our body and soul in eternal life. The Father's plan is ultimately to bring us to Heaven, and He uses everything, especially sickness and suffering, to prepare us to enter His Kingdom, by purifying us of our sinful desires (see Acts 14:22). This purification is necessary, either on earth or in Purgatory, for no sin and no impurity can enter the Kingdom of God (see 1 Cor 6:9; Rev 21:27).

Sometimes the Father will choose not to heal us of a bodily disease because He intends to perform a greater work in our lives and hearts and is preparing us for Heaven. In other words, the Father needs to provide the *empty jars* within us, so that Jesus can fill us with the wine of salvation — the Holy Spirit. Too often, our jars are filled with pride and attachment to the things of this world. The Father allows suffering in our lives so that we might be emptied, and can then be filled.

---

[162]   "*Sălūs:* being safe and sound; a sound or whole condition, health, welfare, prosperity, preservation, safety, deliverance, etc." Lewis and Short, *Harper's Latin Dictionary*, 1621.

[163]   הַעְשׁוּיָ (*yĕšû·'ā(h)*): 1. deliverance, safety, rescue, i.e., to be in a state of freedom from danger (Ex 14:13). 2. salvation, i.e., deliverance in a religious sense (Ps 62:2). 3. victory, i.e., the act. of conquering another entity (2 Sam 22:51). 4. Savior, i.e., a title of God (Dt 32:15; Ps 42:6,12; 43:5; 68:20; 89:27). Swanson, *Dictionary of Biblical Languages with Semantic Domains: Hebrew (Old Testament)*.

The people who came to Jesus seeking healing from their ailments recognized their need for spiritual healing and salvation as well. Encountering Jesus, they acknowledged their misery and accepted that they could not sufficiently take care of their own difficulties and problems (see *CCC*, 1500). Their inability to save themselves did not close them in on themselves and bring them to despair or revolt against the Father (see *CCC*, 1501). Rather, their suffering brought them to their knees, begging and trusting Jesus for help. They realized that Jesus was worthy of their trust, since He is someone who had power over their sickness, demons, and even death. Their trust saved them because it opened them up to a relationship with the living God, from which original sin had excluded them. Mary teaches us to recognize and accept Jesus as trustworthy, and leads us away from discouragement and rebellion in the face of our suffering. She directs our steps to Jesus, so that we might allow His Mercy to touch and transform our every misery.

Consider the woman suffering from a hemorrhage. She was healed, but the story was not over. Jesus asked, "Who touched me?" and sought her out in the middle of a crowd. There were many people surrounding Him, and so the apostles asked the Lord with exasperation how they could know who among the people had touched Him. Nonetheless, Jesus wanted to find the woman and speak to her (see Lk 8:46-48). Her complete healing came when the Lord spoke to her directly, initiating a face-to-face relationship with her.

That is true for us, as well. Our healing, our salvation, consists of more than just being cured of sicknesses or difficulties, and our salvation is more than simply possessing the wine that Mary obtains for us at Cana and Calvary. Healing and salvation come through our entering a personal relationship with the Father by trust in His Word, Jesus Christ. Only then is our healing complete, for that is what we mean by the word Heaven: knowing the Father and Jesus Christ in a relationship of love — the Holy Spirit (see Jn 17:3).

Salvation is therefore not simply a state of mind or soul: It is the interplay between our misery and Divine Mercy. Salvation is what "happens" when we trust and cross the bridge between misery and mercy. Mary is always involved in the process of salvation, for through the Holy Spirit, she leads us to Christ, her Son, in all our needs and difficulties. Satan discourages us and tells us that there is no hope. Mary tells us that hope has a face: Jesus. Mary teaches us that when we take a step of trust, we also crush the head of the serpent, for the two always go together. As we entrust our misery to Jesus' Mercy, through our confidence in Him, we crush the serpent of despair and discouragement.

SIN AND SUFFERING

The suffering endured by individuals in the Gospel is the fruit of original sin (see Rom 5:12; *CCC*, 399-401). People came to Jesus seeking healing of body and soul, acutely aware of their need for the Father. In contrast, the Pharisees attempted to hide their need and misery, and clothed their nakedness with their devotional acts instead of allowing the Father to clothe them with His Mercy.

Pondering our need for the Father helps us to understand the reasons for our illnesses, suffering, and death. By their distrust, Adam and Eve took the first step in creating a world without the Father, a world where they could be self-sufficient, and there would be no need to trust in God: They would need to trust only themselves. To keep this sin from reaching full fruition in eternal damnation, the Father created a world where suffering would be the fruit of sin. He did this precisely to break our illusion of self-sufficiency.

Suffering and death are evil, but they are less of an evil than sin. We are so entrenched in sin, and so accustomed to it, that we do not consider it nearly so great a problem as suffering. We can become blind to the effects of sin, whereas our bodies alert us immediately to the evils of suffering. The saints understood how evil sin is and how incomparably more harmful it is than even the worst suffering. In fact, St. Faustina wrote: "Today, I entered into the bitterness of the Passion of the Lord Jesus. I suffered in a purely spiritual way. I learned how horrible sin was. God gave me to know the whole hideousness of sin. I learned in the depths of my soul how horrible sin was, even the smallest sin, and how much it tormented the soul of Jesus. I would rather suffer a thousand hells than commit even the smallest venial sin" (*Diary,* 1016).

Our good Father never ceases to be merciful, despite our weakness and sinfulness (see Mt 5:45), so He allows suffering to show us how foolish it is to presume to trust in ourselves. Through our suffering and weakness, we are reminded that we are finite creatures who cannot survive without trust in our Father. By seeking a moment's pleasure, satisfaction, or power, we can try to live without trust in the Father, who asks us to be patient; but the greatest suffering from, and punishment of, sin is to be totally without trust, totally self-reliant, totally closed in on ourselves. That is what we call hell.

Earthly suffering prevents the ultimate suffering of hell. Suffering in this life purifies us and brings us back to our original dependence on and need for the Father. It shows us that we cannot live without Him. Suffering, therefore, becomes a school of trust. Remember now the difference between *bios* and *zoe.* God may permit us to have the life of *bios* without Him, as many people in mortal sin do today, but mere *bios* is not true life: *bios* is the water, but *zoe* is the wine. We need both. The wine God gives brings us joy in life, the happiness we desire. Jesus came to bring true life, the life and love that He has shared with the Father since before the foundation of the world (see Jn 17:24). This is the life that is revealed in the Resurrection, the life that death cannot touch, the life that knows no suffering (see Rom 6:9; Rev 21:1-4). This is the life that we beg for in prayer, and the life that Mary teaches us to receive through our trust in the Mercy of the Father.

TRUST AND SALVATION

Salvation consists in being able to possess both *zoe* and *bios*, but that is not possible through our own unaided efforts or power. *Zoe* can be received only as a gift, and to receive it, we first must trust the Giver of eternal life. That is precisely why trust brings salvation. Trust opens the door of our hearts to the workings of the Holy Spirit, the Lord and Giver of Life, who wants to share that eternal life with us. By original sin, by distrusting Him, Adam and Eve turned away from the Father. They lost the life breathed into their nostrils at creation. That breath (*ruah* in Hebrew) is the Holy Spirit Himself, the life they were created to partake of for all eternity in Heaven. That divine life is based on trust and mutual self-giving, so distrust precludes our participation. As Pope Benedict XVI stated, "'Eternal life' is thus a relational event. Man did not acquire it from himself or for himself alone. Through relationship with the One who is Himself life, man too comes alive."[164]

By stating that Mary is the Immaculata, we are saying that Mary never parted from this relationship with the Triune God. She never lost her capacity to receive *zoe*, or the breath of life, from the Father. As she says her unconditional "Yes" to the Father, she also says "No" to Satan, and steps on his head every time she advances along her journey of trust. The Wedding Feast at Cana and Jesus' healings occur in the context of a community. True life is given to us all, not to just one or two. Eternal life is a relationship with the Triune God, but also with all the other saints and angels. When we ponder Mary at the Wedding Feast at Cana, we are reminded that the life God desires to give us is a life shared, not only with Him, but with other adopted sons and daughters of the Father in a wedding banquet where we all feast on the wine of eternal life.

VALUE OF THE CROSS

However, if we trust the Father to fulfill all of our hopes and dreams, no matter what we desire, and to make this life more like the paradise of Eden that we lost, our trust will be disappointed time and time again. In the Gospels, Jesus clearly spoke of the suffering that His disciples would have to endure if they followed Him (see Lk 9:23). He never hid the reality of the Cross. In fact, He spoke so openly about it that Peter attempted to rebuke Him (see Mt 16:23). The Father cannot be trusted to simply do what we would like Him to do. The Father sent His Son to become man and redeem our world by infusing our hearts with the Holy Spirit.

Sometimes, by the power of the Holy Spirit, the Father will heal and remove suffering from our world, as Jesus did during His public ministry. But the will of our Father is not simply to make this world another Eden. The world will indeed be renewed at the Second Coming, but only after intense purification and tribulation. Indeed, we are now in the time of suffering, the time to deny

---

[164] Ratzinger, *Jesus of Nazareth*, Part 2, *Holy Week*, 85.

ourselves and follow Jesus on the way to Calvary, for it is precisely in dying that we are raised to Life in the Spirit and gain the whole world (see Lk 9:24). In this life, we are to battle like knights for the salvation of souls and for the Kingdom of God (see *Diary*, 1489).

If we want to be saved from sin and the second death of Hell, then the Father can be trusted. Indeed, Jesus told Faustina: "**Sooner would heaven and earth turn into nothingness than would My mercy not embrace a trusting soul**" (*Diary*, 1777). The Father ceaselessly works through the Holy Spirit to bring us out of sin and death, and He revealed this intention in the death and Resurrection of Jesus. That is the kind of healing and salvation we are awaiting — salvation from sin and distrust, which are our true worst problems (see *CCC*, 1488). This is precisely why Jesus often states that *faith* brings salvation.

SACRAMENTS OF HEALING

I want to go deeper into the healing of body and soul that Jesus offered to those who sought Him. The two Sacraments of healing in the Church — Penance and Anointing of the Sick — awaken and strengthen our faith and trust in the Father and direct our gaze toward the true healing of the whole person, body and soul. The Sacrament that brings the deepest healing is Penance, which restores us to communion with the Father. Confession requires the admission of our sins; but even more, it requires the acknowledgment and praise of the Father's Mercy toward us: "[This sacrament] is called the *sacrament of confession*, since the disclosure or confession of sins to a priest is an essential element of this sacrament. In a profound sense it is also a confession — acknowledgment and praise — of the holiness of God and of his mercy toward sinful man" (*CCC*, 1424).

In Baptism, we experienced our first conversion. In Penance, we undergo a second conversion, which allows us to experience the Father's Mercy anew. In both Sacraments, water is necessary: fresh water for Baptism, and the tears of contrition for Penance (see *CCC*, 1429). Water, along with the Blood flowing forth from Jesus' side, washes over us whenever we approach the Sacrament of Confession with humble trust (see *Diary*, 1602).

Many turn to the Anointing of the Sick to seek healing during times of illness, and rightly so. There is more than mere physical healing available in this Sacrament, however. The primary effects of Anointing of the Sick include renewal of one's trust and faith in the Father, being strengthened against the temptations of discouragement and anguish, and healing of soul and body, *if such healing is conducive to salvation* (see *CCC*, 1520). The person receiving this Sacrament is thus consecrated by the Holy Spirit to bear fruit by uniting his suffering with Jesus' suffering on the Cross. Suffering thereby gains new meaning when it is consecrated as a participation in the saving work of Jesus (see *CCC*, 1521). By offering up one's suffering, one contributes to the sanctification of the whole Church (see *CCC*, 1522).

People often want to be healed of their sickness in order to minister and serve the Church, but their suffering united to Christ's brings great benefits for the Church, often greater benefits than would the ministry they desire to undertake. Saint Maximilian Kolbe would show guests around Niepokolanów, the monastery he had founded near Warsaw, Poland. He always ended the tour with a visit to the infirmary, for he said that the friars who were suffering there did even more work than those who tended the printing press![165]

Through the Anointing of the Sick, we may seek physical healing, but our Father is much more desirous of our spiritual healing. Just as Jesus touched the sick to heal them, so our Lord touches us through the Sacraments and heals us. The miracles of healing in the Gospels were signs of the coming Kingdom of God (see Lk 11:20). They were meant to awaken faith and trust so the sick person could enter the Kingdom, but ultimately these miracles announced a more radical healing to come — the healing of sin and death by Jesus in His Passover (see *CCC*, 1505). The Anointing of the Sick completes our conformity to Christ in His death and Resurrection — conformity that began in Baptism and was strengthened in Confirmation (see *CCC*, 1523).

His Mercy does not spare us the Cross, however. The Holy Spirit incorporates us into the mystery of Christ's Death and Resurrection. The Spirit of Mercy is given to us precisely to embrace us and lift us to the Cross with Jesus Crucified — and then to Heaven with Jesus Glorified. We must always remember that where there is suffering and the Cross, there is also the Resurrection. Cana is a visible sign that our emptiness will always be filled, if only we have faith and trust, like Mary. Satan's trick — the sting at our heels — is to turn our suffering into bitterness, despair, and distrust. Mary teaches us to take steps forward in trust regardless, presenting these bites of Satan at our heels to Jesus, knowing that He will bring healing for us in our misery and pain, even if that healing is not immediately apparent.

We must always trust in the Father, bringing Him every empty jar, every sickness, and every pain, knowing that in His time, in His way, He will fill us to the brim with the wine of salvation — the Holy Spirit. We have only to wait, like Mary, and listen to her exhortation to obey her Son: to do whatever He tells us. If we have faith in Him, as she did, we will experience the joy of salvation. Mary is the model of our trust, the ideal of our faith, the perfection of our love, and the hope of our salvation as we follow her in this journey.

---

[165] Patricia Treece, *A Man for Others: Maximilian Kolbe, the "Saint of Auschwitz," in the Words of Those Who Knew Him* (Libertyville, Illinois: Marytown Press, 2013).

CHAPTER 17

Walking on Water

"O you of little faith, why did you doubt?" (Mt 14:31).

As we learn to live trusting in the Father, our faith and trust can sometimes be shaken. Earlier, I pointed out how suffering can be purifying because it reminds us of our need to be baptized daily in the Father's Mercy. Life can feel overwhelming at times, as though we are being called to walk out on the water toward Jesus. Indeed, in continuing our journey of trust, we, like Peter, are invited by the Lord to step out of the boat and "walk on the water" of life in trust. "And Peter answered him, 'Lord, if it is you, bid me come to you on the water.' He said, 'Come.' So Peter got out of the boat and walked on the water and came to Jesus" (see Mt 14:28-29). With St. Peter, we walk toward Jesus while praying, "Jesus, I trust in You."

Fortunately, we have one advantage over St. Peter. Whereas he walked on the water alone toward Jesus, we are called to walk on water with Mary, *Stella Maris,* Star of the Sea, by our side. Just as our biological mothers teach us how to walk, Our Lady, our eternal mother, accompanies us, teaching us to take steps of trust upon the water of the sea of life.

In the Bible, the sea is characterized as the place of evil, and of opposition to the Father's plans: the formless void to which the Father set limits at the creation. The flood in Noah's time undid creation, but the Father had power even over the flood (see Ps 104:9; Prov 8:29). The Psalms speak of God calming the sea (see Ps 107:29-30), and the beast in Revelation comes from the sea (see Rev 13:1). John sees the new heavens and new earth in Revelation, noticing that there is no sea, signifying that evil has disappeared entirely (see Rev 21:1).

"Walking on water" describes the reality of trust in a single image. By walking on water with Mary, we trust in Jesus and walk toward Him, stepping on the serpent. In order to defeat the serpent and reach Jesus, however, we must take more than one step to crush the serpent's head. We must step continuously in trust each day with Mary and St. Peter. When we walk on water with Mary, we share in the Immaculate Conception and the definitive defeat of sin and Satan through the death of Jesus upon the Cross.

Peter's walking on water shows us what happens when we trust: We can do the impossible. Jesus told His disciples that without Him, they could do nothing (see Jn 15:5). But with Jesus, all things are possible (see Phil 4:13). If we trust, we will even be able to walk on water, because the power to do so does not come from us. The divine power of Jesus enters into our lives through trust. That divine power — His love — is capable of conquering evil, allowing us to walk on the turbulent waters of this world of sin, and placing the serpent beneath our feet to be trodden under our heels.

We must keep our eyes on the Lord. With Him, we can conquer sin; we can be immaculate, like Mary. Without Jesus, we will drown and spiritually die. Jesus will ask you to do many things that seem impossible, but *be not afraid*. If you obey Him, you can do the impossible. You can take that step toward Jesus, stepping on the serpent in the process.

There is no question about it: Most of the things that Jesus asks us to do are humanly impossible! So, excuses such as "Who, me? I can't do that. I'm not qualified" do not work. When something is impossible for us in the first place, we should never look to ourselves. We simply cannot walk on water. But with Jesus, we can. With Mary, we can. We can get out of the boat with Peter, grasp Mary by the hand, and focus on Jesus. He makes the impossible possible.

STORMS AND DOUBT

In our everyday life, waves and storms inevitably come, and they may frighten us if we take our eyes off the Lord. The serpent wants to overwhelm us and cause us to drown by tempting us to fall into doubt and distrust amid our difficulties and trials. It is Satan's goal to create enough storms in our lives that we will doubt the Father's goodness and sink. After Peter began to sink, our Lord asked: "O you of little faith, why did you doubt?" This can be asked of each of us (see Mt 14:30-31). Jesus directed His question to Peter, the chief disciple, not someone without faith. Time and again the Lord invited His disciples, just as He invites us, to trust Him. By revealing His divine power over sin, over sickness, even over nature and storms, He shows us that He is trustworthy; and by trusting the Lord and keeping our eyes on Him, we will be saved in our distress: "My eyes are ever toward the Lord, for he will pluck my feet out of the net" (Ps 25:15).

Even if we know better; even if we are prepared; even if we try very hard, we might still doubt and take our eyes off the Lord. Why? We can mentally accept that Jesus is Lord, but when the storm hits, that fact can become obscured and seem quite distant. It is still true, but because of our doubt, this truth does not transform our lives. Mere facts do not conquer the serpent behind the storm — only faith and trust can do that. Satan wants to make us fall amid such storms by showing us how futile it is in real life to have faith. But we know that Jesus is Lord. This reality does entirely transform our lives through the gift of faith!

When the apostles saw their Teacher healing and performing miracles, they could easily believe and trust in Him; but once the storm hit, they stopped trusting, beginning instead to act in terror and fear rather than with faith in Jesus. In moments of trial and difficulty, we must rely on Jesus, the Word of God, who calms the storm. Mary, *Stella Maris,* teaches us how to remain steady during the storm, how to walk on water confidently with our gaze upon her Son. She — the Woman of *great faith* — lived, not on her emotions, but on her deep trust in the Word of God.

Desolation and Self-Sufficiency

We all experience emotional storms in our lives. Like changes in the actual weather, they come and go. In the spiritual life, these storms — the times when we experience trials and lack trust in the Father — are called desolation. Elisabeth Leseur comments that these moments of desolation can be quite beneficial for us: "It is surprising to see how much spiritual progress we make in times of aridity, when no conscious joy of any kind unites our souls with God. It is then indeed God Himself whom we love, and not His consolations; and whatever we do then, requiring constant effort and appeals for grace, is indeed done out of obedience to duty in all its starkness. Then, when the dusty road is over and the way becomes easier, we are astonished to see how far we have come; sometimes we arrive at a gentle resting place, in peace, near the heart of God."[166]

How are we to pass through times of desolation? In the rules for discernment in his *Spiritual Exercises,* St. Ignatius of Loyola gives us some guidance: we ought never to change the good resolutions that we made in times of consolation, and we even ought to increase the time we spend in prayer and in other activities that help us grow in our relationship with the Father.[167]

In times of desolation, we often try to fix things ourselves instead of staying on our course and redoubling our efforts to trust. We live in a highly technological world and are used to finding or inventing solutions to our problems, so we do not give up self-determination easily. Suffering brings us face-to-face with our limitations, our poverty, and our need to trust in God to help bring us through the difficulty. Think about another storm on the Sea of Galilee recounted in Mark 4:35-41. What could the apostles do on their own to control it? Can technology control a hurricane? No. Storms reveal how helpless, defenseless, and impotent we are before the forces of nature, for there are limits to our minds and power.

So too are we powerless on our own before the serpent, Satan, with all his might. We are helpless without our armor of trust. We are defenseless before the forces of evil — the serpent and his minions — without Jesus. The Greek *epetimesen,* "rebuke," is the word describing Jesus' speech that lessened the storm. He used the same sort of rebuke during His exorcisms (see Mk 1:25, 4:39). When we suffer, we are not only up against nature, but also sometimes battling against fallen angels. We have no way of defeating such demonic forces on our own (see Acts 4:12). The only source of true strength for us weak creatures is our *faith* and *trust* in the Lord Jesus. We look to Mary to guide us in the paths of faith and trust that give us true strength.

---

[166] Liesl Bee, "Spiritual Lessons with Elisabeth Leseur," *Ignitum Today*, August 30, 2016, accessed July 11, 2017, http://www.ignitumtoday.com/2016/08/30/spiritual-lessons-elisabeth-leseur/.

[167] Saint Ignatius of Loyola, *The Spiritual Exercises of St. Ignatius of Loyola*, 171.

In the Boat With Jesus

Let us imagine for a moment that we are present for the storm recounted by Mark, there in the boat with Jesus and the apostles on the Sea of Galilee. The waves are crashing over the sides, threatening to eventually sink it (see Mk 4:37). The apostles are terrified for their lives. They wake the Lord, who is peacefully sleeping during the storm. The contrast between the apostles and the Lord could not be greater! The apostles are filled with terror and fear in the face of possible death, while the Lord has been sleeping peacefully. The Lord could sleep through the storm because He trusts in the Father.

Trust during life's storms is the fruit of persevering prayer, and prayer is part of the only appropriate response to any storm. In the face of His Passion, the Lord resorted to prolonged prayer to gain the strength necessary to face that tempest: **"My daughter, consider these words: 'And being in agony, he prayed more earnestly'"** (*Diary,* 157). Earnest prayer is necessary because it sets our gaze upon Jesus, the Face of the Father, and immerses us, not in the waters of doubt, but in the fathomless ocean of His Mercy — the Holy Spirit — who opens our hearts to trust, even in the most difficult situations. If we trust our senses during the storm, we will have reason to despair instead of reason to hope. We will see only lightning, thunder, peril, and suffering (see Mt 14:30). Our reason for hope, Jesus Christ, is not Someone whom we can always see with our eyes (see 1 Tim 1:1); He is spiritual and *seen* only by faith (unless, like St. Faustina and other saints, we are privileged to see Him in a vision).

In the face of a storm, the response of our Lord was not to frantically try His best to control it by human efforts. The apostles' human efforts were failing, and so they became even more terrified of dying, but the Lord remained calm, trusting in the merciful Father, knowing that everything that happens is in accord with His Providence. That is why He could sleep in the boat; that is why He could trust in the Father so completely at Calvary that He could endure the sleep of death in peace. We are saved by Jesus' sleep, by His entrustment of Himself to the Father, even unto death upon the Cross. As the Psalmist prays: "I lie down and sleep; I wake again, for the Lord sustains me" (Ps 3:5).

In the Resurrection, the Father awakens Jesus from the sleep of death by the Holy Spirit, just as, during difficulties and storms, we are called to "sleep," let go of control, and patiently wait until the Father intervenes. We are called to "rest" in the truth that our good Father orders all things for our good. Even storms are used by the Father to help us grow! The storms, and all of the serpent's attacks, serve our spiritual growth so that we can share once again in the divine life. Jesus still comes to us in Holy Communion to be within the boat of our hearts and help us in the midst of our storms: "Do not have any doubt, that when today Jesus enters the boat of your heart, He will guide you, grant you His help, and save you."[168]

---

[168] Saint Papczynski, *Pisma Zebrane* [*Collected Works*], 528.

It has been said that the goal of the captain is not to keep the ship safe, but to reach the harbor — Heaven. Jesus was the one who told the disciples to cross the Sea of Galilee (see Mk 4:35); their voyage represents our own passage from the shore of this life to the shores of eternal life. During storms, often we want to turn back, to return to the safe harbor of our routines and normal lives, but we are called instead to put out into the deep, to make our pilgrimage to Heaven. Jesus directs us to make our journey in the boat of the Church, but even in the Church we can expect storms. As Pope Benedict XVI stated: "The ways of the Lord are not easy, but we were not created for an easy life, but for great things, for goodness."[169]

We were created to weather storms and conquer them by trust in the Father. His Providence does not always stop or prevent storms, but it does see us through them. If we are aware of our royal dignity, aware that we are created in His image and likeness, we will be able to say with St. Faustina: "I am going forward through life amidst rainbows and storms, but with my head held high with pride, for I am a royal child. I feel that the blood of Jesus is circulating in my veins, and I have put my trust in the great mercy of the Lord" (*Diary*, 992).

If we are to reach our destination — Heaven — we must pass through the sea, the symbol of evil. Upon that sea, the serpent will attempt to bring about every possible storm to prevent us from safely reaching harbor. He will try time and again, hoping that eventually we will tire out and be shipwrecked. But we are on our voyage in the boat of the Church — the reality that the ark of Noah foreshadowed — upon the sea of this world, traveling toward the shores of Heaven. Jesus has promised that this boat will never fail and never sink. We have only to remain in her, for her course is always directed by the Holy Spirit toward Jesus our Lord (see Mt 16:18).

Unfortunately, many abandon the ship of the Church because of the storms she must endure — and many abandon the Church because of those on the boat. We must not give in to Satan's temptation to leave the Church. This is exactly what the serpent wants, for he knows that outside this boat, the storm will overwhelm us and prevent us from safely reaching harbor. Alone, we will drown; but in the boat of the Church, we will survive. As St. Boniface once wrote, "In her voyage across the ocean of this world, the Church is like a great ship being pounded by the waves of life's different stresses. Our duty is not to abandon ship but to keep her on her course."[170] Jesus is always present in the Church, although it can often seem that He is asleep and that He does not care that we are perishing. But are we truly perishing? What exactly are we perishing from?

---

[169] Pope Benedict XVI, "To the German Pilgrims Gathered in Rome for the Inauguration Ceremony of the Pontificate," April 25, 2005, accessed July 11, 2017, https://w2.vatican.va/content/benedict-xvi/en/speeches/2005/april/documents/hf_ben-xvi_spe_20050425_german-pilgrims.html.
[170] Saint Boniface (Ep. 78: MGH, Epistolae, 3, 352-54) in ICEL, *The Liturgy of the Hours*, Vol. 3, 1456-457.

The disciples were indeed perishing, but not because the storm was too strong. They were perishing of fear and doubt. Their lack of faith allowed them to think that the storm would destroy them. They feared that the Lord had forgotten about them or was incapable of helping them. The real problem was not the storm, but their lack of faith. They were in the boat with the Lord, who, by a command, calmed the storm. So often in our own lives, we complain about storms as if they were the real problem, but they are not. The storms are never the problem.

The real problem is our unwillingness to step out, like Peter, in faith. In the first account I mentioned, the Lord comes walking on water to the disciples who are in a boat during a storm, and calls Simon Peter to walk on water to meet Him (see Mt 14:22-33). Saint Peter fell because of his doubt. But even though he fell, we ought to imitate him because he dared to take steps toward Jesus. We will probably fall through doubt also — not once, but many times, just like children learning to walk. Indeed, as Blessed Michael Sopocko said: "We ourselves are mere children — or less than children — where supernatural things are concerned, and must trust the merciful Savior boundlessly and wholeheartedly."[171]

If we do fall through distrust, Mary will be watching over us, and Jesus will lift us up out of the water. We must not give in to the fear that would prevent us from even getting out of the boat. Indeed, because Jesus has now conquered sin through His death, the *sea*, which was seen as a symbol of evil by the Jews, now becomes a symbol of the Father's Mercy. As St. Faustina wrote: "O Jesus, make the fount of Your mercy gush forth more abundantly, for humankind is seriously ill and thus has more need than ever of Your compassion. You are a bottomless sea of mercy for us sinners; and the greater the misery, the more right we have to Your mercy. You are a fount which makes all creatures happy by Your infinite mercy" (*Diary*, 793). So, if we do fall, we don't fall into water or into the clutches of Satan, though he may grasp at us. As long as we trust in the Lord, even our falls immerse us in the "bottomless sea of mercy for us sinners," because "steadfast love surrounds him who trusts in the Lord" (Ps 32:10).

Many of our complaints about storms are in fact nothing but an objection to being moved out of the status quo. We would prefer that the Father not "rock the boat" of our lives, so we gripe like the Israelites in the desert, who preferred the status quo of Egypt with its food, rather than looking forward to the promised freedom.

Amid the storm, the boat is a symbol of the Church. However, we must remember: The Church is not a physical place, like a parish building, but rather the very People of God who are on this pilgrimage of trust with Mary, walking toward Jesus. Pope Francis has rightly complained that the Church can become too "self-referential" — meaning that we simply stay in our "boats," e.g., going to Sunday Mass at the parish, but doing nothing more. Think, for instance, of how often we consider ourselves to have "done our duty" if we simply go to

---

[171] Blessed Sopocko, *The Mercy of God in His Works*, Vol. 3, 173.

the parish on Sunday for Mass. We are called, like St. Peter, to get out of the physical buildings and evangelize, as the priest says at the end of Mass: "*Ite, missa est*" — literally, "Go, you are sent forth," sent forth on a mission.

Even more, when the storm comes, we need to remember that we *need* to get out of the boats of our lives: our comfort zones, our attachments, our safety. True safety is not in such "boats" or in the Church as an institution; rather, safety is in Jesus and in the People of God, who walk upon the waters of this world toward Him. We have no choice. During storms, the boat will sink if, because of fear, we choose to remain in it. The Church, too, will begin to sink if we are concerned in a selfish, self-referential way about it — if we only go to Mass or are concerned only about our own salvation, but forget about evangelizing and walking in faith and trust every day of our lives. Sometimes the Father allows such situations, and permits the serpent to attack us, to nudge or even push us to "walk on water" in faith and trust toward His Son. The Father knows our complacency, our mediocrity, our lukewarmness.

"According to Father Faber, the chief cause of the spiritual stagnation of Christians today is lack of trust in God. And indeed, people today trust only in themselves — in their intelligence, their inventions, their strength: trust in God lies dormant, or dies away altogether. Even in our [spiritual] life we rely more on natural factors than on those that are supernatural."[172] God knows we are slow to leave everything behind and just trust. What we ought to dread is not so much falling as Peter did, but rather never getting out of the boat at all. Remember that when storms come, you may complain — but let the complaint always burst forth in confident prayers of trust in the Father (see Ps 69:1-2, 13-15, 29-33).

Do complain about your lack of faith and trust, however! Complain and then praise, expecting with confident trust His deliverance and His help. Such confident trust is more pleasing to God than any other sacrifice, so ask the Holy Spirit to help you have the courage to step out of the boat and grasp Mary's hand, confident that the Lord will sustain you. The Lord may not calm the external storm, but He will calm the storm within you and give you *peace* that even the worst storm cannot take away.

There were in fact two storms in the stories of the Sea of Galilee. The first was the external storm that affected the waves. The second was the storm within the disciples' souls — the howling wind of doubt and the crashing waves of despair. Only Jesus can control the hurricanes of our lives in both senses. Hence, the best solution in such storms is to simply repeat, "Jesus, I trust in You." The serpent causes external storms in order to trigger the perfect internal storm, prompting us to lose trust in Jesus and drown in our doubt. Ask Mary to stabilize you as you attempt to walk upon the choppy waters. As St. Francis de Sales wrote, "Let us run to her, and, as her little children, cast ourselves into her arms with a perfect confidence."[173] Storms humble us and help us realize our

---

[172] Ibid., 178.
[173] Francis W. Johnston, *The Voice of the Saints: Counsels from the Saints to Bring Comfort and*

deepest poverty and lack of trust, but the Father is happy to pour forth the balm of trust — the Holy Spirit — into our hearts to strengthen our faith as we walk toward Jesus upon the water of life.

At times it feels as though Jesus has forgotten us or is simply asleep. Sometimes it seems that we endure thick heavy storms, even hurricanes, without His intervention, without hearing His voice commanding the storm to be still. Saint Thérèse was so firmly convinced of Jesus' goodness and love that she resolved *not* to wake Jesus up when He was asleep in her boat.[174] She could wait through the storm with courage because she trusted. She knew the truth of who Jesus is and acted on that knowledge.

Saint Bernard of Clairvaux has a beautiful exhortation to those who have difficulty not awaking the Lord amid the storm: Go to Mary!

> If the winds of temptation arise; if you are driven upon the rocks of tribulation, look to the star, call on Mary; if you are tossed upon the waves of pride, of ambition, of envy, of rivalry, look to the star, call on Mary. Should anger, or avarice, or fleshly desire violently assail the frail vessel of your soul, look at the star, call upon Mary. ... In dangers, in doubts, in difficulties, think of Mary, call upon Mary. Let not her name depart from your lips, never suffer it to leave your heart. And that you may obtain the assistance of her prayer, neglect not to walk in her footsteps. With her for guide, you shall never go astray; while invoking her, you shall never lose heart; so long as she is in your mind, you are safe from deception; while she holds your hand, you cannot fall; under her protection you have nothing to fear; if she walks before you, you shall not grow weary; if she shows you favor, you shall reach the goal (St. Bernard of Clairvaux, d. 1153).[175]

Guidance in Daily Living (Rockford, Illinois: TAN Books and Publishers, 1986).
[174] Saint Thérèse of Lisieux and T. N. Taylor, *The Story of a Soul* (London: Burns and Oates, 1912), 118.
[175] Father Johann Roten, SM, "Star of the Sea," International Marian Research Institute, accessed July 11, 2017, https://udayton.edu/imri/mary/s/star-of-the-sea.php.

CHAPTER 18

Calming the Storm

"Who then is this, that even wind and sea obey him" (Mk 4:41).

The main question in our relationship with Jesus Christ is captured by the rhetorical question of the disciples after they witnessed Jesus calm the storm: Who exactly is this? Because the Father is the only one who set limits to the sea at creation and who could calm the sea, the fact that Jesus calmed the storm by the word of His command points to His divine power (see Ps 104:9; Prov 8:29). In addition, God alone walked on the waters (see Ps 77:19). This did not escape the apostles. They began to grasp more and more fully who Jesus is, both God and man. That's why they were filled with awe — the kind of awe that we call the "fear of the Lord."

Thus the Lord rebukes the apostles for having the *wrong kind* of fear: "Why are you afraid, O men of little faith?" (Mt 8:26). What kind of fear? The apostles were probably afraid of dying — a legitimate fear, given that they were enduring a terrible storm. However, we ought to remember the words of Jesus: "Do not fear those who kill the body but cannot kill the soul; rather fear him who can destroy both soul and body in hell" (Mt 10:28). Who ought we to fear? We are to fear God alone, and not like a slave, but like a son who fears ever hurting his beloved Father or disappointing Him by distrust.

Amid storms, then, what are we to fear? We fear being found wanting or lacking in faith and trust — but we do not fear the storm, or death, or even Satan himself (who can kill only the body, but not the soul). We are to fear Jesus; we are never to lose sight of who He is. Fear in this sense means deep reverence and respect for Him. This fear does not domesticate Jesus or remake Him in our likeness; we cannot do away with those aspects of Jesus that don't fit into our image of Him (for instance, John's falling down as though dead before Jesus in His majesty; see Rev 1:17). Such fear is necessary for true love; reverence and respect allow Jesus to be who He is, and we learn to love Him as He is — not as we might want Him to be. Then we learn to trust Him because we recognize Him as the one who has the power and authority that we lack.

Never Losing Awe

Although today, we overuse the word *awesome*, Jesus' calming of the storm is truly awesome — an event that ought to fill us with awe. But just as the word is overused and emptied of its meaning, so, too, is awe itself often absent from our lives. We ought never to lose our awe before Jesus. Like the apostles, every

day we must ask: "Who then is this?" Saint Stanislaus Papczynski urges us to ask this question as we approach Jesus in the Eucharist: "You ask, who is This, whom you have received in the Eucharist? He is living, immortal, mighty, sweet, invincible; He is good, merciful, full of compassion, and the highest of all; He is kind, gentle; He is Wisdom, Love, Truth, full of all Life and all Goodness. ... He is the One who created you; He is the One who redeemed you; He is the One who will judge you."[176]

If we do not ask this question every day, but instead remain content with the faith we already have in Jesus, then our knowledge of Him is insufficient. If our relationship with Jesus does not grow richer daily in awe and wonder, then our knowledge of Him is dead and has become mere information. We ought to desire, like the Apostle St. Thomas, not merely to know about Jesus from others; we ought to insist on meeting Him and coming to know Him ourselves (see Jn 20:24-29).

Even atheists and agnostics have information about Jesus from the Gospels; even demons know who Jesus is and shout it out before everyone (see Mk 1:24). Only His disciples, however, *know* who He is — by sharing their lives with Him, by being with Him, by giving up *all* to follow Him. We can gain that same knowledge of Jesus by being with Him in prayer and remaining in His love each and every day (see Jn 15:9). Without such intimate knowledge, we will sink in times of trial during storms.

Do we have this *intimate knowledge* of Jesus in our hearts? Do we recognize His voice (see Mk 9:7)? Many of us know that Jesus is Lord, but our reaction during stormy times reveals whether that is merely information or a living faith in Jesus. Giving in to fear and allowing storms to remove our peace does not please Him (see *Diary*, 453). If we know Jesus intimately, we will not let any storm disturb our peace, for we will know that even the worst storm must obey His Word.

Precisely because Mary never lost this attitude of wonder and faith in the face of her Son, she never wavered during the storm. This is a lesson for us: It is easy to become accustomed to Jesus, to domesticate Him, to say, "Oh, yes, I know Jesus!" In doing so, we close off the mystery of Jesus, attempting to place Him in the box of our own finite understanding. We take Jesus for granted. Mary, however, lived in close proximity to Jesus, day in and day out, and never lost her awe of Him. She was not like Jesus' other relatives, who claimed to know Him simply because they knew Him in the flesh (see Mt 13:55). She lived in the spirit of faith each day in Nazareth, contemplating the mystery of her Son, who was flesh of her flesh.

If we want to have a similar intimate and familiar knowledge of Jesus, we must go to Mary and learn from her how to know Him without putting Him in a box, without foreshortening our knowledge of Him, without losing sight of the mystery of who He is. Mary's intimate knowledge and unflagging awe

---

[176] Saint Papczynski, *Pisma Zebrane* [*Collected Works*], 530.

before the Son are revealed to us when Luke writes that she held all these things, meditating upon them in her Heart. She always opened her Heart to the mystery of her Son (see Lk 2:19).

Because our trust is directly proportional to our conviction regarding the trustworthiness of the One whom we trust, prayer is important — the kind of prayer that involves meditation on the Gospels, which reveal who Jesus is. If we do not read the Gospels and are not familiar with the stories of Jesus' life, it is no surprise that when the storms come, like the apostles we begin to doubt and sink. If we do read Scripture, we will recognize the trustworthiness of Jesus.

We know from the Gospels that with but a word, Jesus could do something that would be attributed to God alone: calm a storm. But Jesus not only *spoke* the word; He *is* the Word of God. When Jesus speaks, what He says happens. Jesus' word not only describes reality; it creates and changes reality. For that reason, before receiving Holy Communion, we profess, "Lord, I am not worthy that you should enter under my roof, but only say the word and my soul shall be healed."[177] All it takes is a word for Jesus to heal our souls and calm the storm of our doubts, worries, and anxieties. One of the admirable qualities of St. Peter is his willingness to take risks. At the command of the Lord, Peter let down the nets yet another time: "Master, we toiled all night and took nothing! But at your word I will let down the nets" (Lk 5:5). "At your word" — this is St. Peter's strength. At Jesus' word, St. Peter also left the boat and began to walk on water. We would do well to take Jesus at His word, get out of our comfort zone, and walk on water.

Prayer trains us to act according to faith, according to trust in Jesus and the power of His word. Prayer opens our hearts to trust in Jesus, because it is in prayer that we come to know Jesus more fully. Without prayer, the storm seems to be intensely real and immediate, to have more power and influence in our lives. Without prayer, Jesus seems to be only an idea or head knowledge, whereas the storm is something we experience, something we feel, something that surrounds us and all our senses. But remember: Jesus not only surrounds us; He dwells within us (see Eph 3:17).

The Father surrounds us with His Love and Mercy more closely than our own skin, as Julian of Norwich wrote: "For as the body is clad in the clothes, and the flesh in the skin, and the bones in the flesh, and the heart in the breast, so are we, soul and body, clad in the goodness of God and enclosed — yea, and even more intimately, because all these others may waste and wear away, but the goodness of God is ever whole, and nearer to us without any comparison."[178]

Because He is Spirit, we must learn to meet Him in our own spirit, in the depths of our souls, for God is found not in the earthquake or in the fire, but in the gentle whisper of our hearts (see 1 Kings 19:11-12). If we do not find Him in times of peace in our hearts through prayer, when there should be nothing to

---

[177] Roman Missal, 669.
[178] Julian of Norwich, *Revelations of Divine Love*, 18.

distract us from listening to His whisper, we should not be surprised when we cannot hear the voice of the Lord amid a storm.

God's Light

It is always important to remember that the Father reveals Himself by saving His people from their distress and suffering. Psalm 107 recounts the many times God delivered His people, repeating the refrain: "Then they cried to the Lord in their trouble, and he delivered them from their distress" (Ps 107:6, 13, 19). The Father's Mercy is dramatically revealed against the backdrop of our storms, just as we read about the Father's saving Mercy in the Books of Exodus and Esther. The storms on the Sea of Galilee were no exception. In theological terms, the storm on the sea is an "epiphany," a manifestation of who Jesus is. Jesus shines with His brilliant light, the Holy Spirit, precisely in our darkest moments. Is this not what the Divine Mercy Image illustrates for us? The light of Christ shines forth most radiantly against a completely dark background! Think about the liturgy of the Easter Vigil: The priest enters the dark church with the paschal candle. He prays, "May the light of Christ rising in glory dispel the darkness of our hearts and minds." He then chants three times, "The light of Christ."[179] This liturgical action proclaims the victory of Christ exactly at the moment of greatest darkness (Jn 1:5).

With that in mind, we can approach the storms in our lives, not with fear or doubt, but with courage, confidence, faith, and — above all — trust. When we have allowed Jesus to dwell not only in our heads but in our hearts, then His Love will be more real to us than the worst of storms. We will know, and even sing, that nothing except sin and distrust can separate us from the love of Christ (see Rom 8:35-39). When we truly know Jesus, we will trust Him, especially in the midst of life's storms. We will wait with confidence and patience for the moment when Jesus will appear in His glory and save us.

Saint Faustina wrote this beautiful prayer: "O my Jesus, nothing can lower my ideals, that is, the love which I have for You. Although the path is very thorny, I do not fear to go ahead. Even if a hailstorm of persecutions covers me; even if my friends forsake me, even if all things conspire against me, and the horizon grows dark; even if a raging storm breaks out, and I feel I am quite alone and must brave it all; still, fully at peace, I will trust in Your mercy, O my God, and my hope will not be disappointed" (*Diary*, 1195).

Entrusting Our Whole Selves

The only appropriate response we can offer our loving and merciful Father is that of faith and trust — committing our whole lives to Him, entrusting our whole selves to Him (see *CCC*, 142-143). The rich young man was asked to leave everything and follow Jesus, but he was not willing to do so, even though Jesus

---

[179] Roman Missal, 346.

is more precious and reliable than all riches and wealth (see Mk 10:21). Are we willing to offer Him our *all*? The counterpart to the Father's Mercy is our trust, which requires that we live in all circumstances with confidence that the Father is Love and Mercy. As we pray at the end of the Divine Mercy Chaplet: "Eternal God, in whom mercy is endless and the treasury of compassion inexhaustible, look kindly upon us and increase Your mercy in us, that in difficult moments we might not despair nor become despondent, but with great confidence submit ourselves to Your holy will, which is Love and Mercy itself" (*Diary*, 950). Like Peter, we are invited to leave our boat, escape our comfort zone, and walk on water, even amid a storm. We can do that only in faith. We cannot control the storm in the least.

Jesus cannot be trusted if we simply want an easy comfortable life, but He can be trusted if we want to make it to the other shore — to Heaven. Many people would rather stay on the shore of this world and enjoy its temporal blessings, but Jesus leads us away from this temporal world into the eternal world, from this life (*bios*) to eternal life (*zoe*). We grow in faith and holiness only through trials, and much as with physical exercise — in which we gain strength only by increasing speed, resistance, or distance — our virtues are tried by confronting their opposite.

The Father allows these storms so that we can exercise our ability to entrust ourselves to Him. Though such storms as war, genocide, or abuse can and ought to stir up reactions of pain and sorrow, looking at such evils through the prism of trust, we can be certain that the Father will bring us through them to enjoy life with Him forever. That will be our eternal song in Heaven — a song of eternal gratitude for His salvation, which frees us from the storm. Such praise is, in fact, the "sacrifice" that He desires (see Ps 50:22). Therefore, even the storms should not interrupt our thanksgiving to Him, for all things work for our good — that is, for our growth in holiness and union with Him (see Rom 8:38).

The storms we encounter provide opportunities to learn who Jesus truly is and how to trust Him more and more, until our trust is strong enough for that moment when we will hand everything over to our Lord at death. If we feel a reluctance regarding this final surrender, it is a sign that we do not fully trust Him in our hearts, that we dread death, and that we fear Jesus will take us away from everything we have when we die. Unfortunately, this means that our hearts love the world more than the Father. If we trust and love Jesus, we will approach death, not with fear, but with the joy of knowing that we gain everything when we gain Him. The same is true if someone we love dies. There will be natural sadness because we miss someone dearly beloved, but we must not mourn like those who have no hope (see 1 Thess 4:13). Our hope is in Jesus, and by trusting Him, we stand firm, even in the face of death.

The trials, difficulties, and sufferings of life are intended to purify and empty the soul, so that it has absolutely nothing left except trust in the infinite Mercy of the Father. The serpent — despite all the havoc that he can wreak in our lives — plays a key part in the Father's plan because he tests us, showing us our poverty and misery, making sure we know just how weak we really are. The Father permits the serpent to stir up some storms, in the face of which we are indeed helpless, and leaves us with only one solution: to trust in the Mercy of the Father. Like St. Faustina, we will be able to weather all storms if we have the anchor of trust that is cast deep into the ocean of His Mercy: "I want to love You as no human soul has ever loved You before; and although I am utterly miserable and small, I have, nevertheless, cast the anchor of my trust deep down into the abyss of Your mercy, O my God and Creator! In spite of my great misery I fear nothing, but hope to sing You a hymn of glory for ever. Let no soul, even the most miserable, fall prey to doubt; for, as long as one is alive, each one can become a great saint, so great is the power of God's grace. It remains only for us not to oppose God's action" (*Diary*, 283).

OUR LADY, STAR OF THE SEA

Our Lady has been invoked for centuries as Star of the Sea for centuries, and there is a ninth-century Latin hymn called "*Ave Maris Stella*," "Hail, Star of the Sea." As St. Thomas Aquinas wrote: "As mariners are guided into port by the shining of a star, so Christians are guided to heaven by Mary."[180] During a storm, she still shines brightly. Though clouds may cover her light, we know that she watches over us and guides us along our path.

Pope Benedict XVI writes beautifully about Our Lady as Star of the Sea: "Human life is a journey. Towards what destination? How do we find the way? Life is like a voyage on the sea of history, often dark and stormy, a voyage in which we watch for the stars that indicate the route. The true stars of our life are the people who have lived good lives. They are lights of hope. Certainly, Jesus Christ is the true light, the sun that has risen above all the shadows of history. But to reach him we also need lights close by — people who shine with his light and so guide us along our way. Who more than Mary could be a star of hope for us?"[181]

Our Lady not only leads us through storms; she also helps us walk upon the waters of sin and conquer evil with great trust and faith in her Son, Jesus. She enables us to live the words of Isaiah: "When you pass through the waters I will be with you; and through the rivers, they shall not overwhelm you; when you walk through fire you shall not be burned, and the flame shall not consume you. For I am the Lord your God, the Holy One of Israel, your Savior" (Is 42:2-3).

Various saints and leaders of the Church have written about how important it is to follow Our Lady as a guiding star on the journey of life. I will let one of

---

[180] "Mary, Mother of God Quotes," Jesuit Resources, Xavier University, accessed July 11, 2017, http://www.xavier.edu/jesuitresource/online-resources/Mother-Mary-Quotes.cfm.
[181] Benedict XVI, *Spe Salvi*, n. 49-50.

them explain the importance of following Mary on our pilgrimage of trust in Jesus:

> Mary, Star of the Sea, must be followed in faith and morals lest we capsize amidst the storm-tossed waves of the sea. She will illumine us to believe in Christ, born of her for the salvation of the world (Paschasius Radbertus, d. 865).[182]

Holy Mary, Mother of God, our Mother, teach us to believe, to hope, to love with you. Show us the way to His Kingdom! Star of the Sea, shine upon us and guide us on our way!

---

[182] Father Johann Roten, SM, "Star of the Sea," International Marian Research Institute.

CHAPTER 19

The Zenith of Trust

"Unless we are ready through his power to die in the likeness of his passion, his life is not [fully] in us"
(Ignatius of Antioch, Letter to the Magnesians).

At times, God intervenes to save His people: Jesus healed the sick, raised the dead, and calmed the storm on the Sea of Galilee. In this chapter, we are going to explore those situations when He does not seem to intervene. The prime example is the abandonment and misery of His Crucified Son, when the Father *seemed* to have completely withdrawn. We learned at the Resurrection, however, that He came to redeem His people and show His trustworthiness by walking with us through the "valley of death."

The path of trust we are on takes us along the *Way of the Cross*, as well. Stepping on this path with Mary means setting our faces firmly toward Jerusalem with Jesus, knowing that we will undergo trials and temptations with Him (see Lk 9:51). We will face opposition from Satan through the world and the flesh. Just as the serpent tested Adam's and Eve's trust by tempting and threatening them, he lies in wait to bite us. He prowls about, ready to test us, as he did Job, to see whether our trust is unconditional or has limits.

His threat is intimidating, and he makes his message clear: "If you intend to trust in Jesus, then I will make your life miserable. *Trust me,* you will give up your trust in Him. I know your limits, and I will break that trust." Jesus and Mary show us how to crush the serpent's head, and together we take one step, and then another, along the path to Calvary. We do defeat Satan, not in a single struggle once and for all, but through every step of trust that we take, through maintaining the kind of trust that Mary had in her Son. The serpent's fangs will bite us and cause much suffering, but *do not be afraid* of the devil or of suffering. *Do* be afraid of his poison, of distrust!

WHEN PRAYERS ARE NOT ANSWERED

The Cross teaches us to trust in the Father and His eternal love for us, even when He does not move mountains, part waters, or give answers. Sometimes He remains silent, at least for a while.

The Father may seem to be silent, but the Cross is never His last word. Possibly because we have a crucifix at the center of our faith and in our churches, we may see the Cross as the end of the story. I struggled with this myself during my retreat in Lublin. I think the Lord wants to correct our focus. In giving us the Divine Mercy Image, He calls us to remember that the end of the "greatest story ever told" is the Resurrection and Ascension of Jesus.

The miracles the Lord performed during His life serve to give rise to our faith and trust in Him. Many of the miracles involved physical healing, but Christ came to give people more than just physical healing. While the miracles Jesus performed are important, they still leave the recipient of a miracle in this world of sin. Even Lazarus had to die again one day. Eternal salvation is the true healing, and that means the restoration of one's trusting relationship with the Father. The story of His friend's death and return to life is a powerful example of trust in the Mercy of the Lord, for it begins with Jesus purposefully delaying His visit to Lazarus. He waits so long, in fact, that Lazarus dies. Both Martha and Mary complain to Jesus that if He had only come earlier, Lazarus could have been healed and would still be alive. But Jesus had arranged events as a test of trust, just as the Father in His Divine Providence allows all things so that we might grow in faith, hope, and charity, and learn to trust in Him ever more fully.

Distrust is what the serpent wants above all. The serpent will even use this very book and the message of Divine Mercy to bring about distrust. He will bring forward thoughts such as: "Have you not been reading about how the Father is moved by misery? How the Father would never disappoint someone who trusts in Him? Have you not heard how He is Mercy itself? But look: You are suffering. You have called out to Him. You have tried. And nothing, absolutely nothing in response. Why trust in Him?"

I can only imagine the difficulties Martha and Mary endured in waiting for Jesus to come — the similar thoughts they probably had: "Does Jesus not love Lazarus? Did He not know that he was dying? Yet He waited days before He finally came. Does He not care?" Yes, Jesus cared. In fact, Jesus wept. He wept before the tomb of Lazarus, and the Jews all commented about how much Jesus must have loved Lazarus. Why, then, did Jesus wait?

The key to understanding Jesus' delay — and all such delays in responding to our prayers — is His statement to Martha: "Did I not tell you that if you would believe you would see the glory of God?" Martha had just told Jesus that Lazarus had been in the tomb for four days, and his body was probably already emitting a stench. The point is clear: Jesus waited until Lazarus was completely, indisputably dead, to the point that his body was being corrupted. Lazarus, and all those who are enwrapped and bound in sin, are placed in the tomb. What is the tomb? The tomb symbolizes our sins of distrust and doubt. If we only *believe*, or *trust*, we will see the glory of God — His Mercy, transforming our misery. Jesus delayed going to Lazarus in order to reveal just how powerful He is. He has complete control, even over death. The lesson of Lazarus is clear: Trust and wait to see the glory of God, no matter what. Sometimes we must die to our sin of doubt and distrust before we are able to see God's glory made manifest; but without trust, we will see only suffering and misery — and we will rebel.

We must understand this interaction between our misery and the Father's mercy to have appropriate expectations about how the Father responds to our misery. I have said throughout the book that if we expect the Father to simply wipe away our misery and fix all our problems, we are bound to be disappointed in our trust and feel deceived. The Father indeed responds, but just how He responds and when He will resolve our misery is up to Him alone.

Notice the difference between the serpent, who sows doubt, and Mary's attitude of faith, especially as she traversed the path to Calvary with her Son. I imagine that Mary — like Jesus in His Agony, asking the Father to be spared — prayed fervently for the Father to save her Son, yet, despite her petitions, the Father was silent. Her Son was silent; all was silent. She could have complained to the Father, "You saved so many others through Him. Why can't you save Him, too?" Because Mary was His mother, her desire for her Son to be saved from His Passion and death was completely legitimate. Yet when the Father did not respond, she kept trusting. She continued to trust and trust — and Mary's trust never gave way to assent to the serpent's suggestion to distrust and rebel in anger. Quite the contrary: At Calvary, Mary fully assented to her Son's death, offering Him to the Father for the salvation of souls.

I imagine the Resurrection as a response, in part, to Mary's prayer outside the tomb of Jesus. Because Mary trusted, she saw the glory of God manifested in her Son. She did not dictate when or how the Father should take care of the misery of death and sin. Rather, she took steps of faith and trust along that path to Calvary, and each time she did so, she stepped upon the serpent with her Son. Each step of trust is always a step upon the serpent's head. When we simply take those steps, we pave the way for the glory of God to be revealed in our lives, as it was in Mary's life.

If the Father were to perform all the miracles of physical healing we desire in our lives, we would still remain in a world infected and wounded by sin. What we need is a deeper miracle — the miracle not of being freed from the woes of this life, but of being freed from our slavery to sin, which is what Lazarus, wrapped in cloths, symbolizes. The serpent not only bites but also constricts and binds, wrapping himself around us to cause our deaths by distrust. At times, it seems that the Father is not moving mountains, but He is — namely, the mountains of pride and distrust in our souls. We may not notice this, especially if we relate to Him superficially or want immediate satisfaction. When we do that, we are like Martha and Mary, who asked the Lord, "Why did you wait?" The Father waits to reveal His glory. Saint Irenaeus wrote that God's glory is "a living man" — a man *"fully alive,"* for we come to true life only when we gaze upon the Father as does Jesus, in adoration and praise.[183]

That is why it can sometimes seem that the Father does not hear our prayers. It is not that He does not hear prayers, but that He has two ways of answering them. The Father can respond to each of our requests and repair the

---

[183] Saint Irenaeus of Lyons, "Irenæus Against Heresies," in *The Apostolic Fathers*, Vol. 1, 490.

broken world here and now without helping us grow in sanctity, but this ulti-mately would not provide us with happiness. Or He can seemingly *not* answer our prayer and *not* give us what we ask.[184] The Father does this when what we ask for is not what is best for us (see Jas 4:3). Everything is secondary compared with the surpassing good of knowing the Father and spending eternity with Him (see Phil 3:8), so if the Father does not answer our prayer, this may be because it would interfere with His plans for us to be with Him in Heaven. Saint Augustine warns us against praying "in the flesh," against asking *Abba* for things that do not endure and are not beneficial to salvation.[185] Jesus instructs us to desire and pray only for what endures (see Col 3:1-3; Jn 6:27).

In the Father's original plan, we were never meant to remain on this earth forever. In other words, even without sin, Adam and Eve were not yet in Heaven; they had yet to make a choice of love to enter more fully into the Trinitarian life. The major heresy or lie of the world today is that this fallen world is *it*. You have one life, so make sure you use it well — such is the logic of this passing world. But this is not our only world, nor our only life. We should live well now, in order that we may live for eternity in union with the Trinity in a new Heaven and new earth.

Remember that the Father did not create death as we know it: He destined us for life, but man, through his sin, brought death into the world (see Rom 5:12). If we see death as Jesus saw it — as the door to the next life — we will be able to embrace it as freely and confidently as He did. We are reminded of this next life in the Funeral Mass when the priest prays, "For your faithful, Lord, life is changed not ended."[186]

The fact that the Father allows suffering is, paradoxically, one of the greatest mercies He could provide for His sinful children. Death provides a limit to the suffering we endure in this life. Without death, we would live in this suffering forever, with no gate to enter Heaven. Death provides a pathway to salvation. Pope Benedict XVI, quoting St. Ambrose, wrote: "Death was not part of nature; it became part of nature. God did not decree death from the beginning; he prescribed it as a remedy. Human life, because of sin ... began to experience the burden of wretchedness in unremitting labor and unbearable sorrow. There had to be a limit to its evils; death had to restore what life had forfeited. Without the assistance of grace, immortality is more of a burden than a blessing. ... Death is, then, no cause for mourning, for it is the cause of mankind's salvation."[187]

Ironically, while we would rather not die, none of us would like to live on this earth marked with sin and suffering forever. Pope Benedict XVI continues: "It is true that to eliminate death or to postpone it more or less indefinitely

---

[184] For a good discussion of this topic, see C. S. Lewis, *Letters to Malcolm, Chiefly on Prayer* (San Francisco: HarperOne, HarperCollins Publishers, 2017).
[185] From the Letter of St. Augustine to Proba (Epistolae 130, 11, 21-12, 22: CSEL 44, 63-64). ICEL, *The Liturgy of the Hours*, Vol. 4, 417-18.
[186] Roman Missal, 622.
[187] Benedict XVI, *Spe Salvi*, n. 10.

would place the earth and humanity in an impossible situation, and even for the individual would bring no benefit. Obviously there is a contradiction in our attitude, which points to an inner contradiction in our very existence. On the one hand, we do not want to die; above all, those who love us do not want us to die. Yet on the other hand, neither do we want to continue living indefinitely, nor was the earth created with that in view."[188] Indeed, to live indefinitely in this world filled with sin and suffering would be not a blessing but a curse!

So, what do we really want? Our attitude gives rise to deeper questions. What in fact is life? What does eternity really mean? There are moments when what we desire — true life — suddenly seems clear to us, when we experience the beauty of creation or true love in a relationship. In those moments, we have a foretaste of what true life is — the eternal Beauty and Love of the Triune God. But what we call life in our everyday language is not life in its fullest measure. In the extended letter on prayer that he addressed to Proba, a wealthy Roman widow and mother of three consuls, St. Augustine wrote: "Ultimately, we want only one thing — 'the blessed life,' the life which is simply life, simply 'happiness.' In the final analysis, there is nothing else that we ask for in prayer."[189]

Let us ponder these questions as well. Why must death be the gate into the next life? Is it not a bit cruel for our good Father to demand such a painful exit from this life? Why does the Father allow such tragic deaths? Why would He allow His Son's tragic death? Sin is punished by death and suffering because, by their very nature, they detach us from this world and from ourselves. Everything in this world is passing away, and inevitably, all that it contains will return to dust (see 1 Jn 2:17; 1 Cor 7:31). By accepting this truth, we come to know that it is foolish to set our hearts solely upon the fragile reality of creation. By sinning, we choose this world over the Father. We declare that this world is our goal. Suffering gives us the opportunity to get back on the original path toward Heaven and eternal life, reminding us that this world is not our true home. Death is the moment when the effects of our sins appear to us in all their clarity, for death confronts us with the reality of our vocation to live with the Trinity.

Our Father places forks in the road — suffering and death — to remind us to reflect on where we are going. Death forces even more questions upon us, such as: Do I trust in the Father? Do I trust Him enough to commend all that I have, even my very self, into His hands? Do I trust myself, others, or this world rather than God? Death is harrowing because its power exceeds anything we or the world can do. It is the bluntest reminder of our own weakness and poverty, of our status as creatures, and it reveals the lie pronounced by Satan in the fall: You will not die; you will be like God (see Gen 3:4-5). But only the Father has power over life and death. Thus trusting in God is essential at the moment of death. For that reason, an important work of mercy is to pray for the dying, for they have the most need of trust (see *Diary,* 1777).

---

[188] Ibid., 11.
[189] Ibid.

Was it necessary for Jesus to undergo suffering to enter the life of the Resurrection? The answer is yes, given the plan of the Father for our salvation. Our life is a gift meant to be returned to the Father in praise of His goodness, for in Heaven we will join "the thanksgiving of Christ, who lives for all eternity."[190]

Sometimes it seems that Satan — the serpent — is given free rein, permitted to test us beyond our limit. We know, however, that the Father will never allow us to be tried beyond what we can bear (see 1 Cor 10:13). The Father is always in control, even when it seems that He is not. Jesus could entrust Himself into the hands of sinners — into my hands and your hands — because He knew that even we fall under the Providence of the Father. The reality of the Father's Providence — His power over the serpent's attempts to destroy us — is seen in the Gospels. Several times, especially in the Gospel of John, those who plot against Jesus attempt to capture Him or even stone Him. They were never able to do so until the appointed hour (see Jn 7:30). Satan is not the one who appoints the hour of the Cross — not in Jesus' life, Mary's life, or our own lives. Satan is not the one in control. The Father is the one who appoints the hour of the Cross from all eternity, designating exactly when He will permit suffering to begin, when He will not allow it to continue any further, and how heavy and miserable He will allow it to be for us.

The lie of the serpent is that he is in control, that there will be no end to the Cross. But we know that he is not in control, and the light of the Resurrection shines. Our role is to trust the Father and submit ourselves to His will, most especially at those moments when we cannot even pray. Jesus grants us a living share in His Passion, when He, too, was assailed by Satan and experienced the pain of abandonment (see *Diary*, 1697).

We ought not to be discouraged if we cannot pray as well as we desire in moments of suffering. It is enough in such difficult moments to trust by simply uttering, "Amen," as Mary did; "Thy will be done," as in the Our Father; or "Jesus, I trust in You," as in the Divine Mercy Image prayer. In such moments, we need not pray at length, nor need we meditate deeply about the Passion; we are living the Passion.

Nevertheless, when we can meditate on and contemplate the Passion, this is worthwhile, especially as a preparation for those moments when we are called to live the Passion (see *Diary*, 1184; see also 654). Unfortunately, though, He admits: **"There are few souls who contemplate My Passion with true feeling; I give great graces to souls who meditate devoutly on My Passion"** (*Diary*, 737). It is no surprise, then, that few souls are able to trust in the Lord and follow Him to Calvary! Let each of us strive to be one who does follow Him to the Cross with Mary.

---

[190] Roman Missal, 764.

CHAPTER 20

Crucified Trust

"Love one another as I have loved you" (Jn 13:1).

In the Father's plan of salvation, death and the lesser forms of suffering were not intended to cause the separation of the soul from the body or, more excruciatingly, to cause hell: the separation of the soul from God. Death was, and is again through Christ, the gate to an eternal share in God's divine life. However, for those who are weak in faith and in trust, death can be an occasion for worry, anxiety, and fear. Through confident trust, we can walk through death, holding Our Lady by the hand, asking her to fulfill a petition we have asked so many times: "Holy Mary, Mother of God, pray for us sinners, now and at the hour of our death."

We see this original plan of the Father in regard to death in the way the Blessed Virgin passed from this life to the next. When Pope Pius XII proclaimed the dogma of Mary's Assumption, he did not state whether Our Lady had died or simply passed on to eternal life directly. The passing of one filled with divine grace is called by the Church Fathers, not death, but *dormition*, the English version of the Latin word for "falling asleep" — falling asleep in the arms of God, who lifts us up to Himself in Heaven.

Mary reveals to us the full flowering of baptismal grace: the divine life here on earth. How often we must give things up and suffer unwanted crosses! How often, when we must die to ourselves in small things, we complain and murmur! But Mary teaches us how to carry these crosses in silence and peace, knowing that they are nothing in comparison with the glory to be revealed. There is nothing written in the Bible about Mary's death, but Our Lady shows us what is essential about Christian death: the ability to die to oneself in peace and quiet, without complaining, without letting everyone know. Instead of complaining, she offered up her suffering to God for His glory. She is an example of how to live in communion with the death of Christ, a communion where "death to self" is synonymous with "entrance into the divine life."[191] The divine life of the God who is Love is nothing other than the reciprocal gift of oneself (Father) and reception of another's gift of self (Son) in the Holy Spirit.[192]

---

[191] M.D. Philippe, *The Mysteries of Mary: Growing in Faith, Hope, and Love with the Mother of God* (Charlotte, North Carolina: Saint Benedict Press, 2011).

[192] "Love is the unconditional reception of the beloved in oneself; the affirmation of the longed-for beloved for his own sake; and the gratuitous reciprocation of the gift of his person with that of one's own life. Thus, analogically to what happens in God, where the Father's love is eternally received and reciprocated by the person of the Son, the divine love for man that

Love of the Trinity

Sin destroys the Father's original plan for our transition from this world to Heaven: Death was to be the definitive moment in which we entrusted ourselves entirely to the Father. Without sin, this would have happened in peace, as with Mary. Because of sin, however, death often seems to us to be, not an entrance into eternal life, but a separation from that to which we are disorderedly attached. What could be greater than entering definitively into the Trinitarian life? But because of sin, instead of being the greatest moment of life upon earth, death has become the moment of fear — the fear of losing all that is dear to us. Christ's suffering and death are intimately linked to the Father's Love, which was fully revealed in the Crucifixion (see 1 Jn 4:9-10). Let us return to our understanding of the Trinity. The Father loves the Son and hands everything over to Him (see Jn 3:35). The Son receives and returns everything with that love to the Father in gratitude and thanksgiving. The Crucifixion is the point in time and history when we see this exchange taking place — the Son returning the Spirit of Love to the Father (see Jn 19:30). This return of love is the Son's "thanksgiving" — *eucharistia* in Greek — for all that the Father has given to Him. Jesus, as man, entrusts Himself entirely and completely into His Father's hands on the Cross (see Lk 23:47).

Mind you, this act of entrustment follows immediately on the heels of His earlier cry of abandonment (see Mt 27:46; Ps 22:1). Jesus experiences the full depth of the agony of death. He experiences the full weight of all the evil in the world and still chooses to entrust Himself completely to the Father. At the time when we would probably give up trusting in the Father, under such extreme suffering, Jesus perseveres and surrenders Himself completely to the Father. For this reason, He is called the pioneer of our faith (see Heb 12:1-2).

Jesus envelops our own misery and sinfulness in that eternal exchange of Love, the Holy Spirit, between Himself and the Father. Jesus burns up our own sinfulness in the furnace of Love in His Sacred Heart, and so takes away our sins: **"Your minor faults will disappear in My love like a piece of straw thrown into a great furnace"** (*Diary*, 156). The battle between His love for the Father and our sinfulness has been finished. Jesus' Love has conquered our death (see Song 8:6-7). By His self-entrustment to the Father, He has conquered our distrust and the serpent's venom.

What does His Crucifixion have to do with eternal life? If Heaven is participation in the inner life of the Trinity, an infinite and eternal exchange of love, then in order to enter Heaven, we must learn to love as Jesus does. In other words, unless we want to love as Jesus loves, we do not really want to enter Heaven, for St. Faustina clearly identified the gate to Heaven: the pierced Heart

the Logos is to personify in history must be recognized and welcomed by a human person." Antonio Lopez, "'Blessed Is She Who Believed': Mary's Faith and the Form of Christian Existence," *Communio: International Catholic Review,* Winter 2013, doi:10.18411/a-2017-023.

of Jesus. We witness, visibly and historically, this invisible life of the Trinity displayed at Calvary, in the complete gift of self of the Son to the Father for our salvation. Calvary depicts just how strong the Love (Holy Spirit) is between the Father and the Son, and that it is infinite.

In contrast, we might imagine Heaven to be like a perpetual vacation in a resort such as Cancun, where there is no work, no responsibility, and no cares. Though we will gasp before the reality of the ocean of the Father's Mercy, Heaven is the place where there is an unending, eternal exchange of self-sacrificing Love. For this reason, the Crucifixion is the first and necessary step to enter Heaven. The Crucifixion teaches us how to love to the end, as did Jesus (see Jn 13:1). Indeed, on Judgment Day we will stand before the crucifix once again and be judged on whether we gave ourselves in love to others and to the Father as Jesus did upon the Cross.

LOVING AS JESUS DOES

Jesus gave us one commandment at the Last Supper: to love one another as He has loved us (see Jn 13:34). This commandment was not given simply as a moral requirement. Rather, it represents the goal of Jesus' life on earth: to enable us to participate in the Love of the Trinity, the Love that goes to the end: Giving one's life for one's friends (see Jn 15:13). Sacrificial love — putting the other first — is not easy, but it does bring us true happiness.

Saint Teresa of Avila defines love in this way: "When He sees a soul who loves Him greatly, He knows that soul can suffer much for Him, whereas one who loves Him little will suffer little. For my own part, I believe that love is the measure of our ability to bear crosses, whether great or small. So if you have this love, sisters, try not to let the prayers you make to so great a Lord be words of mere politeness, but brace yourselves to suffer what His Majesty desires. For if you give Him your will in any other way, you are just showing Him a jewel, making as if to give it to Him and begging Him to take it, and then, when He puts out His hand to do so, taking it back and holding on to it tightly."[193]

How exactly do we love as Jesus loves in our daily lives? We love the Father and each other by offering our jewel — our free will — undergoing our own daily crucifixion of self-denial and offering this up in union with Jesus in the Eucharist. Suffering is necessary to enter Heaven because suffering is the school of true love: "Suffering is a great grace; through suffering the soul becomes like the Savior; in suffering love becomes crystallized; the greater the suffering, the purer the love" (*Diary*, 57). For that reason, the Father will not always say "yes" to our prayers when we ask Him to spare us the Cross. Wanting Him to do so would mean that we want Him to spare us from learning true, sacrificial Love — symbolized by the Blood and Water that flow from His pierced Sacred Heart. Saint Faustina wrote: "I do not ask, Lord, that You take me down from

---

[193] *Teresa of Ávila: The Way of Perfection*, 2nd Edition (London: Thomas Baker, 1919), 192.

the cross, but I implore You to give me the strength to remain steadfast upon it" (*Diary*, 1484).

SUFFERING AS THE THERMOMETER OF LOVE

As St. Faustina wrote: "True love is measured by the thermometer of suffering" (*Diary*, 343). How does suffering teach us true love? We are all born with a predominant ego at the center of our being. Newborns are not aware of anyone else's needs. Even in their relationship with their parents, infants are consumed by their own desires: food, rest, a clean diaper, etc. As time goes on, the infant learns how to grow in awareness of others and their needs. Eventually, a mature adult learns to put the needs of others above his or her own. That is true love. Love seeks the good of the other for the sake of the other person, regardless of whether it brings us any tangible benefit. As St. Thomas Aquinas wrote: "An act of love always tends towards two things: to the good that one wills, and to the person for whom one wills it, since to love a person is to wish that person good."[194] Love means giving oneself to another — to the Father and to our neighbor. We are to give ourselves to the Father without reserve and without limit. We are to give ourselves to our neighbor with *prudent charity*, seeking the good of the other without putting ourselves in danger of sin.

To repay the Father — whom we can never fully repay — we are to love others who cannot repay us. As the Father told St. Catherine of Siena: "I require that you should love Me with the same love with which I love you. This indeed you cannot do, because I loved you without being loved. All the love which you have for Me you owe to Me, so that it is not of grace that you love Me, but because you ought to do so. While I love you of grace, and not because I owe you My love. Therefore to Me, in person, you cannot repay the love which I require of you, and I have placed you in the midst of your fellows, that you may do to them that which you cannot do to Me, that is to say, that you may love your neighbor of free grace, without expecting any return from him, and what you do to him, I count as done to Me, which My Truth showed forth when He said to Paul, My persecutor — 'Saul, Saul, why persecute you Me?' This He said, judging that Paul persecuted Him in His faithful."[195]

Jesus told St. Faustina the same: "**My daughter, in this meditation, consider the love of neighbor. Is your love for your neighbor guided by My love? Do you pray for your enemies? Do you wish well to those who have, in one way or another, caused you sorrow or offended you? Know that whatever good you do to any soul, I accept it as if you had done it to Me**" (*Diary*, 1768).

Given our limited resources and time, putting someone else's needs above our own means self-denial, and therefore suffering. Love requires that we forgo

---

[194] Saint Thomas Aquinas, *Summa Theologica*, I, q. 20, a. 1, ad. 3.
[195] Saint Catherine of Siena, *The Dialogue*, 134-35.

fulfilling some of our own needs so that someone else's might be fulfilled. Such love finds perfection in loving our enemies and forgiving those who cause us harm, precisely because doing so requires accepting suffering out of love for them.

At our birth into this world, we are egocentric. By the time of our birth into the next world, we ought to have become theocentric, with the Triune God at the center. That shift occurs only through self-denial, suffering, and crucifixion (see Mk 8:34-35). Why is such extreme suffering as crucifixion necessary? In this world, the pure love of the Father can be expressed only by the Cross — by the extreme love of the Son denying His own will and obeying the Father, regardless of how much obedience costs. Such a radical love reveals that at the center of the Son's being is not Himself, but the Father.

Some might object that such self-denial is necessary in giving up sin and even in giving up some of the good things of life, but that we must not deny ourselves completely. However, St. John of the Cross instructs us differently — that we ought not to stop denying ourselves only in external or obvious things (e.g., being silent instead of raising our voice or gossiping), but that self-denial must be present in every aspect of our being. Every aspect of our being — our entire person — must die with Christ to rise to new life with Him and become a new creation (see Rom 6:9; 2 Cor 5:17). For this reason, our trust in Him must be absolute and without reserve, for there is nothing on to which we can hold; rather, we must, by entrusting ourselves to Him without reserve, let Him hold on to us.

In the Trinity, the Father dwells in the Son, and the Son in the Father, through the bond of the Holy Spirit. This mutual indwelling is called *perichoresis,* a Greek word for "rotation," indicating how the Persons enter each other and dwell within each other. Among humans, mutual indwelling is manifested when we put others — God and neighbor — at the center of our life. By means of love, we dwell in others and others dwell in us. Consider how often we think of those whom we love! Such mutual indwelling is the effect of Love. As Aquinas taught, "It is written (1 Jn 4:16): *He that abideth in charity abideth in God, and God in him.* Now charity is the love of God. Therefore, for the same reason, every love makes the beloved to be in the lover, and vice versa."[196]

To love someone, I must take myself out of the center of my life, displace my own needs and wants, and put someone else's there. The Crucifixion is a necessary prelude to the Resurrection because it reverses what happened in Eden, when we humans placed ourselves and our own desires before the Father and His will. Remember: Sin causes us to focus on our own interests and place ourselves at the center. The serpent whispers his lies into our minds and hearts, saying that we will be happy if we take care of ourselves first and leave others to the side as we pursue our goals. The Crucifixion annihilates our old self, burdened as it is with inordinate desires that place us at the center. We crush the head of the serpent when we entrust ourselves to the Father unconditionally.

---

[196] Saint Thomas Aquinas, *Summa Theologica,* II-I, q. 28, a. 2, sed contra.

In death, we even have to give up ourselves. We cling to ourselves and our life on earth because of our fallen human nature with its residue of original sin; but death is the medicine that heals us of our sinful clinging, that we might learn to entrust ourselves entirely to our Heavenly Father. Death then raises this question: Are we our own treasure, so that we dearly want to hold onto ourselves? Jesus teaches the paradox of life, that if we attempt to hold on to it, we will lose it; if we give it away in love and with trust, we will find true life. "This likeness reveals that man, who is the only creature on earth which God willed for itself, cannot fully find himself except through a sincere gift of himself."[197] We are made in the image of the Triune God, and only by giving ourselves do we truly find ourselves — and God.

The Pierced Heart

What is the greatest proof that Jesus can be trusted? If we look at the Divine Mercy Image, we see the Blood and Water flowing from Jesus' pierced Heart. Father Rózycki suggests that the Divine Mercy Image could be painted differently to emphasize its biblical roots: Instead of Jesus Risen, the Blood and Water could be depicted gushing forth from Jesus Crucified, as happened in John 19:34. This alternative image is a lesson in the Mercy of God our Father: When the Father is pushed to His limits, as it were, by our sins, what is His response? Mercy. Jesus Crucified had already undergone His agony, the mockery, the trial, the scourging, the crowning with thorns, the carrying of the Cross, and finally the Crucifixion. After He died, the soldier pierced His Heart, and what flowed forth from His Heart? Mercy. What's in the Blood and Water? Only Mercy.

Why did Jesus permit His Heart to be pierced? Saint Catherine of Siena asked this question of the Father, and He responded: "Because My desire towards the human generation was ended, and I had finished the actual work of bearing pain and torment, and yet I had not been able to show, by finite things, because My love was infinite, how much more love I had, I wished you to see the secret of the Heart, showing it to you open, so that you might see how much more I loved than I could show you by finite pain."[198]

Jesus wanted to show us that His Love truly is infinite, that no sin of ours can exhaust it or cause Him to respond to our sins with anything other than Love and Mercy! Jesus loves us so much that He considers His Passion to be a joy: "It is a joy, a bliss, an endless delight to me that ever I suffered the Passion for thee."[199] This infinite love of Jesus conquers Satan and crushes the head of the serpent — only this extreme love can rout our enemy. Any lesser Love than this cannot conquer Satan. Love that does not entail giving oneself completely to the Father and to one's neighbor without reserve, without conditions, cannot

---

[197] *Gaudium et Spes: Pastoral Constitution on the Church in the Modern World*, in *Vatican II Documents* (Vatican City: Libreria Editrice Vaticana, 2011), n. 24.
[198] Saint Catherine of Siena, *The Dialogue*, 154-55.
[199] Julian of Norwich, *Revelations of Divine Love*, 71.

conquer the serpent. For this reason, St. Faustina calls Jesus a madman of love (see *Diary*, 124, 278).

Jesus can be trusted because His reaction to our sinfulness always remains the same: Mercy. Even if Jesus chastises us, it is a proof of His Love and Mercy (see Prov 3:12; Heb 12:6; Rev 3:19). When we cause Him immense suffering, crucify Him, and even pierce His Heart, His response remains constant: forgiveness and Mercy. This is evidenced by how Luke recounts Jesus' words of forgiveness, uttered right at the moment of crucifixion (see Lk 23:34). Mary also forgives us for crucifying her Son: "Sharing his deepest feelings, she counters the arrogant insults addressed to the crucified Messiah with forbearance and pardon, associating herself with his prayer to the Father: 'Forgive them, for they know not what they do' (Lk 23:34)."[200]

This is a challenge — and we must ask ourselves some questions. Are we trustworthy and merciful as Jesus is trustworthy and merciful? What flows forth from our hearts when we are pierced by the sins of others? Often, what flows from our hearts is a flood of bitterness, anger, hatred, unforgiveness, jealousy, and a host of other sins. We need to stand beneath Jesus' flood of Blood and Water, trusting these sins to Him, asking that He would make our hearts like His own. In this way, bathed in His Blood and Water, which we receive in Baptism, Confession, and the Holy Eucharist, we can come to allow these streams of grace to flow upon others when they hurt or injure us.

Causes of Suffering

What causes suffering? We suffer when we cannot attain something or have lost something we desire. We want so many things that we often lose sight of the one thing we want most of all: true and eternal love. That is obtained only when we divest ourselves of false substitutes for God's love. Penance is intended to empty us of the things of this world and lead us to surrender our trust in ourselves so that we can be filled with and always remain in God's love. That is the purpose of self-denial and mortification. The word "mortification" comes from the Latin *mors, mortis* ("death") and *facere* ("to cause or produce"). Mortification produces the death of unruly passions or of inordinate desires caused by sin.

Remaining in His Love means staying at Calvary with Christ on the Cross. The suffering and wounds of Christ are the physical manifestations of His Love, which conquered death. His wounds bring healing because through them — especially the wound in His Pierced Side — the Love of the Father is poured forth into our hearts. Our hearts are thirsty for that Love because we were made to receive it — but we so often reject it through sin (see Is 53:5).

How does this relate to trust? To be able to trust the Father during suffering as Jesus and Mary did, we must understand the dynamics of trust. Trust opens the door to sacrificial love, to giving oneself completely to another. Such

---

[200] Saint John Paul II, *Audiences of Pope John Paul II*. Catechesis given on April 2, 1997.

trust allows us to enter the relationship of dialogue and love. The greatest act of worship we offer the Father is to entrust ourselves entirely into His hands, as Jesus did, at death. When we die, it is not by chance or because the Father is cruel. We die, and are crucified daily with Christ, because the Father wants to rid us of all of our sinful desires and the habits by which we place ourselves in the center of the universe, and so deprive ourselves of the true life of God.

Results of Suffering

Suffering can lead to distrust and bitterness, or to trust and love. It leads to bitterness if we seek the things we no longer have or if we cannot let go of our desires. If I lose my health (and that is all I care about), I can become bitter. In contrast, suffering can lead to Love and therefore to the Father, if in place of what I have lost, I seek the one thing that always remains: the Triune God. If there is bitterness in our hearts because of suffering, we ought to remember that the Paschal Mystery must "become imprinted in the fabric of daily life,"[201] and this takes place through daily death and resurrection with the Lord Jesus. That participation in the life, death, and resurrection of Christ is salvation.

"You cannot belong to Christ unless you crucify all self-indulgent passions and desires" (Gal 5:24). We must take this teaching of St. Paul to heart. We ought not only to celebrate the Paschal Mystery, but to live it, for it is a mystery of trust. Saint Gregory of Nazianzus wrote: "So let us take our part in the Passover prescribed by the law, not in a literal way, but according to the teaching of the Gospel; not in an imperfect way, but perfectly; not only for a time, but eternally … let us join the choirs of angels in offering God upon his heavenly altar a sacrifice of praise … we must sacrifice ourselves to God, each day and in everything we do, accepting all that happens to us for the sake of the Word, imitating his passion by our sufferings, and honoring his blood by shedding our own. We must be ready to be crucified."[202]

At each moment of self-denial during our daily lives, we face a choice. Do I let go of what is precious to me and entrust myself and all I have to the Father? Or do I hold on to things, not trusting that the Father has something better in store for me? If we give ourselves completely, we allow the Paschal Mystery to "become imprinted in the fabric of daily life." Even if we die on account of such trust, we can be assured the Father will raise us to new life — just as He raised His beloved Son.

For those who trust imperfectly and cannot leave everything behind at the final moment of death, there is Purgatory. The saints who have seen Purgatory

---

[201] Cardinal Joseph Ratzinger, "Letter to the Bishops of the Catholic Church on the Pastoral Care of Homosexual Persons," October 1, 1986, accessed July 11, 2017, http://www.vatican.va/roman_curia/congregations/cfaith/documents/rc_con_cfaith_doc_19861001_homosexual-persons_en.html.
[202] Gregory of Nazianzus, Oratio 45, 23-24, from ICEL, *The Liturgy of the Hours,* Vol. 2, 392-93.

affirm that one second in Purgatory involves worse suffering than all possible sufferings here in this life! It is in our own self-interest to be rid of all our shallow, sinful desires as soon as possible. There are two reasons for this. First, worldly desires only disappoint, for they promise happiness that they do not provide. The serpent may promise us happiness if we give in to self-love and pride, but these never lead to happiness. Second, we must suffer our purification from such desires either now through penance, or in Purgatory. Purgatory is the place to purge these desires so the soul becomes empty and ready to be filled with one thing alone: the Holy Spirit. Like Shadrach, Meshach, and Abednego, we are in the fiery furnace, consumed with fire. If we trust, we will be able to withstand the flames, for Jesus is with us. But if we fail to trust, we will perish and burn (see Dan 3).

In the Sacrament of Penance, we set out on the path of conversion that, if completed, will help us enter Heaven without passing through Purgatory. The absolution given by the priest does not remedy all the disorders caused by sin, so we must also make satisfaction for and expiate our sins by penance. Such penances can include prayer, fasting, almsgiving, and acts of self-denial. Above all, we perform penance through patiently bearing our daily crosses. Through penance, we allow ourselves to be configured to Christ Crucified, to die with Him to sin, and to rise with Him to new life. Moreover, by voluntarily placing ourselves before Christ in Confession, we anticipate our personal judgment after death. If we walk the path of trust and penance in this life, we will not come under judgment or go to Purgatory when we die (see *CCC*, 1470).

The Passion of Jesus Christ is understandable, as are our own daily sufferings, only when we look at the Father as a Father of Love. In other words, suffering, sin, and the serpent can be conquered only by unconditionally trusting in a good Father who allows us to suffer, but uses our suffering for good by teaching us how to receive Love and give Love.

PERSONAL WITNESS

To illustrate this important aspect of trust — being crucified with Christ — I want to share another step of my own journey of trust. It is common throughout the seminary process to experience that doubt of wanting to live the life of the Cross, and I was no exception. In the beginning of this book, I described the doubt I felt when I was about to be ordained as a priest, but I had experienced doubt before. When I was in the Philippines as a young seminarian (22 years old), I was discerning whether to leave the Marians and enter the diocesan seminary where I was studying at the time. Due to various factors, I was experiencing a lot of suffering — internal and external — and my heart very much wanted to leave. During formation, I was taught that at times of trial I should simply kneel before the crucifix for fifteen minutes and gaze upon Jesus without saying anything in particular.

With my heart heavy, one morning I went to the chapel. I knelt. And as my mind filled with various thoughts, I began a dialogue with the Lord. "Lord, this is too much suffering for me. What do I do?" As is typical of the Lord in the Gospels, He responded with a question: "Did you not take vows?" I answered, "Yes." "And are not the vows the three nails that affix you to the Cross with Me?" Again, I answered, "Yes." "And you are complaining that your vows to Me are causing you suffering? You are complaining that you are crucified with Me?" I answered, "Yes" ... yet again.

Jesus' point was clear. I was complaining about the very thing I had promised to do: to be crucified with Christ (see Gal 2:20). How often we tell the Lord that we want to trust Him, we want to become saints, we want to love Him ... but then when the Lord answers our prayers and grants our desires, we want to escape. Saint John of the Cross warns of this attitude: God cannot fill us with His Mercy if we doubt and waver when He answers our prayers for growth in holiness and fulfillment. James teaches us the same lesson — that we must ask with faith, not with doubt.

I endured the same temptation while I was still in Steubenville, and Fr. Donald Calloway, MIC, my superior at the time, listened to my doubts and said: If you stay, you are going to stay because of your love for Our Lady. Jesus was mocked and told to come down from the Cross. He stayed on the Cross. Do you want to be like Him, or do you want to come down from the Cross? The serpent tempts us to become impatient and get down from the Cross (see Mk 15:30). We are tempted to doubt the Father's goodness because amid the storm, He seems not to be responding and even seems to want the suffering. The temptation is to think that salvation and mercy mean being saved from the Cross, rather than being saved through the Cross. How often in our daily lives do we need to look to the Lord upon the Cross! Satan is all too eager to offer us another path to happiness and suggest that we are simply crazy for wanting to be crucified with Christ.

To follow Christ, I realized I needed to be a fool for Him. As Blessed Francis Xavier Seelos wrote: "This life is full of obstacles, difficulties for one whose purpose is the close following of Christ. O how few start on this road of the following of Christ! And for this reason it may sometimes appear that the true Christian life is something excessive. Our poor human nature may even call it at times a stupidity to despise a pleasure for God. It is as if somebody said to us: 'How stupid you are to deny yourselves all innocent pleasures which others enjoy without scruple of conscience. Do you only want to go to Heaven? O what a dry, uninteresting form of existence!' To such whisperings of the devil, you must never pay attention."[203]

As the serpent tempted me with a more appealing life that didn't include such a heavy cross, he will be likely to tempt you with the same thought: "How stupid to deny yourself so constantly! Does God not want you to be happy? Seek

---

[203] Blessed Francis Xavier Seelos, CSsR, "Wise Words of Francis Xavier Seelos."

happiness; enjoy life; don't worry about the Cross." But to trust in the Lord means to entrust everything to Him and to "only want to go to Heaven."

The serpent waits to lead us down the wrong path, but Mary takes us by the hand to lead us home to Heaven. Although the Father will not let us escape the Cross, He is not indifferent to our suffering, nor does He delight to see us in pain. We suffer on the Cross, but Mary stands by us and teaches us not to escape the pain, but to entrust ourselves with Jesus to the Father. As Mary told St. Faustina, amid her dark night and intense suffering: **"I know how much you suffer, but do not be afraid. I share with you your suffering, and I shall always do so"** (*Diary*, 25).

CHAPTER 21

Trust at the Cross with Our Lady

"Standing by the cross of Jesus were his mother ..." (Jn 19:25).

At the Annunciation, the Archangel Gabriel promised Mary that her Son would reign on the throne of David forevermore (see Lk 1:32-33). We do not know whether Mary expected that Jesus' royal throne would be the Cross,[204] but she was no doubt familiar with the Song of the Suffering Servant from Isaiah 53 and listened intently to the words of her own Son, who foretold His suffering and death. Nevertheless, standing at the foot of the Cross, Mary witnessed the seeming negation of the words of the Archangel, because on the wood of that Cross, her Son hung in agony as one condemned. "He was despised and rejected by men; a man of sorrows ... he was despised, and we esteemed him not" (see Is 53:3–5). As St. John Paul II wrote, "How great, how heroic, then, is the obedience of faith shown by Mary in the face of God's 'unsearchable judgments'! How completely she 'abandons herself to God' without reserve, offering the 'full assent of the intellect and the will' to him whose 'ways are inscrutable' (see Rom 11:33)! And how powerful is the action of grace in her soul, how all-pervading is the influence of the Holy Spirit and His light and power!"[205]

We recall also that at the Visitation, Elizabeth named Mary *he Pisteusasa*: "Blessed Are You who believed." Saint John Paul II offers his interpretation: "This blessing reaches its full meaning when Mary stands beneath the Cross of her Son." He continues and says that this happened "not without a divine plan," and that by "suffering deeply with her only-begotten Son and joining herself with her maternal spirit to his sacrifice, lovingly consenting to the immolation of the victim to whom she had given birth," Mary "faithfully preserved her union with her Son even to the Cross."[206] Their union, based upon faith and trust, was blessed indeed.

At Calvary, Mary, as any good mother would be, was probably praying with all her heart that her Son would be spared death, just as Jesus had asked this of His Father in the Garden of Gethsemane (see Lk 22:42). We imagine that she was praying constantly and yet finding no answer to her prayers. She watched her Son suffer increasingly painful torments and witnessed Him crucified upon

---

[204] "The Cross is his throne, from which he draws the world to himself. From this place of total self-sacrifice, from this place of truly divine love, he reigns as the true king in his own way — a way that neither Pilate nor the members of the Sanhedrin had been able to comprehend." Ratzinger, *Jesus of Nazareth;* Part 2, Holy Week, 211-12.

[205] Saint John Paul II, *Redemptoris Mater,* n. 18.

[206] Ibid.

the Cross. As she looked upon the naked Jesus, the words of the angel seemed to be false, but Mary did not doubt. She did not downplay the real horror and drama of His human suffering. She did not trust her senses more than the Word of God, nor did she presume to have all the answers.

Mary also did not flee as most of the apostles did (see Mk 14:50). She was concerned, not about herself, but only about her Son. By fleeing, the apostles revealed their priorities — they were concerned mostly about themselves and their own lives. Mary did not rebel against the will of the Father to prevent Jesus' Passion. She did not use the tactics of the serpent, who proposes ways to avoid the Father's will when He asks us to accept the Cross with His Son. No. Mary accepted and surrendered her will to the Father's will in silent faith and trust.

This surrender required her complete self-emptying, in participation with Christ's own kenosis (see Phil 2:7). If we are to truly participate in Mary's faith and trust, we must pass through a similar kenosis. "Through this faith Mary is perfectly united with Christ in his self-emptying. At the foot of the Cross, Mary shares in the shocking mystery of this self-emptying. This is perhaps the deepest 'kenosis' of faith in human history. Through faith the Mother shares in the death of her Son, in his redeeming death; but in contrast with the faith of the disciples who fled, hers was far more enlightened."[207] Kenosis is necessary to receive the fullness of the Holy Spirit, the gift conferred in the Blood and Water at Calvary; at the Resurrection, when Jesus breathes upon the apostles; and at Pentecost, when the Holy Spirit descends upon the Church.

Mary did not go back on her *fiat*, the full surrender she gave at the Annunciation. She remained faithful to the Father's will to the very end. As with Mary, all we can do during suffering is surrender, trust, and wait until the Word of God is fulfilled. We are to imitate Mary's dignity and strength, as well as "her unfailing constancy and extraordinary courage in facing suffering. In the tragic events of Calvary, Mary is sustained by faith, strengthened during the events of her life and especially during Jesus' public life."[208]

What did Mary do? "There she stood, in keeping with the divine plan, enduring with her only begotten Son the intensity of his suffering, joining herself with his sacrifice in her mother's heart, and lovingly consenting to the immolation of this victim, born of her."[209] She simply stood by her Son at the Cross, compassionately sharing in His suffering. The word "compassion" comes from the Latin *cum* ("with") and *passio* ("suffer"). As St. John Paul II said: "[I]n her heart reverberates all that Jesus suffers in body and soul, emphasizing her willingness to share in her Son's redeeming sacrifice and to join her own maternal suffering to his priestly offering … her consent to Jesus' immolation is not passive acceptance but a genuine act of love, by which she offers her Son as

---

[207] Ibid.
[208] Saint John Paul II, *Audiences of Pope John Paul II*. Catechesis given on April 2, 1997.
[209] *Lumen Gentium*, n. 58.

a 'victim' of expiation for the sins of all humanity."[210] With unfathomable trust and love, Mary offered her Son for us sinners, accepting that she would lose Him through the Crucifixion, rather than consenting that we should lose our souls in Hell. She willingly offered up her Son for you and me, so that our sins might be forgiven and our souls redeemed.

The experience of interior darkness and abandonment by God that St. John of the Cross called the "dark night of the soul" is a share in Christ's suffering during His Passion. Mary lived through her own dark night at Calvary, where only sheer faith and trust could provide sufficient strength to endure it. She did not doubt the Father's plan, did not become angry at the Father, and did not presume to know better than God. She humbly submitted herself to His plan while pouring out her heart and maternal pain, trusting that the Father would not allow her Son's death to be the last word (see Jas 4:7-8). When we pass through such trials, whether we are crucified with Christ or are witnessing the suffering of another, all we can do at times is simply look upon Mary, speechless. But it is enough to seek refuge under her Immaculate Heart, offering up all that we (or others) suffer with love, knowing that she perfects what is lacking in our sacrifice.

With her nearby, we will be able to heed the counsel of Blessed Michael Sopocko: "Let us trust God in all our needs, temporal and eternal — in all our sufferings, dangers, and derelictions. Let us trust Him, even when it seems as though He Himself has abandoned us; when He withholds His consolations, leaves our prayers unanswered, crushes us beneath a heavy cross. It is then that we should trust God most, for this is the time of trial, the testing time, through which every soul must pass."[211]

Distrust and pride often impede our surrender to and trust in Divine Providence. The assumption that in this broken, sinful world *we* know how to manage things better than an infinitely merciful, loving, and wise Father is prideful and a major cause of our rebellion in the face of suffering. Humility is a prerequisite for trust because as finite creatures, we cannot comprehend the Father's infinite wisdom. We can only trust in our Father's goodness, knowing that even if we cannot understand why He permitted such evils, we can trust that the Father can bring good out of them, as He brought us salvation through the suffering of the Cross. Because Mary was humble, she could trust, and only through such humble trust will we be able to remain on the Cross with Christ, with Mary our side. As Mother Teresa is known to have said, "God does not require that we be successful [but] only that we be faithful." [212] I would add: especially during suffering.

---

[210] Saint John Paul II, *Audiences of Pope John Paul II*. Catechesis given on April 2, 1997.

[211] Blessed Sopocko, *The Mercy of God in His Works*, Vol. 3, 180.

[212] Jessica Harris, "Faithful, Not Successful," Catholic News Agency, accessed July 11, 2017, http://www.catholicnewsagency.com/cw/post.php?id=564.

LETTING GO

In the film *The Passion of the Christ*, Mary clenched her hands, full of rocks and dirt, while kneeling before her Son's Cross. Looking up at Jesus, she opened her hands and let go of the rocks and dirt. Her hands were empty, showing her surrender. In her emptiness, she did not cling to the earth or pursue the fulfillment of the normal human desires of a mother. She did not hold on to the rocks with which to "stone" the Father because He had handed His Son over to death. Instead, she opened her emptiness and her misery to the Mercy and Love of the Father in the Blood and Water that poured forth from the Sacred Heart.

By opening her hands in surrender, Mary uttered her "Amen" once again, entrusting herself to the Father and His plan. Her "amen" is not spoken in passive submission or in resigned sadness. No. Mary's "Yes" is "radiant with trusting hope in the mysterious future, begun with the death of her crucified Son."[213] And it is her "amen" at Calvary that definitively crushes the head of the serpent, for she hopes against all hope (see Rom 4:18). "Mary's hope at the foot of the Cross contains a light stronger than the darkness that reigns in many hearts: in the presence of the redeeming Sacrifice, the hope of the Church and of humanity is born in Mary."[214]

Mary did not trust her intellect to explain what was happening, did not employ her willpower to stop it, and did not wallow in her own emotions of sorrow and pain as a mother. She trusted in the Word of God, walked faithfully on her pilgrimage, and lived in faith, just as we must do: "Thus the Blessed Virgin advanced in her pilgrimage of faith, and faithfully persevered in her union with her Son unto the cross."[215]

BELIEVING BY FAITH WHAT WE DO NOT SEE

In contrast, Mary Magdalene could not let go. Her world was imploding and, like the Blessed Virgin Mary, she could not make heads or tails of all that had happened that day. Her sorrow gave way to despair because she did not trust the Lord's promise that He would rise from the dead (see Mk 10:34). Her sorrow clouded her trust — a lesson for us to be on guard against giving in to sorrow. This is a lesson that St. Faustina learned as well: "I understood that I should not give in to such sorrows" (*Diary*, 129). When we forget the truth by failing to cling to the Lord's words, we may believe the lies of the enemy and make our suffering even worse. The Holy Spirit is present during times of suffering to strengthen us with the consolation of the truth, but the evil spirits — the serpents — are present also to lead us astray by whispering lies. Their most basic lie is that suffering is all there is, it will not end, it has no meaning, and therefore we should give up our "hope against hope" (Rom 4:18). But that hope is our

---

[213] Saint John Paul II, *Audiences of Pope John Paul II*. Catechesis on April 9, 1997.
[214] Ibid.
[215] *Lumen Gentium*, n. 58.

anchor during the storm and assures us that no suffering is wasted when it is united to Christ Crucified (see Heb 6:19).

The Gospels do not record any appearance of the Risen Jesus to His mother, Mary, but she knew in faith that the Lord would rise from the dead, just as He had promised. She needed no proof of the Word of the Lord; she simply trusted! On the other hand, Mary Magdalene's excess of sorrow was most evident in the immediate aftermath of the Resurrection. It was she who received the first appearance of the Risen Jesus, but she could not recognize our Lord (see Jn 20:15) because she was looking for the Jesus whom she had known during His earthly life. She could not let Him die and rise from the dead. She was looking for the Jesus who had died, and wasn't immediately open to the Jesus who had risen from the dead, to hope against hope! She could not entrust Jesus to the Father, as the Mother of God did, and was weeping and unable to fully experience the joy of the Resurrection. Similarly, we cannot enjoy the glory of the Resurrection if we do not fully surrender and walk the Way of the Cross with faith.

The Blessed Virgin Mary, on the other hand, remained still and silent, for her strength was in patient trust (see Is 30:15). She could trust because she held on to the truth as she pondered all the events of Christ's life in her heart (see Lk 2:51) and sought their deeper meaning in light of the Word of God. Every event is a *word* of the Father; in Hebrew, *dā·ḇār* ("word") also means "event."[216] We are called, like Mary, to listen to the words of our Father that come to us in the events of our daily lives. We can understand these words only in light of the Word of God that comes to us in Scripture. Without this interplay between words/events and the Word, we will not understand the Father's plan for our lives. If we seek the words of the Father in light of His Word, then, like Mary, we will remain firm and stand erect at Calvary. If we do not, we will be shaken in our faith, as were the apostles and other disciples who fled from Calvary.

Saint Augustine wrote, "Faith is to believe what we do not see; the reward of this faith is to see what we believe."[217] Pious Catholic tradition holds that Jesus appeared to the Blessed Virgin Mary even before He appeared to Mary Magdalene.[218] By waiting in patient trust, the Mother of God received her reward — the sight of Jesus Christ risen from the dead. All that the Lord allows in our life is intended to purify us and strengthen our faith so that we too will

---

[216] "דָּבָר (dā·ḇār) : happening, event, matter, thing, something, anything, i.e., an event to which one may refer (Num 31:16)." Swanson, *Dictionary of Biblical Languages with Semantic Domains: Hebrew* (Old Testament).

[217] "Augustine," *Lapham's Quarterly*, accessed July 11, 2017, http://www.laphamsquarterly.org/contributors/augustine.

[218] "He appeared to the Virgin Mary. This, although it is not said in Scripture, is included in saying that He appeared to so many others, because Scripture supposes that we have understanding, as it is written: 'Are you also without understanding?'" St. Ignatius of Loyola, *The Spiritual Exercises of St. Ignatius of Loyola*, 160.

be prepared for the reward of faith: the vision of Christ risen from the dead (see 1 Pet 1:6-7).

We cannot skip from Good Friday to Easter Sunday, however. The time of suffering and waiting didn't end with the Crucifixion. We must spend Holy Saturday with Our Lady — the day dedicated to Mary because that is the day when she, as Daughter Zion, the greatest descendant and fulfillment of all the people Israel in their hope for the Messiah across the centuries, waited in trusting faith for her Son's Resurrection. On Saturday, we honor Mary and ponder with her the life of Jesus. Not surprisingly, at Fatima Our Lady asked us to spend 15 minutes with her on the First Saturdays of each month to meditate on the mysteries of the Rosary, which focus on her memories of her Son. Saint John Paul II describes the beautiful meaning of the Rosary: "Mary lived with her eyes fixed on Christ, treasuring his every word: 'She kept all these things, pondering them in her heart' (Lk 2:19; see 2:51). Memories of Jesus were impressed upon her heart so that the various moments of her life at her Son's side were always with her. Those memories were the 'Rosary' which she lived and thus recited throughout her earthly life. Even now, amid the joyful songs of the heavenly Jerusalem, the reasons for her thanksgiving and praise remain unchanged and they inspire her maternal concern for the pilgrim Church, in which she continues to relate her personal account of the Gospel. Mary constantly sets before the faithful the 'mysteries' of her Son, with the desire that their contemplation will release all their saving power. In the recitation of the Rosary, the Christian community enters into contact with the memories and the contemplative gaze of Mary."[219] The Rosary is an excellent way to live one's life in the light of the Word of God.

---

[219] Saint John Paul II, "*Rosarium Virginis Mariae: on the Most Holy Rosary*," n. 11.

CHAPTER 22

Waiting in Trust for the Answer

*"Wait for the Lord; be strong, and let your heart take courage;
yes, wait for the Lord!"* (Ps 27:14).

We can join Mary at the Cross when we wait before the Blessed Sacrament during times of suffering, as St. Faustina did (see *Diary,* 73, 226, 1037). By resting on His Sacred Heart, we will find true consolation and comfort: **"Now, rest your head on My bosom, on My heart, and draw from it strength and power for these sufferings because you will find neither relief nor help nor comfort anywhere else. Know that you will have much, much to suffer, but don't let this frighten you; I am with you"** (*Diary,* 36). Sometimes prolonged and persevering prayer is necessary if we are to receive that consolation, as St. Faustina also describes: "There are times in life when the soul finds comfort only in profound prayer. Would that souls knew how to persevere in prayer at such times. This is very important" (*Diary,* 860).

Mary knew that the Holy Spirit would bring her true consolation and peace. One of the Holy Spirit's names in Greek, *Paraclete,* can be translated as "Comforter." The Greek word for consolation and encouragement is *paraklēsis,* and the English words "consolation" and "comfort" both come from Latin words that mean "to strengthen." *Comfort* is from the Latin *cum,* "with" + *fors/fortis,* "strength." Thus the Holy Spirit provides comfort or strength during suffering. The very words tell us that the Holy Spirit is given so that we might have the strength to faithfully suffer with Christ (see 1 Pet 4:14), and that comfort is offered according to the measure of our suffering.

Jesus promises this comfort to those who weep in times of suffering and mourn over the sins of the world (see Mt 5:4). Such consolation comes when we turn, not to creatures, but to the Holy Spirit for help in times of suffering (see *Diary,* 279).

Moreover, as St. Faustina describes her own feelings: "Amid the greatest torments, I fix the gaze of my soul upon Jesus Crucified; I do not expect help from people, but place my trust in God. In His fathomless mercy lies all my hope" (*Diary,* 681). In the difficult moments of our lives, our strength and hope flow from the unfathomable Mercy of the Father. This does not preclude the Holy Spirit from working in and through other people and all of creation to shower His Mercy upon us and help us; however, we must remember that other people, *as fallen sinners,* can provide only *some,* not *all,* of the help we need. In moments of need, we must turn to the Crucified One, as well as to those who help us to remain faithful to Him.

If we desire to have others help us, we must remember where we will find such help: at the Cross. There, we find the consolation of the Holy Spirit in Christ's Mystical Body, the Church, just as Mary found some solace in St. John and St. Mary Magdalene at the foot of the Cross, for Christ never abandons us at Calvary. He is present to us through others who help us, as Our Lady herself helped our Lord by her presence and prayer. When we seek help from others, then, we ought to seek help from those who will bring us to the Pierced Heart of Jesus — and not take us away from it.

Nevertheless, in moments of suffering, we ought to keep in mind the words of St. Faustina: "I have come to know that every soul would like to have divine comforts, but is by no means willing to forsake human comforts, whereas these two things cannot be reconciled" (*Diary*, 1443). In other words, self-seeking and self-giving cannot be reconciled, or as St. Paul writes, the Spirit and the flesh are opposed (see Gal 5:17). Hence, because Mary did not give in to the serpent's suggestions to seek false comforts, she was filled with the true comfort and strength of the Holy Spirit as given in and through the Church.

WAITING WITH CONFIDENCE

We express our trust in the Father by waiting upon His Word, for He fulfills His promises: "Wait for the Lord; be strong, and let your heart take courage; yes, wait for the Lord!" (Ps 27:14). In his book *A Father Who Keeps His Promises*, Scott Hahn tells a story about a child under the rubble of a school shattered by an earthquake. The child's father had always promised his son that he would be there for him, and so he went digging in the rubble of his son's school, even though all seemed lost. When his son's classroom was uncovered after three days of digging, he heard his son's voice say, "See, I told you my father was coming!"[220] That is the attitude we need to have — confidence to wait patiently for the moment the Father chooses to fulfill His promises. As Isaiah prophesied: "It will be said on that day, 'Behold, this is our God; we have waited for him, that he might save us. This is the Lord; we have waited for him; let us be glad and rejoice in his salvation'" (Is 25:9). The prayer "Jesus, I trust in You" is so important because it reminds us that Jesus will fulfill His promises in due time — in His time.

Waiting with Mary at the tomb of Jesus gives us an immeasurable exposure to the greatest human example of trust. Her patience is impossible to fathom. The word "patience" comes from the Latin *pati*, "to suffer."[221] Patience is the virtue of being able to endure suffering with abiding trust that, in the Father's timing, the suffering will cease: "If you seek patience, you will find no better example than the cross. Great patience occurs in two ways: either when one

---

[220] Scott Hahn, *A Father Who Keeps His Promises: God's Covenant Love in Scripture* (Cincinnati, Ohio: St. Anthony Messenger Press, 1998), 13-14.

[221] "pătĭentĭa, ae, f. [patior], the quality of bearing, suffering, or enduring, patience, endurance." Lewis and Short, *Harper's Latin Dictionary*, 1314.

patiently suffers much, or when one suffers things which one is able to avoid and yet does not avoid. Christ endured much on the cross, and did so patiently because when he suffered he did not try to avoid — he was led like a sheep to the slaughter and he did not open his mouth. Therefore, Christ's patience on the cross was great."[222]

Patience is required every time we do not get *what* we want, *as* we want it, or *when* we want it. With patient trust, we will no longer be unhappy with anything the Father permits, for *all* He permits will be a joy to us. To grow in patience, it is helpful to thank the Father for those times when others provide moments to practice it! As the Carmelite St. Miriam of Jesus Crucified said: "Always remember to love your neighbor; always prefer the one who tries your patience, who tests your virtue, because with her you can always merit: suffering is Love; the Law is Love."[223]

Whenever things do not go our way, we need to remember that the Lord will judge our life not by our successes, but by our love and patience. When St. Faustina was concerned that her spiritual director, Blessed Michael Sopocko, was suffering too much as a consequence of his work with her, Jesus told her: **"Write that by day and by night My gaze is fixed upon him and I permit these adversities in order to increase his merit. I do not reward for good results but for the patience and hardship undergone for My sake"** (*Diary*, 86). The Lord indeed gazes upon us and knows the adversities we undergo. He allows them so that our merit might increase along with our patience in adversity — the proof of our love for Him.

An easy way to practice patience is to repeat Mary's words at the Annunciation: "Amen! Let it be done to me according to *your* word." Each time something happens that spoils our plans, causes us difficulty, or places a cross upon our shoulders, let us give thanks for the opportunity to grow in patience through such suffering, for the two — patience and suffering — always go together. In a word, our trust is proven by patience, which in turn is proven by gratitude to the Father for *everything* —without exception.

IMPATIENCE, ANGER, AND MEEKNESS

However, even with the best of intentions, we may sometimes fail to be patient, and our feelings may take control. As an emotion, anger is not a sin. There are times when anger can be justified — as when the Lord Himself cast out the money changers in the Temple (see Mt 21:12-17). In our own times there is righteous anger that seeks to redress the wrongs of social injustice and come to the defense of victims. However, for such anger to be righteous, it must be based upon love, meaning that the anger must be an expression of God's Love.

---

[222] Saint Thomas Aquinas, *Collatio 6 Super Credo in Deum,* in ICEL, *The Liturgy of the Hours,* Vol. 3, 1335-336.
[223] "Saintly Quotes," accessed July 11, 2017, http://www.catholictradition.org/Saints/saintly-quotes13.htm.

When the Father is portrayed as angry in the Bible, the point is not that God is emotional, but that the Father's Love can sometimes be felt as anger: He strongly opposes evil and seeks to root it out.

For us, however, our anger can become sinful when our hearts are hardened by resentment and hate, especially when anger is an expression of our rebellion against the Father's will. Such anger is built, not upon Love or Mercy, but upon hatred. Often we become angry when things do not go our way, or the way we think they should go. We must learn to direct that anger toward the offense and not toward the offender. How vastly different we are from Jesus, who, without complaint, embraced the Cross! How little we trust that the crosses imposed by others are part of the Father's plan for our salvation! There are numerous proverbs in Scripture against anger, encouraging us not to let our anger become sinful and not to let it lead us to distrust the Father (see Prov 14:29, 15:1, 15:18, 16:32, 19:11, 22:24, 29:11; see also Ps 7:11, 37:8-9). Jesus Himself warns us against such anger (see Mt 5:22; see also Eph 4:26-31; Jas 1:19-20; Col 3:8).

The opposite of patience is, of course, *impatience*: "Let it be done according to *my* word, *my* will" — the primary manifestation of which is unrighteous *anger*. When we are impatient with others, it may be not because of the evil they have committed, but because we are unwilling to carry the cross they impose upon us through their faults or actions. In those moments, we ought to remember the second station of the Way of the Cross, when Jesus accepts and carries His Cross. In *The Passion of the Christ,* the two thieves fight against the Roman soldiers who impose their crosses upon their shoulders. The soldiers have to tie the crosses to their arms with a rope. Jesus does not fight. He does not even wait for the soldiers to impose the Cross upon Him. He kneels and embraces the Cross while kissing it.

This is true patience: Jesus willingly undergoes His Passion. It seems that Pilate, the Jewish leaders, and the soldiers have control, but Jesus is actually the one in control. Nothing is forced upon Him. He willingly carries the Cross, as Eucharistic Prayer II reminds us at Mass. Jesus "entered willingly into his Passion." This willingness is marked by the constant repetition in the Gospels that for much of His public ministry, it was not yet Jesus' hour to suffer and die. The hour for His death was not appointed by men, nor by Satan. His hour was appointed by the Father (see Jn 7:30). We always ought to remember this when we lose control of our lives and seem to drown amid suffering and evil — that although things may happen that surprise us, they are never a surprise to the Father, who organizes everything, even the evil that happens, according to His will to bring about good.

How then do we explain the Father's anger and wrath? The Father's anger is His love directed toward our sinfulness. His love becomes anger or wrath to remove evil from our lives by means of discipline or punishment; it is other-centered. Our anger is too often directed toward overcoming obstacles to achieving our desired outcome; it is self-centered. Patience is the art of waiting so that the Father's will is fulfilled. Such waiting requires trusting that the Father will act in due time. According to St. Thomas Aquinas, *wrath* is a virtue, but requires the tempering of our emotions so that our anger motivates us to correct the evil at hand rather than merely leading us to self-indulgence, to pouring out a flood of emotions that brings more harm.

What is distinct about the Father's wrath is that His anger is always connected to His Mercy and Love, whereas our anger is often connected to selfishness, pride, bitterness, and lack of forgiveness. Looking upon the evil we have done, Jesus desires to correct it. But notice how He goes about it: He takes our sins upon His own shoulders. He does not tell us to correct the evil on our own, unaided. He takes our infirmities upon Himself because only He, our Savior, can heal us by His wounds (see Is 53:5).

With His Mercy in mind, think about how often we do not fulfill Jesus' commandment to love one another as He has loved us (see Jn 13:34). We refuse to carry the sins of others or to bear their burdens (see Gal 6:2) because we flag in our trust in the Father's Providence. Our impatience with the weaknesses and sins of others drives us to be like the Roman soldiers on the Way of the Cross. When Jesus fell, instead of assisting Him to rise, the soldiers scourged, beat, and mocked Him further, demanding that He rise on His own.

How often do we, in our impatience, look down on those who have fallen into sin and are unable to arise! We fail to see in them Christ weighed down with His Cross, and instead mock them, scourge them, and leave them to continue their path of trust alone. We must remember that we cannot get out of our sins on our own. We all need a Savior, and Jesus uses our hands and arms to lift up the fallen and the weary. When countless brothers and sisters fall under their crosses, He asks us to be like Simon of Cyrene, willingly taking their crosses upon ourselves.

The fruit of such patience is *meekness,* the ability to endure an injury with patience and without resentment. It can be very helpful in times of impatience and anger to repeat the prayer from the Litany to the Sacred Heart: "O Jesus, meek and humble of heart, make my heart like unto your own Heart!" By pausing to pray, we can remember that the Lord is in control, and we need to surrender and listen before acting. In her *Diary,* St. Faustina often wrote of the need for silence, particularly in relationships (see *Diary,* 477).

Saint Faustina also asked the Lord to heal her tongue, so that the same tongue which receives Jesus in Holy Communion would not harm Jesus in His Body, the Church: "When I receive Holy Communion I entreat and beg the Savior to heal my tongue, that I may never fail in love of neighbor" (*Diary,* 590).

Pride can impel us to react strongly and swiftly, not pondering the Father's will, but acting on our own. One of the greatest ways to grow in humility — the soil necessary for trust to grow — is to learn to guard our silence when things do not go our way or we are ridiculed or misjudged (see *Diary,* 1164). By keeping silent, we show our trust before the Lord, having confidence that He sees our situation and pain, and will come to our aid (see *Diary,* 1701). If others abuse our goodness, as they abused the Lord during His Passion, then we are in good company!

We ought to use the words of our mouth to express our confident praise of the Father, as did Mary in the Magnificat, rather than imposing bitter criticism and judgment on our brothers and sisters. "With [our tongue] we bless the Lord and Father, and with it we curse men, who are made in the likeness of God. From the same mouth come blessing and cursing. My brethren, this ought not to be so" (Jas 3:9-10). Saint James even goes so far as to write: "If anyone thinks he is religious, and does not bridle his tongue but deceives his heart, this man's religion is vain" (Jas 1:26). The same is true of trust: If anyone thinks he trusts in Jesus and does not bridle his tongue, this man's trust is in vain.

ON SUFFERING AND ABANDONMENT

Suffering enables us to be more closely united with Jesus. Saint Faustina tells us: "If the angels were capable of envy, they would envy us for two things: one is the receiving of Holy Communion, and the other is suffering" (*Diary,* 1804). Ask yourself some important questions now: Do I approach my suffering and daily crosses as willingly and joyfully as I approach Holy Communion? Do I trust and believe that Jesus is hidden under what looks like bread in the Eucharist, and therefore also trust and believe that He is hidden in my daily crosses?

Saint Faustina also writes: "A soul in love with God and immersed in Him approaches her duties with the same dispositions as she does Holy Communion and carries out the simplest tasks with great care, under the loving gaze of God" (*Diary,* 890). Am I grateful to Jesus for giving me a share in the Cross, as much as I am for giving me Himself? Jesus cannot be separated from the Cross that leads to the Resurrection. If I receive Him in the Eucharist, I receive Jesus Crucified and Risen. Am I willing to receive Jesus Crucified, hidden in my brothers and sisters, weighed down by their crosses (see Rom 15:7)?

In Holy Communion, we are called to accept even the heaviest cross of our suffering and join it to that of Christ Crucified, accepting this suffering with the same appreciation as our greatest blessing: Jesus Himself in the Eucharist. There are times, however, when complaining about our suffering feels like the only thing we can do to cope, and the ideals set before us seem unattainable — particularly our calling to follow the example of Jesus Himself, who commanded us to be perfect as the Father is perfect (see Mt 5:48). This can especially seem to be the case regarding suffering perfectly. Some of the phrases the saints use in their writings, including those of St. Faustina and St. Catherine, may leave us wondering whether we are ever justified in complaining about our suffering. The example of Mary Immaculate is beautiful and inspiring, but we wonder how we can ever live up to it.

Even though we have no record of her complaining aloud to others, we can be sure that she poured out her heart to the Father, expressing herself in the words of the many psalms of lament that cry out to Him for help and mercy in the midst of suffering. In her silence, she trusted in the Lord and waited upon Him for salvation. Her complaints, however, did not close her heart to the Father in bitterness, but rather opened her up to expect His Mercy.

If anyone had a reason to murmur and become bitter over all the suffering and obstacles placed in her life, it would be Mary. We call her "most blessed among women," and rightly so, but would we recognize her life as blessed if we saw it being lived out before us? Let us consider some details of her life for a moment. Her parents appear to have had difficulty having children. She grew up in a country dominated by Roman occupiers. At around the age of 12, she became pregnant through no natural cause, experiencing the confusion of St. Joseph and possibly many others. While heavily pregnant, she had to make a long journey to a town where there was no room for her to give birth indoors; instead she had to deliver God's Son in a stable and bed Him in a manger. After giving birth, she was forced to flee to a foreign country (Egypt) and then had to leave everything again to return to Nazareth. She lived in poverty, most likely in a home made from a cave.

Little notice was taken of Mary during her earthly lifetime. There's barely any mention in the Gospels of her life with Jesus when He was a child and young man in Nazareth. During His public life, He did not allow her immediate access to Him such as she had had in Nazareth; He reminded her of the new dynamics of their relationship. Imagine the pain that must have seared her Heart when she sought to talk to Jesus and could not draw near to Him whom she loved so much. She followed Jesus to Calvary, where she witnessed her only Son being stripped naked, scourged, mocked, spat upon, crowned with thorns, and crucified. She suffered the loss of her only Son and of her husband, Joseph, who was not at the Cross because he had predeceased his foster Son. Jesus rose from the dead, only to leave Mary once more, 40 days later. She would not see Him again until she herself entered Heaven. Such was Mary's pilgrimage of faith.

THE WORD FULFILLED

That does not sound like a very "blessed" life, so why do we say that it was? Mary is "blessed among all women" because she is the Mother of Christ, and she is "most blessed," not because she gave human flesh to Jesus, but because, as Elizabeth states, she believed. Mary's journey toward God began at her Immaculate Conception and took its definitive shape at the Annunciation, and her trust kept her united to the Lord to the very end. Her obedience, often heroic, enabled the Word promised her to be fulfilled. Through her trust, Mary converted into blessings all the curses, trials, and crosses that she faced. This is the mystery of our Christian faith: transforming evil into good. We allow the Father to draw evil out of good through our trust. We allow the Father to fulfill His promises to us by giving Him our trust and obedience, for these conquer the serpent and crush his head. Without such trust, evil simply remains evil and will spread like a contagious disease, but as Christians we have an antidote, an antivirus: trust.

Mary's Immaculate Conception is most visibly displayed at Calvary. Standing beside her Son, she was washed in spirit with His Blood and Water. The crucifix I gaze upon here at the Our Lady of Mercy Oratory on the grounds of the National Shrine of The Divine Mercy displays Jesus Crucified with Mary by His side, holding a chalice to collect His Blood and Water. Already bathed in this Blood and Water at her Immaculate Conception, Mary was preserved from all stain of sin. This gift of the Holy Spirit is one that she had to keep aflame throughout her life. While Eve was immaculate at the moment of her creation, as well, she failed through disobedience and distrust. In contrast, Mary always walked in the grace given to her at her conception. Mary's unfailing faith and trust precede and enable our own.

Indeed, Mary remained faithful when so many did not because she never doubted the Father's Mercy, and she continued to trust even when so many others failed — notably the apostles. By our faith and trust, we participate in the great mystery of Mary — the mystery of the Immaculate Conception. This mystery is sometimes narrowed down to one historical moment — the moment when Mary was conceived without original sin — but that is much too limited. The mystery of the Immaculate Conception is the great Mercy and Love of the Father — the Holy Spirit — that pours itself out upon Mary in the Blood and Water of Jesus' Sacred Heart, and through Mary and in the Church's Sacraments, this same Blood and Water pours itself upon us.

The mystery of the Immaculate Conception is the Holy Spirit, burning within the Immaculate Heart of Mary like a fire, a fire never extinguished by pain, suffering, or sin. The fire of the Holy Spirit burned brightly and grew ever brighter amid Mary's trials and difficulties, which for her were only tinder to make the fire grow. This fire of the Holy Spirit shone forth in her "amen" to Christ's immolation at Calvary.

TRIUMPH OF THE IMMACULATE HEART

Does this mean that Mary was immune to suffering? No. I remember being in Rome, standing in front of Michelangelo's Pietà at St. Peter's Basilica. A mother turned to me and asked, "How could she do it?" Of all the statues of Our Lady, this Pietà is perhaps the most famous because it epitomizes, at one and the same time, the greatness and the sorrow of Mary. Mary has lost everything at that moment, yet by her faith she remains united with her Son, who, though physically dead, is still alive — for death could not conquer the Word made flesh.

We also wonder how Mary did it. How did she trust? It is hard for us to comprehend Mary because she is immaculately conceived and radically different from us in her way of thinking, acting, and feeling. But Mary did not deny her emotions, and she undoubtedly felt sorrow. As St. Bernard of Clairvaux stated, she is the Queen of Martyrs: She passed through more suffering than any of us could possibly imagine.[224] What was her secret? How was she able to feel the full weight of suffering and yet still persevere in her trust? Mary allowed her Heart to be pierced.

In our lack of trust, we assume that suffering and death are worse than sin. But Mary's Immaculate Heart revealed something different: a decisive choice to accept death and whatever suffering would come in order never to sin, in order always to remain perfectly united to God. Mary's Immaculate Heart represents a triumph of trust over distrust at the moment of total darkness and doubt. This was the triumph of the Immaculate Heart at Calvary 2,000 years ago. Trust that flees from the Cross cannot step upon the serpent. Trust that has a limit cannot crush Satan's head. No. Only Mary's unlimited trust triumphs over Satan, and our task as Christians is to share in her unlimited trust *today*, and crush Satan's head again *today*.

Is this triumph glorious? There was no external semblance of glory. Mary's triumph was internal, within her Heart. She could feel intense pain and sorrow and at the same time not close her Heart to God. She kept her Heart open with love and trust. Often, the serpent tempts us to distrust, and we close our hearts in order to avoid further pain. Mary stepped on the serpent because she did not avoid further pain.

This is the reason St. Stanislaus could write about Mary that *she herself would want to fasten Jesus to the Cross.* Such a statement astounds us today because our focus is on what Mary must have felt as a mother losing her only Son. Her pain was profound, but remember: Mary is Immaculate. There is no self-pity in her, no "Woe is me!" What does Mary sorrow over, even today, as we see at Fatima? She sorrows over the sins that caused her Son to die. She sorrows over our lack of conversion — that even after the death of her Son, we are still reluctant to trust in Him. Jesus spoke to Faustina about how certain souls still do not trust Him, even after His death — the greatest proof of His love: **"Distrust on the part of souls is tearing at My insides. The distrust of a chosen soul causes Me even greater pain; despite My inexhaustible love for them they do not trust Me. Even My death is not enough for them. Woe to the soul that abuses these"** (*Diary*, 50).

For us sinners, what is to be done to remedy this sorrow? We are to participate in the mystery of Mary's Immaculate Conception. This means that we run to her at Calvary to hide under her mantle, to seek refuge in her Immaculate Heart, so that she can teach us how to trust and be cleansed by the torrent of Blood and Water from Jesus' side. We are to accept the real pain and suffering we must endure in this life without whitewashing it, without saying, "Well, it is not

---

[224] ICEL, *The Liturgy of the Hours*, vol. 4, 1401-402.

really suffering." No. It is suffering, and suffering is difficult. Though suffering is used in the Father's plan of salvation, we know that we are not destined to suffer eternally: We were created for joy and for happiness.

Saint Faustina had a devotion to the Immaculate Conception, and in imitation of Our Lady, she tells us simply: Trust in Jesus. We must do so while realizing that the very hand we hold when we trust is a crucified hand — the hand of Jesus Christ. Mary — whose hand we grasp — also knows pain. Her Heart was pierced, yet she continued to trust in the Father. We see this trust manifested in Jesus when He was dying naked upon the Cross and would have had every reason to give up. After an eternity of loving service and obedience to the Father, Jesus seemed to be ruthlessly rejected and completely abandoned by Him. That is hard to understand because we expect someone who loves us to be loyal no matter what (see Sir 6:14-16). The Father's loyalty was revealed in the Resurrection.

CHAPTER 23

Trust Amid Abandonment

"Immerse yourself in My Passion, particularly in My abandonment at the moment of agony"
(*Diary*, 1320).

Jesus entered into the drama of our sin, the worst aspect of which is abandonment. But let us be clear: Sin does not prompt God's abandonment of us — sin is our abandonment of Him. The hideousness of sin is that, at its worst, when we have turned away from Him, we accuse Him of abandoning us. Jesus never sinned. He never turned away from the Father, but He did experience the abandonment we all endure. He did not hide this from the Father and openly cried out to Him at the Cross: "Why have you abandoned me?"

Despite His cry to the Father, Jesus was, in fact, not entirely abandoned. "If Jesus felt abandoned by the Father, he knew however that that was not really so. Jesus himself said, 'I and the Father are one' (Jn 10:30). Speaking of His future passion, He said, 'I am not alone, for the Father is with me' (Jn 16:32)."[225] Jesus had a clear vision of God and the certainty of His union with the Father in His mind. The Father was present to Jesus in a particular way through Mary during those painful and punishing moments at Calvary.

Saint John Paul II wrote this regarding Jesus' cry of abandonment: "In hearing Jesus crying out his 'why,' we learn indeed that those who suffer can utter this same cry, but with those same dispositions of filial trust and abandonment of which Jesus is the teacher and model. In the 'why' of Jesus there is no feeling or resentment leading to rebellion or desperation. There is no semblance of a reproach to the Father, but the expression of the experience of weakness, of solitude, of abandonment to himself, made by Jesus in our place. Jesus thus became the first of the 'smitten and afflicted,' the first of the abandoned. ... At the same time, however, he tells us that the benign eye of Providence watches over all these poor children of Eve."[226]

Jesus teaches us how to cry out in moments of difficulty, trial, and temptation. We are entitled to cry out "Why?" and voice our excruciating experiences of abandonment to the Father, but we must always remain children and never rebel. Jesus asks this poignant question with trust and surrender, quoting, in His anguish, a psalm that begins in desolation but ends with praise, already thanking God for His deliverance, which will surely come.

---

[225] Saint John Paul II, *Audiences of Pope John Paul II*. November 30, 1988.
[226] Ibid.

After my dad had died, there were many moments where the question "Why?" burst forth from my aching heart. For some years, there was seemingly no response as to why the Father's will included such a horrible death. Later, however, I learned from one of my brothers a detail that unraveled for me this particular mystery of God's Providence. As I shared earlier, my dad had suffered heart attacks and strokes when I was 12 years old. While he was in the hospital, aware of the considerable danger that he might die during surgery (or really, at any moment), he had asked the Father to let him live to see me graduate from high school. This was in the year 2000. Looking back, I can see that the Father had perfectly fulfilled his request: Two weeks after my high school graduation, my dad passed away. What originally had looked like an utterly and completely awful event was in fact the result of the Father's Mercy toward me: He had granted my father those extra years to live, to watch over me until I was ready to enter religious life. Hence, what originally began as a lament — "Why?" — ended with praise and thanksgiving for His Providence and love.

ACCEPTING AND REMEMBERING

We have only to look at the two thieves hanging crucified next to Jesus to see the great difference between the attitudes of trust and distrust. One thief mockingly tells Jesus to save him and Himself. The other thief recognizes that he ought to suffer because of his sins and entrusts himself to Jesus. This is the attitude we are to have before Jesus. If only we recognize our faults like the Good Thief, Jesus opens the gates of Heaven to us through His pierced side, through His Sacred Heart (see Lk 23:43). Like the Good Thief, our duty is to accept the Cross and know that Jesus is not powerless, that His power is manifested upon the Cross in His Love and Mercy, by which He crushed Satan's head. Nor is Mary powerless. Her power is in her unconditional trust and surrender, by which she, too, stepped upon the serpent.

It is precisely this abandonment that Jesus asks us to remember at three o'clock each day (see *Diary*, 1320). In describing the agony of abandonment that Jesus experienced, St. John Paul II points out that Jesus did not contest His fate. He did not call upon the untold legions of angels at His disposal, blocked Peter's sword raised in His defense, and did not encourage Pilate's failed efforts to rouse support for Him. Although His agony was all the more excruciating because His strength and greatest joy came from His union with His Father who seemed to be silent, Jesus endured by having confidence that Crucifixion would lead to Resurrection. He asks that we immerse ourselves in His agony and sorrow, so ask yourself now: Do I desire to do that? How can I fathom what He experienced in His moment of agony and abandonment? What experiences have I had that help me ponder the depth of His suffering and the gift He has given me and mankind? How can Jesus' confidence apply to my own life circumstances?

How often we experience the silence of God when external events all seem to go wrong and work against us! How often, too, at precisely those moments, does all interior consolation seem to evaporate! Saint John Paul II reflects upon the silence and abandonment of God in his audience given on April 2, 1997, which I highly recommend. The Pope points out that the perfection of Jesus' sacrifice upon the Cross is precisely His entrustment of Himself to the Father at the height of His abandonment and separation, and that abandonment and separation are the effects of our sin. Mary teaches us to share with her His experience of abandonment and surrender to the Father's will, expressed in His last words on the Cross, "Father, into your hands I commend my spirit!" (Lk 23:46). Thus she offers loving consent "to the immolation of this victim which was born of her."[227]

Abandonment is perhaps the worst sting of the serpent. When we experience desertion, it can be very difficult to trust the Father, especially when the serpent feeds us the lie that the Father has truly abandoned us, leaving us alone as orphans, without love, direction, or help. This experience was one through which St. Faustina successfully navigated by her trust, declaring: "Jesus, You said that a mother would sooner forget her infant than God His creature, and that 'even if she would forget her infant, I, God, will never forget My creature.' O Jesus, do You hear how my soul is moaning? Deign to hear the painful whimpers of Your child. I trust in You, O God, because heaven and earth will pass, but Your word will last forever" (*Diary*, 23).

In the name of all who have felt abandoned by God, Jesus speaks forth these words of abandonment and cries out "from the depths" (Ps 130) to the Father. Many commentators have noted that Jews of Jesus' day often would refer to an entire psalm by quoting only the first verse. With this in mind, we notice that immediately after the first verse of Psalm 22, the psalmist remembers the goodness of the Lord shown throughout history, the trust His people had in Him, and His rescues of the people time and again. The psalmist returns to words of complaint, but ends by giving praise for God's work of deliverance, stating that the Lord will free him, and he will thus be able to recount His goodness to others in the future.

WORSHIP, TRUST, AND LAMENTATION

At every Eucharist, we proclaim how the Father did indeed *save* Jesus when He cried out to Him. You see, the Father did not *spare* Jesus, but He did accompany Him through the trial. Jesus' trust in the Father was not based on the idea expressed by the psalmist: "*If* the Father is good, He will spare me." No. Jesus knows that the Father is good and walks with us through every trial. Notice also how, soon after Jesus complains of abandonment, He concludes His entire life with the words: "Into your hands, Father, I commend my spirit." Even amid

---

[227] Saint John Paul II, *Audiences of Pope John Paul II.* April 2, 1997.

abandonment, Jesus continues to entrust Himself to the Father, as evidenced by the way John describes Jesus' death: "he bowed his head and gave up his spirit" (Jn 19:30).

The Greek word for "gave up" is *paredoken,* which means "to hand over" and "to entrust." The final act of Jesus' life was entrusting His Spirit to the Father. Even amid total darkness, Jesus trusts in the Father. This is His greatest act of worship of the Father and the reason why the Eucharist is our own greatest act of worship. In the Eucharist, Jesus comes to dwell in us so that He might once again trust in the Father through us, His Body on earth. The worship we offer the Father is the consummate worship of Jesus and Mary: of perfect and total trust amid darkness, pain, and abandonment.

This worship extends beyond our own crosses, at which we ask Our Lady to be present and to guide us. Our worship extends also to our love of neighbor, so we must ask: Are we willing to be like Mary and stand by others who are crucified? Are we willing to be the presence of the Father, to comfort and provide tender care for others, even if we cannot remove their suffering? Like Mary, are we willing to be a living Ark of the Covenant, bringing the presence of God to those who are abandoned?

For all her tenderness and love, Mary does not simply take away our suffering. In the *Diary,* there is a passage where Faustina is enduring one of the most difficult forms of suffering: the dark night. When Mary appears, she states that she suffers with, and has compassion for, Faustina. Mary's presence makes all the difference. Our presence may make all the difference for others in their moment of abandonment and agony as well. Mary teaches us how to walk through the dark valley under the care of the Father, and to walk beside others who suffer and travel in darkness.

Is it wrong then to complain and plead with the Father amid suffering? If we understand complaining as expressing "grief, pain, or discontent" to God, then such complaint is not evil. The word "complaint" comes from the Latin *plangere,* "to lament." In the Bible, such complaints always end in praise and blessing. However, if we understand "complaint" in its second meaning, "to make a formal accusation or charge," then we ought not to accuse God of having done evil or wrong. Such a complaint expresses lack of trust, which is wrong. For this reason, we ought not to complain in the sense of "building a case" for how unjustly we have been treated by God or others, accusing Him or them of having done wrong. This kind of complaint ends only in bitterness.

But in the sense of lamenting, Jesus Himself complained in the Garden of Gethsemane, and at least one third of the Psalms are complaints. We ought to complain in this way to the Father and pour out our hearts, for He is our refuge in times of trial (see Ps 55:22, 62:8). Before entering freely into His Passion, Jesus spent three hours in intense prayer — intense to the point of agony — as He accepted that He was to bear the full weight of sin. During His prayer, Jesus' human will, by its very nature, balked at such excruciating suffering (see Mt

26:39). But this human will embraced His divine will — one with the Father's will — so that in His humanity, He could peacefully accept the chalice of suffering. You see, even in Jesus, embracing the Father's will does not erase the weakness of humanity; yet, by the Holy Spirit, through persevering prayer, our weak humanity can be strengthened to embrace the Father's will in all things.

We might be tempted to ask now: Are we not called to simply accept without complaint whatever the Father sends us? No. Not even Jesus did so. In Gethsemane, He poured out His Heart to the Father, and His agony (from the Greek *agon,* meaning "struggle," "fight") was so intense that He sweat Blood (see Lk 22:44).

We know that the Father did not remove the chalice of suffering. So what was the point of Christ's prayer? The point is that we trust not a monolith, nor an idea, nor an ideal, but a living Person: the Father, who hears our prayers and answers them in His own time and according to His will. Jesus could step into His Passion because He knew that the Father always hears His prayers (see Jn 11:42). Although the Father's answer to Christ's prayer came only after Christ's suffering, we see in the Resurrection that Jesus was heard and answered precisely because of His reverence, His humility, and His filial love for the Father (see Heb 5:7). We cannot trust a Father who is insensitive and indifferent to our suffering, who is unwilling to listen to our complaints. No. And we are not asked to do so. We trust those who walk with us and help us, even if, in their infinite wisdom, they will not solve the situation obviously and immediately.

When we ask for the chalice of suffering to pass, we must learn to imitate Christ by joining our request onto complete trust in the Father and His plan. In the same prayer, Jesus expressed both His desire to be delivered from His Passion and His determination to be obedient to the Father's will, no matter what would befall Him. These are both necessary, for only when we trust the Father enough to pour our hearts out to Him will we trust Him enough to walk according to His will along the Way of the Cross. Lamentations 3:1-33 portrays lament, complaint, and trust in the Father's Mercy in a powerful and vivid manner. I would even recommend putting down this book to read and reread that chapter before continuing!

We all need to unburden ourselves and share our pain with a loving other, even as Jesus did by inviting Peter, James, and John to Gethsemane, but we ought not, as we typically do, simply complain in order to complain, without ending in praise. Good complaining always ends in praise; the psalms of lament begin with deep cries of pain, but always end in praise and confidence in deliverance by the Father — sometimes even ending simply, "Amen, Amen!" (see Ps 89). Blessed Solanus Casey, a Capuchin priest on the path to sainthood, said that we ought to give thanks to God for answering our prayers, even before He answers them.

What are we to do in the midst of suffering? First, we are to complain to the Lord Himself. Saint Teresa of Avila said: "The only true friend is Jesus Christ; when I rely on Him, I have such strength that — as it seems to me — I could resist the whole world, were it to rise up against me."[228] We can seek that help of Jesus in a good friend who will sincerely help us, not by rejecting our cross and telling us to get rid of it, but by being like Simon of Cyrene and helping us carry it. Our suffering may not cease as or when we want in this life, but when we surrender to God, our suffering ceases to be suffering as we know it. It is no longer just something bad to be thrown away, but an opportunity that God, our provident Father, gives us to grow in love and charity and to heal us of the sin of not loving as Jesus loves. We ought to rejoice, or at least acknowledge, that the Father offers us forgiveness of our sins through Christ's suffering and healing of the effects of sin through our penitential suffering, spiritually united to the suffering of Christ.

EVIL AND GOD'S WILL

Does anything happen that is not God's will? No. The Father allows every-thing, even suffering, to help us grow into loving as Jesus loves. As Jesus told St. Faustina: **"And know this, too, My daughter: all creatures, whether they know it or not, and whether they want to or not, always fulfill My will"** (*Diary*, 586). This does not mean that the Father wills sin; it simply means that the Father can and does use everything, even sin, to help us grow in holiness and trust. We need not ponder why He does this, but should ask instead how we can transform the terrible curse of sin and suffering into a wonderful blessing, as Mary and Jesus did. How can we trust as they did? By God's grace, and by taking Mary as our model. At the Cross, she did not seek to explain everything away. She simply remained silent, humble, in pain.

We will learn to trust our Father by imitating Mary's Immaculate Heart. Our hearts are intended to be pierced by a sword. If our hearts are never pierced, we will never learn to trust. What are we to do amid suffering, then? Do not ignore it. Do not blame it on God. Do not say, "It is just His will." Say rather: "The Father can use this. No matter what the source of this suffering is, I am to do something with it by entrusting it into His hands." This is the scandal of the Cross — that a good, loving, merciful Father would allow the terrible torture and crucifixion of the Son that He loves; that the Father would hand over His Son to sinful men. Yet the Father continues to hand His Son over to us sinful humans each day in the Holy Eucharist! This love is inconceivable to us because we associate love with wanting to prevent such things. But there is a reason for it: our salvation. It is scandalous that the Father allowed His Son to undergo such suffering and be the victim of human sin for us, but we, too, will undergo such pain if we want to be called His beloved sons and daughters.

We ought not be discouraged, however, for Jesus Himself is our Simon of Cyrene — He helps us carry our cross. And just as she helped Jesus, Mary accompanies us along the Way of the Cross. Many are tempted to question

---

[228] Blessed Sopocko, *The Mercy of God in His Works,* Vol. 3, 173.

why God allows violence and evil — they lose patience with Him and find it difficult to trust. Saint John Paul II offers a Polish proverb as an answer to our impatience: "*God takes his time, but he is just.*"[229] He further suggests that with faith, this patience will conform us to Christ and that, just as she helped Jesus, Mary will accompany us along the Way of the Cross.

PETER AND JUDAS

But what do we do if we fail in our trust? What do we do if, like Peter, Judas, and the other apostles, we flee, deny Jesus, or betray Him? Daily, we sin! The Bible states that the just man falls seven times a day (see Prov 24:16). We can expect to fall, but we must always look to Jesus and decide to get up again. Judas despaired because after his fatal kiss he could no longer look Jesus in the face or discover His Love and Mercy. Peter converted and wept bitterly because he gazed into the eyes of Jesus. Amazingly, according to St. Catherine of Siena, St. Peter even grew in holiness that night because of his bitter tears, as Father Garrigou-Lagrange explains: "Everything leads us to think that by the fervor of his repentance Peter not only recovered the degree of grace that he had lost, but was raised to a higher degree of the supernatural life. The Lord permitted this fall only to cure him of his presumption so that he might become more humble and thereafter place his confidence, not in himself, but in God."[230]

If we come to Jesus instead of fleeing from Him, our sins can actually help us grow in holiness. Saint Faustina herself experienced this: "If it hadn't been for this small imperfection, you wouldn't have come to Me. Know that as often as you come to Me, humbling yourself and asking My forgiveness, I pour out a superabundance of graces on your soul, and your imperfection vanishes before My eyes, and I see only your love and your humility. You lose nothing but gain much" (*Diary*, 1293).

So, the question is not whether we will fall — it's a given that we are sinners and at times deny Jesus. The question is what we will do then. Will we, like St. Peter, look into His eyes to be set afire and purified by His love and mercy? Or will we, like Judas, avoid His gaze, believing ourselves unlovable and unforgivable? The pain of looking at Jesus' face after we sin is Purgatory, which is not so much a place as it is the pain we feel gazing into the eyes and wounds of Jesus, who has loved us so.[231]

The image of Jesus looking at Peter, who begins weeping bitterly in the aftermath of his denial, is an icon of the pain of Purgatory (see Mt 26:75). When we fall on the path to God, as Jesus did along the way to Calvary, we are to look at Jesus and Mary beside us, ask for their help, stand up again, and continue along the path.

---

[229] Saint John Paul II, *Homilies of Pope John Paul II*. Homily from October 8, 1995.
[230] Fr. Reginald Garrigou-Lagrange, OP, "The Three Ages of the Interior Life," accessed July 11, 2017, http://www.christianperfection.info/tta52.php.
[231] Benedict XVI, *Spe Salvi*, n. 47.

If our encounter with Jesus in Confession arouses perfect contrition (namely, sorrow for our sins because we have wounded the Beloved, rather than simply because we fear hell), we will have no need to endure Purgatory, no need to endure the pain caused by our sins. We will endure that pain already here on earth by freely turning to Jesus and weeping bitterly for our sins, so that, like Peter, we can grow in holiness through repentance and trust in the Father's Mercy. The best course of action is to humbly allow Jesus to gaze upon us when we sin and ask for His pardon in our personal prayer and especially in Confession.

All too often, like Peter, in our pride we assume that we will not sin — that we, of all people, will remain faithful to the Lord (see Mt 26:35). Peter fell precisely because of his pride, because he relied on himself. Ironically, we, too, fall because we assume that we will never fall! Jesus tells St. Faustina: **"You see, My child, what you are of yourself. The cause of your falls is that you rely too much upon yourself and too little on Me. But let this not sadden you so much. You are dealing with the God of mercy, which your misery cannot exhaust. Remember, I did not allot only a certain number of pardons"** (*Diary*, 1488). We must humble ourselves before the Lord in repentance and in that way grow in holiness. This is the secret of the saints: never to give in to discouragement when we sin, but to simply turn to Jesus and allow His gaze of love and mercy to purify us of our sin.

Our Lady and the Eucharist

At Calvary, some of the last words of Jesus were, "Behold, your Mother." In our own Calvary, whatever that may entail, we are never alone. We are always accompanied by Mary, who comforts and consoles us. She is one of the greatest gifts of the Father's Mercy: our Mother, given to us by Christ. This means that our duty is to accept her, receive her in our daily lives, and invite her presence and intercession in all our sufferings.

In one of his writings on the Eucharist, St. John Paul II tells us that Jesus' gift of Mary is renewed at each Holy Mass: "'Do this in remembrance of me' (Lk 22:19). In the 'memorial' of Calvary all that Christ accomplished by his passion and his death is present. Consequently, *all that Christ did with regard to his Mother* for our sake is also present. To Mary, He gave the beloved disciple and by extension each of us: 'Behold, your Son!' To each of us He also says: 'Behold your mother!' (see Jn 19:26–27). In this memorial of Christ's death in the Eucharist, we continually receive this gift of Mary and like John, are to accept the one given anew as our Mother. It also means taking on a commitment to be conformed to Christ, putting ourselves in the school of His Mother, and allowing her to accompany us. Mary is present as the Mother of the Church at each of our celebrations of the Eucharist. If the Church and the Eucharist are inseparably united, the same ought to be said of Mary and the Eucharist."[232]

---

[232] Saint John Paul II, *Ecclesia de Eucharistia,* Encyclical Letter (Vatican City: Libreria Editrice Vaticana, 2003), n. 57.

This means that in Holy Communion we accept and receive not only Jesus, but also Mary as our Mother!

We notice that it is precisely in His moments of suffering, darkness, and pain that we are asked by Jesus to receive Mary into our hearts. Thus there is a link between Mary's being our Mother and the Christian way of suffering. Mary's maternal relationship to the Church and the adopted children of God, willed to us by Jesus in His dying moments, is particularly manifested in moments of suffering, when she is a living icon, a face of the Holy Spirit, the Gift of the Father. Indeed, we call Mary the Mother and Queen of Mercy, and Mercy, as I have shown, is another name for the Holy Spirit. Mary's Immaculate Heart is the temple of the Holy Spirit. By her example and with her encouragement, she enables us to stay near to Jesus and not flee as the apostles did. She is always with her Son, so it is impossible to be beside the pierced side of Christ without at the same time being near Mary, herself beside that wounded Heart.

Mary had to pass through all the events of Holy Week just as we do today when we face our crosses and trials. She had to endure those moments through faith, hope, and charity, continuing to walk along the path of trust. Standing at the foot of the Cross, Mary experienced her own extreme poverty and, in a way unlike that of any other person, stood in need of the Mercy of God, in need of His overflowing love at that crucial moment. She knows exactly what it means to suffer; she knows how painful the agony of abandonment is; she knows how much we need the Mercy of God.

We must learn from Mary's profound obedience to "do whatever He tells you" (see Jn 2:5). By obedience, we surrender to the will of God, giving up our own plans and entering the Father's plan, trusting Him as Jesus trusted — even unto death — knowing that God can bring good out of every evil. That cannot happen when we trust in ourselves, when we try to find our own ways of resolving evil. Mary teaches us to offer up our sufferings in union with Jesus, transforming our daily lives into moments of trust in the Lord, all for the salvation of souls. With her encouragement, let us say these three prayers daily and let them become one prayer: "Jesus, I trust in You!" "Let it be done to me according to your word, your will!" "Amen! Amen!"

CHAPTER 24

The Reward of Trust

"He ... suffered that He might deliver the sufferer who trusted in Him ... and reveal His Resurrection"
(Anaphora of the Apostles).

In the preceding chapters, we have traversed the Way of the Cross with Mary and, with her, we patiently awaited the day of the Resurrection — the day the Father answered His Son's prayers and consummated the Crucifixion by raising Him from the dead. The Resurrection is also the Father's response to Mary's "Amen," her "Yes" that resulted in her entrusting Jesus, her dearly beloved Son, to the Father, even throughout His Passion and death. As I was pondering the crucifix before my ordination as a priest, I could not see beyond the suffering of the Cross, due to my lack of trust in the Father. But even on Calvary, Jesus and Mary could see beyond the crucifix to the third day, and wait with patience for the Father's response to their complete surrender to His will.

The Resurrection and Ascension of Jesus are the fulfillment of the promise given by the Archangel Gabriel that He would indeed reign as king — a promise made to Mary some 33 years earlier. How great must Mary's patience have been for her to wait so many years to see the fulfillment of the Lord's promise — and how much she had to trust each day! We can likewise anticipate our own resurrection if we entrust everything to the Father, as Jesus and Mary did.

Resurrection is not the end of the journey; it is only the beginning of *zoe*, of eternal life with God. All that precedes our death is intended to help us grow in trust, so that we might live no longer according to our selfish and worldly desires born of the distrust of original sin, but according to the Father's will. The very first paragraph of the *Catechism* tells us that His plan is for us to share in His divine life (see *CCC*, 1). The life of the Resurrection is *zoe*, the life of Heaven, life spent fulfilling, moment by moment, the Father's will, which will be fully manifested only in the new Heaven and the new earth when we share glorified bodies with Christ (see Rom 8:11; Phil 3:21).

We must first be convinced that His will is good if we are ever to want to fulfill it constantly, yet when we speak of God's will, how often do we think only of suffering and pain? What do we think of when we say, "Thy will be done"? The serpent's trick is to have us associate the Father's will with everything that is evil and bad. Ironically, that is not the Father's will, but the serpent's. The Father may *use* evil and suffering, but He does not *will* it to happen in the first place. In contrast, the serpent desires sin and even helps cause it to occur, along with all of its attendant suffering. Our sinful desires and worldly outlook often tell us that the Father's plan — His will — is not so good.

In Chapter 1, I talked about not being sure about the goodness of the Father's plan for me. Praying before the crucifix, I knew I needed to die to my own false plans, false hopes, and self-will so that my deeper desires for happiness could be fulfilled. Through prayer and experience, I have come to know that when I am faced with suffering, it is only by embracing the Cross and dying to myself that I can understand and truly receive the blessing the Father has in store for me: the Resurrection. The Christian who unites his own self-denial or death to self with that of Jesus Crucified takes a step toward the Risen Jesus, for the Cross is the entrance into everlasting life (see *CCC*, 1020). Thus suffering is a necessary prelude to the Resurrection because it is Christ's Cross that frees us from living in the flesh and enables us to live by the Father's will (see 1 Pet 4:1-2). We must allow our Father to crucify our flesh and its desires, so we may live with the Risen Christ (see Gal 5:24). Only when we cease living the life of sin, by dying to sin, can we live with the Father in union with Jesus Christ (see Rom 6:10-11).

"Flesh" here does not mean simply the human body, which is good and is to be used to glorify God (see 1 Cor 6:20). Rather, *flesh* — as St. Paul uses this term in his letters and as I am using it here — refers to all fallen human nature, with its disordered desires. Nevertheless, we are crucified in the body, and our entire person is crucified with Christ. Even our good desires may be crucified in this broken world, but we can be certain that any suffering we endure, if united with Christ, will bear fruit in sharing in the glory of His Resurrection — even now upon earth. This is the dichotomy that St. Paul teaches: to crucify the flesh so as to live according to the Spirit — namely, to live the life of the Resurrection.

At every Easter Vigil, we renew our baptismal promises. In Baptism, we died with Christ in order to be raised to new life with Him by the Holy Spirit; we died to the empty assurances of this fallen world and to the lies of Satan. By hoping to rise with Christ in His Resurrection, we live with faith and trust in the Father. We express this trust by living in obedience to the Father's will. The serpent tempts us to make the best of both worlds: to have a little bit of God and a little bit of this world.

If we love the world, however, we are not friends but enemies of God, for the world, though created by God, is disfigured by sin and can lead us away from Him (see 1 Jn 2:15). If we want to experience the power of the Resurrection, we need to die with Christ and live through Him, with Him, and in Him, for the glory and honor of the Father. Then we will be able to live in this world, not according to our sinful desires, but according to the will of God, which means that we will be able to use the world — and all of creation — with peace and joy for the glory of the Father. In this way, we anticipate even now the new Heaven and the new earth — the fulfillment of Jesus' Resurrection — when this world will no longer lead us away from God, but rather speak to us incessantly of His Beauty and Mercy.

SLAVERY OF SIN

The Resurrection of Christ is the fulfillment of the Exodus. As we sing in the *Exsultet*, "This is the night, when once you led our forebears, Israel's children, from slavery in Egypt and made them pass dry-shod through the Red Sea." In the original Exodus, the Israelites were enslaved in Egypt, incapable of serving the living God because of the harsh demands and labor imposed on them by the ruler of this world, Pharaoh. When we distrust the Father and put our trust in human flesh, we fall into slavery ourselves, but by trusting the Father and fulfilling His will, we make our own spiritual exodus from slavery to freedom — freedom gained by obedience, even unto death on the Cross.

Saint John Paul II wrote about the great paradox of this freedom: "The Crucified Christ reveals the authentic meaning of freedom; he lives it fully in the total gift of himself and calls his disciples to share in his freedom."[233] Jesus' freedom is the freedom to give Himself fully and without reserve to the Father. Saint Faustina experienced this same freedom of love: "Now I understand that even in prison there can burst forth from a pure heart the fullness of love for You, O Lord! External things mean nothing to pure love; it cuts through them all. Neither prison doors nor the gates of heaven are strong enough to stop it. It reaches God Himself, and nothing can quench it. It knows no obstacles; it is free like a queen and has free access to all places. Death itself must bow its head before it" (*Diary*, 201).

Nothing external — not even the worst suffering, such as the Crucifixion — can imprison and enslave the one who loves. Only sin, manifesting lack of trust, can take away the freedom of love. The serpent whispers in our ear that freedom is external and comes from having things go our way, but how often are those who have external freedom enslaved internally by sin! Mary teaches us to embrace true freedom with trust. Saint Faustina describes the joy that flows from it: "One hour spent at the foot of the altar in the greatest dryness of spirit is dearer to me than a hundred years of worldly pleasures" (*Diary*, 254).

Suffering is unavoidable in both slavery and freedom — either we will suffer from the cruel "mercy" of this world and the devil, or we will suffer under the merciful Providence of our Heavenly Father (see 2 Sam 24:14). Suffering in a life ruled by the world, the flesh, and the devil leads to despair and slavery, but suffering in union with Christ brings the freedom of the children of God and eternal life.

The entirety of the Christian life is an exodus out of ourselves and this world into the divine life of the Holy Trinity: "Love is indeed 'ecstasy,' not in the sense of a moment of intoxication, but rather as a journey, an ongoing exodus out of the closed inward-looking self towards its liberation through self-giving,

---

[233] Saint John Paul II, *Veritatis Splendor*, Encyclical Letter (Vatican City: Libreria Editrice Vaticana, 1993), n. 85.

and thus towards authentic self-discovery and indeed the discovery of God." [234] The word "exodus" comes from Greek words meaning "the path out of," but every path also leads *to* a destination. The Cross is the exodus, the path out of distrust and sin that leads to the Resurrection, to the new life of *zoe* — restored dialogue and communion with the Father. Just as the many trials in the desert were the prelude to the Father's deliverance of Israel out of Egypt into the Promised Land on earth, our sufferings are the plagues that weaken our sinful desires and set us free to enter the Promised Land of Heaven.

Are we still living in slavery to sin? Are we willing to be crucified with Christ, trusting that crucifixion is necessary for our salvation, since the Father can bring good out of evil? Are we willing to do what God requires to set us free from sin so that we can live for Him (see Rom 6:6)? Have we truly experienced the power of Christ's Resurrection? The life of the Resurrection is summed up in the words of St. Paul: "My old self has been crucified with Christ; now I live by trust in the Son of God who has loved me and given himself up for me" (Gal 2:19-20).

Our sinful desires enslave us because our hearts are designed for the Triune God (see Tit 3:3). When we doubt that God satisfies our deepest longings, we seek ultimate satisfaction in a multitude of created things. Such things were meant for our health and refreshment, but to find true satisfaction, we must let go of our false pleasures and substitutes for the Father. Then we will be able to experience the joy of the Resurrection and restored communion with our Father.

CONFIDENCE IN THE SURPASSING POWER OF GOD

Sometimes it is difficult to see what the Resurrection has changed in the world, since much of creation is still enmeshed in sin, death, and suffering. The most profound change takes place first and foremost in our hearts and souls through the trust that flows from faith, hope, and charity. This change can be summed up by the Greek word *parrēsia*, "confidence" (see *CCC*, 2778). In Latin, the word is *confidentia*, meaning "full trust or reliance."[235] Thus confidence is another way to express the reality of trust. The Resurrection shows us that we can have confidence or full trust in the Father *no matter what*. There is no earthly situation in which He cannot save us and bring us home; He allows us to suffer trials, but then provides relief (see Ps 66:12).

We must pray for our hearts to be open to having confidence in the surpassing power of the Holy Spirit at work in us, because He is the Power of the Resurrection (see Eph 1:18-21). Power (might, strength, force) in Greek is

---

[234] Benedict XVI, *Deus Caritas Est*, Encyclical Letter (Vatican City: Libreria Editrice Vaticana, 2005), n. 8.

[235] "Confidence" from Latin *confidentia*, from *confidentem*: "firmly trusting, bold," present participle of *confidere* "to have full trust or reliance," from *com-*, intensive prefix, + *fidere* "to trust." "Confidence," Online Etymology Dictionary, accessed July 11, 2017, http://www. etymonline.com/index.php?term=confidence.

dynamis, the root of the English word *dynamite.* The Power of God, the Power of the Resurrection — the Holy Spirit — is more powerful than dynamite, capable of bursting asunder all strongholds, all chains that bind us, the stone in front of the tomb, and even the very gates of hell. As with Christ in the Agony in the Garden of Gethsemane, it is normal for us to experience fear, anxiety, and sorrow in the face of suffering (see Mk 14:34). We were made for life, so death brings fear. However, we no longer need to live under the dominion of fear; rather, we can live with courage in the freedom of the Kingdom of the Father, where life has the last word (see Heb 2:14-15). There is nothing to fear, because if that Power of God conquered all sin and death in Christ Crucified, and that Power is at work in our hearts through trust and Baptism, then surely all our own sin and its effects will be conquered, too!

This surpassing power of God dwells in our hearts through confidence in the Word of God. "The gates of hell shall not prevail" against such power, but we must remember that the Father's surpassing power is hidden in the wounds of Christ Crucified (see Mt 16:18). In truth, such power of the Spirit is made perfect in our weakness (see 2 Cor 12:9). We will conquer sin and death by what may seem like defeat and crucifixion. We can be glad and even boast of our weaknesses and suffering, for it is then that the surpassing power of the Holy Spirit, the Power of God, dwells within us.

This surpassing power flows from the transcendent wisdom of our Father, for His wise plan for our salvation takes our sins into account. In our sinfulness, you and I have crucified Jesus, but the Crucified Jesus is precisely the One who rose from the dead and brought us new life. He knew that we would try to sabotage His plans, because that is what sin does. The Father therefore used what He knew we would do — sin. He used our sin to bring about His greatest work, the Resurrection of Christ. We should never lose our awe before this paradox: The Father used our sins to accomplish His plan of salvation. The Father allowed sin in the first place to reveal His infinite mercy (see Rom 11:32), as we exclaim in the *Exsultet* at Easter: "O happy fault, that gained for us so great a Redeemer!"

Marvel with me at this amazing fact: The Father would rather send His own Son to die for our sins than see us die in sin in hell (see Jn 3:16). How could we not trust in the Father? All that happens, both good and evil, serves His purpose and plan. "So that in worldly men My mercy and charity shine, and they render praise and glory to My Name, even when they persecute My servants; for they prove in them the virtues of patience and charity, causing them to suffer humbly and offer to Me their persecutions and injuries, thus turning them into My praise and glory. So that, whether they will or no, worldly people render to My Name praise and glory, even when they intend to do Me infamy and wrong."[236]

---

[236] Saint Catherine of Siena, *The Dialogue,* 168.

God is our Father. From all eternity, He has foreseen each cross we bear and chosen it specifically for us: "Your Cross: The everlasting God has in His wisdom foreseen from eternity the cross that He now presents to you as a gift from His inmost heart. This cross He now sends you He has considered with His all-knowing eyes, understood with His divine mind, tested with His wise justice, warmed with loving arms and weighed with His own hands to see that it be not one inch too large and not one ounce too heavy for you. He has blessed it with His holy Name, anointed it with His consolation, taken one last glance at you and your courage, and then sent it to you from heaven, a special greeting from God to you, an alms of the all-merciful love of God."[237] Remember the lesson from the storm on the Sea of Galilee: Our enemy is not the cross, but our lack of trust that our Father can use all that happens for our good.

We begin to see that sin — our own and that of others — is used by the Father to help us grow in holiness. Even the sins of others are used to help us die to our own sinfulness and rise to new life with Jesus Christ. We will be most grateful for trying people at death, for without the crosses they provide, we would not be able to enter Heaven. Without the Cross, there is no ladder to Heaven (see *CCC*, 618), so the worst cross is not to have a cross at all! As Blessed George Matulaitis, MIC, wrote: "Without crosses and sufferings, there is no path to Heaven."[238]

This does not mean that at every moment we must find some way to suffer; Still, we must remember that there is no way to reach the Resurrection except through the Cross. The only way to obtain the true peace, happiness, and life that we desire is through the Cross. There is simply no other way. We must not forget that days of blessing come not by "chance" but through the choice to follow Christ to Calvary, for He will lead us from Golgotha to unending joy and happiness, even in this life. For what are this true joy, happiness, and blessings if not true love — *agape*, self-donating love? When we learn to love as Christ loved on the Cross, when this love becomes second nature to us, then we will have unending days of blessing and peace because that love is Heaven. And we have a foretaste of Heaven every time we learn to love as Jesus loved on the Cross. If we die daily with Christ, we also experience the joy of rising daily with Him — in a life of self-giving love.

In St. Faustina's vision of her beatification, the people around her began to throw whatever they could at her: mud, stones, sand, brooms. Because of that, she rushed to the altar, and once she'd reached it, the same people who had hurled stones at her stretched out their hands asking her for graces. Paradoxically, she felt a special love for those people because they had forced her to go more quickly to her appointed throne beside Jesus in Heaven (see *Diary,*

---

[237] Cardinal Christoph Schönborn, ed., *Youcat English: Youth Catechism of the Catholic Church,* trans. Michael J. Miller (San Francisco: Ignatius Press, 2011), 158. www.ignatius.com. Used with permission.

[238] Blessed George Matulaitis, *Zło dobrem zwyciężaj: 365 myśli o życiu duchowym,* ed. Janusz Stanisław Kumala (Licheń: Centrum Formacji Maryjnej "Salvatoris Mater," 2009), 47.

31). In the same way, only at our judgment will we see how beneficial were all the trials imposed on us by others. If we are valiant and bold in our trust in the Father, both fortune and misfortune will be of benefit to us, for they both spur us on to holiness, as St. Catherine of Siena said: "For the valiant man, fortune and misfortune are like his right and left hands; he uses both."[239]

SUFFERING OF SPOUSES

This point is particularly true of marriage. Marriage is a Sacrament because it incarnates in the world the love of Christ for His Church (see *CCC*, 1617). This love of Christ for the Church is precisely the forgiving, merciful love with which He freely accepted His death upon the Cross to redeem sinners (see Rom 5:6-8). The question for those who are married or considering marriage is this: Is my love for my spouse stronger than their sinfulness? Sacramental matrimony fills a spouse's heart with the Love of Christ for the other spouse, and the Holy Spirit is present wherever there is true *agape* love between humans. This is expressed in the hymn *Ubi caritas, Deus ibi est:* "Where there is charity, there is God." Only His Love is stronger than sin and death (see *CCC*, 1642). If we try to love the other with our love alone, we will love them too little. (This unfortunately manifests itself in the high divorce rate, even among the baptized.)

Because two spouses live so closely together and share every aspect of their lives, marriage often reveals the weaknesses of both and is a constant lesson in trust in the Father and each other. Marrying someone means that you have each decided to become a bridge builder (*pontifex*) between yourself, your spouse's misery, and the Father's Mercy. The other's failings become opportunities to grow in love and determine whether your love comes from the Sacred Heart of Jesus, which enables you to help the other on their road to sanctification, to lift your loved one through your love and prayers out of his or her misery into the Father's Mercy. This should not be one-sided, however: For it to work well, both spouses must agree to this — one cannot simply bear the cross imposed by the other. Nevertheless, even when this does become one-sided, the Holy Spirit is still present and can work miracles.

There are cases when there is a justified reason for separation, such as abuse. Apart from such cases, in many marriages that are relatively healthy, the serpent wants to convince us that the weaknesses and sins of our spouse are the reasons why we are unhappy. He tempts us to impatience, giving us a myriad of reasons why our anger is justified. We lose our patience mainly because placing the good of the other person first in our priorities will not allow us to always get what we want, but we have to remember to ask: What is it I truly want? Do I want my will and desires to always be immediately satisfied, or do I want to lay down control of a situation in order to love the other, even if that requires suffering?

---

[239] Cardinal Christoph Schönborn, ed. *Youcat English: Youth Catechism of the Catholic Church*, 158.

True Christian marital love requires a willingness to die to self out of love for the other, to recognize that the other is worth the sacrifice of laying down one's life, wants, and desires. Instead of losing patience, try to see opportunities to love your spouse as Christ loved us on the Cross, even though we were sinners. In that way, you will live the grace of matrimony. Marriage is a lifelong commitment that demonstrates the supremacy of love: that everything else can be lost, but not love for the Father expressed through love for one's spouse and children.

Marriage requires one of the greatest acts of trust, for in marriage, spouses surrender themselves to each other. This mutual entrustment is expressed bodily through the marital act, an expression of complete and mutually trusting self-gift, imitating Jesus' unconditional entrustment of Himself to us in the Incarnation. Because the marital act is to be an icon of this total self-gift, holding back part of oneself vitiates trust. In addition, not only must we trust the Father and each other, but He also trusts us! In marriage, He entrusts our spouse to us, as well as the children whom love produces in that union. He entrusts our neighbors (our children, our families, our friends, our enemies) to us to love and care for in His stead.

We are stewards of His love for each other, and for that reason, trust is essential in our relationships with others, especially between spouses, parents, children, and friends. There might even be times when we are called to radical trust by following Jesus' example of entrusting Himself even into the hands of sinners — as in martyrdom. For Jesus entrusts His very self to us in the Eucharist. And think how much the Lord trusts His priests! He comes to earth at their command, and He entrusts His Spouse, the Church, to their care: "**I have come to do My Father's will. I obeyed My parents, I obeyed My tormentors and now I obey the priests**" (*Diary*, 535).

FORGIVENESS

Forgiveness is essential to allowing the Father to use the sins of others to help us grow in holiness. By forgiving others, we commend their sins to the Mercy of God, opening wide the door for Him to draw good out of evil and help them grow in holiness. Forgiveness indicates that we willingly accept, not the sin, but the sinner and the suffering imposed upon us, thus lifting our pain to the Father as a plea for their healing and salvation, just as Christ did for us upon the Cross (see Lk 23:34).

On the other hand, rebelling against suffering places us outside the Father's plan to bring good out of evil. This is the serpent's trick: to give us seemingly just and valid reasons to remain in bitterness, unforgiveness, and rebellion, which only enclose us in the evil of a given situation. There *are* ways to alleviate suffering in accord with the Father's will, and in some situations we *ought* to relieve suffering, e.g., by leaving an abusive relationship or seeking proper medical care in sickness. When such means are sought out with trust and obedience, we cooperate with the Father to bring good out of any situation and manifest the Power of the Resurrection. In such a situation, we do not rebel against suffering so much as use it as an opportunity to manifest the Love of the Father, as did Jesus on Calvary.

This is the lesson we learn from Jesus during His Agony in the Garden of Gethsemane: By humbling ourselves before the Father, by accepting His will and submitting to drinking from the chalice of bitter suffering, we allow Him to exalt us (see Lk 14:11; 2 Pet 5:5-6). Jesus connected drinking from His cup with acceptance of suffering: "**I want to teach you how to suffer. ... You are allowed to drink from the cup from which I drink. I give you that exclusive privilege today**" (*Diary*, 1626). Do we fully understand that we pledge to accept the chalice of "Jesus" when we drink from His Precious Blood (see Mt 26:39)? We gladly say "amen" to the Chalice of His Precious Blood, but do we say "amen" with as much joy when the chalice of suffering is offered to us in our daily lives?

This is the only path to being exalted, and it is the greatest blessing the Father can bestow upon us: being conformed to His Son, as St. Teresa of Avila stated: "For His Majesty can do nothing greater for us than grant us a life which is an imitation of that lived by His Beloved Son."[240] By embracing the Cross and being more like Jesus in His Passion, we will be more like Him in His glory: "**Do you see these souls? Those who are like Me in the pain and contempt they suffer will be like Me also in glory. And those who resemble Me less in pain and contempt will also bear less resemblance to Me in glory**" (*Diary*, 446). Part of this glory is forgiveness — not holding the suffering others cause us against them, but making our suffering at their hands a plea for their salvation.

During trials, we must always trust that if the Father allows us to suffer greatly, it is because He is supporting us with even greater grace and desires us to be near Him in Heaven: "Have great trust in the Lord Jesus. ... Have great confidence; God is always our Father, even when He sends us trials" (*Diary*, 23-24). Indeed, as St. Teresa of Avila wrote: "Since God leads those whom He most loves by the way of trials, the more He loves them, the greater will be their trials."[241] Saint Ignatius of Loyola further reminds us: "If God sends you many sufferings, it is a sign that He has great plans for you and certainly wants to make you a saint. ... If God gives you an abundant harvest of trials, it is a sign of great holiness which He desires you to attain. Do you want to become a great saint? Ask God to send you many sufferings. The flame of Divine Love never rises higher than when fed with the wood of the Cross, which the infinite charity of the Savior used to finish His sacrifice. All the pleasures of the world are nothing compared with the sweetness found in the gall and vinegar offered to Jesus Christ. That is, hard and painful things endured for Jesus Christ and with Jesus Christ."

---

[240] Saint Teresa of Ávila and John Dalton, *The Interior Castle* (London: T. Jones, 1852), 193.
[241] *Teresa of Ávila: The Way of Perfection*, 101-02.

Only one who has experienced the Power of the Resurrection with its enduring peace and joy can say that the pleasures of the world are "nothing compared with the sweetness found in the gall and vinegar offered to Jesus Christ." We must take saints at their word, for of all people, they would not lie or exaggerate! True peace and enduring joy come from dying with Christ and rising to new life in trust. This does not mean we must never fight against suffering in accord with the Father's will: We ought to remedy injustice and alleviate suffering, as did Jesus during His earthly ministry, but we must remember that the greatest suffering is that of sin, which is uprooted through union with Christ Crucified and Risen. The greatest suffering is the lack of divine love — gushing forth in the Blood and Water — in the hearts of men and women throughout the world.

We grow in humility, and therefore trust, the more we partake of Jesus' sufferings in our daily lives, as St. Ignatius teaches: "The third is most perfect Humility; namely, when ... in order to imitate and be more actually like Christ our Lord, I want and choose poverty with Christ poor rather than riches, opprobrium with Christ replete with it rather than honors; and to desire to be rated as worthless and a fool for Christ, Who first was held as such, rather than wise or prudent in this world."[242] We must remember, however, that our humiliations do not automatically provide humility. It is only by joyfully offering our humiliation to Jesus Crucified and by identifying ourselves with Him that we turn humiliations into humility. Hence we ought not to hold on to bitterness if someone humiliates us. If we do, we lose the opportunity to embrace humility; we close our hearts to trust in the Father's plan that permits such humiliations — as He permitted the humiliation of His Son.

Notice how on the day of the Resurrection, Jesus greets the apostles after having been abandoned by all but one of them. Jesus' first words are not, "Where have you been?" Jesus does not excoriate them. He simply uses the traditional Hebrew greeting: "*Shalom*! Peace be with you!" (see Jn 20:21). Jesus greets them with peace because He dwells in peace that cannot be disturbed nor taken away by the world (see Jn 14:27) and because He always forgives. Mary did not become indignant at the Apostles either. She shares her Son's attitude of trust and forgiveness, and if we accept her into our home, as John did, she will teach us to forgive as Christ forgives. How often, though, do we greet those who cause us difficulty, not with peace, but with irritation and frustration!

"Trust gives us inner peace, such as the world cannot give. And so Christ, showing Himself to the Apostles after the Resurrection, greeted them with the words: 'Peace be to you!' (John 20:19), for they had great trust in their Master."[243]

To draw this point further: God can bring good out of evil, even out of our sins and the sins of those around us, through His Divine Mercy. Now, this does

---

[242] Saint Ignatius of Loyola, *The Spiritual Exercises of St. Ignatius of Loyola*, 84.
[243] Blessed Sopocko, *The Mercy of God in His Works*, Vol. 3, 178.

not give us permission to sin in order to see God bring good out of it (see Rom 6:1, 15); our sinfulness itself does not please the Father. But if we daily renew our Baptism by immersing ourselves and our sinfulness in the Spirit of Mercy, washing them in the Blood and Water, we have an opportunity to accomplish our sanctification by growing in humility and giving glory to Jesus, whose glory it is to forgive sins and save sinners. Our glory as Christians is to forgive others, as Christ has forgiven us (see Eph 4:32; see *Diary*, 1628).

It is important to remember that loving those who cause us suffering does not mean that we will feel the emotions of love. Rather, we can recognize the *presence* of love in our hearts if we pray for those who cause us suffering, wish them well, and do not lose our peace.

IMPORTANCE OF GRACE

All of this makes sense when we read it, but can we profess and live it in our own lives? Do we stand with confidence before the storms and crosses of our everyday lives? If we trust that the Father's Love is at work in our crosses, we will carry them more easily on our path toward the joy of the Resurrection. To speak of the Father's Love — the Holy Spirit — at work in our lives is one simple way of describing *grace*. In Greek, the word for grace, *charis*, is related to the word for joy, *chara*. If we trust in the Father's Love, *charis*, at work in our suffering, then we will experience true joy: *chara*.

When the Archangel Gabriel greets Mary, he calls her *kecharitomene* — a word naming Mary the one who has been completely transformed by grace, by joy. The Church sees in this name of Mary an indication of her Immaculate Conception. To be immaculate like Mary means to be completely transformed by grace, the joy of the Father's Love, at each moment, in every circumstance. Such joy causes much harm to Satan and crushes the serpent's head, because if we find our joy in the Lord (see Is 61:10), we will not need to seek such joy in any sinful pleasures or delights of this world. This joy in the Lord does not exclude but rather includes the beautiful delights of this world, inasmuch as they are echoes of the infinite beauty of God, a hymn of praise to His glory (see Dan 3:57-90). Saint Ignatius of Loyola in fact urges us to see how God labors to manifest His goodness and love for us in all creation![244]

Mary is the cause of our joy, for she bore Jesus Christ, the source of all grace and joy, even during suffering. She teaches us to carry the joy and peace of the Resurrection within our hearts wherever we go, not allowing the serpent to take those away by his lies. Just as Mary shared in a unique way in the sufferings of her Son, so she shared in the glory of His Resurrection, as Jesus told St. Faustina: **"You have taken a great part in My Passion; therefore I now give you a great share in My joy and glory"** (*Diary*, 205).

The key to joy is not to see our problems as the center or focus of our lives, but to see Jesus, risen from the dead, as Pope Francis exhorts us:

---

[244] Saint Ignatius of Loyola, *The Spiritual Exercises of St. Ignatius of Loyola*, 117-22.

May the Lord free us from this trap, from being Christians without hope, who live as if the Lord were not risen, as if our problems were the center of our lives. We see and will continue to see problems both within and without. They will always be there. But tonight it is important to shed the light of the Risen Lord upon our problems, and in a certain sense, to "evangelize" them. To evangelize our problems. Let us not allow darkness and fear to distract us and control us; we must cry out to them: the Lord "is not here, but has risen!" He is our greatest joy; he is always at our side and will never let us down.[245]

Transformed by joy, Mary takes our hand amid our problems to lead us to her Son, to teach us to take a step of trust toward Him, stepping upon the serpent of sadness and hopelessness.

The serpent lies to us, attempting to convince us that in the end, evil has the last word, but Mary teaches us to wait in patience and silence for the glory of the Resurrection, confident in our trust that the Father will resolve all problems and conquer all evil in His time and in His manner. We have only to trust as Mary trusted, that the Father who created this beautiful world with its natural wonders out of nothing can raise us from the dead and create a saint out of the nothingness of our sins (see 2 Macc 7:28-29).

While we are away from the Lord in body in this world of suffering, we must walk by faith and trust, not by sight (see 2 Cor 5:6-8). We must already sing, "Alleluia" (Hebrew for "Praise the Lord!"), confident of the victory of Christ over sin and death. If we judge according to what we can see, we will not notice what is invisible, yet present, in the crosses we carry: the joy of the Holy Spirit. If we do not see the Father's grace hidden in our sufferings, it is no surprise that we find no joy in our sufferings, either. How often, because we lack faith and trust, we fail to see Christ, risen from the dead, hidden amid our daily crosses and difficulties. The saints considered suffering to be a joy because they allowed the Father's grace to be at work in them and trusted that the Holy Spirit was transforming them through suffering (see Jas 1:2).

Saint Faustina relates a story from her life that illustrates the connection between suffering and joy: The more she suffered, the more she felt she had an opportunity to love God, and hence the more joy she felt. She said that this seems impossible, but love can do such amazing things in souls who love God (see *Diary*, 303).

That suffering could ever become a delight seems quite impossible to most of us. But "love can work such things in pure souls" (*Diary*, 303), and we have only to trust that the Holy Spirit *will* work such things in our souls, for what He is doing far surpasses what we ask for or imagine (see Eph 3:20-21). In fact, He

---

[245] Pope Francis, "Easter Vigil in the Holy Night" (March 26, 2016), accessed July 11, 2017, http://w2.vatican.va/content/francesco/en/homilies/2016/documents/papa-francesco_20160326_omelia-veglia-pasquale.html.

often wants to do more than we want Him to do — He wants to make us into saints that shine like stars in a world of darkness (see Phil 2:13-16). May we not make His work be in vain. Rather, may we allow Him to mold us through suffering like the potter, and purify us like gold in the furnace (see Is 48:10, 64:7).

It would be foolish for us to presume to know better than God. He leads us to Heaven, for He is our Father and knows what He is doing (see Is 45:9-11). As St. Ignatius of Loyola stated: "Few souls understand what God would accomplish in them if they were to abandon themselves unreservedly to Him and if they were to allow His grace to mold them accordingly."[246] On the other hand, if our plans differ from God's, we often become frustrated, impatient, and upset when things don't go our way because we are going against God Himself (see Acts 5:39).

GOD'S PLAN VERSUS OUR PLAN

The Resurrection reveals that the ultimate answer to our suffering is not to be found in this life, and that we cannot demand an answer from the Father this side of the grave. Job tried to find an answer from the Lord for all that he endured, but he did not receive a specific response. Instead, the answer was that God Himself came down to Job — a foreshadowing of the Incarnation. And God reminded Job of the infinite wisdom of our Father, wisdom we cannot fathom (see Job 40:2). When we look for an answer to suffering, the only answer we receive this side of the grave is Jesus Christ. All our trials serve to point us toward Jesus, our Light amid the darkness of this life.

The suffering we endure darkens all the false lights, so we can see the one true light, Jesus Christ. Ultimately, we can only trust in the Father, knowing that all our heart's longings and desires will be answered fully in the next life. We must be patient, knowing that if we hold out to the end, we will receive the crown of life (see Jas 1:12). Since we are children in God's sight, we cannot possibly know the reasons why He allows everything — only at the Last Judgment will everything be made clear (see CCC, 1040). For now, we are asked to trust and be confident that He uses everything to accomplish His will: our sanctification (see 1 Thess 4:3).

I want to introduce you to another Greek word from the New Testament: hypomonē, which means "perseverance, endurance, or patience" — literally, "standing under" difficulties and trials. Trust enables this endurance and perseverance so we can attain victory during a trial.[247] This perseverance is so

---

[246] Quoted in Joseph M. Esper, *Saintly Solutions to Life's Common Problems: From Anger, Boredom, and Temptation to Gluttony, Gossip, and Greed* (Manchester, New Hampshire: Sophia Institute Press, 2001).

[247] "[*Hypomonē*] is not what we today call theological hope, but a constancy in desire that overcomes the trial of waiting, a soul attitude that must struggle to persevere, a waiting that is determined and victorious because it trusts in God." Ceslas Spicq and James D. Ernest, *Theological Lexicon of the New Testament* (Peabody, Massachusetts: Hendrickson Publishers, 1994), 414.

important that Jesus promises salvation to those who persevere in trust unto the end (see Mk 13:13). The Resurrection shows that our persevering trust will always be rewarded and proves that no one who has turned with trust to the Mercy of the Father has been deceived (see *Diary*, 1541).

Let us ponder now how Jesus did not upbraid or punish the apostles for deserting Him. Instead, He forgave them, just as, from the Cross, He forgave His executioners (see Lk 23:34). We can trust the Lord because no matter how terrible our sins are, no matter how far we have fallen, Jesus will forgive us (see *Diary*, 1059). Jesus encourages us to approach Him with confidence, for He is our High Priest who knows our human weaknesses and sufferings (see Heb 4:15-16).

Because the Resurrection is not merely a return to Eden and to what was lost by Adam and Eve, even after Baptism we must endure the consequences of sin (see *CCC*, 1264). The Father allowed man to sin, foreseeing that through faith in Christ we would receive greater blessings than those lost by Adam and Eve (see *CCC*, 412). In Eden, they enjoyed a relationship of trust with God as Father. We enjoy that relationship anew in Jesus Christ, as His adopted sons and daughters (see Gal 4:4-7). We know, in a way that Adam and Eve did not, how trustworthy, good, and merciful our Father is, even in the face of our sinfulness! Our sins have served the purpose of revealing the very Face of Mercy: Jesus Christ. Despite our worst misery and sins, He remains merciful and compassionate.

Since the Lord promised us plans for our welfare and a future of hope, we ought never to look at our crosses without faith or without looking also at the Crucified One. By means of faith, our gaze penetrates beyond the suffering we are given to bear, to the grace and joy hidden within it. What may seem, superficially, to be senseless and pointless in fact offers a step toward dying to ourselves and an opportunity to enter more deeply into the divine life (see *Diary*, 1599).

Without trust, we may profess the Resurrection with our lips, but we aren't living it. Without trust, we are not living in *zoe*. Without trust, we are not living out our Baptism. The Resurrection shows us that we can lose everything, and yet gain everything: for if we have Christ, we have all we need (see Mt 10:39; Phil 3:8).

In Chapter 3 of this book, I discussed how we can trust what someone says because of the kind of person he is. We believe in Jesus, not because we can verify everything He says, but because we know what kind of person He is. We trust Jesus because of His infinite love and mercy, revealed to us when He offered Himself for our sake. We trust Him because even when we did our absolute best to hurt Him and even kill Him, His only response was (and remains) one of mercy and pardon. When we pierced His Sacred Heart with the lance of our sins, Blood and Water poured out — a sign of His Mercy and forgiveness. Let us ask now: "When I am pushed to my limit, when others lance my heart, what flows forth — mercy and forgiveness or anger and bitterness? Which has greater power in my life — sin or Mercy? Have I died to myself, and how much do I trust? Not only is trust *receptive*; trust leads to *active obedience*. Living the Resurrection requires that we obey the will of the Father by denying ourselves and loving others as Jesus has loved us (see 1 Jn 3:16-18).

DISAPPOINTMENT AND DISCOURAGEMENT

Previously, I discussed how discouragement and anxiety can be obstacles to trust and to our advancement in the spiritual life. In the Gospels, we see time and again how Jesus "disappoints" people's hopes in Him. We naturally hope that Jesus will bring worldly blessings, peace, and temporal welfare. However, Jesus bluntly states that He came, not to bring false peace, but to bring the sword (see Mt 10:34). This is not a sword of worldly violence, but the sword of trust in God amid a sinful world, for our trust in God requires sacrifice — just as a sword pierced Mary's heart because of her unconditional trust in the Father.

What are we to do when this sword pierces our hearts and we are tempted to be disappointed and discouraged? In the Gospel of Luke, we see how Jesus reacts to our disappointment. When Cleopas and another disciple were walking to Emmaus, Jesus came to them, hidden. They were astonished that He had not heard about all that had happened in Jerusalem — referring to the death of Jesus. Imagine how disappointing the death of the Messiah would be! They had placed hope and trust in Him, only to see their hope and trust dashed to pieces by the authorities. Jesus listened to their disappointment.

How often are we like them! We place our trust in Jesus, and what happens seems to be the complete opposite of what we expect. What could be a harsher way to shatter the disciples' dreams and hopes than by the Crucifixion of the Liberator? Yet Jesus has great patience with them. He understood their disappointment as He understands our disappointment today. He proceeds to explain to them all that was foretold about Him in the Scriptures. Often we focus on only part of what was foretold — the "nice" things: prophecies and promises of blessings — and glide over the promises of persecution, suffering, and death. I imagine that the disciples focused on the Messiah who would be a great military king and would destroy the power of the oppressors, conveniently glossing over the prophecies of Isaiah, Daniel, Zechariah, and others with their predictions of a suffering servant, a Messiah and Son of Man who would die and so redeem His people.

We often do not live our lives in the light of the full Word of God. We trust only the part that appeals to us: eternal life. When we do this, we become easily disappointed and confused, and it is harder to trust. Living in the light of the whole Bible is so important because if we don't know His Word, inevitably we will be like the two saddened disciples going to Emmaus, and the serpent will seize us in our ignorance, disappointment, and distrust. He will attempt to point out apparent contradictions in God's promises: "Look, He promised you a Messiah, and there He is, crucified!" Or even: "Look, He promised that your trust would never be disappointed, and here you are in such suffering! Could you trust such a Father?" Such are the taunts of Satan, the serpent of old, whose only goal is to capture us in our ignorance of the Scriptures. By explaining the Scriptures to the two disciples, Jesus reignites their hearts with the fire of the Holy Spirit, teaching them to trust once again that the Father's plan is always fulfilled.

The Word had such a home in Mary that the Word Himself came to dwell in her physically in the Incarnation. Mary teaches us to be Christians of the Word, immersed in the words of God, that we might trust the Word of God. Mary teaches us to trust, to step upon the serpent, by the daily reading of Scripture and allowing that Word to take on flesh. I can only imagine her preparation for Pentecost: how she taught the disciples many stories about her Son that they had never heard before, or explained the Bible to them in new ways. May we allow Jesus to walk with us in our disappointment and discouragement, confident that Mary aids us even then, showing how all the contradictions of the serpent are just fog intended to cloud the path before us.

CHAPTER 25

Trust as Spiritual Worship

"Glorify My Mercy"
(*Diary*, 1485).

Trust is not an easy path and not for the fainthearted (the *pusillanimous*). As a concrete sign of her total trust in Him, Jesus asked Faustina for the sacrifice of her own will as a whole "burnt offering," meaning that she would fulfill His will always, everywhere, and in everything (see *Diary*, 923).

This request is not specifically to St. Faustina or a few select Christians, for we are all called to offer ourselves up as living sacrifices to the Father (see Rom 12:1-2). The Holy Spirit is the fire from Heaven that consumes the holocaust offering of our will. This is our spiritual worship — that our humanity and our bodies filled with the Holy Spirit become an offering to the Father as victims of love. Moreover, if we trust Him and allow Him to work freely in our lives, the Holy Spirit transforms our suffering into salvific love, into blessing.[248]

Our Lady, the one "thoroughly transformed by grace," was just such a holocaust at Calvary, for she completely entrusted her will and her Son to the Father. Hence, the Fathers of the Church saw Mary as symbolized by the burning bush that Moses had seen: set ablaze with fire, but not consumed (see Ex 3:1-17). The Holy Spirit transformed her suffering into blessing through the Resurrection. Mary was on fire with the Holy Spirit — but she was not consumed, not destroyed. There is always this dual movement in the Christian life: suffering followed by Resurrection to new life and the descent of the Holy Spirit.

We may be afraid, but Mary is with us to teach us to allow the Holy Spirit to set us ablaze. We are to be afraid, not of the fire or suffering, but only of sin and of closing our hearts to the Spirit of Love. The Spirit falls upon us, but does not destroy or consume us. Like Mary, we are called to be burning bushes, giving off the light of Christ to the world, setting it ablaze with that same Spirit of trust and love (see Mt 5:16; Lk 12:49). Christ came to set the world ablaze with the Holy Spirit, and He desires to continue to do so through us!

Our spiritual worship is defined by our trust, expressing itself in joyful obedience to the Father's will and self-donation through our love of God and neighbor at every moment of our lives. We often think of the Father's will in terms of the big or necessary moments, such as going to Mass on Sundays or not eating meat on Fridays in Lent. But if God is our Father and we dwell in His

---

[248] Saint John Paul II, *Dominum et Vivificantem*, n. 39-41.

house, the Church, then we are under His roof and we ought to obey Him, not just in obvious or important instances, but above all in the small moments of everyday life, just as we ought to obey our parents.

We trust and obey the Father's will every day by listening to the inspiration of the Holy Spirit and fulfilling our duties out of love for Him and for His glory (see Col 3:17). As St. Faustina tells us, such trust in the Holy Spirit is the shortest route to holiness (see *Diary*, 291). This way to grow in holiness requires only attentive listening to the voice of Jesus and trust in His inspiration (see *Diary*, 584).

Our spiritual worship exercised through trust and obedience requires the "burnt offering" or complete sacrifice of entirely uniting our will to His. This personal sacrifice of our will through the Holy Spirit unites us to the one sacrifice of Christ that brings about our salvation. Our redemption occurred not by the mere suffering of Christ, but by the loving obedience of Jesus, who freely undertook such suffering. We are opened to Christ's salvation through trusting obedience, by allowing the Holy Spirit to unite our will with the Father's will, even when that includes suffering. The sacrifice of obedience is the sacrifice of the Son, and by the Holy Spirit and Baptism, His sacrifice becomes our sacrifice, too.[249]

Our spiritual worship extends the Liturgy of the Mass in our lives, for we are all royal priests by Baptism (see *CCC*, 1268), and we participate in the Mass, not merely by doing things, but by uniting ourselves with Christ as a living sacrifice to the Father for the salvation of souls. The priest asks this of the Father during Eucharistic Prayer IV — that we, together with Christ, would become a sacrifice to the praise of His glory: "Look, O Lord, upon the Sacrifice which you yourself have provided for your Church, and grant in your loving kindness to all who partake of this one Bread and one Chalice that, gathered into one body by the Holy Spirit, they may truly become a living sacrifice in Christ to the praise of your glory."[250]

Just as the bread and wine are transformed by the Holy Spirit into the Body and Blood of Christ as an offering acceptable to the Father, so we, too, are transformed into the Body of Christ in the Eucharist and become a sacrifice to the Father. This offering of ourselves in union with Jesus in the Eucharist is the fulfillment of our Baptism, by which we are united to Christ as members of His Body. We are called through the celebration of the Eucharist to entrust ourselves completely and entirely to the Father in union with Jesus upon the Cross. This is our worship: imitation of Jesus' complete entrustment of Himself and Our Lady's trust in her Son.

Such spiritual worship is the full, conscious, and active participation of the laity in the Liturgy emphasized by Vatican II: "Mother Church earnestly desires that all the faithful should be led to that fully conscious, and active participation

---

[249] Ratzinger, *Jesus of Nazareth*, Part 2: *Holy Week*, 161.
[250] Roman Missal, 865.

in liturgical celebrations which is demanded by the very nature of the liturgy. Such participation by the Christian people as 'a chosen race, a royal priesthood, a holy nation, a redeemed people,' is their right and duty by reason of their baptism."[251]

Active participation does not mean simply exterior involvement in the Liturgy of the Mass, such as being a lector or an Extraordinary Minister of Holy Communion. Although those are ways of participating in the Holy Mass, they can be distractions for people performing the ministry if not understood properly.

The Holy Mass is primarily about interior, not exterior, reality. Many of us tend to focus on the external and practical, so we think participation must mean doing something, rather than *being* a certain way. To actively participate in the Eucharist, we need to be united with the Lord in His offering of Himself to the Father for the salvation of souls. By uniting ourselves and all our pain, joy, suffering, and crosses with those of Christ, we participate in the redemption of the world (see *CCC*, 1368). Indeed, our true problem is not that we suffer, but that we love so little when we suffer and thereby participate in Christ's redemption.

If we do not embrace our crosses during the week, what will we unite to Christ Crucified and Risen at Sunday Mass? We must not appear before the Father empty-handed (see Ex 23:15), nor should we leave Holy Communion with an empty heart! Our Lord is saddened when He comes to souls in Holy Communion with all kinds of graces, but they do not receive them because they do not recognize His love. After receiving Our Lord in the Eucharist, we hurt Jesus if we quickly occupy ourselves with other things and forget about Him (see *Diary,* 1385). How often we abandon Jesus, seeking our temporal pleasures and joys as consolation, instead of remaining with Him!

We can take all the evils of our lives — sin and suffering — to Mass, and ask the Father to redeem and bring good out of them just as He did by raising His Son from the grave. When we actively participate at Mass, our lives gain eternal significance, and our small actions of love and daily crosses gain value and merit by being united to those of our Lord (see *Diary,* 1512). In fact, just as the bread and wine undergo transubstantiation and so become the Body and Blood of Christ, in our daily acts of trust and love, even amid suffering, we undergo a similar transformation by the Holy Spirit and become an offering to the Father.

When we undergo this transformation, we ourselves become the Body of Christ. Where do we find the Body of the Risen Christ? *We* are the Body of the Risen Christ: We are His hands, His feet, His members upon earth. Do we trust Jesus enough to let Him use us, even unwittingly and without our knowledge? Part of the Resurrection is learning to trust that Jesus can use us — even in our sinfulness — as His Body; the only obstacle to this is our lack of trust!

---

[251] *Sacrosanctum Concilium: Dogmatic Constitution on the Sacred Liturgy*, in *Vatican II Documents* (Vatican City: Libreria Editrice Vaticana, 2011), n. 14.

PAYING THE PRICE

Those who live in a capitalistic society know that things cost money; the more valuable something is, the more one must pay to obtain it. This is also true for the most valuable thing of all: human souls, which are purchased only by sacrifice. "**Every conversion of a sinful soul demands sacrifice**" (*Diary*, 961). When we complain about suffering, we must ask ourselves just how precious is our own soul, or that of another. If souls are precious to us, there will be no price too high to pay for them. If souls are not precious to us, then we will consider the Cross much too heavy a price to pay.

Are we willing to unite our sufferings with those of Christ for the salvation of souls? Are we willing, with Paul and countless saints across the millennia, to complete what is lacking in the sufferings of Christ (see Col 1:24) by uniting our daily sufferings with His when we join our brethren in celebrating the Eucharist? Simply by fulfilling her daily duties out of obedience, St. Faustina saved many souls without preaching or doing any apostolic work. With every stitch of her crocheting, St. Faustina converted a soul because she united her work to Jesus' work and obedience to the Father in His hidden life (see *Diary*, 961).

How many souls can we convert by offering up our daily duties for the glory of God and the salvation of souls? We do not know how many souls have been entrusted to us and our prayers, so it behooves us not to miss a single opportunity in our ordinary lives (see *Diary*, 245). How many opportunities there are each day to offer up countless sacrifices as we let go of our own will, deny ourselves, and entrust ourselves to the Father's will! We need not do great things, but rather fulfill our normal duties for the glory of God (see Col 3:17). This basic acceptance of duty and the will of the Father is the fundamental form of penance that God asks of us.[252] In return for a little suffering that ends, we can gain, for ourselves or for another, life that never ends!

There is nothing written about Mary's daily life as such, but we can assume that she was caught up in the normal activities of a woman and mother of her time — cooking, cleaning, conversing with others, helping her neighbor and the poor — and that she lived her days in self-denial, humility, surrender, trust, and docility to the Holy Spirit. Mary offered spiritual worship constantly and without ceasing by her gratitude, as sung in the Magnificat, and by her constant "amen" of trust in the Father's will, yet she was perfected in grace and virtue precisely because of the Holy Spirit at work in her everyday life.

All of this leads us to the essential element at the heart of *zoe:* thanksgiving. Through gratitude, we participate in the Eucharist each day — not only during the Mass, but throughout our entire day, for *eucharist* is the Greek word for "thanksgiving." With Jesus, we are called to give thanks always and everywhere

---

[252] Pope Paul VI, *Paenitemini* (February 17, 1966), accessed July 11, 2017, http://w2.vatican.va/content/paul-vi/en/apost_constitutions/documents/hf_p-vi_apc_19660217_paenitemini.html.

for all that the Father has done, is doing, and will do. Our daily lives, then, become one long thanksgiving, or Eucharist, to the Father. Saint Ignatius of Loyola wrote that the root of all sin is ingratitude.

How important, then, is gratitude in order to avoid sin! The prefaces of the Eucharistic Liturgy proclaim that it is our "duty and our salvation, always and everywhere to give you thanks, Lord, holy Father." Indeed, it is not only our duty to give the Father thanks; it is our *salvation* to give Him thanks, always and everywhere! Heaven will be a ceaseless hymn of thanksgiving to the Father for the gift of salvation in Jesus Christ. If we want to be ready for Heaven, we must begin today by giving thanks — not sometimes; not often; but "always and everywhere." As St. Gianna Molla exhorts us: "Also in suffering, let us say: Thanks be to God."[253]

Since we are saved by faith in Jesus Christ, we fulfill the Father's will and demonstrate our trust by doing the good works prepared for us by the Father from all eternity (see Eph 2:10). We perform those good works precisely out of gratitude for all that the Father has done. The greatest "good work" we can do is to endure suffering in union with Christ, for Christ redeemed the world by His entire life, but most especially by His death upon the Cross.

As Blessed George Matulaitis, the Renovator of the Marians, said, "If you are seriously ill and bedridden, do not worry that you cannot work. You already have something to do — to bear the pain and discomfort of your illness patiently and peacefully. … Suffering in the spirit of Christ is very worthwhile. Our Savior never accomplished so much as when he appeared to be doing nothing — on the cross."[254] Similarly, we may do all sorts of good works for the Lord, but the one work that outweighs all the rest is obedience that embraces suffering in union with the offering of the Eucharist. We can curb the flood of evil in the world by our trust, expressing itself in the surrender of ourselves into the hands of the Father, particularly on behalf of all those who distrust Him.

KEEPING THE SABBATH HOLY

Early in Christian history, the day of rest shifted from Saturday to Sunday, from the last day of the week to the first. Understood as an encounter with the Risen Lord, the Eucharist was celebrated on Sunday morning, the time when our Lord appeared to the disciples and apostles. Jesus celebrated the Eucharist as an act of thanksgiving, in gratitude to the Father for hearing His prayer and plea for deliverance. We often give thanks *after* the fact, *after* we have received a gift from our Father in Heaven, but Jesus teaches us by His example to do otherwise.

---

[253] "Reflections of Saint Gianna Beretta Molla."
[254] "Blessed George Matulaitis-Matulewicz (1871-1927), Renovator of The Marians," accessed July 11, 2017, http://www.matulaitis-matulewicz.org/hislife.php.

We notice that on Holy Thursday, Jesus was already giving thanks to the Father for the Resurrection on Easter Sunday.[255] We are called to give thanks already for the gift of the Resurrection that awaits us. When we receive Jesus in Holy Communion, we already receive the pledge of our own resurrection: "Hidden Jesus, glorious pledge of my resurrection, All my life is concentrated in You. It is You, O Host, who empower me to love forever, And I know that You will love me as Your child in return" (*Diary,* 1427). Every Holy Communion increases our share in eternal life (see *Diary,* 1811). The Eucharist and Sunday ought to be privileged times to trust and receive strength from the Risen Lord, and with Mary ponder the face of her Risen Son, begging her that we may share in her faith and trust.

By giving thanks before He underwent His Passion, Jesus transformed His violent death into an act of love, showing that in His Passion, He does not lose control, but instead enjoys total freedom through His self-surrender to the Father upon the Cross.[256] Unlike Jesus, we cannot foresee the future, but we can offer up everything that will happen to us, so all that happens will be transformed into an offering to the Father.

When we fail to rest on Sundays — fail to worship Jesus in the Eucharist, fail to spend time in communal prayer and rest — we also fail to orient our lives toward the Resurrection, and thus we fail to trust throughout the week. Our lives become enslaved to this world, to its work and its demands, and we fail to trust that the Father will always provide for our needs. On Sundays, we need not only to rest by spending time with family and loved ones, but also to rest with the Lord and in the Lord by reading the Bible and praying together, for the Lord promised His presence to those who gather in His name (see Mt 18:20).

Saint John Paul II recommended that Sundays be not only days of rest for ourselves, but also days of witnessing to the Resurrection, suggesting that we evangelize on Sundays. We should visit the poor, the sick, the elderly, and the imprisoned, and so give witness that Christ, risen from the dead, works through His Body, the Church. We are privileged to encounter Christ in the underprivileged, and I would highly recommend reading St. John Paul II's letter on the Lord's Day, *Dies Domini,* to understand how to properly live the Day of the Lord.[257] We have a moral duty to share our wealth with others as a way to encourage them to trust in the Father. We do this by manifesting His goodness through our own good works (see Mt 5:16; 1 Pet 2:12; Phil 2:5). Just as Jesus, the Son of God, is the human face of the Heavenly Father, so should we, sons and daughters in the Son, put a human face on Divine Providence (see Jn 12:45).

---

[255] Ratzinger, *Jesus of Nazareth; Part 2, Holy Week,* 140.

[256] Ibid., 130.

[257] Saint John Paul II, *Dies Domini,* Apostolic Letter (May 31, 1998), accessed July 11, 2017, https://w2.vatican.va/content/john-paul-ii/en/apost_letters/1998/documents/hf_jp-ii_apl_05071998_dies-domini.html.

We are given money to use it well, not to hoard it as our source of security. Our attitude toward the poor is decisive for our eternal salvation; indeed, our final judgment by Jesus hinges upon our relationship with the poor: "Our Lord warns us that we shall be separated from him if we fail to meet the serious needs of the poor and the little ones who are his brethren" (*CCC*, 1033). Jesus states clearly that where our treasure is, our heart is also. We are to gain for ourselves treasure in Heaven, not on earth (see Mt 6:19-20).

We should ask now, as St. Faustina described her own experience, if the most solemn moment of our lives is the moment when we receive Holy Communion. Do we, like her, long for each Holy Communion? Do we remember how it hurts Jesus when we are indifferent to Holy Communion and to His presence in the Eucharist (see *Diary*, 1447)? How often do we give thanks for Holy Communion itself? What are we to do when we receive Jesus in Holy Communion? How are we to give Him proper thanks? Saint Faustina teaches us: "Jesus, living Host, You are my Mother, You are my all! It is with simplicity and love, with faith and trust that I will always come to You, O Jesus! I will share everything with You, as a child with its loving mother, my joys and sorrows — in a word, everything" (*Diary*, 230).

If we remain with Jesus in Holy Communion and receive all the graces He desires to lavish upon us, we will have the strength necessary to endure whatever may befall us (see *Diary*, 1489). Saint Faustina, whose full name in religion is Sr. Maria Faustina of the Most Blessed Sacrament, experienced this strength: "When my strength begins to fail, it is Holy Communion that will sustain me and give me strength. Indeed, I fear the day on which I would not receive Holy Communion. My soul draws astonishing strength from Holy Communion" (*Diary*, 1826). Without strength from Holy Communion, we cannot possibly carry the crosses that befall us throughout the week. She continues: "Jesus-Host, if You Yourself did not sustain me, I would not be able to persevere on the cross. I would not be able to endure so much suffering. But the power of Your grace maintains me on a higher level and makes my sufferings meritorious. You give me strength always to move forward and to gain heaven by force and to have love in my heart for those from whom I suffer adversities and contempt. With Your grace one can do all things" (*Diary*, 1620).

Fortified with this strength, we are called to give thanks in advance for all that will befall us, so that we are not unwilling to undergo difficulties, but rather embrace such crosses with great trust for the glory of our Father. If we adopt this practice of giving thanks in advance for everything that will happen to us, then whenever we encounter an unexpected cross during the week, we have already given thanks to the Father for it and willingly accepted it by drinking of the chalice of the Lord! Just as Jesus entrusts Himself without reserve to the Father and to us in Holy Communion, so we are called to imitate Him by placing ourselves unconditionally in the hands of the Father as a Host. We are called to be transformed into living Hosts, as Jesus instructs St. Faustina (see *Diary*, 1629, 1826).

Only then can we truly live what the priest says at the end of every Eucharistic prayer: "Through him, and with him, and in him, O God, Almighty Father, in the unity of the Holy Spirit, all glory and honor is yours, for ever and ever."[258] To which we respond, as did Mary at the Annunciation, with great trust and confidence: "Amen!"

---

[258] Roman Missal, 662.

CHAPTER 26

The Courage to Trust

"[Behold] I am sending the promise of my Father upon you; but stay in the city until you are clothed with power from on high"
(Lk 24:49).

Having read thus far, you might be convinced of the need to trust in the Lord, but your heart may still be filled with fear. Do not be ashamed if you are afraid, for even after seeing Christ raised from the dead, the apostles were still not courageous enough to trust in the Father and face the Cross as Jesus did. Why was that? Why do we, with all that we now know about suffering, still cower before our daily crosses?

As Thomas à Kempis exhorts us in the *Imitation of Christ:*

> Why, then, do you fear to take up the cross when through it you can win a kingdom? In the cross is salvation, in the cross is life, in the cross is protection from enemies, in the cross is infusion of heavenly sweetness, in the cross is strength of mind, in the cross is joy of spirit, in the cross is highest virtue, in the cross is perfect holiness. There is no salvation of soul nor hope of everlasting life but in the cross. Take up your cross, therefore, and follow Jesus, and you shall enter eternal life. He Himself opened the way before you in carrying His cross, and upon it He died for you, that you, too, might take up your cross and long to die upon it. If you die with Him, you shall also live with Him, and if you share His suffering, you shall also share His glory.[259]

Why do we still complain? Why do we, as Paul so famously put it, "do what we do not want to do, and not do the things we do want to do?" (see Rom 7:15-19).

TRUST AND FEAR

Let us look at the accounts of the Resurrection. The apostles were gathered in hiding in the Cenacle where the Lord had His Last Supper. Sometimes they locked the door out of fear of the Jews (see Jn 20:19). We see that, even after being decisively defeated by Christ, the serpent still possessed the powerful weapon of fear that enslaved the disciples themselves. We know, however, that

---

[259] Thomas à Kempis, *The Imitation of Christ* (Oak Harbor, Washington: Logos Research Systems, 1996), 87.

all but one of these fearful and timid apostles would suffer martyrdom for Jesus Christ. So what wrought such a change in them? Pentecost: the day when the Father sent forth the Holy Spirit upon Jesus Christ's apostles.

The apostles not only knew Jesus as a Person with whom they lived, but they also were united to Jesus Christ in their hearts through the same Spirit of Jesus that enabled Him to suffer His brutal death (see 2 Tim 1:7-8). The Holy Spirit that filled Jesus fills our own hearts with the surpassing power that is found only in God and is manifested in our lives through our apparent weakness and defeat — namely, the Cross. The Holy Spirit gives us the courage to trust, even when it seems that the serpent has conquered.

This is Mary's greatness, that even before Pentecost, while standing beneath her Son at Calvary, when all seemed lost, she did not lose hope nor stop trusting in the Father. It is no accident that she was gathered in the Upper Room with the apostles and disciples on Pentecost. Mary, who was entrusted to John at Calvary, who watched over the new Church, and who poured out her maternal self-giving love upon the disciples, was there on the day the fire fell.[260] Mary, who was forever filled with the Holy Spirit from the very first moment of her conception and overshadowed by Him at the Annunciation, gathered in prayer with the Church to teach her early members how to receive that same Holy Spirit, so that they, too, might learn to trust. Mary who, through the grace of the Immaculate Conception, always walked in the light of the Resurrection and in newness of life, now teaches us to do the same — to be always open to resurrection to new life by the Holy Spirit.

The Immaculate Conception is nothing other than the mystery of the Resurrection, already present in this life. It is victory over the serpent and over evil. The eternal Immaculate Conception is the Holy Spirit who raises us to new life. At Pentecost, that same Holy Spirit comes upon us to sanctify us, lift us to new life, and fill us with the balm of trust.

If we still waver and have a spirit of cowardice, it means that we are not yet fully alive in the Holy Spirit. In the Eucharist, we are united to Jesus Christ and strengthened by His Love. In Baptism, we are immersed in the Mercy of the Father to wash away our sins. In Confirmation, the mystery of Pentecost is repeated: The Holy Spirit is given to us in full measure by the laying on of hands[261] and anointing with oil. *Masiah* (Messiah) and *Christos* (Christ) both mean "one anointed by the Holy Spirit," and to say that we are Christians is to say that we are the "anointed ones," because we are disciples of the Messiah, the "Anointed One" (see *CCC*, 1287). If we are to live a life of trust and not cower before the Cross as the apostles did before Pentecost, we need to ask the Holy Spirit to renew within us His presence and grace given through Baptism and

---

[260] Saint John Paul II, *Redemptoris Mater*, n. 40.

[261] Blessed Paul VI, *Divina Consortium Naturae*, Apostolic Constitution, August 15, 1971, accessed July 11, 2017, http://w2.vatican.va/content/paul-vi/la/apost_constitutions/documents/hf_p-vi_apc_19710815_divina-consortium.html.

Confirmation (see *CCC*, 1300). This can be done by offering a prayer to the Holy Spirit every morning and evening, or simply repeating throughout the day, "Come, Holy Spirit!"

The surpassing power of God is not just an attribute: It is a Person, the Holy Spirit. "Life in the Spirit" means a life of trust and obedience to the Father's will; it means walking in the light of the Resurrection and the grace of Our Lady's Immaculate Conception; it means grasping her hand and walking along the path of trust while firmly and confidently stepping upon the serpent of distrust and fear.

Obedience and God's Will

Obedience does not mean that I choose to do the Father's will only because it is *His* will and I want to please Him. No. As Jesus taught Faustina, in true obedience *His* will becomes *my* will. True obedience is not denying myself and obeying the Father while still preferring my own will. Such obedience is imperfect. It may be a step forward, but unless we purposefully aim at perfect obedience, we may fall into complacency and make compromise after compromise, choosing our will instead of the Lord's (see Rev 3:15-16).

What is the Father's will? Saint Paul makes the Father's will explicit: He wants us to give thanks, to do all for His glory, and to become saints (see 1 Thess 4:3, 5:18). We discussed the need to be thankful always and do all for His glory, but I want to return once more to fighting the vice of pusillanimity because, since we are burdened with sin and its effects, we must consciously make the decision to become a saint; otherwise it will not happen. According to St. Faustina, holiness and sanctity can be summed up in one word: *obedience*. "The essence of the virtues is the will of God. He who does the will of God faithfully, practices all the virtues. In all the events and circumstances of my life, I adore and bless the holy will of God. The holy will of God is the object of my love. In the most secret depths of my soul, I live according to His will. I act exteriorly according to what I recognize inwardly as the will of God. Sweeter to me are the torments, sufferings, persecutions, and all manner of adversities by divine will than popularity, praise, and esteem by my own will" (*Diary*, 678).

Perfect obedience means completely aligning my will with that of the Father — in all things, at all times. As St. Faustina describes it: "Today during meditation, God gave me inner light and the understanding as to what sanctity is and of what it consists. ... Neither graces, nor revelations, nor raptures, nor gifts granted to a soul make it perfect, but rather the intimate union of the soul with God. These gifts are merely ornaments of the soul, but constitute neither its essence nor its perfection. My sanctity and perfection consist in the close union of my will with the will of God. God never violates our free will. It is up to us whether we want to receive God's grace or not. It is up to us whether we will cooperate with it or waste it" (*Diary*, 1107).

This sacrifice of obedience pleases God more than any other (see Ps 40:6-8; 1 Sam 15:22). No other sacrifice can compare with this, for living exclusively by the will of God brings particular delight to the entire Holy Trinity: "**Host pleasing to My Father, know, My daughter, that the entire Holy Trinity finds Its special delight in you, because you live exclusively by the will of God. No sacrifice can compare with this**" (*Diary*, 955). Such trust manifesting itself in submission to His will brings the greatest glory to Jesus: "**It is when you submit yourself to My will that you give Me the greatest glory and draw down upon yourself a sea of blessings. I would not take such special delight in you if you were not living by my will**" (*Diary*, 954).

Jesus taught St. Faustina that in order for her to live out this sacrifice of obedience, her will must no longer exist. She retained her free will, but whenever there was a divergence between the two wills, Faustina would choose the Father's. This was to be her daily sacrifice (see *Diary*, 372). This daily sacrifice of fulfilling the Father's will in obedience and gratitude for all He has given us is consummated in our participation in the Eucharist, the liturgical thanksgiving of Jesus to the Father. By living this sacrifice, we ourselves become the host offered to the Father. In this way, our lives are carried out in union with Jesus — the perfect Host, the Eucharist — and we are burning inside with the consuming fire of the Holy Spirit, a holocaust to the glory of God (see Heb 12:29; see also *Diary*, 483).

As the bread and wine are transubstantiated by the Holy Spirit and become the living Host — Jesus — so the Holy Spirit transforms us to be living hosts. Mary had an ordinary life, but inside her Heart, she burned with the Holy Spirit. Saint Gianna wrote: "One earns Paradise with one's daily task."[262] Saint Faustina was a sacrificial host to the Father, although her transformation was hidden from her sisters. Saint Thérèse of Lisieux wrote that she hoped for an army of little victim souls, souls who are "burnt offerings" of the overflowing Mercy of the Father, receiving all the love that is rejected by other souls.[263] May we, by daily trust, obedience, and gratitude, become such victim souls, such offerings for the glory of the Father.

Love and the Holy Spirit

What are the various authentic forms of human love if not reflected participation in the divine Love, the Holy Spirit? When we truly love, we no longer count the cost, and we joyfully carry all things for the sake of the beloved; we are focused no longer on ourselves and what we endure, but on them (see 1 Cor 13:7-8).[264]

If this sounds impossible, it is — without the Holy Spirit. The Holy Spirit is Love; we cannot trust unless He is supporting us, because such Love enables

---

[262] "Reflections of Saint Gianna Beretta Molla."
[263] Saint Thérèse of Lisieux and Taylor, *The Story of a Soul*, 133.
[264] Thomas a Kempis, *The Imitation of Christ*, trans. Leo Sherley-Price (London: Penguin Books, 2005), Book 3, chapter 5.

us to do many things we would not ordinarily choose to do. In other words, if we are to trust, we must first be open to His Love, so that we may participate in this Love. Just as St. Peter could not walk on water without trust in Jesus, so we cannot fulfill the Father's will without trust. With love, we trust, and exchange our weakness for His omnipotence: **"Yes, when you are obedient I take away your weakness and replace it with My strength. I am very surprised that souls do not want to make that exchange with Me"** (*Diary*, 381). Jesus promises extraordinary things to disciples who believe and trust in Him: "And these signs will accompany those who believe: in my name they will cast out demons; they will speak in new tongues; they will pick up serpents, and if they drink any deadly thing, it will not hurt them; they will lay their hands on the sick, and they will recover" (Mk 16:17-18).

The Holy Spirit is also the Spirit of adoption. At Baptism we are made children and heirs of the Father, coheirs with Christ. Like Him, we are to live in the full love of the Father. Through the Spirit of adoption, we learn to trust and endure the Cross as obedient — not rebellious — sons and daughters (see Rom 8:14-17). We have the privilege and duty of believing and professing Christ by obediently suffering with Him, and thereby witnessing to Him before the world (see Phil 1:29). The strength to bear one's cross and witness to Christ is one of the main effects of Confirmation (see *CCC*, 1303). Thus it is that, whereas in Baptism we receive the Spirit for our own sanctification, in Confirmation we are sealed with the Spirit so as to give witness to Christ before the world so that others might believe.

In Greek, the word for "witness" is *martys*, the root of the modern word "martyr." The Holy Spirit leads us to be witnesses of Jesus by giving our lives in testimony to Him. We testify through our trust in the face of difficulty and suffering! What differentiates Christians from everyone else is how we react to the Cross. Others scorn the Cross, flee from the Cross, or rebel against the Cross; Christians venerate the Cross and kiss the Cross, embracing it as the source of salvation. Only the Holy Spirit can enable us to do this, for in our weakness, we are no different from non-Christians. Our primary testimony is our suffering, just as the martyrs, by their deaths, witnessed with singular power. We are willing to suffer and witness because of our love.

"All who are led by the Spirit are children of God" (Rom 8:14). Only those who trust and are docile to the Holy Spirit can truly live as children of the Father. The Holy Spirit led Jesus to Jerusalem and His death on Calvary (see Lk 9:51). Are we willing to allow the Holy Spirit to direct our steps along this path of trust toward Calvary? We can have no greater love for Jesus than to lay down our lives for Him through martyrdom (see Jn 15:13). This does not mean that only those who physically die for Jesus love Him so much. We are called to daily martyrdom and, by denying ourselves and our will, we show our trust in Jesus. Without daily self-donation, we cannot expect to stand firm should the moment of real martyrdom come! Hidden moments of self-denial prepare us for the public moment of witnessing: martyrdom.

If we desire to trust in the Mercy of God and share that mercy with others, we need to be ready for martyrdom. At the World Apostolic Congress on Mercy in the Philippines, Bishop Villegas stated: "The destiny of people who show mercy is martyrdom and martyrdom is a great act of mercy. We must be ready to die for one another. There is no greater act of mercy than to die for those who do not even deserve mercy."[265]

MARTYRDOM

If you think that such martyrdom is not likely, contemplate the countless Christians in the world *today* who lay down their lives for Christ. Are we willing to do the same? There is no greater act of trust in the Father than to entrust one's very being to Him, uniting oneself with Jesus on the Cross. In fact, there is no greater worship we can offer to the Father than the radical faith by which we entrust ourselves entirely to Him in such moments of abandonment, suffering, and pain. As St. Faustina states: "One act of trust at such moments gives greater glory to God than whole hours passed in prayer filled with consolations" (*Diary*, 78).

Lest you think that this is masochistic, remember that suffering ceases to be suffering as we know it when we let go of our distrust and our own will, as the Father teaches St. Catherine of Siena.[266] Most of our suffering stems not from the actual cross itself, but from being at variance with the Father's will. Remember that patience leads to obedience, and obedience leads to joy, even in suffering, for when we have no other will than the Father's, we are no longer upset if things do not go our way. Instead, we have deep peace. When we accept that things *always* go the Father's way, we are *always* filled with joy, because we rejoice in His will — whatever it might be and whatever it might bring, even in the most difficult moments. A modern example is Mother Teresa, who, even in the midst of darkness and pain, smiled with joy and peace that flowed from her obedience and trust in the Father.

Christian joy is not giddiness, nor is it superficial happiness. No. True Christian joy is the fruit of the Holy Spirit and can be experienced even amid sorrow and pain (see Gal 5:22). Joy is deeper than emotions, because it flows from grace, which comes to us from sources outside our direct experience. Christian joy is the result of possessing the Beloved — namely, Christ. Saint Thomas Aquinas states that "joy is caused by love … through the presence of the thing loved" whereas sorrow arises from the "absence of the thing loved."[267] The more we love, then, the more we will experience joy. At the same time, however, the more we love, the more we will experience sorrow when what we love is hurt or lost. We can rejoice in the Lord always, since we rejoice in

---

[265] Melanie Williams, "The Church Is the Body of the Face of Divine Mercy," Day Two of WACOM 4, January 18, 2017, accessed July 11, 2017, http://www.thedivinemercy.org/news/Day-Two-of-WACOM-4-7058.
[266] Saint Catherine of Siena, *The Dialogue*, 161-65.
[267] Saint Thomas Aquinas, *Summa Theologica*, II-II, q. 28, a. 1.

God Himself, whose goodness is everlasting and never changes (see Phil 4:4; Ps 136); but because we live in a sinful world, we sorrow when we see how His goodness is distrusted by ourselves and others. Christian love causes both great joy (because we possess what truly satisfies us: the Triune God) and great sorrow (because we see how we distrust Him).[268]

Hence, even while suffering physically or psychologically, spiritually a Christian rejoices in being in union with Christ Crucified. According to St. Catherine of Siena, Christ was both happy and sad upon the Cross: sad because of the suffering in His Body and the sins of mankind, and joyful in His soul because He always remained united to the Father through the Holy Spirit.[269] While enduring our own crosses, we may feel sorrow and sadness, but, like Christ, we endure this for the sake of the joy of union with the Father that is possible only through Christ Crucified (see Heb 12:2). We may sorrow that we have lost certain good created realities, but we nonetheless rejoice that we still possess Goodness itself: the Creator, who is the source of all created realities and who can transform every sorrow into joy (see Jn 16:20). The joy of the Triune God is so great that it makes the soul completely forget, upon entering Heaven, all the sorrows it endured: "At the end of the road there was a magnificent garden filled with all sorts of happiness, and all these souls entered there. At the very first instant they forgot all their sufferings" (*Diary*, 153).

Saint Augustine argues that the distinctive mark of Christians is that even while we are in this vale of sorrow, we sing because we are confident of our victory over suffering through Christ Jesus.[270] The sign that one has joy, even during such sorrow, is that we offer such praise and experience peace undisturbed by suffering — a foretaste of the peace of Heaven.

DELIGHT IN THE LORD

Our relationship with the Father is not one-sided. It is reciprocal, like His relationship with His Son. The Bible teaches us that when we begin to fear the Lord and delight in Him always, He grants the desires of our hearts (see Ps 37:4, 145:19; Prov 10:24). We do not fulfill our deepest desires ourselves; instead, the Father fulfills them for us — often in beautiful and unimaginable ways! When we fulfill His will, He wants to fulfill ours. We can trust that if we seek the Father's will and suffer on that account, He will not leave us in our misery. He will raise us to new life. As Pope Francis said:

> This is the foundation of our hope, which is not mere optimism, nor a psychological attitude or desire to be courageous. Christian hope is a gift that God gives us if we come out of ourselves and open our hearts

---

[268] Ibid., a. 2.

[269] Romanus Cessario, *Compassionate Blood: Catherine of Siena on the Passion* (Paris: Magnificat, 2016).

[270] ICEL, *The Liturgy of the Hours*, Vol. 2, 864-65.

to him. This hope does not disappoint us because the Holy Spirit has been poured into our hearts (see Rom 5:5). The Paraclete does not make everything look appealing. He does not remove evil with a magic wand. But he pours into us the vitality of life, which is not the absence of problems, but the certainty of being loved and always forgiven by Christ, who for us has conquered sin, conquered death and conquered fear. Today [Easter] is the celebration of our hope, the celebration of this truth: nothing and no one will ever be able to separate us from his love (see Rom 8:39).[271]

In her account of the Passion, Blessed Anne Catherine Emmerich describes how Jesus lovingly thanked the Father for each stage of His Passion, offering it up with love for the redemption of mankind. If we are grateful for all that God allows, our suffering will turn to joy, for within all suffering is the opportunity to love — and love is the source of all joy. When there is great love, suffering ceases to be suffering. In the words of St. Faustina, "Great love can change small things into great ones, and it is only love which lends value to our actions. And the purer our love becomes, the less there will be within us for the flames of suffering to feed upon, and the suffering will cease to be a suffering for us; it will become a delight! By the grace of God, I have received such a disposition of heart that I am never so happy as when I suffer for Jesus, whom I love with every beat of my heart" (*Diary*, 303).

All this is accomplished by the surpassing power of divine Love, which is the Holy Spirit. Without the Holy Spirit, we can know all of this in our heads, but we will not experience it in our hearts. We will know the truth intellectually, but without the Holy Spirit, we will not be able to trust that suffering and even death serve our Father's plan to bring us eternal happiness. Mary was united to the Father's will entirely and always, and the Holy Spirit enables us to unite ourselves to His will at each moment of our lives. Ask therefore that this *divine Love* come into your heart many times a day: *Veni, Creator Spiritus!* "Come, Creator Spirit!" *Veni, Sancte Spiritus!* "Come, Holy Spirit!" I recommend saying these simple prayers every day to ask for His light and guidance, especially during times of suffering, so that He may burn in your heart and make you a holocaust of trust, a burning bush that emits His light and grace amid the darkness of this world.

---

[271] Pope Francis, "Easter Vigil in the Holy Night," March 26, 2016.

CHAPTER 27

Trust in the Father's Will

"I have placed all my trust in Your will which is,
for me, love and mercy itself"
(*Diary*, 1264).

To live by the Father's will, we must know what His will is. The will of the Father is expressed first and foremost through the Church, her teaching, and the duties of our state in life. These provide the structure of the Father's will for our lives, but moment by moment we rely on the inspiration of the Holy Spirit for specifics. How do we discern what is of the Holy Spirit and what is not? Jesus said that we know a tree by its fruits (see Mt 7:20), so we can recognize what kind of spirit is operating in us by asking if our actions and decisions yield the fruits of the Holy Spirit (see Gal 5:22-25). If not, then what we have done is not in accordance with the Father's will.

The most fundamental criterion for understanding the Father's will is found in the new commandment Jesus left with us at the Last Supper — to love one another as He has loved us. All that we do as Christians must be in accord with that one commandment. How has Christ loved us? He has loved us to the end, by dying for us upon the Cross (see Jn 13:1; 1 Jn 3:16). We can begin loving as Christ loves by meditating upon the Passion of Christ, and I also recommend praying the Divine Mercy Chaplet daily.

The story of the Passion is a book from which we can learn how to love others: "O my Jesus, my only hope, thank You for the book which You have opened before my soul's eyes. That book is Your Passion which You underwent for love of me. It is from this book that I have learned how to love God and souls. In this book there are found for us inexhaustible treasures. O Jesus, how few souls understand You in Your martyrdom of love! Oh, how great is the fire of purest love which burns in Your Most Sacred Heart! Happy the soul that has come to understand the love of the Heart of Jesus!" (*Diary,* 304). Meditating upon the Passion is one of the best ways to honor Mary's sacrifice of her Son and receive the Holy Spirit, for that same Holy Spirit gushed forth in the Blood and Water from the Heart of Jesus.

Loving as Christ loved us means not only that we would die for someone should the need or opportunity arise. It also means we are called to lay down our lives for our brethren through imitating the Passion of Christ in our interactions with others. It means showing others the same kindness, meekness, patience, humility, long-suffering, and forgiveness that Jesus manifested in His Passion (see 1 Pet 2:20-23). When we are too quick to defend ourselves instead of entrusting difficult situations to the Father, we forget that those who call upon the Mercy of the Lord are defended by God Himself! "Happy is the soul that calls upon the mercy of the Lord. It will see that the Lord will defend it as His glory, as He said. And who would dare fight against God?" (*Diary*, 598).

CONQUERING EVIL WITH GOOD

We are called to conquer evil with good, just as Christ did in the Passion (see Rom 12:21). Meditating on the Passion is one of the most beneficial things we can do as Christians, and heartfelt compassion for our Lord in His suffering is worth more than many penances (see *Diary*, 369).

Carrying our own crosses is the surest way of penance; and meditation on the Passion strengthens us to carry them as we obey Jesus (see *CCC*, 1465). It also helps us repent of sin, not only because sin is bad, but because *my sin* wounded *my Lord*. Meditating on the Passion reveals precisely how much we love the Lord. If the Lord is merely someone we hear about at Mass, we will not have heartfelt compassion for Him while meditating on His Passion. If the Lord is truly dear to us, we will weep, not only for His Passion, but for our sins that caused it — we can fully understand sin only by looking at it against the backdrop of the suffering Jesus endured for us out of love (see *CCC*, 1432). The more we love Jesus, the more we will meditate on His Passion, and the more we will see the gravity of our sins that were washed away by His Blood and Water.

Does our Father enjoy testing us and sending us suffering? No. The suffering we endure helps us grow in trust and love so we can enter more deeply into the divine life that was lost in Adam and Eve. Remember that the suffering of this life cannot be compared to the glory that will be revealed (see Rom 8:18). We cannot see the truth of this statement now, but we can believe the testimony of others that this is indeed true. We can know that God, as a good Father, is looking out for our eternal good. In the words of St. Sebastian Valfre: "When it is all over you will not regret having suffered; rather you will regret having suffered so little, and suffered that little so badly." Blessed George Matulaitis expressed this same attitude: "We should fear one thing only: to die without having suffered, struggled, and toiled for the Church, for the salvation of souls, for the glory of God" (*Journal*, 45).

HUMILITY

Especially in moments of suffering, happiness in this life is intimately linked to humility and trust. Saint Faustina expresses how only a truly humble soul can be happy (see *Diary*, 593).

Humility is a prerequisite for trust because only by recognizing my own poverty and misery can I recognize my need to trust in the Mercy of the Father. A humble soul that recognizes its misery has every reason to be joyful and happy, for God pursues such humble souls with His greatest blessings. We will be truly happy only when we embrace our own poverty, immersing ourselves in the infinite Mercy of the Father. When things go "our way" — in opposition to the Father's way — we ought to watch out, because that is the worst possible scenario (see *Diary*, 1728).

Does all this seem beyond your grasp? Such a life of love and suffering *is* beyond what we are capable of by nature, and without the Holy Spirit it *is* impossible (see Mk 10:27). Many Christians think that what is needed is more effort, but what is actually needed is acceptance of one's poverty and greater trust in the Holy Spirit. In St. Faustina's words: "During Holy Mass, offered by Father Andrasz, I saw the little Infant Jesus, who told me that I was to depend on him for everything; '**No action undertaken on your own, even though you put much effort into it, pleases Me.**' I understood this [need of] dependence" (*Diary*, 659).

We can trust the words of our Lord that His burden is indeed light (see Mt 11:28-30). By trusting, we let go of our burden and enter the Lord's rest, even during moments of suffering — for we already have what our hearts long for: Love, which is the Holy Spirit (see Heb 4:11).

AWAKENING THE HOLY SPIRIT

Although we received the gift of the Holy Spirit in Baptism and Confirmation, His grace may be lying dormant in our souls. The power of the Holy Spirit is awakened by daily Mass, the Rosary, and private prayer in silence, among other means. As St. Faustina tells us: "There is no soul which is not bound to pray, for every single grace comes to the soul through prayer" (*Diary*, 146). Notice that when the apostles prayed and fasted for nine days, the Holy Spirit came upon them! Beyond set times of prayer, we can pray *always* by rejoicing and giving thanks to the Father in all circumstances (see 1 Thess 5:16-19). Our salvation consists of constant thanksgiving! The source of our joy is the Lord's nearness, and He desires to make our joy complete (see Phil 4:4-7).

When we find that we are not joyful or cannot rejoice, we must ask ourselves what happened to cause us sadness. The ultimate reason for sadness is sin, which should lead us to conversion, rather than to condemnation. When the Father's will includes tragedy or death, sadness is normal, but a deeper joy and *peace* remain because the Father is with us in such sadness. There is a different kind of sadness, however — the sadness produced by sin. When we do not accept His will and when we rebel against it, we experience sadness without peace or love, a feeling that flows from mourning over things that did not go our way. Preferring our will to His will is what causes us true distress and sadness. Such sadness flows from pride, from not getting what we want. The solution is to praise the Father and thank Him for all that He allows, even suffering and daily crosses (see Ps 43:5). Saint Paul's instruction mentioned above — to give thanks — is categorical: There is no time or circumstance in which we are not to give thanks to the Father, even if only for accompanying us through our suffering.

When we give thanks to God even amid suffering and trials, the Holy Spirit unites our thanksgiving to that of Jesus at the Last Supper, when He praised and thanked the Father for the gift of being able to love Him and us through suffering, and for His Resurrection (see *Diary*, 684). Praising the Father for everything is a sign of deep trust in His Providence, that the last "word" in every situation is resurrection. When we praise, we direct our gaze to the Father instead of focusing on the situation at hand. Praise and thanksgiving can seem irrelevant as a solution to real, practical matters. But praise is eminently practical, because it helps us leave the prison of our own hearts and enter now into the bliss of eternal life in Heaven, where there is ceaseless praise of the Trinity.

What does joy have to do with the Holy Spirit? The Lord tells us not to be fearful and draw back, for such fear and cowardice lead to death (see Heb 10:39). Joy and praise of the Father are the mark of the Holy Spirit and a sign that He is at work in our lives. The apostles were locked in the Upper Room before Pentecost, but later rejoiced to suffer for the sake of Christ (see Acts 5:41). Paul was even able to sing hymns of praise while in prison (see Acts 16:25). Thus trust is marked not only by perfect obedience, but also by ceaseless praise and a spirit of gratitude. The Holy Spirit can work such a change in us that obedience and suffering become "sweeter than honey" (Ps 19:10, 119:103). Instead of experiencing the Father's will as a burdensome law imposed on us from outside, we begin to fulfill the Father's will joyfully; it is almost second nature, because the Holy Spirit is the interior Law of the New Covenant in Christ Jesus.[272] The Holy Spirit moves us out of fear and trepidation into confidence and joy; from a defensive to an offensive position.

Jesus promised that "the gates of Hell shall not prevail against" the Church. We often imagine this promise of the Lord to mean that the gates of the Church will not crumble before the attacks of Satan and the world, but that is not what the Lord intended. He meant that the gates of the netherworld shall not prevail against us. We are called not merely to defend ourselves and our own salvation, but also to *harrow hell* along with Christ by offering ourselves up each day with Him in our sacrifices of trust, self-denial, and obedience (see *Diary*, 639). We are called to march forward with bold confidence and trust in the Lord Jesus — even unto the very gates of hell. We are not to wait until hell comes to us: We are to go forward, confident that we possess the surpassing power of the Holy Spirit and are ready to do battle for the salvation of souls. Concretely, that means we are called to share the Gospel and to witness to Christ.

In his speech to the cardinals before the conclave that led to his election, Pope Francis said that what ails the Church is that we are often closed in on ourselves and have forgotten the joy of the Gospel.[273] Witnessing to Christ and

---

[272] Saint Thomas Aquinas, *Summa Theologica*, I-II, q. 106, a. 2.

[273] "When the Church does not come out of herself to evangelize, she becomes self-referential and then gets sick. ... In Revelation, Jesus says that he is at the door and knocks. Obviously, the text refers to his knocking from the outside in order to enter but I think about the times in which Jesus knocks from within so that we will let him come

evangelizing in today's culture cost us dearly, but it is only by sharing our faith that it increases. And it is only by sharing the Father's Mercy that we receive more of His Mercy. The only way to grow spiritually is by sharing what the Father has given us. That is the *law of the gift*. If we share and give away material possessions, we possess less. But spiritually, when we share and give what we have to others, it increases and multiplies. If we want to be able to trust more in the Lord, we need to encourage others to trust in Jesus, too.

Trust is the essential ingredient for the Divine Mercy devotion, and from that trust flow *works of mercy*. We are called by our Lord to practice both the corporal and the spiritual works of mercy (see *Diary*, 742).

According to Pope Benedict XVI, "It is important, however, to remember that the greatest work of charity is evangelization, which is the 'ministry of the word.' There is no action more beneficial, and therefore more charitable, towards one's neighbor than to break the bread of the word of God, to share with him the Good News of the Gospel, to introduce him to a relationship with God: evangelization is the highest and the most integral promotion of the human person."[274] I would add that teaching others how to trust in the Father's Mercy is the greatest act of mercy and a key part of evangelization. Saint Faustina's mission was precisely to encourage souls to trust in the Father's Mercy through her writings and her sufferings on their behalf.

The mission entrusted to Faustina has not ended, however. She continues her mission from Heaven while we fulfill our role on earth. We are to unite our mission of trust with hers and, in so doing, offer ourselves up as a living sacrifice to the Father for the salvation of souls (see *Diary*, 482-83).

MARY, THE MOTHER OF THE CHURCH

When I was overwhelmed as a seminarian and could not figure out what to do, my novice master taught me to do something very simple: Sit down for a few minutes and ask myself, "What do I feel? Why do I feel that way?" I have since added a third question: "What is the Holy Spirit moving me to do?" When I become overwhelmed now as a priest and, like Peter, begin to sink amid the waves of life, I try to sit down for a few minutes or go visit the Lord and kneel, asking those questions, which are a short form of the Ignatian examination of conscience.

Often along this path of trust, we will feel overwhelmed and exhausted! We have only to look at St. Paul's list of sufferings endured for Christ in order to see

---

out. The self-referential Church keeps Jesus Christ within herself and does not let him out." "Bergoglio's Intervention: A Diagnosis of the Problems in the Church," Vatican Radio, March 27, 2013, accessed July 11, 2017, http://en.radiovaticana.va/storico/2013/03/27/bergoglios_intervention_a_diagnosis_of_the_problems_in_the_church/en1-677269.

[274] Benedict XVI, "Message of His Holiness Benedict XVI for Lent 2013," October 15, 2012, accessed July 11, 2017, https://w2.vatican.va/content/benedict-xvi/en/messages/lent/documents/hf_ben-xvi_mes_20121015_lent-2013.html.

that not even great saints are immune to such moments (see 2 Cor 11). Where do we go in such moments? I invite you to return in spirit to the Upper Room, to the Cenacle, and be present with Mary and the saints (see Acts 1:14). Allow Mary to take you by the hand when you cannot take a step farther; allow her as your Mother to carry you upon her sweet, Immaculate Heart. If you cannot embrace the Cross and overcome your fear, remember that near every cross is Mary. There she stands, waiting for you, looking upon you with great love. Her love will make every cross sweet and easier to carry! As she told St. Faustina during her intense suffering: "*I know how much you suffer, but do not be afraid. I share with you your suffering, and I shall always do so*" (*Diary*, 25). Often, we are exhausted because we are working on fumes — the little strength we can muster by our own, unaided effort. We work alone upon our crosses, when in fact we should remember that at Calvary we are never alone: Mary stands by our side. With her, we will be filled with the breath of the Holy Spirit, who fills us with love and eternal life.

Throughout the day, Mary teaches us how to remain open to the Holy Spirit, to be docile to Him, to trust Him, and to obey Him. All this requires is a simple acknowledgment of her presence — sitting down for a moment and calling upon her name. I have a good friend who, in moments of need, simply prays, "Mary, I need you, and I need you now!" Consistently, Mary helps her in such moments. Call upon Mary, ask her for help, and invite her into your heart so that she may teach you to be ever more open to the Holy Spirit, the *Paraclete,* who will strengthen you. The Holy Spirit is the Comforter, the one who gives us strength when we have no strength left!

Saint Faustina made this resolution regarding her work — and it would be wise for us to do the same: "I will not allow myself to be so absorbed in the whirlwind of work as to forget about God. I will spend all my free moments at the feet of the Master hidden in the Blessed Sacrament" (*Diary*, 82). I would add: Never allow yourself to be so absorbed in problems as to forget about Mary; spend your free moments with her, for she will teach you to trust and to be open ever more to the Holy Spirit. One Catholic even made this question a part of his daily examen: "How often have I felt weak today and asked Mary to intercede for me, that the Holy Spirit might come and help me?" I recommend the same practice: Never forget about Mary, and never forget the Holy Spirit, lest you wander off her path of trust that leads to Heaven.

PERSONAL WITNESS

Those words can seem almost unfeeling and inhuman, so let me illustrate them with my own personal experience. On June 6, 2005, my brother and I sat at a table at Methodist Hospital in Houston for lunch. My dad had been readmitted to the hospital a week before, after I had called 911 when he'd fallen unexpectedly at home. I asked my brother, "Do you think there's any chance that Dad could die suddenly?" He said no, that the doctors had given Dad some months to live. My concern about the possibility of sudden death persisted, even though I didn't mention it further. I was comforted that my father had received the Sacraments in the hospital earlier that day.

That evening, my brother and I had a changing of the guard. He had spent the week with my father in the hospital, sleeping there at night because he was taking care of tying up all the loose ends in the face of my father's coming death. That night, I encouraged my brother to go home; I would stay. That evening, I fell asleep at my dad's bedside while praying the Rosary. I then awoke around 1:45 a.m. to find my dad needing to use the bathroom, which he couldn't do easily, so I asked the nurse to come in. While I waited outside for the nurse, I heard some heavy breathing, and thought that a patient in another room was having difficulty. Only after some time did I realize that my father was the one having difficulties.

As I entered the room, I realized that my dad was having a full heart attack before my eyes. I called the nurse, who called, "Code blue!" and in the blink of an eye, a whole team arrived. After asking quickly, "What happened?" I was escorted out — but not without first seeing and hearing my father's last breath; he died before they could even try to resuscitate him.

As I stood by the door for a moment, I prayed the *Suscipe* of St. Ignatius of Loyola: "Take O Lord, and receive … ." Receive my dad, receive everything. I walked to the waiting room and began to pray a Rosary for my father in Purgatory. It was Sunday and I was praying the Glorious Mysteries, and during the Third Glorious Mystery, I sensed that my mother — who had also died of cancer in 1990 — had greeted my father at the heavenly gates. Amid such terrible pain and confusion, I was consoled.

What I learned from this experience is that by entrusting even what I held most dear — my father — to the eternal Father, I could have deep peace and joy even amid such pain and loss. Yes, there was sadness because of my father's death, and that sadness continued off and on for years. However, as I struggled in the coming years not to give in to anger and bitterness toward God, I realized that the worst sadness came, not from my father's death, but from my lack of faith and lack of trust in the Father. The greatest darkness that I experienced was not my father's death, but rather the sin that the Father later confronted me about: "Do you simply call me Father, or do you really believe that I am your Father?"

Indeed, at age 18, I had the majority of my journey of trust ahead of me, without my parents. It was "unfair" and hard, since my siblings all had the advantage of navigating the difficult years of college with Dad's helping hand and advice. But the Father wanted me to learn at a young age that He is truly my Father, and I can take His hand — and Our Lady's — in all doubts and difficulties, if I only trust. In fact, the more I began to trust and to praise the Father, even amid such sorrow and sadness, the more those clouds of darkness lifted and I began to find joy, because I could accept the will of the Father, who had not left me an orphan but guided me to the Marian Fathers, my new family.

CHAPTER 28

The Weapon of Trust

"Prepare for Great Battles"
(*Diary*, 1760).

Much of this book has been focused on the *past* as we have looked at stories of salvation history in Scripture to give us examples of how to trust in the Word of God. In the previous few chapters, we have discussed the *present* need to live the Resurrection each day as a sacrifice of obedience to the Father. Before ending this book, I want to consider the future.

The story of salvation history is not over. If we look at Adam and Eve, Mary and Joseph, Jesus, St. Peter, St. Paul, and so on as the relevant actors in this story — without including ourselves — we are missing the bigger picture. *Salvation history has not yet ended. You and I are also actors in the story of salvation.* Are we ready to take our roles? Are we ready to step forward with Mary in trust and tread upon the serpent with her? Are we ready to do battle with St. Michael against the dragon, Satan, and his demons?

This world's morals are rapidly declining. Economically and socially, the world is becoming more and more unstable. The battle lines are being drawn between good and evil, and it can be tempting to think that evil is stronger. This battle is depicted symbolically in Revelation 12, where we get a glimpse of the spiritual conflict between the Woman and the dragon. By all appearances, the dragon should be the winner — a woman giving birth is not exactly able to defend herself or her son! But we must remember: victory *always* belongs to the Lord. The Lamb who was slain was worthy of victory (see Rev 5:12).

Neither the size of our army nor that of the enemy counts — what matters in this decisive battle is only the strength that comes from Heaven (see 1 Macc 3:18-19). In the time of the judges of Israel, the Lord told Gideon that he had too many soldiers. He commanded him to send most of them away, and Gideon went into battle with only 300 men. The Lord did this specifically to show that Israel's victory was due, not to the army's size, but rather, to the Lord Himself (see Judges 7:2). Likewise, the Lord uses our weakness, our smallness, and our being outnumbered to show His surpassing power (see 2 Cor 4:7). In this way, He makes sure that we are not likely to fall back into the original sin of Satan: attempting to steal some of the Father's glory and claim it for our own. We are to trust, not in our own resources or our own strength, but solely in the Holy Spirit, who comes to our aid in our weakness (see Rom 8:26).

THE WORLD, THE FLESH, AND THE DEVIL (PART 1)

To understand our current battle, we need to consider the story of the fall. Adam and Eve did not decide on their own to sin; they were deceived by a cunning serpent (Satan). Similarly, in the world today, many people fall, not simply because they have a malicious desire to commit evil, but rather at the instigation and temptation of a demon. The title of this book, *Stepping on the Serpent*, reflects this familiar drama, which began with the fall of the angels and has repeated itself ever since Adam and Eve's sin.

The story of the Garden of Eden and of our temptation today features a demonic serpent and its innocent victims. In the story, the serpent attempts to lead us astray by striking from a hidden position. His goal is to catch us unawares. We must be vigilant and know who our enemy is, because he is cunning, and if we do not recognize him, we cannot step on his head. Our task is to trust Jesus and Mary to keep us from being seized, and to trust in God's Mercy that we will be protected and saved from our misery. We need to keep an eye on Satan, however, because wherever Jesus and Mary are at work, the devil is nearby to attempt to destroy all that they do.

In Revelation, the dragon cast down a third of the stars in the sky with its tail (see Rev 12:4). If we remember that there are myriads upon myriads of angels attending the throne of God, and if a third of them fell, that means there are plenty of demons roaming the earth (see Dan 7:10; Rev 5:11; 1 Pet 5:8-9). As we say in the prayer to the Archangel Michael, these demons "prowl around the world seeking the ruin of souls." To defend ourselves, we first must recognize their presence, for in any battle, we are weakest when we cannot discern our enemy.

Demons are rarely discussed, because it is assumed that they attack only a few people. However, demons take on various forms to trouble us. The Tradition of the Church teaches that we have three key enemies opposing our salvation: the world, the flesh, and the devil. The world, in this sense, is not the good creation of the Father as it came forth from His hands, designed to reflect His glory and goodness (see Gen 1-2); the world in the negative sense is the world as imprinted and deformed by sin. Hence, the world, although good as created by God, now bears the marks of human sin and has "structures of sin" that can systematically lead one away from the Father (see *CCC*, 1869).

No one can think that he is immune to the attacks of the devil, for all of us are sinners. Each time we commit a mortal sin, we shift ourselves away from the Kingdom of God and toward the kingdom of Satan; we damage the work Jesus did of freeing us from the kingdom of darkness and bringing us into His Kingdom (see Col 1:13). Jesus Himself clearly tells us: "Truly, truly, I say to you, every one who commits sin is a slave to sin" (see Jn 8:34). Strictly speaking, Satan has no authority over us, but by our sin, especially mortal sin, we freely place ourselves under his dominion. Once he gains that dominion, he will do his best never to let us go.

Satan hates the Immaculate Conception so much because Mary was never under his dominion. She not only was conceived without sin, but throughout her entire life, chose never to sin. Satan's position in Mary's life was always under her heel, because Mary trusted the Father's will for her. If we ask Our Lady, she will teach us how to place Satan where he belongs — under our feet. This victory over Satan was not solely a result of Mary's efforts. It was a victory of the Father's Mercy. His Mercy frees us from sin and from the serpent's bite, the venom that tempts us toward evil, and this is precisely why Satan hates Mercy so much. As St. Faustina tells us: "I have now learned that Satan hates mercy more than anything else. It is his greatest torment" (*Diary*, 764).

We often think that once we cease a particular sin, the evil resulting from that sin also ceases, but we do not realize that the tempter does not always depart. After the temptation of Jesus in the desert, Satan regrouped to launch a fresh attack at a more opportune time (see Lk 4:13). In a similar way, after the devil has tempted us, he hides and waits for another opportunity to entice us toward a particular sin, and continues to tempt us until we make a habit of it. Once we have a sinful habit, the devil can begin to bind us so that, even with our best efforts, we cannot shake it off. Such habitual sin is called "bondage."

Although we know there are psychological factors behind sin, factors that need to be dealt with through counseling or by other means, we often forget the spiritual factors. Whenever a serious sin keeps recurring despite one's best efforts or human help, that is good reason to ask for deliverance prayers from a priest, because once we are trapped in a pattern of sin, we cannot free ourselves: We need the help of the Church, especially through her priests. For most, this help is provided in sacramental Confession, the Eucharist, or a deliverance prayer. Sometimes, however, more extraordinary means — such as exorcism — are required to break any spiritual bondage that is keeping someone from enjoying freedom as a child of the Father. In either case, like the paralytic, we need the Church to bring us to Christ for healing from sin and to relieve suffering (see Mk 2:1-12).

THE WORLD, THE FLESH, AND THE DEVIL (PART 2)

Let us consider the three enemies mentioned above: the world, the flesh, and the devil. We can flee the world by creating in our lives a safe haven where the Triune God may dwell. For some, leaving the world means entering religious life in a monastery, but for most of us, it means making our home itself a little "monastery," a place of refuge where the sinful world cannot enter. The serpent slithers into our homes through many pores: TV, movies, music, the Internet, etc. We ought to ensure that the world does not have unrestricted entrance into our private lives. In this battle of trust against distrust, we must ask ourselves: Do we allow the world, which thrives on distrust, into the sanctuary of our homes and our families?

As I mentioned previously, the world itself is not all evil. After all, the Father created it and redeemed mankind (see Jn 3:16). Nevertheless, as I use the word in this chapter, the *world* refers to the world in opposition to the Father, dominated by Satan (see 1 Jn 2:17). The family is called the *ecclesia domestica*, the "domestic church." Families are meant to be centers of living and radiant faith where children see, by the Word of God and the example of their parents, that faith is alive in the modern world (see *CCC*, 1656). We ought indeed to be "in the world," but not "of the world" (see Jn 17:14-16). Our homes ought to be oases of Christian faith rather than more houses among others belonging to those who live only for this world. In Acts 1-2, we discover an image of a faithful Christian home, with the family of the disciples gathered together in prayer. Communal prayer offered each day at home — particularly including communal reading of the Scriptures and the Rosary — is a powerful way to experience Pentecost, when the Holy Spirit descends upon a family.

Our Lady prays with us and for us when we gather as a family at prayer, teaching us how to allow our families to be domestic churches filled with the Holy Spirit. Do we create this sense of spiritual sanctuary and unity in our homes? We must ask ourselves: How porous are the walls of our life and our home? The goal is not necessarily to be secluded from the world (which is impossible for most of the laity), or to be like ostriches with our heads in the sand, ignoring the world; rather, we are to be witnesses to Christ in the world, always keeping in mind, however, that we are not of the world (see Jn 17:16). In other words, we are to have a beneficial effect; we are to bring salvation to the world in Christ without allowing the sinful world to have a deleterious effect upon us. Jesus speaks of this in calling us salt: We are to salt the world, but we must be careful not to lose our flavor (see Mt 5:13).

Religious orders maintain the practice of silent hours precisely as a time to turn the mind away from this world and focus on the Triune God, a necessary step in preparation for Heaven. The gift of Heaven is what theology calls the *beatific vision* — literally, the vision that makes us happy. This vision is not something we see with our eyes; rather it is a gaze of the heart inflamed with love. If our minds and hearts are not focused on Jesus while we are on earth, it is hard to imagine that we will want to lovingly contemplate Him once we die. Purgatory exists for just that reason — to help those who have not focused on God make the transition from what is earthly to what is divine. Are we prepared for the beatific vision? Do we daily gaze upon Jesus, as we will do for all eternity? Or do we daily gaze upon TV, movies, Facebook, etc.? How often do we visit Jesus in the Blessed Sacrament and adore Him? Such adoration is a participation in what the angels and saints already do in Heaven as they gaze upon the Face of Mercy.

How Demons Attack

Saint Thomas Aquinas teaches us that angels and demons have only an indirect influence on our will, and that they primarily influence us through our thoughts.[275] To arouse our senses, demons can present things to our minds in very tempting ways, but as the old saying goes, "Out of sight, out of mind." If our mind is filled with earthly things, the devil will tempt us even more. If the world is out of our sight, it will be out of our mind, and we will suffer less the temptation not to trust in the Father. Angels will fill our minds with thoughts of Jesus; the more He is in our sight, the more He will be in our mind. Silence and prayer are necessary for Jesus to be in our sight and mind.

Evil spirits prowl about the earth, tempting us to distrust the Word of God. Today, their most common temptation seems to be making us so busy that we are not able to find time for prayer or reading the Word of God. Busyness is particularly useful to Satan because he wants to thwart persevering prayer, by which we can get away from him. Our flesh is always with us, however, and even if the world and the devil are absent, we still have the "old man" that inclines us toward sin (see Eph 4:22-24). Of our three enemies, our flesh — our fallen human nature — is the worst, because we cannot escape from ourselves. We can only put ourselves completely in the hands of the Father, trusting that He will preserve us from sin as He preserved Our Lady by His Mercy.

The devil attacks us precisely because our flesh is weak, so the way to bolster our defense against the devil is to be filled with the surpassing power of the Holy Spirit through solid, constant trust in the Word of God (see Mt 26:41). Jesus conquered the temptations of the devil in the desert precisely by this method: To every temptation offered by the devil, Jesus responded with the Word of God (see Mt 4:1-11). With each temptation, the devil intended to question Jesus' identity and His relationship with the Father, but He remained loyal to His bond of obedience and trust, and successfully repelled the attacks of the devil (see *CCC*, 538). Like Jesus, we can conquer the temptations of the world, the flesh, and the devil by firm trust in the Word of God, thereby remaining in our own relationship of trust and obedience to the Father by the power of the Holy Spirit received through the Sacraments. Such confident trust and obedience are the way to win the battle in the world today, for in this way Jesus Christ conquered Satan on Calvary.

When Mother Teresa was asked: "What has to change in the Church?" she responded, "You and I."[276] We can easily complain about the faults of others, as seen in the media — fraught with accusation, condemnation, gossip, and all sorts of needless chatter that is not of God. So as a way of helping to change the world, I would recommend taking time away from watching TV programs and instead pray. In the past, fasting — abstaining from food — was the most important

---

[275] Saint Thomas Aquinas, *Summa Theologica*, I, q. 111.
[276] Schönborn, *Youcat English: Youth Catechism of the Catholic Church*, 33.

way to focus one's attention upon God, but I think that today, "fasting" from TV, radio, and other media is very important. *Silence* is necessary to trust, for in order to trust, we must be able to hear the Word of God.

Saint Faustina had much to say about the useless noise and eternal damage caused by excessive use of the tongue (see *Diary*, 118). Even though St. Faustina writes as a religious, it would be wise for us to heed her words. Although some of us may be extroverts, the key to silence is not simply *not talking*, but rather talking first and foremost with the Creator. In fact, as St. Faustina notes, we can break silence by being too quiet, and we can speak a great deal without breaking silence. The important factor is not the quantity of words but their quality: whether they flow from the Holy Spirit for the glory of the Father or not.

Without silence, we cannot hear or trust Jesus: "The Lord gave me to know how displeased He is with a talkative soul. **I find no rest in such a soul. The constant din tires Me, and in the midst of it the soul cannot discern My voice**" (*Diary*, 1008). If we cannot hear Jesus, we cannot have faith, for faith comes from hearing (see Rom 10:17-18). Maybe it is for this reason that we hear so little from Mary. As a woman of trust, she kept silence and prayed.

Saint Faustina recognized how she could talk less and pray more, especially for the souls in Purgatory: "The second light concerns speaking. I sometimes talk too much. A thing could be settled in one or two words, and as for me, I take too much time about it. But Jesus wants me to use that time to say some short indulgenced prayers for the souls in purgatory. And the Lord says that every word will be weighed on the day of judgment" (*Diary*, 274). She is referring to Matthew 12:34-37: "For out of the abundance of the heart, the mouth speaks. The good man out of his good treasure brings forth good, and the evil man out of his evil treasure brings forth evil. I tell you, on the day of judgment men will render account for every careless word they utter; for by your words you will be justified, and by your words you will be condemned."

Hence, if we simply talk about current events or the evil in the world, we are not conquering that evil. Rather, when we take steps of trust with Mary, steps that include prayer, sacrifice, "fasting" from noise, and encouraging others to trust, we will join her in crushing the head of the serpent. The primary battle in the world today is a spiritual battle over the truth. Demons do their best to deceive us, giving us many reasons not to trust the Father and trying to convince us that what He has said is not true. Is this not part of the reason for so much negative news every day? Is this not part of the demon's tactic: to flood us with all that is going wrong, trying to convince us that in the end, evil wins? Angels do the opposite: They remind us of the truth and thereby try to encourage us to place our trust in the Word of God.

If we listen to news, but not to the Word of God about Christ's victory over evil upon the Cross, we should not be surprised if we fall into discouragement at the state of the world. If we want to win this battle of trust, we must recognize both our enemy and our comrades, for we must remember that the voice of the Lord is most clearly heard in silence and not in the commotion of the world (see 1 Kings 19:11-13). Such silent listening to the Lord requires us, not to retreat from the world physically, but rather to hold a cell within our hearts for the Lord that enables us never to forget His gentle voice of love. Saint Faustina says: "From that moment I set up a little cell in my heart where I always kept company with Jesus" (*Diary*, 16). Every event is a "word" of God, but to understand what He is attempting to say through the events of history, we must have time to discern His voice. Without such silence and discernment, we are prone to misinterpret and misunderstand Him!

MYRIADS OF ANGELS

Our comrades are the angels: personal, immortal creatures surpassing all visible creatures in their perfection and the splendor of their glory (see *CCC*, 330). In his discussion on angels, St. Thomas Aquinas states that more angels were faithful to the Father in their moment of trial than those who fell.[277] The fact that only a third of the stars fell from Heaven because of the dragon is consoling. The angels are given to us to protect and help us during our spiritual battle with the world, the flesh, and the devil. Their presence is yet another reason to trust in our Heavenly Father, who surrounds us with His mighty angels to guide us along our journey, just as an angel led the Israelites through the desert (see Ex 13:21). Let us call upon them and ask for their aid so that we may cling to the truth and not give way to the deceit of Satan.

To win the battle we face, we need the help of the angels. One powerful way to invoke their help is through the Chaplet of St. Michael, given in a private revelation to a Portuguese Carmelite nun, Antónia d'Astónaco, and approved by Pope Blessed Pius IX in 1851. Saint Michael promised his protection and help, and that of all the holy angels, during their lifetime and at their death for all who recite this chaplet. In addition, he promised that when receiving Holy Communion, someone who said the St. Michael Chaplet daily would be attended by an escort of nine angels, one from each choir.

Traditionally, the Church has held that there are choirs of angels, each with their own respective duties and characteristics. Sacred Scripture distinguishes nine choirs: seraphim, cherubim, thrones, dominations (or dominions), powers, virtues, principalities, archangels, and angels (see Is 6:2; Gen 3:24; Col 1:16; Eph 1:21; Rom 8:38). While we often forget about the angels and focus on the saints, angels are assigned to help us journey to our heavenly homeland. In this way, our good Father supplies us with angelic help, supplementing human help, to protect us from all evil. We each have a guardian angel who protects us throughout our life (see *CCC*, 336). Saint Michael and the other angels will help us fulfill the Father's will; as St. Faustina wrote: "I have great reverence for Saint Michael the Archangel; he had no example to follow in doing the will of God, and yet he fulfilled God's will faithfully" (*Diary*, 667).

---

[277] Saint Thomas Aquinas, *Summa Theologica*, I, q. 63, a. 9.

To Change the World

Amid such a spiritual battle, what are we to do? How can we change the world? We take the advice of Mother Teresa (cited above) that if we want to change the world, we ourselves need to change. The purpose of this book is not merely to help you undergo a personal conversion, however. We will have victory in this spiritual battle only in and through the Church when we gather together by the Holy Spirit into the one Body of Christ (see *CCC*, 751). The Father Himself has called us out of the darkness of this world to enjoy His marvelous light (see 1 Pet 2:9-10), and our vocation as the People of God is to shine the light of Christ into the darkness of this world — precisely to free this world from the tyranny of the devil (see Mt 5:14-16). Our vocation is to share in the victory of the Immaculate Conception of Mary by trusting in the Mercy of the Father — for our surest defense against Satan is trust in God's Mercy! **"My daughter, tell souls that I am giving them My mercy as a defense. I Myself am fighting for them"** (*Diary*, 1516).

Our silent witness of faithful trust will bear much fruit. Remember that Mary changed the world, not by making herself known or heard, but rather by her humble trust and fulfillment of the Father's will in her daily life. We witness through our daily, trusting adherence to the truth, and the truth is what will set us — and the world — free. If we witness to the truth, even in our weakness, we will be filled with the fire of the Holy Spirit, which will renew the world (see *CCC*, 696). According to biblical prophecy, the world will indeed be renewed by fire (see 2 Pet 3:11-13). The question is whether we will let the world be renewed by the fire of the Holy Spirit or by the fire of nuclear weapons and war. There is no doubt that the world must be cleansed of its sins. Our God is a consuming fire, so it is appropriate that the cleansing and renewal of the world will be by fire (see Dt 4:24).

Unfortunately, there are many prophets of doom who speak only of destruction. There is no doubt that the Lord has chastised the world in the past and will chastise it again in the future — the Bible is replete with warnings of impending destruction due to human sinfulness. But such punishment is not a matter of the Father's wrath alone. Much of the death and suffering we undergo as punishment is the natural consequence of sin and distrust. The Father's wrath is His love directed against sin. In human terms, we see this when a doctor must apply alcohol to a wound. The treatment will hurt, but it is necessary to clean the wound for it to be healed. All chastisement is healing. If we lack this understanding, we become discouraged when we undergo sufferings. But we ought not be surprised when we undergo a "trial by fire" (see 1 Pet 4:12-13). Rather, we should rejoice, because trial by fire is the result of the action of the Holy Spirit, cleansing us of our sinfulness and preparing us for the coming of Christ, either at death or at the end of time.

When Christ returns at the end of time, His Bride, the Church, must be immaculate. While we may be upset at the state of affairs in the world, the trials we endure are intended to bring about the return of goodness and to purify the Church, making her immaculate so that the Wedding Feast of the Lamb can commence (see Rev 19:6-9). **"The bride must resemble her Betrothed"** (*Diary*, 269). The Church must live the mysteries of Christ, her Head. She must be born, must grow, and must preach, as Jesus did, but she must also be crucified and resurrected.[278] Even though the crucifixion of Christ has taken place once and for all, the Church is to partake in that crucifixion, too (see *CCC*, 677). People may be surprised that things are getting so troubled, but we should *expect* that the Church will be crucified. We should *expect* that the Church will have her own Holy Saturday — a period of darkness and the seeming absence of the Lord, when evil appears to have won and God is completely silent. We accept the fact of Jesus' Crucifixion, but often forget just how scandalous the Cross is until the crucifixion occurs in our own life (see 1 Cor 1:18). We realize how scandalous the Crucifixion is when we look at the Church and see how she suffers, even at the hands of her own members — just as Jesus suffered at the hands of His Chosen People.

If we can anticipate and even expect these things, we have a much greater chance of not giving in to discouragement. Remember that discouragement and anxiety, whether regarding our own faults and sins or those of the world, are the greatest obstacles to our trust and growth in sanctity (see *Diary*, 1488). Discouragement uproots our trust in the Lord's mercy and makes us lose heart. *Courage* comes from the Latin *cor*, meaning "heart," so encouraging one another is an important work of mercy (see 1 Thess 5:11; Heb 3:13). We must have courage and take heart. We must *trust* that the risen Lord has conquered the world and that through our trust in Him, we too will have victory over the world (see Jn 16:33; 1 Jn 5:4). This requires that we trust as Mary did — and trust that victory will come through her help.

---

[278] ICEL, *Liturgy of the Hours*, Friday of 33rd Week of Ordinary Time: "We must strive to follow and fulfill in ourselves the various stages of Christ's plan as well as his mysteries, and frequently beg him to bring them to completion in us and in the whole Church. For the mysteries of Jesus are not yet completely perfected and fulfilled. They are complete, indeed, in the person of Jesus, but not in us, who are his members, nor in the Church, which is his mystical body. The Son of God wills to give us a share in his mysteries and somehow to extend them to us. He wills to continue them in us and in his universal Church."

CHAPTER 29

Mary, Our Help and Trust

"Then the dragon was angry with the woman, and went off to make war on the rest of her offspring"
(Rev 12:17).

In the battle against Satan, Mary leads us by her example of humility and trust. Just as she was present at the first Calvary, Mary is present each time the Church experiences her own Calvary, to teach us to trust during the difficult and dark moments that occur in this battle. Remember that salvation history is a battle of the Woman — Mary and the Church — not simply against sin as an abstract idea, but against the serpent, Satan and his fallen angels, as depicted in Revelation 12. The war is won not by force or by strength, but by trust and confidence in the Mercy of God! The end times are the dramatic conclusion of this history, and we may be privileged to be part of it!

Saint John Paul II wrote of Mary's involvement in our battle: "For Mary, present in the Church as the Mother of the Redeemer, takes part, as a mother, in that monumental struggle against the powers of darkness which continues throughout human history. ... Hence, as Christians raise their eyes with faith to Mary in the course of their earthly pilgrimage, they strive to increase in holiness. ... Mary, the exalted Daughter of Sion, helps all her children, wherever they may be and whatever their condition, to find in Christ the path to the Father's house."[279] Mary not only helps us find the path but walks along the path with us, repeating her own journey of trust with us as we learn to step upon the serpent.

Notice that in John's vision of Revelation 12, Mary does not battle the dragon directly; rather, through her holiness and trust in the Lord, she is given a refuge and is safe from all the attacks of the enemy. This is true for us also — our quiet trust in the Lord is our refuge (see Is 30:15). In this story from Scripture, Mary is giving birth to a Son in pain, recalling the Cross, where Mary gave birth to the members of the Mystical Body of Christ, the Church. Mary conquered Satan and evil, not by violence, not by force, not by fighting back or attacking, but rather by her quiet trust in the Word of the Lord. She stepped upon the serpent through her trust. Jesus defeated Satan in precisely the same way: Through what seemed like defeat, Jesus conquered the prince of darkness. It may seem at times that we are not capable of winning the battle, that we have been defeated, or that we may even die as martyrs in the process, but that does not mean we

---

[279] Saint John Paul II, *Redemptoris Mater*, n. 47.

have lost. Jesus died, but He also rose from the dead. We, too, will die, but if we trust in Him, we will rise also, and live forever (see Jn 11:25-26).

How, then, will the victory come? Victory will come through entrusting ourselves entirely to the Lord, not from our efforts alone (see Zech 4:6). Mary has appeared, and continues to appear, to teach us how to conquer Satan in our times, just as she defeated him at the Cross. By remaining in the "school of Mary" — praying the Rosary and allowing her to teach us to trust in her Son, Jesus Christ — we will remain faithful to the Crucified Christ and defeat the enemy.[280] We see by Mary's example that what defeats the devil and demons is our trust in the Mercy of the Father and fidelity to His will at each moment. Mary never stopped giving her "amen," her "fiat," even to the Cross. Like her, we will conquer evil by remaining humble and trusting, not in ourselves, but in the infinite Mercy of the Father, even when all *seems* lost. At His death, Christ redeemed us, and at the darkest moment of history, the victory of Christ will come (see *CCC*, 677).

If our trust remains unshakable, we will win the battle against evil and one day be inhabitants of the New Jerusalem, the holy city that John foresaw in Revelation (see Rev 21:1-4). By keeping our eyes on that destination, our destiny, we will be filled with hope, for in that city there will be no suffering, no weeping, no death, and no sin (see Is 25:6-8). If we take our eyes off the heavenly Jerusalem — as St. Peter took his eyes off the Lord Jesus — we will become discouraged and drown amid the flood of sin in the world. Trust is the foundation for the hope with which we await the future the Father has planned for us. Living in hope, we now have the Holy Spirit already and participate by grace in the glory of God. Knowing that we have something indestructible waiting for us in Heaven gives us the freedom to lose everything here on earth, trusting that we will receive a hundredfold in return (see 1 Pt 1:3-5).

Early Christians gladly underwent the confiscation of their property for the sake of Christ. Why would they so willingly endure that? They hoped. They already possessed the Holy Spirit, who was leading them to Heaven and giving them a foretaste of life with the Triune God.[281] Hope enables us to be poor, to be completely dependent upon the Father, knowing that He will provide for all our needs. Hope sets our heart's desires, not on earthly things that pass away, those things we often lose in any case through unexpected suffering, but upon what is truly good: the Triune God, and possessing Him for all eternity. Hope enables us to lose everything, so long as we do not lose God, for if we possess Him, we possess everything we need. The more we suffer and are emptied of all earthly desires, the stronger our hope can become. When we are empty and no longer have any possession except hope in the Father's abundant Mercy — that is when the Holy Spirit comes to dwell within us in His fullness (see 1 Pet 4:14). While we have great reason to hope, we must do so with a conscious desire to

---

[280]   Saint John Paul II, *Rosarium Virginis Mariae*, n. 1.

[281]   Benedict XVI, *Spe Salvi*, n. 7.

live according to the grace of Baptism and Confirmation — filled with the Holy Spirit. Without that mindful focus, we will lack the necessary courage to witness to Christ in the face of suffering and martyrdom.

In the face of all this, what are we to do? We are in a spiritual war, so how do we protect ourselves? Saint Faustina was given instruction by the Lord Himself on spiritual warfare and how to live in trust in this battle. Although His instruction is long, it is worth reading in full several times so that we take to heart Jesus' words (see *Diary*, 1760).

We are called to prepare in times of consolation for the desolation that will come. We are even called to be so prepared that we will be able to help others during the battle! **"I want you to become like a knight experienced in battle, who can give orders to others amid the exploding shells. In the same way, My child, you should know how to master yourself amid the greatest difficulties, and let nothing drive you away from Me, not even your falls"** (*Diary*, 1823). This battle is not against other human beings, but against the spiritual powers of evil: namely, the demons that roam the world seeking the ruin of souls. We must take the shield of faith and trust, and employ it in our daily lives, for this shield will stop all the arrows of the enemy and protect us from all attacks (see Eph 6:10-17). Without trust, we will fall in the battle. "St. John Chrysostom calls trust a helmet, to protect the soul against the arrows of hell — a shield in times of temptation, which, if one trusts, one can vanquish with a swift [prayer]: 'Show us, O Lord, thy mercy; and grant us thy salvation' (Ps 84:8) — a strong force, as the Apostle says: 'I can do all things in him who strengthens me' (Phil 4:13)."[282]

Trust in Mercy

As the People of God, we must trust in His Mercy! We know from the *Catechism* that times of great trial must come upon the earth; indeed, in the *Diary*, angels were sent to unleash His justice. Saint Faustina's mission is to prepare the world for the second coming (see *Diary*, 635).

Jesus cannot hold back His judgment and justice upon those who do not trust in His mercy: **"Tell sinners that no one shall escape My Hand; if they run away from My Merciful Heart, they will fall into My Just Hands"** (*Diary*, 1728). The future will be a time of great purification and the Church herself may appear to be in ruins. But from such ruins and ashes, the Father will raise up the Immaculate Bride for His Son Jesus, just as the Father raised the body of His own Son from the dead.

We must prepare for that day when Jesus returns by growing in our trust in His Mercy — especially by participating in Divine Mercy Sunday, when Jesus grants the forgiveness of all sins and temporal punishment so that His Bride will be immaculate and ready for His coming: **"[W]hoever approaches the Fount**

---

[282] Blessed Sopocko, *The Mercy of God in His Works*, Vol. 3, 177.

of Life on this day will be granted complete remission of sins and punishment" (*Diary*, 300). Indeed, the goal of Divine Mercy Sunday is to make us like Mary: immaculate and ready to receive Him when He comes, as she was at the Annunciation. Divine Mercy Sunday is the eighth day of the Easter Octave. On Easter Sunday, we celebrate the Resurrection of Christ. On the following Sunday, Divine Mercy Sunday, we seek His infinite Mercy as we await the participation of the Church in the victory of Christ over sin and death. That victory will be complete at the Second Coming, when we will see Jesus as we see Him in the Divine Mercy Image: coming toward us. For now, that same Jesus comes to us hidden in Holy Communion at each Mass. Are we ready to receive Him? Let us prepare ourselves for Him by repeating, over and over, at all times and in all circumstances, in trials and in blessings: "Jesus, I trust in You!"

The path to victory is the path of trust in Jesus. This is not a path of defending oneself, attacking others, or coming up with complicated plans. No. The path to victory is Mary's path of silent, calm trust in the Lord, fulfilling His will, knowing that He Himself will come to defeat all our enemies. Our only defense and sure victory is the infinite Mercy of God: "**My daughter, tell souls that I am giving them My mercy as a defense. I Myself am fighting for them and am bearing the just anger of My Father**" (*Diary*, 1516).

"*Jesus, I trust in You*." This prayer is essential for the Christian life in the times to come. Those who do not trust in Jesus will not be sustained by His Mercy, and judgment and justice will come upon them. That will happen, not because the Father wants to harm His own children, but because He cannot help those who do not trust and believe in His Love and Mercy. We must make known to everyone the message of His Divine Mercy and the blessings available to all who trust in Him, especially in times of temptation and trial. Jesus' Mercy will sustain those of us who trust in Him if only we say, "Jesus, I trust in You."

If you are afraid, if you cannot face the battle, remember that Our Lady is with you. Pope Leo XIII said about Mary, "We know that there is sure help in the maternal goodness of the Virgin, and We are very certain that We shall never vainly place Our trust in her."[283]

Mary will teach you to speak the words "Jesus, I trust in You," just as earthly mothers teach their children to speak. By her side, you have nothing to fear, for she is "fair as the moon, bright as the sun, terrible as an army with banners" (Song 6:10). Her very presence conquers Satan and steps upon his head. Call upon her in battle, and she will teach you to step on his head as you say along with her: "*Jesus, I trust in You!*"

---

[283] Leo XII, *Quamquam Pluries: On Devotion to St. Joseph*, Encyclical Letter (August 15, 1889), in Claudia Carlen, ed., *The Papal Encyclicals: 1878–1903* (Ypsilanti, MI: Pierian Press, 1990), 207.

Jesus, I trust in You

Conclusion

We have walked a long path of trust with Our Lady: from the beginning of time in Genesis all the way to the end of time in Revelation. We asked Mary to be present at the beginning of our pilgrimage together, and I hope that you have made your journey of trust with her in your personal life as well.

We will offer the greatest glory possible to the Father if we trust as Mary has taught us and live the prayer "Jesus, I trust in You" — walking with Peter upon the waters of our storms and suffering, and stepping on the serpent's head with Our Lady. If we are still inclined to live this prayer only superficially, however, we will not give that glory to Him, so we must ask ourselves: Precisely how solid is our trust in Jesus? And do we trust Him with sincerity? Let us ponder the points made in this book:

> *Trust* is simply placing everything in His hands, especially when it is out of our control.
>
> *Trust* is an attitude that encompasses our entire life as a Christian; it is a virtue.
>
> *Trust* is the door of our hearts that allows Jesus to give us salvation; it is the gift of the Holy Spirit.
>
> *Trust* is the weapon that conquers suffering and defeats Satan.
>
> *Trust* is our veneration of the Divine Mercy and our proper worship of God.
>
> *Trust* allows us to grasp Mary's hand and so participate in the Immaculate Conception.

By sharing in Mary's Immaculate Conception, we walk upon water and overcome evil, crushing the head of Satan.

We must remember, however, that in our everyday lives, trust and suffering are two sides of the same coin. On good days, we can say, "Jesus, I trust in You" quite easily. But when we are crucified together with Christ on the Cross, reciting this prayer can be a bit more difficult. We may not be able to explain all the suffering of this present life, but we can nevertheless trust in our good Father, for we have no sufficient reason to doubt the good plans He has for us. Sometimes we are shocked by world events — such as the two world wars in the past century — tragic and horrific events that give us apparent reasons to doubt His goodness and Mercy. However, the worst possible event has already happened — the death of Jesus Christ — and the Father revealed that His Mercy is greater than even that, and greater than all sin and suffering, if we but trust, instead of doubting. His Mercy is also revealed in Mary, our Mother, who stands by our crosses and silently encourages us to trust. The Resurrection of Christ has proven that our trust will never ultimately be disappointed!

By accepting suffering as a key means of our purification and a way to grow in divine love through union with Christ Crucified, we return to our original vocation: to share in the divine life. That vocation shines forth in all its splendor in Mary Immaculate. If we take her hand, she will walk the path of trust with us and enable us to once again share in the life of the Trinity. It is the Father's will that we be saved, that we be able to enter fully into the divine life given to us in Baptism. All that the Father permits is directed toward the one goal of allowing us to enter His own eternal bliss and happiness. Let us consider the rewards of suffering:

> *Suffering* is the means to wash away our sins and increase our love.
>
> *Suffering* provides opportunities that allow us to entrust ourselves to the Father and to others.
>
> *Suffering* becomes a means to express our love of Christ, uniting ourselves to the Lord Jesus in the Eucharist in an act of thanksgiving to the Father.

The fact that so much suffering is present in the world can be scandalous to many. We are tempted to doubt the Father's goodness, especially when we consider that many innocents suffer. But sin and distrust are burdens of fallen humanity, and it is suffering that gives us the opportunity to be purified and prepared to enter Heaven. That is why suffering can be a great consolation. If the Cross is indeed the path to eternal life, and suffering is the means of being saved, the door is open for everyone on earth. By uniting our sufferings to those of Jesus and Mary and associating ourselves with the Paschal Mystery, we can walk through that door to Heaven. In this sense, we can be "co-redeemers" by uniting our sufferings with those of Mary, the "Co-Redemptrix" who through her faith and trust cooperated with Christ in His Passion.

Not all who suffer amid storms are saved, however. Those who do not trust cannot be saved by their suffering, for their distrust closes them off from Christ, whose Love, manifested in His suffering, brings salvation. Such distrust causes them to drown in the choppy waters. Distrust allows the serpent to bite us and, with his venom, constrict our hearts. For suffering to become a means of salvation, we need to trust in God the Father. For suffering to bring about good, we need to trust in Jesus Christ. We need also to trust in the Holy Spirit and allow His purifying fire to cleanse us of our sins and make us immaculate like the Blessed Mother, ready for Jesus to come.

Evangelization is important because so many suffer, but very few know the great treasure that is suffering or the strength that trust provides to carry the Cross. The greatest work of mercy we can do is to help others trust in the Mercy of the Father. As Jesus promised, it is only when humanity turns with trust to His

Divine Mercy that mankind will have peace (see *Diary,* 300). Let us bring peace to the world by tearing aside the veil of Heaven with Faustina and convincing everyone that the Father is good and worthy of our trust!

Indeed, if Christianity could be summed up in a phrase, I argue that it would be "Jesus, I trust in You." In it is contained our faith entire. We have a Father we can trust, who shares with us His Beloved Son and His Holy Spirit, who lead us to eternal life and walk with us upon the waters of our suffering and trials. We have a Father who has given us Mary as our mother, a mother who walks the journey of trust with us each day, stepping upon the serpent as we advance toward Heaven. We are true children of our Heavenly Father and heavenly Mother if we imitate Mary's great virtue: her unconditional trust.

Jesus said that the world would know we are Christians by our love (see Jn 13:35). May the world also know we are Christians by our boundless trust in our Father!

APPENDIX

PRAYER

From the belief that I have to earn Your love …
>*Deliver me, Jesus.*

From the fear that I am unlovable …
>*Deliver me, Jesus.*

From the false security of believing that I [alone] have what it takes …
>*Deliver me, Jesus.*

From the fear that trusting You will leave me more destitute …
>*Deliver me, Jesus.*

From all suspicion of Your words and promises …
>*Deliver me, Jesus.*

From the rebellion against childlike dependency on You …
>*Deliver me, Jesus.*

From refusals and reluctance in accepting Your will …
>*Deliver me, Jesus.*

From anxiety about the future …
>*Deliver me, Jesus.*

From resentment or excessive preoccupation with the past …
>*Deliver me, Jesus.*

From restless self-seeking in the present moment …
>*Deliver me, Jesus.*

From disbelief in Your love and presence …
>*Deliver me, Jesus.*

From the fear of being asked to give more than I have …
>*Deliver me, Jesus.*

From the belief that my life has no meaning or worth …
>*Deliver me, Jesus.*

From the fear of what love demands …
>*Deliver me, Jesus.*

From discouragement …
>*Deliver me, Jesus.*

Choosing to accept that You are continually holding me, sustaining me, loving me,
>*Jesus, I trust in You.*

Choosing to accept that Your love goes deeper than my sins and failings, and transforms me,
>*Jesus, I trust in You.*

Choosing to accept that not knowing what tomorrow brings is an invitation to lean on You,
>*Jesus, I trust in You.*

Choosing to accept that you are with me in my suffering,
> *Jesus, I trust in You.*

Choosing to accept that my suffering, united to Your own, will bear fruit in this life and the next,
> *Jesus, I trust in You.*

Choosing to accept that You will not leave me orphaned, that You are present in Your Church,
> *Jesus, I trust in You.*

Choosing to accept that Your plan is better than anything else,
> *Jesus, I trust in You.*

Choosing to accept that You always hear me, and in Your goodness always respond to me,
> *Jesus, I trust in You.*

Choosing to accept that You give me the grace to accept forgiveness and to forgive others,
> *Jesus, I trust in You.*

Choosing to accept that You give me all the strength I need for what is asked,
> *Jesus, I trust in You.*

Choosing to accept that my life is a gift,
> *Jesus, I trust in You.*

Choosing to accept that You will teach me to trust You,
> *Jesus, I trust in You.*

Choosing to accept that You are my Lord and my God,
> *Jesus, I trust in You.*

Choosing to accept that I am Your beloved one,
> *Jesus, I trust in You.*

Adapted from the Litany of Trust *by Sr. Faustina Maria Pia, SV (reprinted with permission from the Sisters of Life).*

Mary and Divine Mercy Resources

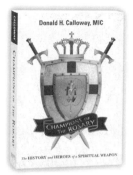

- DVDs
- CDs
- Bibles
- Books
- Prayercards
- and more!

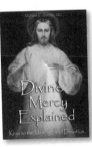

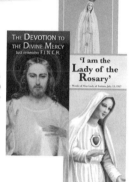

Diary of Saint Maria Faustina Kowalska:
Divine Mercy in My Soul

Large Paperback:
Y72-NBFD

Compact Paperback:
Y72-DNBF

Deluxe Leather-Bound
Edition
Y72-DDBURG

Audio Diary MP3 Edition
Y72-ADMP3

Also available as an ebook —
Visit shopmercy.org

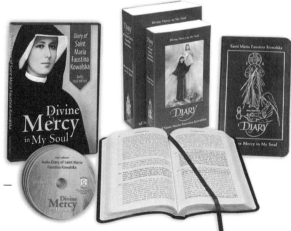

The *Diary* chronicles the message that Jesus, the Divine Mercy, gave to the world through this humble nun. In it, we are reminded to trust in His forgiveness — and as Christ is merciful, so, too, are we instructed to be merciful to others. Written in the 1930s, the *Diary* exemplifies God's love toward mankind and to this day, remains a source of hope and renewal. Keep the *Diary* next to your Bible for constant insight and inspiration for your spiritual growth! Also available in Spanish.

For our complete line of books, prayercards, pamphlets, rosaries, and chaplets, visit ShopMercy.org or call 1-800-462-7426 to have our latest catalog sent to you.

Join the
Association of Marian Helpers,
headquartered at the National Shrine of The Divine Mercy, and share in special blessings!

An invitation from Fr. Joseph, MIC, the director

Marian Helpers is an Association of Christian faithful of the Congregation of Marian Fathers of the Immaculate Conception. By becoming a member, you share in the spiritual benefits of the daily Masses, prayers, and good works of the Marian priests and brothers.

This is a special offer of grace given to you by the Church through the Marians. Please consider this opportunity to share in these blessings, along with others whom you would wish to join into this spiritual communion.

The Marian Fathers of the Immaculate Conception of the Blessed Virgin Mary is a religious congregation of nearly 500 priests and brothers around the world.

Call 1-800-462-7426 or visit marian.org